The Yellow Peril

The Yellow Peril

Dr. Fu Manchu
& The Rise of Chinaphobia

Christopher Frayling

60 illustrations, 37 in color

 Thames & Hudson

PAGE 2: Boris Karloff brandishing the sword of Genghis Khan in Hollywood's *The Mask of Fu Manchu* (1932). For captions to the chapters' opening images see Sources of Illustrations.

The Yellow Peril: Dr. Fu Manchu & The Rise of Chinaphobia © 2014 Christopher Frayling

Designed by Karin Fremer

First published in 2014 in hardcover in the United States of America by Thames & Hudson Inc., 500 Fifth Avenue, New York, New York 10110

thamesandhudsonusa.com

Library of Congress Catalog Card Number 2014932768

ISBN 978-0-500-25207-9

Printed and bound in China by Toppan Leefung Printing Limited

Contents

Yellow Peril

1: a danger to Western Civilization held to arise from expansion of the power and influence of Oriental people;

2: a threat to Western living standards developed through the incursion into Western countries of Oriental labourers willing to work for very low wages and under inferior working conditions.

Webster's New International Dictionary, 1971

If there were no more than twenty Chinese people dwelling in Chinatown, the accounts of the sensation-seekers would without fail magnify their number to five thousand. And every one of those five thousand yellow-faced demons will smoke opium, smuggle arms, commit murder – hiding the corpses under their bed – rape women – regardless of age – and commit an endless amount of crimes, all deserving, at the very least, gradual dismemberment and death by ten thousand slices of the sword. Authors, playwrights and screenwriters are prompt to base their pictures of the Chinese upon such rumours and reports . . .

Lao She: Mr Ma and Son, first published in China, 1929;
Penguin translation by William Dolby, 2013

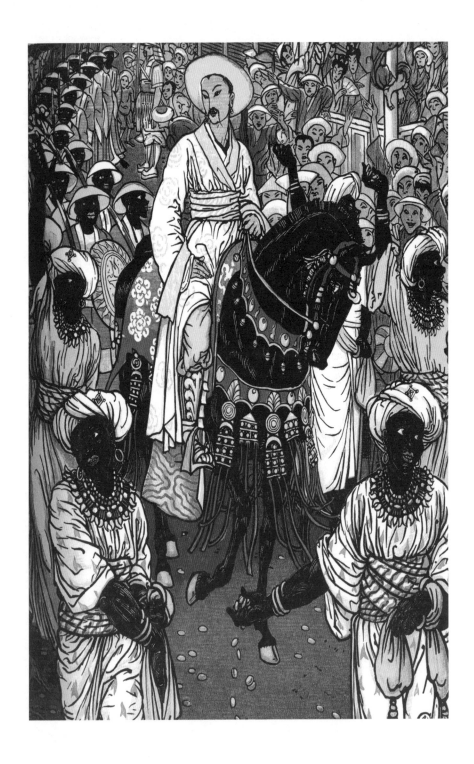

Preface

The seeds of this book were first sown over a genial lunch with Edward Said in Paris on 7 July 1995. We had been discussing the 'cinema of Empire' in the context of postcolonial ideas, for a BBC radio documentary series, then our discussion turned to Said's very influential book on *Orientalism* (1978), one of the few academic studies to have changed the meaning of a word in common parlance – in this case, from description of a specialism to a pejorative. I suggested that there were two very significant gaps in *Orientalism*: any analysis of the role of popular culture in diffusing (or even creating) orientalist prejudices and reinforcing stereotypes, and any case-studies from or about China. Said's main interest, it seemed, was confined to academic writing by intellectuals in serious literature/high culture, and to the Middle East and North Africa. He tended to see high-table orientalists of the late nineteenth and early twentieth centuries – especially those from France and Britain – as the main culprits, busy projecting their own parochial assumptions and racist myths onto 'the Orient' through their specialist writings, which would then somehow trickle down, or so it was implied, into popular culture.

Edward Said readily agreed with the point about the absence of popular culture in *Orientalism*, most notably film:

> . . . there is definitely a connection *of some sort* between the mass media, literature and serious novels. And the mass media, certainly the films, have a much more powerful, simplifying and reductive effect. Because they are *visual*. I mean, when you see an American-Indian with feathers and paint across his face he looks terrifying and it doesn't matter whether you've read about him in Fenimore Cooper or not . . . it fixes the image in your mind forever. It also, if you receive these as I did growing up – medieval films about the Crusades, *Arabian Nights* films, Imperial films, films with exotic Chinese – all of them are very difficult to remove from your head when later on you grow up and you *read the books*.

Someone ought, he said, seriously to examine the diffusion of orientalism – in his view usually originating in academe – through the media of popular and mass culture, and to question whether such ideas ever *originated* there: pulp literature, song lyrics, comics, films, cartoons, postcards, melodrama, music hall and pantomime. There had been a few studies of this kind, but nothing really substantial. Maybe I would be interested in taking on such a project?

He agreed with the point about China as well. Some of the most indelible visual images from popular culture were of 'Chinamen'.

> I remember their effect on me [when growing up in Egypt and British Palestine], the Fu Manchu films and Charlie Chan . . . We just didn't know. We didn't interact with Chinese people. So in a certain way these films also created divisions within the non-European world. But the most powerful thing about them is that they established the norm, which became unquestioning. And everything else was deviant, frightening and eccentric. They were and are very strong . . .

There was much to be written about the assumptions of sinologists in the Victorian and Edwardian periods, their defence of their own guilty consciences, and about the received wisdom among connoisseurs that the ancient glories of Chinese culture peaked in the Tang dynasty – around the seventh and eighth centuries – and had been in decline ever since; about how the wonderment of Marco Polo in Cathay morphed into the contempt of the nineteenth century and beyond; about how it was thought to have been the Jesuits and European administrators who prevented the savage Genghis Khan tendency from resurfacing.

In America, the *literary* image of the Chinese as alien 'other' – as sinister villain or dragon lady or comic laundryman or threatening heathen or broken blossom or doomed prostitute or member of a brutalized horde – grew out of Bret Harte, mining stories from gold-rush California, railroad and urban myths about bachelor societies, the Exclusion Act of 1882, and the anxieties the images embodied were mainly about immigration. In Britain and the rest of Europe, however, the repertoire of 'Chinese characteristics' also reflected anxieties about the decline of Empire and the rising dragon. The stories were about 'us' – they were not really about China at all. By the time Edward Said first encountered them, during his schooldays in Cairo, British occupation was nearing its end and Arab Nationalism was on the rise:

When I was growing up in the early 1940s, I must have been six or seven, and seeing films such as *Gunga Din, The Lives of a Bengal Lancer* and *The Four Feathers*, there were no comparably powerful images yet being produced in the Egyptian cinema . . . no costume dramas, nothing exotic, only films about local Egyptian life. I don't remember *ever* seeing any of these films in the framework of colonialism in which I was on the side of the colonized. Rather I saw them as a kind of replica of the schools I went to – which happened to be English schools – where the master looked like those guys in the films, the leading characters. Gunga Din looked like a recalcitrant schoolboy who had his moment of glory at the end, his apotheosis. That was the best you could do. There wasn't a moment's doubt that I should question any of this. It was the height of 'sportsmanship', of 'behaving well' – those are the words we used. Sacrificing yourself for *the cause*. There was no other cause on offer, you see. The other thing is that the *others* were identified with torture, with sneakiness, and it was very important not to be a sneak. All of that was fortifying everything we were taught at school.

So the impact of popular culture was not just a simple question of 'them' versus 'us'. Identities did not remain as stable as that, local cultures absorbed and adapted the narratives of Hollywood; 'the other' meant different things under different historical circumstances, and much depended on the *context* in which the images were consumed:

There's a fascinating footnote in Franz Fanon's book *Black Skins, White Masks* [1952] in which he talks about watching Tarzan films in Martinique as he is growing up and he says that when he saw these films in which Tarzan was abusing all the blacks, he identified with the white man Tarzan. It was only when he came to Paris and saw the films again that he identified with the blacks. Seeing the films in France, he felt his black identity more acutely and became upset by the sight of a white man abusing a lot of natives. But seeing them in Martinique, as an exported, approved version of reality, even a man like Fanon himself identified with the white man, so powerful was the image. Extraordinary. Tarzan is the hero in one setting and the racial enemy in another.

This conversation triggered memories of my own childhood, in the early to mid-1950s, when Sax Rohmer's Fu Manchu stories were a popular feature of my Sussex boarding school's library – nestling next to clubland heroes such as Bulldog Drummond and Richard Hannay, Imperial boy-wonders in the dusty works of G. A. Henty (*With the Allies to Pekin*, 1904) and Percy F. Westerman (*When East Meets West: A Story of the Yellow Peril*, 1913), not to mention Biggles flying in the Orient and across the Gobi. Flash Gordon serials, with the evil, inscrutable Ming the Merciless (Charles Middleton) were still doing the rounds at Saturday morning scrambles; Charlie Chan (J. Carrol Naish) on television was now working with Inspector Duff of Scotland Yard rather than the Honolulu police; the mysterious 'Chinese conjuror' with his mischievous daughter Tiger Lily and Pekingese called Pong-Ping plus pet dragon Ming were regulars in daily Rupert Bear drawings in the *Daily Express* (they lived, improbably, in a pagoda in Nutwood); small-format war comics featured savage 'Japs' and, if set in the past, equally savage Chinese warlords and pirates; we played a game called Chinese Chequers – with a Fu Manchu lookalike on the box, complete with long moustache and mandarin robe – and had Chinese conjuring sets, which were supplied with an ornate faux-ivory wand; we gave each other Chinese burns in the playground, bowled sneaky 'Chinamen' on the cricket field and joked in pidgin Chinese ('Confucius, he say . . .'); and prints of Tretchikoff's *The Chinese Girl* (painted in 1951, prints from 1956) with her copper-green face, lipstick and unfinished torso, were beginning to be sold in Woolworths. I can remember a river cruise up the Thames through London, in the school holidays, during which the amplified commentator pointed out that Limehouse was 'the headquarters of Dr Fu Manchu, where he planned to take over the world'.

All of this was, indeed, very difficult to remove from my head when I grew up. It stayed with me. There were, needless to say, no East Asian or Chinese-British pupils in the school. China even as a tourist destination was all but inaccessible. So the images became the norm, and they were unquestioned by the members of staff at the school. At one level, this book is a kind of exorcism.

That was some sixty years ago. China is now accessible, the sun has long since set on the British Empire and many of the stereotypes which were acceptable yesterday have either been discredited or reclaimed by their opposites – Eve by feminists, Caliban by postcolonials, macho signifiers by gay rights. What about the Yellow Peril? Has it survived the rise of China as a global superpower and the opening up of China to foreign tourists? Does the colonial, white, public school view of Chinese people linger on? Has Dr Fu Manchu remained the ultimate personification of exotic villainy, in an age which still likes to give a single face to diffuse terrorist threats? Scare stories about Chinese perfidy continue to fill broadsheet newspapers, financial pages and tabloid headlines alike. Some right-wing politicians, especially in the United States, use the rhetoric of China-bashing to gain populist approval. Strategists talk and write of the 'Coming China Wars' over Taiwan or South Korea or the islands off South Japan or even Africa. There's the cliché that 'China must learn to become a respectable world nation', like – it is assumed – the other members of the World Trade Organization. Buried just beneath the surface of acceptable discourse lies the deep, long history of the Yellow Peril – like a reflex.

The US Postal Service, in 1995, issued a stamp prominently featuring Ming the Merciless, as part of a 'comic-strip classics' series; in 2008, Royal Mail in Britain issued a stamp of the dust-jacket of Ian Fleming's *Dr No* to commemorate Fleming's centenary. Such official visual imagery reveals – among many other things – that there is much less sensitivity about depictions of Chinese villains than there is about those from other ethnic groups. Dr Fu Manchu, progenitor of Ming and Dr No, lingers in the popular consciousness more than any other twentieth-century villain – whether or not the generation of 2000 can actually put a name to him.

At a cultural level, there have been angry controversies about the casting of non-Asians in East Asian roles, a practice which now goes by the unappealing name of 'yellowface'. A play about *The Arrest of Ai Weiwei* by Howard Brenton (2013) is criticized for presenting Chinese officials, in their secret garden, as stereotypically sinister and inscrutable. The controversy about casting in the musical *Miss Saigon* (1989) even inspired the farce *Face Value* (1993) by David Hwang, author of *M. Butterfly* (1988), about a white actor in yellowface playing a Fu Manchu lookalike in a Broadway musical: this play in turn inspired the same author's semi-autobiographical *Yellow Face* (2007). Non-Asians acting roles such as 'the Engineer', the Eurasian pimp played by Jonathan Pryce in the original West End and Broadway pro-ductions of *Miss Saigon*, are seen as heirs to the tradition of Warner Oland (Swedish) or Boris Karloff and Christopher Lee (British) playing Fu Manchu in the movies, to the forty-four Charlie Chan films with non-Chinese actors in the lead role, or to David Carradine (American) playing the heroic Shaolin monk in the television series *Kung Fu* (1972–75). Meanwhile, the episode 'The Blind Banker' in the updated *Sherlock* television series (2010) – which included nasty goings-on in 'the Dragon Circus', a spiderwoman acrobat, 'the Tong of the Black Lotus' and a double-gourd-shaped Ming vase – was treated by angry members of the Chinese community in Britain as if it was a latter-day Fu Manchu story without the wit. *Team America: World Police* (2004) thought that pidgin English, sung by a puppet, was in itself hilarious. Quentin Tarantino in 2007 put Fu Manchu (Nicolas Cage) into a grindhouse setting – which he must have thought made it all right. Paperback thrillers about snakehead gangs cast the Chinese gang masters as the sole villains, rather than the supermarkets which insist on the cheapest possible products of their slave-like labours.

And then there is the cultural battle over the contemporary meaning of Charlie Chan, the overweight detective from the Honolulu Police Department with the sing-song voice who first appeared in 1925. To some Asian-American writers, he became in the 1980s a yellow Uncle Tom – along with the more obviously unpleasant Fu Manchu, one of the most deeply disliked characters in American popular culture, a symbol who got in the way.

Against this, literary scholar Yunte Huang's book *Charlie Chan: The Untold Story* (2010) argues that Chan can be a positive role model for Asian-Americans, as they resettle or assimilate into American society. He quotes the Canton-born Keye Luke, who played Charlie Chan's 'number one son' in seven of the Warner Oland films in the 1930s, as saying that the films in no way 'demean the race'. 'Demean! My God! We were making the best damn murder mysteries in Hollywood.' Wayne Wang's remarkable 1982 film *Chan Is Missing*, the first American feature film made by an entirely Asian-American cast and crew, is about the search for a man called Chan, missing for a week in San Francisco's Chinatown: he leaves clues everywhere, but no one can find him. The film is full of references to Charlie Chan and his number one son, a relationship echoed by the cabbie Joe and his nephew Steve (who watches old Chan films 'for laughs'). It ends on a discussion between the two men about 'finding an identity'. Should this identity come 'from China'? Is that the way 'to find yourself'? Steve: 'That's bullshit, man. That's old news, ten years ago. . . . The Chinese are all in the city now.'

Has there been an equivalent attempt to reclaim Dr Fu Manchu? After all, he was presented by Sax Rohmer as an archangel ruined and often likened to Milton's Satan. He always keeps his word, to the letter. He bears no personal grudges. He speaks 'the purest English I have ever heard'. He is a nobleman, appalled by the chaos of contemporary China. He wants China to be *someone* on the world stage again. Some young Chinese scholars working in Britain today are beginning to consider reclamation. In the Rohmer novels, it is his adversary Nayland Smith who these days comes over as the fanatic – like Van Helsing in *Dracula*. Are the stories about much more than the protocols of the elders of Peking? Are they about an *admiration* for pre-Revolutionary Chinese culture? As I write this, a play called *The Fu Manchu Complex* has just opened in London, written by actor and playwright Daniel York, himself with East Asian roots, in which the old stories are re-enacted – in white half-masks – by Chinese-British actors: Fu Manchu is kidnapping highflying financiers from all over Europe, and turning them into stereotypical Chinese people with the aid of his magic mushrooms. One of the punchlines is that, confronted by daily insults in newspapers, on stage and screen, members of the Chinese community should not 'stay invisible'. 'I am the god of *assimilation*,' shrieks Dr Fu Manchu at the climax, played for the first time by a Chinese *actress*. The Yellow Peril is very much alive in the culture wars of the early twenty-first century, and so is Sax Rohmer's indestructible creation.

This book begins with the 'Hong Kong handover' in 1997 and its presentation in the British media – which contained distant echoes of fears about the Yellow Peril in the late nineteenth and early twentieth centuries and showed that such prejudices are still firmly if subtly embedded in Western culture. It then flashes back to a meeting in 1971 between the author and Rose Elizabeth Sax Rohmer, widow of the creator of the Fu Manchu stories and novels, which raises the curtain on the cultural origins of the Yellow Peril in Britain and America in both senses of the phrase – Chinese immigration and Chinese belligerence/expansionism. The origins of Dr Fu Manchu are explored, and placed within the contexts of nineteenth-century literature and pop-orientalism. A chapter on Charles Dickens and the invention of the seedy 'opium den' in the East End of London – which had become an unavoidable literary and journalistic cliché by the end of the nineteenth century – includes an analysis of how the image of 'Limehouse' as Chinatown came to be constructed, on the rebound from the Chinatowns of New York and San Francisco. This leads to a detailed examination of the late-Victorian and Edwardian music hall, the popular weekly press and pulp literature. Sax Rohmer was deeply involved in all of them. But, beyond his contribution, these were the main incubators of the attitudes and anxieties of the Yellow Peril in public consciousness, disseminated by new media and exaggerated by new patterns of consumption. Rohmer's classic description of Fu Manchu, repeated in several of his novels like a signature tune, is unpicked phrase by phrase for the assumptions it contains, and where they came from. Finally, the afterlife of Dr Fu Manchu in films since the 1920s is shown to have *amplified* the sinister elements, and the racism, of the original stories, before turning them into camp nostalgia. He is still present in cinematic shorthand. Surrealist artists, meanwhile, have celebrated the dreamlike quality of Sax Rohmer's fiction, and its improbabilities, while forgetting all about its skewed perceptions of Chinese people. The overarching themes of the book are: What were the origins of Yellow Peril thinking? How did they come to be distilled into one fictional character, Dr Fu Manchu? Why has the Yellow Peril proved to be so resilient, over the last 150 years? How and why has the Peril changed its meaning over the years since it was first conceived: similar repertoire of images, different connotations?

A word about the phrase 'Yellow Peril', the noun 'Chinaman' and the adjective 'oriental'. They were all in common parlance during the historical period which is the main focus of this book. Both 'Yellow' and 'Peril' are of course deeply problematic, as sections of this study point out. It was especially ironic that the phrase should be applied to China at precisely the time when the country was in chaos, divided against itself, victim of successive famines and utterly incapable of being a 'peril' to anyone, even if it had wanted to be. 'Chinaman' – as distinct from 'Chinese' or 'Chinese person' – was already being treated as a slur by a few enlightened commentators in the late nineteenth century. 'Oriental' has made way for 'East Asian'. In the 1920s, it would have been 'Asiatic', a racial category which emerged within eugenics in the 1910s and which – in the United States – was first codified by the Supreme Court in 1923. It seemed too arch, and even smug, always to put these words into quotation marks, to distance myself from what they connoted and in some quarters still connote. I hope the reader will not be tempted to shoot the messenger.

A word, too, about the name 'Fu Manchu'. In the first three books by Sax Rohmer, published in quick succession in 1912–17, it was always hyphenated: 'Fu-Manchu'. But following the release of the first Hollywood film version,

The Mysterious Dr Fu Manchu in 1929, Rohmer dropped the hyphen from all subsequent books – perhaps as a result of the seeming confusion in the film about the name: references to the 'House of Fu' made it sound like a family name; other characters used 'Fu' as a first name; the emphasis in 'Manchu' was always on the first syllable for some reason. To avoid needless complications, I have adopted the unhyphenated form for all references to Fu Manchu.

As will be evident from the outset, this book has been written in the hope that the more we can openly examine, discuss and unpack racial stereotypes, the more likely we are to understand each other. And mutual understanding has never been more important. Part of this process is, I believe, to admit to ourselves – whether we are 'us' or 'them' – as Prospero said of Caliban, 'This thing of darkness I acknowledge mine.'

Christopher Frayling

INTRODUCTION

The Setting of the Sun

I t felt like the last day of the British Empire, 100 years – to the week – after Queen Victoria's Diamond Jubilee. At 4.35 p.m. on 30 June 1997, the Union flag was ceremoniously lowered from above the portico of granite, neoclassical Government House on the steep slope of the Crown Colony of Hong Kong. Chris Patten, who had been Governor for five years – last in a long line that went back to when China was forced at gunpoint to surrender first rocky Hong Kong Island in 1842, then the Kowloon Peninsula in 1860, followed by the negotiated lease of the New Territories in 1898 – stood in a plain blue suit on a podium on the front lawn, which faced Victoria Park. The last Governor, the twenty-eighth, was a politician rather than a diplomat or 'old China hand' – a controversial decision much resented by crusty veteran sinologists and old colonialists. The first Administrator, self-appointed on 26 January 1841, had been an Admiral. Patten's remit, when he was sworn in, July 1992, had been to prepare for the Colony's future under Chinese rule, to help arrange the transfer of sovereignty and to achieve both with as much dignity as possible. 'The last main chapter in the story of this country's empire . . . should not end in a shabby way,' said then-Foreign Secretary Douglas Hurd. As the Union flag was lowered that June afternoon, the Last Post bugled; and as the flag was handed to the last Governor by his aide-de-camp, furled and on a royal-blue cushion, in the fine tropical rain the Royal Hong Kong Police Band struck up 'God Save the Queen', followed by 'Auld Lang Syne' in a slow-march tempo. Then the official vintage Rolls-Royce took Patten through the iron gates and stone pillars, down to the farewell Sunset Parade on the waterfront. For the first time since 1854, Government House would no longer be the home of the representative of the Queen: twenty-five Governors out of twenty-eight had resided there, since Sir John Bowring, the multilingual fourth Governor who among his other achievements ignited the Second Opium War (1856–60).

The Farewell Ceremony, which began at 6.15 p.m. on a soaking esplanade with the Royal Yacht *Britannia* and HMS *Chatham* moored beyond – the monsoon by now had gathered force – included speeches on a red carpet: 'Sometimes we should remember the past the better to forget it . . . our own nation's contribution here was to provide the scaffolding to enable the people of Hong Kong to ascend . . .' The theatre of the event, said *The Times* the following morning, was 'lifted unchanged from every retreat-from-empire textbook'. The twilight-themed music ranged from 'The Day Thou Gavest, Lord, Is Ended' to the Sunset Hymn to 'Goodnight, Irene' as the Prince of Wales in his white uniform and the Governor in his suit walked, under umbrellas, up the gangplank of the Royal Yacht. The formal business included a banquet, boycotted by the Chinese delegation, a summit meeting, and the solemn official handover from Prince Charles on behalf of his mother to President Jiang Zemin – all in the new Convention Centre on the harbour front, known locally as 'the Flying Cockroach'. Privately, Prince Charles wrote of the 'ridiculous rigmarole', and the 'propaganda' speech cheered to the echo by the rent-a-crowd of party officials, and the 'appalling old waxworks' on the podium. Meanwhile, pro-democracy advocates protested outside the Legislative Council and tried to tie a giant yellow ribbon round the building: a police band played Beethoven's Ninth very loudly indeed so the Chinese delegation would not be able to hear the sound of the demonstrators.

At midnight, there was the raising of the Chinese 'Special Administrative Region' flag, and the Yellow Star, and the playing of the national anthem 'March of the Volunteers'. The police all over Hong Kong took the colonial insignia from their uniforms and replaced them with new SAR ones, while flags and numberplates were changed on official cars. The Royal Yacht steamed away, under escort, while the Royal Marines Band played 'Rule, Britannia'. Chris Patten sent his final communiqué to London, from *Britannia*: 'I have relinquished the administration of this government. God save the Queen.' Prince Charles was filled with 'a kind of exasperated sadness', he wrote, but it had all been palpably anachronistic.

The BBC television coverage – reluctant to become too misty-eyed, perhaps, in an era of political correctness – kept contrasting the pomp and circumstance of Government House and the waterfront esplanade with the soldiers and sailors of the Chinese People's Liberation Army (PLA), in their new trucks, armoured cars and coaches, 'amassing on the border' between China and Hong Kong, their headlight beams cutting through the rain. Five hundred and nine of these troops – the agreed figure, after much diplomatic wrangling about the number to be deployed before the actual handover: why 509 is anybody's guess – crossed the border without inspection, drove through the tunnel and along the dual carriageway to the centre of Hong Kong at 9 p.m. The rest waited for the stroke of midnight, revving up their engines. The Chinese hordes, it seemed from the coverage, latter-day heirs to Genghis Khan's cavalry, were at the gates – presented as faceless, incomprehensible, overwhelming, vast in number like Chairman Mao's 'human sea': an image of pent-up energy which went back a very long way, since the days when 'Mongol horde' was equated with 'oriental'.

The Farewell Ceremony on the shiny esplanade certainly aroused a lot of emotion – more, perhaps, than any previous de-colonization, because it was so obviously the last. But its coverage on television came across as a fancy-dress operetta, a spectacularly designed production of *The Yeomen of the Guard* on ice, crossed with an Olympic opening ceremony – an outward and visible sign, at full volume, of the loss of Empire and the struggle to find a role in the modern world.

Meanwhile, as the 'retreat-from-empire textbook' was being re-enacted in Hong Kong, crowds were simultaneously watching on giant screens in Tiananmen Square – where for weeks there had been a countdown on a digital signboard of the days, hours and seconds to 'return' – a $15 million, 153-minute epic film, *The Opium War*, directed by seventy-three-year-old Xie Jin, veteran of the Cultural Revolution, and publicly endorsed by President Jiang Zemin. The most expensive film ever made in China up to then told the story of the war (1839–42) from the points of view of Commissioner Lin Tse-Hsu (Bao Guo'an), a nationalist, scholar and honest government official, and British diplomat and naval commander Charles Elliot (Simon Williams), later the island's Administrator. The most spectacular sequence showed Lin dissolving 20,000 cases of 'foreign mud' (opium) in a solution of seawater mixed with quicklime. Another sequence pointedly showed the British takeover ceremony, on the barren rocky island, with the raising of the Union Jack and a wooden notice 'Hong Kong British Territory' to the strains of the national anthem – with a portrait of Queen Victoria placed nearby, in a gilt frame. Victoria herself, following advice from a bellicose, stolid and hypocritical Foreign Secretary Viscount Palmerston, when asked what the next move should be, replies, 'Whoever gets hold of China will have the entire East,' and walks away. Enough said. For Elliot, 'Hong Kong will be invaluable to us – we reckon it is the finest port in the whole Far East.' In 1842, it was – the film shows – an unequal struggle: bows and arrows, grotesque masks, aged matchlock rifles, medieval cannons and 'a fleet of fishing boats' versus very well-armed British warships. *The Opium War* concluded on shots of the Emperor weeping at his abject humiliation, and of rampant stone lions symbolically guarding the Imperial Palace in Peking. Then the caption: 'July 1st 1997: the Chinese government takes back sovereignty of Hong Kong, 157 years after the Opium War.' In its first few months of domestic release, *The Opium War* was the highest-grossing Chinese film, ever.

And while the broadcasters were on the subject of Tiananmen Square . . . there were of course the events of 4 June 1989, when the PLA had been ordered to clear the square of 'subversive elements' by opening fire on protesters. Tiananmen Square had marked a sea-change in broadcasters' attitudes towards the Crown Colony. Up until then, television had not shown much interest. But now, suddenly, there was a lot to debate. Much more importantly, Tiananmen Square had decisively raised the political temperature – and the anxiety levels – in Hong Kong.

But the key visual contrast on television that evening, partly as a result, was between the fine upstanding public school chap, the muddled grandeur of the British troops, and those faceless and nameless lorries and armoured personnel carriers revving up, under their red flags, at the border. The following morning, one BBC correspondent reported on the 'robotic waves and fixed smiles' of the troops as they crossed the bridge. It was like the old illustration in *Ripley's Believe It or Not* of 'The Marching Chinese': 'If all the Chinese in the world were to march four abreast past a given point, they would *never* finish passing though they marched for ever and ever.' When a billion Chinese jump . . .

Watching this coverage was – to me – also like, more like, watching a live-action Fu Manchu thriller, written eighty-five years before, around the time of the First World War, in which the fine, upstanding, heroic District Commissioner, late of Burma, stands alone against the faceless secret army of 'the devil doctor', an army equipped with the products of the latest scientific research as well as of ancient esoteric wisdom, and the fate of the entire British Empire is in the balance.

Dr Fu Manchu was still by far the dominant and best-remembered fictional personification of the merciless, inscrutable, vengeful and cunning Chinese – of 'Chineseness' – all over the world, thanks to countless books, comics, cartoons, serials and feature films: a stereotypical image, which went deep, standing for an entire people who had killed girl infants, bound women's feet, enjoyed the torture of a thousand cuts, massacred Christian missionaries during the 'Boxer uprising' of 1900, eaten dogs and cats, and who had more recently become 'the awakening giant' with Communist ambitions of global domination. All distilled into a public character and a fearsome name. There had been a celebrated letter to *Time* magazine on 14 February 1969 which complained about the widespread use of the shorthand term 'Hong Kong 'Flu': 'Since it was probably manufactured in secret laboratories on mainland China – it should be called Flu Manchu.' In 1997, this was an image to be recognized – part of a culture of quotations – and put into inverted commas. A slightly anxious semiotic game to be played in the shadow of China . . .

Shortly *before* the handover, on 24 February 1997, James R. Lilley – CIA Station Chief in Beijing 1973–75, US Ambassador to China 1989–91 – made a similar connection, this time from an American perspective, in a *Newsweek* article entitled 'The "Fu Manchu" Problem: Why America and China Tend to Think of Each Other as Cartoonlike Enemies'. It was 'The "Fu Manchu" Problem' because this fictional character was better known than any real-life Chinese character other than Chairman Mao himself. Lilley wrote of how for decades America and China had been sniping, suspecting and spying on each other. But recently the rhetoric and the posturing had been getting considerably worse. Both sides were becoming less cooperative and more confrontational:

> Columnists and Congressmen portray the Chinese as rabid abortionists and iron-fisted thugs – a gang of Fu Manchus who relish ripping out their enemies' fingernails. The hostility is very much on people's minds throughout the culture.

The political rhetoric of China-bashing, especially at times of economic hardship and anxiety about East–West relations, was deeply embedded in American political life, he added – a classic modern example of the tradition of anti-intellectualism. Meanwhile, the Chinese were ratcheting up the argument by blaming America for 'wanting to keep it down', even after President Nixon's recognition of the People's Republic in 1972. The roots of mutual misunderstanding, from the Chinese point of view, lay in nineteenth-century businessmen and Christian missionaries who followed trade and the flag, brushed aside Confucianism, forcibly broke down the mercantile doors, and encouraged the opium habit while looting the Middle Kingdom. They also propped up the discredited Manchu regime for their own capitalist purposes. American animosity had gathered momentum during the Cold War (fighting the Red Chinese in Korea; alarmed about Chinese ambitions in Asia), fanned by John Foster Dulles conjuring up 'images of yellow hordes seeping south to turn all of Asia communist . . . we still haven't entirely shaken that old view'.

One of the problems to which Lilley referred was how little most Americans really understood about China – close personal acquaintance, at home or abroad, was the exception rather than the rule, and this opened the way for crude stereotypes, the fruit of inexperience, on both sides. So it was worth asking: where did information about China come from, at a popular level? School textbooks emphasized the American perspective: the Opium Wars, the Open Door, the Boxers, the 1911 revolution, Dr Sun Yat Sen, Chiang Kai-Shek and Formosa, the rise of Communism, Korea, Chairman Mao Tse-Tung – as one astute commentator put it, from the Age of Respect (during the eighteenth century) to the Age of Contempt (1840–1905) to the Age of Benevolence (1905–44) to the Age of Disenchantment (1944–49) to the Age of Hostility (1949–). Most Americans' knowledge of 'Confucianism' seemed to be confined to the pedantic aphorisms of the philosophical, fictional, asexual Hawaiian-Chinese detective from Honolulu, Charlie Chan:

Hasty conclusion easy to make, like hole in water.

It is difficult to pick up needle with boxing glove.

Confucius say, 'No man is poor who have worthy son.'

Often, Charlie Chan's fortune-cookie aphorisms were prefaced with the words 'old Chinese proverb', 'ancient Chinese philosopher say' or – of course – 'Confucius he say'. Knowledge of Chinese inventions – such as paper, moveable type, the compass, porcelain and gunpowder – tended to be based on American school textbooks containing colourful retellings of the travels of Marco Polo. Bret Harte's 'heathen Chinee', and Mark Twain's robust reports about Chinese immigrants on the American frontier, were better known – both featuring pidgin-speaking characters whose apparent stupidity masked an inner shrewdness: the deliberate irony of both authors was usually lost, as their work entered the popular bloodstream.

Because of this limited access to understanding, reality and image had a nasty tendency to become confused: China-bashing in public mimicked stories about Fu Manchu. There were two important consequences for America: a tendency to think of 'China' in terms of a generalized set of national characteristics – like the missionaries and officials who wrote about 'the Chinese' with great confidence in the late nineteenth century; and a dominant image which obstructed mutual understanding. Even distinguished Harvard researchers, who wrote of a coming 'clash of civilizations' – sometimes with a question mark, sometimes not – notably between America and China, 'a civilization pretending to be a state', and even of 'a Confucian–Islamic alliance', these academics were not untouched by popular fictions. A guide written for Americans going East, orienting them, had this to say in all seriousness:

> Those who have not done their homework, and have arrived on the scene without a background in oriental philosophy, history, religion, sociology and anthropology . . . often try to make judgements in the limited context of their Western preconception of Fu Manchu, the fictional Oriental arch-fiend.

James Lilley concluded his article:

> There is an old tradition of trying to unify the Chinese spirit by Great Projects – the Great Wall or damming the Yangtze. Saying that we are the enemy could be their next Great Project. As tempting as it may be, we shouldn't respond in kind. Chinese society can be brutal, and their territorial ambitions are real. We must show them that there is no profit in expansion – without reviving old fears about the 'Yellow Peril'!

Even here, there was the assumption ('territorial ambitions . . . expansion') that China would one day be on the march, given half a chance. This mirrored the sentiments of the hero-diplomat of the 1969 thriller by the future Foreign Secretary Douglas Hurd, and Andrew Osmond, *The Smile on the Face of the Tiger*:

> The Chinese? . . . They are the one genuine imperial power left in the world. Even when we were clobbering them a hundred years ago they

went on thinking that China was central and unique. We've all thought that about ourselves at one time or another. But we British stopped long ago, the Russians stopped after Stalin and the Americans never really started. To the Chinese, the foreigner is still someone who owes tribute to the Emperor, and the sooner he pays up the better.

When I asked Chris Patten what, in retrospect, he felt about the media coverage of the Hong Kong handover, he replied:

We tried very hard to get Chinese people to understand that we didn't want goose-stepping soldiers, lorryloads of troops pouring into Hong Kong. If they did this, everyone would find it difficult to accept that this was to be a gentle, civil and civilized acquisition. We were always nervous about how it would look – that it might rock confidence. But actually it didn't.

There had, apparently, been a number of discussions during the twenty-two rounds of formal talks concerning the ceremony about what exactly would happen when the PLA marched in. So, what *did* the Chinese officials think was most appropriate?

Well, they called it 'the return' rather than 'the handover'. Sometimes they called it a 'victory celebration'. They originally wanted a small ceremony in the City Hall, one of the more grotty buildings in Hong Kong, with about 200 guests, during which we would just sign a piece of paper saying, 'Here's Hong Kong – sorry we were here!' Then we'd have a glass of wine and we would leave. Followed by a separate military ceremony behind closed doors . . .

Patten was keen that the ceremony would instead be a very public demonstration of the peaceful transfer of sovereignty from one power to another – something that had never happened before: it should be 'dignified and honourable'. But he says he was not at all tempted to display himself on a podium in the 'Ruritanian' plumed hat and ceremonial court uniform traditionally worn by the senior diplomats who had been Governors of Hong Kong. He wanted to distance himself from the ornamentalism of Victorian times, symbolized by the elaborate uniform:

. . . it would have been entirely the wrong image to give the Chinese in the 1990s: we wanted it to look as though Hong Kong was not a colony but a great Asian city – so better to look like a mayor than a proconsul, a relic of Empire.

Chris Patten's official Chinese name was 'Pang Ding-hong', meaning 'stability and health'. He was also given the Hong Kong-Chinese nickname 'Fat Pang'. This drew attention in a well-meaning way to his portliness – but it also connoted 'prosperity and well-being' and it was said to be something of a compliment to have been given an affectionate nickname. Earlier Governors were far too severe, and remote, to engage in such intimacy. Other names for Patten, uttered by disgruntled mainland Chinese negotiators who were unimpressed by his approach to political reform, were much less affectionate: they included at one time or another 'serpent', 'trickster', 'strutting prostitute' and, for some obscure reason, 'tango dancer'.

But discussions about other aspects of the protocol of handover – every second of it – seemed interminable, not least the weeks of negotiation about the Prince of Wales and the President, and who should take precedence, which was not made any easier by the tendency of the Chinese officials to call him 'the Prince of Charles'. Prime Minister Margaret Thatcher, on her visit to Beijing back in September 1982, had encountered a similar problem: the interpreter was heard to call her 'The Quite Honourable Margaret Thatcher'. On the other hand, she took some persuading to stop using the word 'Chinamen'. In the end, it was decided that Prince Charles and the President should both enter the new Convention Centre at exactly the same moment, with four colleagues each, and sit down. The President would say a few words, then Prince Charles would make some elegant remarks in Chinese, then they would say 'thank you very much' and go their separate ways. When Prime Minister Tony Blair witnessed the real thing, he couldn't quite believe it: 'Is *that* what we've been negotiating about for weeks and weeks?' In 2005, a British tabloid newspaper somehow got hold of the extracts from Prince Charles's private diary which revealed what he *really* thought about the 'ridiculous rigmarole' surrounding the ceremony – the emphasis on 'loss of face' – and generally about 'the handover of Hong Kong – or the great Chinese takeaway . . .'

Surely Chris Patten appreciated Chinese sensitivities – the feeling that a great long-term humiliation, a running sore, was at last coming to an end?

Of course. The 'Yellow Peril' side of things was part of the story. Fu Manchu and all that. And at a higher level, the examples studied by Jonathan

Spence in *The Chan's Great Continent* [1998] – or, for a diplomatic perspective, Lucian Pye's *The Spirit of Chinese Politics* [1968]. The paradox of the 'opium den' view is that opium was indeed forced on the Chinese – to pay for the Indian balance of payments in the mid-nineteenth century. We globalized China to balance the books in India. And that happened remarkably quickly. It was, after all, only in 1793 that Macartney was sent packing with a grand missive from the Emperor to George III saying that they didn't heed him at all, or anyone else for that matter. We had no power, unlike Commodore Perry in Japan for example. But within forty-five years we'd knocked hell out of them in the Opium Wars and contributed to their disintegration. No question about that. Which leads to their view of *us*. For eighteen out of twenty centuries they had the largest economy in the world. The Chinese have a view of us as contributors to the terrible humiliation of their country which we should all know is the Middle Kingdom, the centre of the world. For the first time in 200 years there is now a feel-good factor in China, a sense of national pride – after two centuries which have been calamitously bad for them. The Chinese point of view is that we were a major contributor to this terrible decline. . . . I have slightly more sympathy with their point of view now – now I know more about how appallingly we behaved. You can't defend it in terms of current morality, obviously – but even by the standards of the time it was repellent.

So three months before handover, the Chinese Foreign Minister let it be known at the Chinese People's Congress that there would have to be some serious amendments to the history textbooks used in Hong Kong's schools. At the subsequent press conference in Hong Kong, the soon-to-be Chief Executive C. H. Tung explained that of course the story of 'the colonial past' would need to be rewritten. There was a provocative question from the floor about whether the Tiananmen Square massacre would have to be rewritten as well – to which he replied, 'You may be interested to read what is written about the Opium Wars.' Such tensions about the historical past sometimes distracted meetings with the Beijing 'gerontocracy': at key moments, apparently, the Opium Wars, the 'Unfair Treaties', the Boxers, the burning and sacking of the Summer Palace, the prejudiced treatment of Chinese people in the West, would suddenly be raised. The sense of humiliation went very deep, and was a fixed barrier to mutual understanding. Not victimhood, but humiliation.

Ten years later, and one of my regular visits to China and Hong Kong to give some lectures on Western art schools and the education of designers. On my last day at Tsinghua University in Beijing, I was shown around the glorious Summer Palace northwest of the city – the great complex of Imperial palaces, residencies, temples, gardens and 'a thousand bridges' of the Manchu dynasty, originally built at the beginning of the eighteenth century, partly with help from Jesuit designers – by Dr Fang Xiaofeng, architect and lecturer in environmental design at Tsinghua, as well as being editor of the oldest-established design magazine in mainland China, *Zhuang Shi* (Decoration). The original Palace had been sacked, burned and looted in 1860, at the end of the Second Opium War, to 'punish' the defeated Manchu court – by taking revenge on the Hsien-Feng Emperor personally rather than his people: it was his favourite Palace – and again in 1900 by the punitive expedition known as the 'Eight Power Allied Expeditionary Forces', in reprisal for the destruction caused by the Boxers, on both occasions with boatloads of plunder finding their way to the British Museum, the London antiques market and assorted stately homes. The order to destroy the Palace in 1860 was delivered from the Hall of Probity, of all places, by Lord Elgin – who, by the way, was the son of the Lord Elgin who chipped away the Parthenon marbles: like father, like son. Elgin ordered a notice to be put up near the smouldering ruins, in Chinese: 'This is the reward for perfidy and cruelty.' The British troops, though, left behind the massive sculptural lions guarding the gates of the Palace complex, thinking they were of little value and far too difficult to ship home. In fact, they were made of solid gold. Mark Twain famously wrote of the events of August 1900 – the second sacking of the Palace – that it was a 'pirate raid' by avenging Christendom, her 'soul full of mean-ness, her pocket full of boodle and her mouth full of pious hypocrisies . . .' Knowing all this, I asked the genial Dr Fang if there were still any hard feelings, 150 years later? It was as well to clear the air.

First of all, replied Dr Fang, the Chinese preferred to call the Boxers 'The Righteous and Harmonious Brotherhood of Fists': the British had called them 'Boxers' because their displays of martial arts – which they thought made them invulnerable to foreign bullets and swords – resembled boxing. But, where the burnings and lootings of 1860 and 1900 were concerned, 'many Chinese do not know about this history at all – it was, after all, a long time ago'. As we walked around the post-1860 Palace, and admired the astonishing scenery of Kunming Lake, Dr Fang patiently explained the historical background and architectural significance of each element, and the meaning of each flight of fancy. It was, he said, traditionally known as Yuanming Yuan (Garden of Perfect Brightness). The Emperor had prided himself on his five miles of granite and thousand bridges. I could not help noticing, from my English-language printed guide, that several of the buildings and gardens had been reconstructed after the two holocausts. Some of the fabric seemed to have remained intact, and much of the overall design. But tucked away behind Longevity Hill, there were the broken remnants of marble columns, the ruins of fountains, the overgrown blackened stubble of a small Buddhist temple and gateway, a library and a 'terrace of leisure and tea', overturned stone slabs with elaborate carvings – together known locally as 'the Elgin Masonry' and intentionally since the Communist era as 'Yuanming Yuan Ruins Park'. This was the site of the original Summer Palace, with its mixture of Chinese and Western European architecture and its famed programme of gardens centred on the Garden of Perfect Brilliance. It created the impression, said Dr Fang, that the whole complex was more European-looking than it really was. My printed guide added: 'Stand quietly, and you can easily imagine emperors and empresses in their fabulous court clothes, walking by and enjoying their leisure.' Well, just about. A group of excited schoolchildren was looking at an informa-tion board; with their teacher pointing at the words with a long stick resembling a billiard cue. 'What does it say?' I asked. 'Well, it tells the story of the Second Opium War and of how the Qing court was humiliated in 1860 by Anglo-French Allied troops. And how the Imperial powers broke their way into China at that time. And also of the "Boxer uprising" and its aftermath.' Over a late lunch, Dr Fang explained that, 'Yes, that historical period is still taught in Middle School (twelve to seventeen) – the two Opium Wars, and the "Boxers" – but in not so many details – just the outline of the main story.' But why has the old Summer Palace never been restored? It resembled an overgrown shrine. 'Chinese people like to keep the memory of the past alive, even if they don't all know the his-torical details.' Had much damage been done *since* 1900? Well, over the years some of the stone had been quarried for later projects offsite. This seemed a good opportunity to raise the issue of the terrible sufferings the Chinese people inflicted on one another in the same period – such as the Taiping Rebellion of 1850–64, when literally millions of Chinese are thought to have died. 'Yes, there were bad people in China as well as good people – like everywhere . . .' We raised our glasses to the sentiment that we should all 'remember the past the better to forget it', so that yesterday's mistakes would not lead to tomorrow's.

In Britain, we preferred to keep our memories alive in the maybe too casual use of language: from the 'Chinese burn' in the school playground (with the comic-book reaction of 'aiiieee') to 'bowling a Chinaman' on the cricket pitch – a sneaky, left-arm, unorthodox spin (in baseball, there's the equally sneaky 'Chinese homer'); from the 'Chinese wall' of silence – with a 'chink' in it, of course – to untrustworthy 'Chinese whispers'; from 'I wouldn't do that for all the tea in China' to 'he hasn't got a Chinaman's chance' (he has no chance at all) to the chaotic 'Chinese fire drill' to 'a Chinese compliment' (pretended deference when one's mind is already made up); from infants with Down's Syndrome being called 'Mongoloids' – a doctor in 1866 thought they had 'strongly Oriental' imperfections in their faces – to 'Chinese torture', the devilishly ingenious kind, or in the film business 'the death of a thousand cuts'; from the word 'Chinaman' – originally descriptive, now offensive unless used in an ironic, knowing way – to the now less common 'Chink' (which may have originated from the Qing (Ch'ing/Manchu) dynasty, or from the word 'China', or from chink meaning a slanting crevice) to 'coolie' or 'coolie hat' used as a derogatory, for example when celebrity chefs quip, 'I thought a coulis was a hardworking Chinaman.' The phrase 'yellow journalism' – meaning exploitative, flag-waving journalism – was still around, and it probably owed its origin to a newspaper cartoon character called The Yellow Kid, who first appeared in America in 1896, and who closely resembled contemporary caricatures of Asian people (bald head, toothless face, large ears): 'yellow kid journalism'. Then there's the ancient proverb known as 'the Chinese curse' – 'may you live in interesting times' – much quoted in guidebooks and popular histories and much loved by testosterone-driven businessfolk, usually garnished with a knowing chuckle: this seems to have been first coined, in its current English form, in 1936 – within the English diplomatic community! It is the sort of cod-Confucian proverb that, to Western ears, sounds right – as 'ancient' as the corny aphorisms of Charlie Chan, in fact. Of course, the diplomatic community – like the senior ranks of the Civil Service – is full of 'mandarins', meaning powerful bureaucrats who are especially reactionary or secretive. The word originally described, in Imperial China, the top nine ranks of the civil service. It took the Brits to turn it into a pejorative. The toast 'Chin Chin' was brought from China by British officials too, an approximation of the greeting 'Tsui Tsui'.

The word 'Chinaman' is thought originally to have derived from the contemptuous and all-purpose 'John Chinaman' or 'Jack Chinaman': some restaurants still use the name. Where 'Chink' is concerned, the nursery skipping rhyme survives to this day in variant versions:

> *Chink, Chink, Chinaman, sitting on a rail;*
> *Along comes a white man and cuts off his tail . . .*

or

> *Chinky, Chinky, Chinaman, sitting on a fence;*
> *Trying to make a dollar out of fifteen cents.*
> *Chinky, Chinky, Chinaman, eats dead rats;*
> *Eats them up like gingersnaps . . .*

In television circles, a filming appointment at 2.30 p.m. was until recently known as 'Chinese dentist', as in 'Tooth hurtee?' Among film technicians, the shorthand phrase 'Make it Chinese' means setting the lights with masking metal barn doors, to cut out unwanted beams, so that a horizontal rather than a vertical slit remains. An order for 'fly ry' still seems popular with students on a boozy evening out – a legacy of pidgin English as spoken by Chinese people around Guangzhou who had difficulty pronouncing certain words. 'Pidgin' may be derived from the word 'business' – a Christian bishop was, for example, known as 'No. 1 Heaven Pigeon'. There was no implied insult about pidgin English until the early twentieth century, when it began to be seen as humiliating – because English-speakers and writers of dialect comedy tended to present it as ridiculous. There are still phrases in everyday language – 'long time no see', 'look see', among them – which date from the pidgin era. The cricketing team 'bowling a Chinaman', by the way, is said to date from 1933, and a Test Match with the West Indies at Old Trafford when Ellis 'Puss' Achong (who had Chinese ancestors) bowled Walter Robins with left-arm spin, who was heard muttering as he walked off, 'Fancy being done by a bloody Chinaman.' And so on. Such thoughts rushed through my mind. But they were a tad too convoluted to share with Dr Fang. Besides, they would have spoiled the party.

So, just between us, *were* there still any hard feelings? 'Today's British are so different to the Empire British,' replied Dr Fang. And besides, the Japanese were so much worse, and much deeper in the popular memory. The humiliating Sino-Japanese war of 1894–95; the Russo-Japanese War of 1905; and above all the terrible massacre of Nanking in December 1937. This went much deeper than the 'Treaty of Nanking' of way back in 1842! I turned to my interpreter: 'You have been too nice about the history of our two countries.' 'Yes.' She smiled prettily. 'But it was, as Dr Fang says, all a long time ago.' Maybe so, but photographs of the Yuanming Yuan Ruins Park still appear on countless tee-shirts, bottle labels, posters and calendars.

Later that afternoon, I was shown an illustrated textbook called *A Record of National Humiliation* (1998). Its primary focus was on 'the century of humiliation' – between the start of the First Opium War in 1839 and the Communist victory in 1949. The key historical milestones included:

- The First Opium War (1839–42) and the challenge to Chinese sovereignty ('the invaders')
- The Second Opium War and 'reprisals' (1856–60) ('the pirates')
- The burning and looting of the Garden of Perfect Brightness ('the barbarians')
- The Unfair Treaties, starting with the 1842 Treaty of Nanking, and including Tianjin in 1858, which among other provisions forbad Chinese officials from calling the British 'barbarians' even when they were ('gunboat diplomacy')
- The shameless treatment of hardworking Chinese overseas, who defended themselves in ghettos called Chinatowns ('capitalism')
- The mockery of Chinese people who could not pronounce English words ('their idea of comedy')
- The aftermath of the 'Righteous and Harmonious Brotherhood of Fists' in 1900 ('the frenzied scramble for concessions')

And photographs of 'the Elgin Ruins' were much in evidence. The British seemed to have been responsible for about half of the featured 'humiliations'. The shameless treatment of 'Chinese overseas' was more about California – the gold rush, the building of the transcontinental railroad and the draconian 1882 Exclusion Act (made 'permanent' in 1902) – than about English cities, though they were mentioned too. Apparently, there had been a spate of such high-profile books about 'humiliation' published since 1989 as a matter of party policy under President Jiang Zemin – with his mantras of 'national unity', 'soft power' and 'memories of humiliation leading to national rejuvenation'. They were partly about the century of humiliation, partly about bringing the nation together with thoughts of historical enemies abroad and the traitors at home who had dealings with them, and partly about 'the clash of civilizations' (a popular concept in the United States as well). Following Tiananmen Square, they were much in evidence. The punchline seemed to be: 'We are on our own and always have been: we must set out our own destiny and we must stick together.' And we must welcome the new paradigm of a fast-developing market and with it a ubiquitous state.

On the way back home, I called in to see some friends in Hong Kong. The city was buzzing with Chinese entrepreneurial activity – more, it seemed, than before 1997. The dire predictions about the disruption of business and the threat of 'two countries, one system' had evidently not come true. I went to a bookshop, just before leaving for the airport. In the English-language section, the first thing that caught my eye was the sheer number of jackets on books about *contemporary* China which featured full-face portraits of Mao Tse-Tung (Warhol-style), the red and yellow flag, versions of highly coloured Cultural Revolution posters of Red Guards on the march – and above all, a scaly serpentine dragon. In Chinese folklore, the dragon is a wise, peaceable and helpful creature, a symbol of good luck, but he has become on book jackets threatening, fire-breathing and warlike, to be challenged – presumably – by the likes of St George. The awakening dragon; the rising dragon; the aggressive dragon. The mythical Dragon King Guangrun, enshrined in a temple on Kunming Lake, exercised control over the weather, and the all-important supply of water. The image of the five-clawed dragon was, historically, reserved for Imperial clothing – harnessing its folkloric connotations of good luck, power and beneficence; the four-clawed dragon was reserved for the nobility and the three-clawed for ministers. Today, 'dragon dances' are a distant residue of this. Not so on book covers. Publishers evidently misread the creatures as symbolic of post-Imperial Chinese global ambitions: or perhaps they assume that the equation 'dragon = China' will be interpreted in this way by readers. I could only find a single book featuring an image of up-to-date Chinese civilians going about their business in a modern Chinese city. Chinese marketeers and graphic designers have tried to establish the cuddly panda as an alternative – but he has not, it seems, caught on. Nearly all the books in English about contemporary China seemed to have the words 'power', 'threat' and 'rise' in their titles. Then three books caused a sudden adrenalin rush.

The first, with a cover photo of a Chinese soldier peering down the sight of a fearsome weapon pointed threateningly at the reader, had the very muscular title of *Showdown: Why China Wants War with the United States* and was written by a former Deputy Under Secretary of Defense in George Bush Sr's administration, together with a former US Marine fighter pilot who had held 'high security positions'. The book described a series of fictional scenarios in the form of short stories about 'the Pacific Cold War' and how it may well be warming up: the invasion of Taiwan, the Second Korean War (this time nuclear), the First Oil War (Venezuela plus China), the Sino-Japanese War over the islands off Southern Japan and – again – the Confucian-Islamic alliance. It concluded that China's internal instability under 'ChiCom' – military shorthand for the Communist Party – frantic pace of rearmament (more intense 'than anything since the Nazis', despite the absence of an external military threat) and endemic corruption among officialdom could well ignite any of these scenarios – or, failing those, conflict in the oilfields of the Middle East, the Far East, Africa or South America, which just about covered the globe. Take your pick! 'To win the Pacific Cold War we must first understand that it has begun . . .'

The second, with a fierce golden dragon resembling a hub-cap on the jacket, had the equally direct title *The Coming China Wars: Where They Will Be Fought and How They Can Be Won*. It was by a professor of business at the University of California, Irvine, and it explored the collision course between a rapidly industrialized China ('the world's largest pirate nation') and the West: counterfeit goods and doctored drugs; the '21st century opium wars' – masterminded this time by 'an unholy triangle of Triad gangsters, international smugglers and corrupt Communist Party officials'; the spreading of environmental pollution; blood for oil – 'just business, no political conditions' – especially in Africa; new Imperialism in Latin America, 'with low-interest loans and sophisticated weapons systems as bait', plus weapons of mass construction – 'in a supreme historical irony, one of imperialism's worst former victims has become the 21st century's most relentlessly imperialistic nation'; water wars – the huge dam projects which have led to fierce diplomatic battles between 'upstream' and 'downstream' countries; mass protest from within – students, rural peasants, ethnic separatists; and 'China's ticking time bomb', an ageing population which is becoming 'increasingly sick'. All or any of this, plus the behind-the-scenes manipulation of currencies, the subsidizing of exports and the forcible lowering of wages and conditions of work in the Chinese labour force. 'A better understanding of the complexities of the economic origins of the Coming China Wars will help to lead to their peaceful resolution.' The conclusion felt like an elephant giving birth to a mouse.

Both books claimed to be pleas for 'better understanding'. But both were written in macho, sabre-rattling style – and were basically updated versions of the Yellow Peril literature of the early twentieth century. The Yellow Peril with footnotes, maps and graphs. In this sense, they chimed with reported statements – especially by Republican or Tea Party candidates in the States – about secret plans by China to undermine/take over/purchase America. 'Why should we undermine the American economy?' says the smiling Chinese official. 'We *own* it.' Evidently, the idea of a Yellow Peril has never really gone away from American politics: it regularly emerges from just beneath the surface, with increasing shrillness, when times become hard. 'Better understanding' or attempts to play to the prejudice of voters? In Edwardian times, the threat of 'the rising dragon' was thought to be as much racial as military: today it is – according to these books, countless commentators in the weeklies, and barnstorming politicians – economic and military, on the face of it at least; or medical, in the form of a pandemic spreading from the East. The repertoire of fiendish plots has changed surprisingly little, making allowances for the passage of time: bugs in computers, poisoned medicines, taints in milk, infected chickens, a plague of spam, gluttony of raw materials, unfair trade surpluses, trespasses on intellectual property, secret purchases of strategic assets, huge arms deals, piracy in Western universities, infiltration of Africa, trouble in Tibet, slave labour, unstable tyranny at home, laughter at international trade agreements, opium, plunder of the latest ideas of the West and lack of *real* invention, Mongol hordes ready to eat us for breakfast, lunch and supper, the awakening giant, fantasies of world domination, the clash of civilizations . . . The litany has a very familiar ring. The one element missing is a pictorial personification of these anxieties, an embodiment of Chinese cunning and culpability, a scapegoat for broader economic and social tensions. A suitably exaggerated personification – someone, as it were, ten feet tall.

The third book which caught my eye, nestling nearby, was a paperback omnibus (published in 1998) reprinting the first three novels to feature Dr Fu Manchu, the second most famous Chinese person in the world . . . and the twentieth-century literary villain who lingers in the consciousness more than any other.

CHAPTER ONE

Sax and the Single Chinaman

A s I walked slowly up the short drive, I wondered which of her names would appear beside the door. Rose Elizabeth Knox? Rose Elizabeth Knox Ward? Elizabeth Rohmer? The house was at the end of a quiet leafy road bordering Lewes old town in Sussex. It was a robust redbrick construction. Suburban baronial. Late Victorian by the look of it, probably dating from about twenty years before *The Mystery of Dr Fu-Manchu* was published in 1913 (serialized 1912–13). She lived in the ground floor flat, next to the garden: 'Elizabeth Sax Rohmer' – the name she adopted for her own thriller, when times became harder, *Bianca in Black* (1954), about an 'internationally famous mannequin' who wears black because she keeps losing her husbands. The 1962 paperback referred to her as 'the daughter of master-storyteller Sax Rohmer'. She was in fact his widow at the time, and the marriage was childless. A petite, bonny, curly-haired woman with eyes set wide apart came to the door. She must have been all of eighty-five years old and she certainly didn't look it. Her makeup – rouged cheeks, magenta lipstick – was stuck in the period when she had peaked, the 1930s. Still making an effort. She had the breezy, unselfconscious manner of a pub landlady, with a very faint trace of cockney in her voice – the voice of a vaudevillian who had risen in the world, full of elocution. This was not someone who was about to go gently into that good night.

Elizabeth's sitting room was an Aladdin's Cave, or rather a never-never land, past its best. Sax Rohmer would no doubt have called the room 'orientally furnished, cushioned and perfumed', a private museum of bedazzling memorabilia assembled, maybe, to bring good news as a protection against the everyday world outside. Lacquered tables on spindly legs. Tassels on the curtains. Brocade cushions, and a thick-pile carpet with a patterned Persian rug on it. A wooden casket with ivory inlay. A potted palm. An empty flask which once held oil of jasmine – purchased, I later learned, from a souk in

Cairo during their belated honeymoon in Egypt, 1913. Puffy red couches with footstools, a camel-saddle, a mahogany cabinet full of large-format leather and gilt-bound first editions of some of her late husband's novels, with watercolour illustrations in the soft palette style of Edmund Dulac. Sax Rohmer's polished wooden writing desk which Rose had bought for thirty shillings around 1910 early in their marriage and which had survived their nomadic life since, and on it one of the briar pipes he always smoked. Among the antique brown and white postcards, a photograph of a pretty, fresh-faced girl with auburn curly hair, half smiling as she stared confidently at the camera. A girl with attitude. Most of Sax Rohmer's heroines tended to have auburn hair. And in an alcove, the little dolls she would give him as a reward while he was getting down to his work: his preferred hours were 11 p.m. to 3 a.m. and he wrote in pencil. No joss-sticks or masks or little shrines, though – the overall message was 'Egyptian' rather than 'Chinese'. Rohmer always used the adjectives 'gorgeous' or 'exquisite' to describe such interiors. In one of the early Fu Manchu stories, he attempted to evoke, in characteristic style,

> an exquisitely furnished room, illuminated by the soft light of a shaded lamp which stood upon a low, inlaid table amidst a perfect ocean of silken cushions, strewn upon a Persian carpet.

Elizabeth Sax Rohmer's sitting room was not *that* opulent, but it was striving for a similar effect.

Mr and Mrs Sax Rohmer had once – in the 1930s – lived very well on the proceeds and rights of his books: a Daimler, a Rolls-Royce coupé-de-ville, and a specially built country house just outside Reigate in Surrey – with a dining room panelled in weathered oak, courtesy of the *Mauretania* which had recently been stripped in Southampton. The Rohmers had replaced a Victorian villa there with a house of their own design – complete with multicoloured roof in blue, red and purple, plus a hint of gold. The house cost some £45,000 to build. 'It wasn't at all vulgar,' Elizabeth confided to me, 'and it was a long time ago': dating from before the time when her husband's taste for travel and luxury, his ruinous addiction to finding a 'mathematical or geometrical flaw' in the game of roulette in Monte Carlo (he'd hoped to write a book about 'the system of roulette' which would ensure his readers 'a reasonable profit', but never got round to it), his lack of business acumen, naivety about the taxman and unfortunate choice of advisers had all but exhausted their fortune. As late as 1955, it had been rumoured that Sax had sold the film, television and radio rights of the Fu Manchu character and stories in America for $4 million – a colossal sum for a screenwriter at the time – but that he was cheated by an agent and took home only $8,000 of it. If so, it would not have been the first time. In fact, the Rohmers had already sold their country house, Little Gatton, to the celebrated racing motorist Sir Malcolm Campbell for half the money it had cost them to build it.

According to Elizabeth Sax Rohmer, her husband was something of a gentle dreamer, often out of touch with day-to-day reality; he was 'full of Irish charm and old world chivalry'. He even tried to finish off Dr Fu Manchu after the first three novels, or rather collections of stories (1912–17), but had to keep resurrecting him 'by popular clamourance' from the late 1920s onwards. 'I play Frankenstein to the monster of Dr Fu Manchu,' he admitted. Like Arthur Conan Doyle and Sherlock Holmes. But Doyle wrote under his own name. *He* was the man who reinvented Arthur Ward as the much more interesting and exotic 'Sax Rohmer' and was apparently a disarming person who half-believed the fantasies he had made up. All the newspaper articles about him, in his heyday, were about 'Sax' the authorized persona rather than 'Arthur'. Something like today's John le Carré and spies – where it is difficult to draw the line between real life and fantasy life – only much more so. The vehemence of his prose, the melodrama of his plots, the towering self-confidence of his Fu Manchu novels were, in time-honoured fashion, smokescreens for a much less self-assured, much more friendly person. Even those who despised his writings commented on his immense charm. But his attempts to branch out into theatre, and serious fiction, all ended in disappointment.

I had made an appointment to meet Elizabeth Rohmer, because I had recently written a play based on the first three Fu Manchu novels, a kind of pop-art commentary on the originals, Dick Lester–style, and I sought her permission to perform it during the 1971 summer season in Cornwall, either at the open-air Minack in Porthcurno or at a theatre in Penzance with a group of actors from Cambridge University. The play was a send-up – and nostalgic – both at the same time. The first thing Elizabeth said to me, as we sat down, was that she had sold the film rights of the novels in the early 1960s, after Sax's death from Asian 'flu in 1959, to 'an Englishman from a theatrical family', for not very much money, not nearly as much as they would have fetched in the good old days of Hollywood and mass-circulation fiction magazines.

She thought the figure might be £4,500 (actually it was £2,500), which was much needed because dear Sax had left her 'only £700'. In fact, the legacy was £1,047 and 16 shillings. 'Come to think of it,' she added, she thought she had sold the rights in the characters' *names*, rather than the novels themselves. Maybe the resulting films would stimulate the sales of the novels: 'maybe, dear; who knows these days?' Elizabeth was not at all sure whether her deal with the theatrical Englishman Harry Alan Towers included theatrical rights, and she certainly did not want to jeopardize one of her two main sources of income – the other being paperback reprints of Sax's novels for the dope-smoking generation. Towers had been a tough negotiator, she recalled. But it *was* an amateur production, so maybe that would make it all right. What I *mustn't* do, under any circumstances, was to include the name 'Fu Manchu' in the title . . . How about 'The Devil Doctor' instead? Whatever the finer points of the deal, the film producer had certainly bought the performing rights to the characters' names. She remembered that. So don't mention the Chinaman. Elizabeth was good-humoured, and seemed amused and touched that this young man from Cambridge was interested in her late husband's work. A tad apprehensively – it seemed to me – she agreed to let me write and produce the play. 'But don't advertise it too widely.' Her hands were hyperactive, fidgety, throughout the conversation. Did I know that Sax Rohmer had tried to write a Fu Manchu play? But 'it never saw the light' and instead became the novel *The Shadow of Fu Manchu* (1948). Elizabeth hoped I would have better luck with my play . . .

In summer 1971, the name of 'Fu Manchu' was certainly in the cultural ether again. The Kinks had recently had a modest hit with the Ray Davies song 'The Village Green Preservation Society':

> We are the Sherlock Holmes, English-speaking vernacular.
> God save Fu Manchu, Moriarty and Dracula . . .

This quirky rearguard resistance song, loosely inspired by Dylan Thomas's *Under Milk Wood* (1954), listed some of the old things that should be preserved by this alternative National Trust, including Desperate Dan, draught beer, strawberry jam, vaudeville and variety, winners of the George Cross – and Fu Manchu. The song reapplied *County Life* nostalgia to popular culture – and also accepted that 'the new ways' could sometimes be an improvement.

Anthony Shaffer's play *Sleuth* had opened in London's West End early in 1970 and would eventually play for eight and a half years. Among its many references to classic mystery and detective stories – from Conan Doyle to the 'country house' stories of the interwar years to the police procedurals of the 1950s – was this impassioned plea by Andrew Wyke, creator of the Peter Wimsey-style detective St John Lord Merridew:

> Let's give our crime the true sparkle of the thirties, a little amateur aristocratic quirkiness. Think of all that wonderful material. There's the ice dagger, the poison that leaves no trace, the Regie cigarette stubbed in the ashtray, charred violet notepaper in the grate, Duesenberg tyre marks in the driveway, the gramophone record simulating conversation, the clutching hand behind the arras, sinister Orientals . . .

Wyke also, at one point, spits the words: 'Shuttee shopee . . .' This was a quote from an early chapter of Sax Rohmer's first Fu Manchu novel, when the intrepid heroes visit Shen Yan's barbershop and opium den in the East End of London, 'off the old Ratcliffe Highway' – known in the trade as Singapore Charlie's – cleverly disguised as 'Dago seamen':

> From behind a curtain heavily brocaded with filth a little Chinaman appeared, dressed in a loose smock, black trousers and thick-soled slippers, and, advancing, shook his head vigorously. 'No shavee – no shavee,' he chattered, simian fashion, squinting from one to the other of us with his twinkling eyes. 'Too late! Shuttee shop!'

The pidgin 'shuttee shop!' line was repeated by Rohmer – as was the exact situation – seven years later in his novel *The Golden Scorpion* (1919). This time, the intrepid heroes were French detective Gaston Max accompanied by stolid Dr Keppel Stuart, and the location was beside 'The Pidgin House' in Limehouse, nearer London's docks:

> 'Go off! Too late! Shuttee shop!' chattered a voice out of the darkness. Max thrust his way resolutely in, followed by Stuart. 'Shut the door, Ah-Fang-Fu!' he said curtly . . .

Sleuth was partly about the contrast between pre-war and post-war Britain – symbolized by fictional amateur detectives versus working policemen – and partly about whether the classic detective/mystery story was the normal recreation of noble minds or whether it was more a case of noble minds being the normal recreation of detective stories. Why did people still read them, when their social and racial attitudes were so out of date? When Chinese people could routinely be described as 'simian', as they chattered in music-hall pidgin English? What was the attraction in the late 1960s? Nostalgia? Alienation from the brash modern world? Reinforcement of old attitudes? Imperial longings?

The rival for the affections of Wyke's wife Marguerite, Milo Tindle, is in no doubt where *he* stands:

> Take a look at yourself, Andrew, and ask yourself a few simple questions about your attachment to the English detective story. Perhaps you might come to realise that the only place you inhabit is a dead world – a country house world where peers and colonels die in their studies; where butlers steal the port, and pert parlourmaids cringe, weeping malapropisms behind green baize doors. It's a world of coldness and class hatred, and two-dimensional characters who are not expected to communicate; it's a world where only the amateurs win, and where foreigners are automatically figures of fun.

In his memoir *So What Did You Expect?* (2001), Anthony Shaffer was later to recall that his father advised him, aged thirteen, always to drink Bollinger champagne rather than 'a lot of the other Chinese stuff that's around'. 'Chinese', Shaffer helpfully explains, 'was his word for anything strange, unfamiliar, foreign or dubious.' He also recalled reading Sax Rohmer's mystery and detective stories in his youth. Clearly, part of him despised the world of the classic detective/mystery story, and part of him was still attracted by it. Shaffer dedicated *Sleuth* to ten of the best-known old-style detectives, and all their omniscient, amateur colleagues, 'with regard and affection'. *Sleuth* was playing while Hugh Green's anthologies of *The Rivals of Sherlock Holmes* (1970–73) were sharing shelf-space in the bookshops with paperback reprints of Sax Rohmer's Fu Manchu novels.

In summer 1971, the James Bond film franchise was expanding fast, with the latest, *Diamonds Are Forever,* involving the much-publicized return of Sean Connery, who had driven a hard bargain. The franchise had been kick-started by the surprise success of the film *Dr No* in 1962. The original novel, published four years before, had – by Ian Fleming's own admission – owed a great deal to memories of Sax Rohmer, not just as a forerunner but as a progenitor. Indeed, Fleming's whole approach to crafting spy stories had been partly about updating the clubland heroes of his youth for a consumer age – with the addition of an active sex life for his hero, and memories/fantasies of Intelligence in the Second World War:

> I didn't believe in the heroic Bulldog Drummond types. I felt these types could no longer exist in literature. I wanted my lead character to more or less follow the style of Raymond Chandler and Dashiell Hammett's heroes, who are believable people, believable heroes. I was considerably influenced by those superb masters of the modern thriller . . . and to some extent in my childhood Sax Rohmer.

So, not just *Dr No*. Most of Ian Fleming's villains were descendants in one form or another of Dr Fu Manchu. John Pearson had recently written of *Live and Let Die* (1954), for example, in his biography of Fleming:

> . . . the whole episode of Mr Big with the table that descends through the floor of the Boneyard Strip Club, the supernatural awfulness of his presence and his reliance on voodoo and black magic to keep his followers in order, is a skilful recreation [for the Cold War era] of the world of Sax Rohmer and Fu Manchu which Fleming enjoyed as a boy at Eton.

Actually, Fleming was first introduced to Sax Rohmer's novels even earlier in his life – by the headmaster's wife at his hated prep school, Durnford, near Swanage in Dorset. But *Dr No* went one large step further, according to Pearson. This time it was 'a nostalgic thriller *modelled* on those stories of Sax Rohmer which had made such an impression on Fleming'. The villain became a kind of rich man's Fu Manchu, living in a Caribbean enclave of the British Empire. He is first described to James Bond as 'this Chinaman, who must be a wily devil by the way'. Wily, because he has cornered the market in bird droppings, which make an excellent fertilizer. Bond's next experience of the devil doctor and his cunning methods is via a poisoned nectarine, followed in short order by a five-inch centipede with poison claws crawling around his hotel bed. When Dr No finally appears in his undersea lair on the guano-encrusted island of Crab Key (the chapter is called 'Come into My Parlour'), the description of first impressions could almost have been penned by Rohmer half a century earlier. Fleming had learned to delay the entry of his villain, and strictly to ration his appearances, to enhance the mystique:

> Dr No was at least six inches taller than Bond, but the straight immovable poise of his body made him seem still taller. The head also was elongated

and tapered from a round, completely bald skull down to a sharp chin so that the impression was of a reversed raindrop – or rather oildrop, for the skin was of a deep, almost translucent, yellow. It was impossible to tell Dr No's age. Slanting jet-black eyes stared out of the skull. They were without eyelashes. . . . The thin fine nose ended very close above a wide compressed mound of a mouth which, despite its almost permanent sketch of a smile, showed only cruelty and authority. . . . The bizarre, gliding figure looked like a giant venomous worm wrapped in grey tin-foil . . .

The height, the bald skull, the agelessness, the eyes, the general aura of 'cruelty and authority', the likeness to a venomous creature, read like a carbon copy of all Rohmer's classic descriptions of Fu Manchu. In the film version, stage actor Joseph Wiseman played Dr No in a more streamlined and sophisticated way: his hands have no longer been cut off by the vindictive Hip Sing Chinese Tong in New York, but have been lost in a nuclear accident; his sponsors are no longer the Russians but SPECTRE, a strictly for-profit international terrorist organization; his domination of the workforce on Crab Key – described in the novel as made up of Cuban and Jamaican labourers under 'Chingroe' ('Chinese Negro') overseers, who have 'some of the intelligence of the Chinese and most of the vices of the black man' – is mercifully not emphasized. And his death – drowned in tons of bird shit: he who lives by the guano will die by the guano – becomes in the film version a drowning in radioactive liquid in the middle of a nuclear water-reactor. Joseph Wiseman thought that *Dr No* would turn out to be 'just another grade B Charlie Chan mystery'. It featured British actress Zena Marshall as a most improbable 'Miss Taro', Dr No's seductive Eurasian secretary: apparently 'thirty Asian actresses' were tested for the part, but they were all found wanting.

Although all the good guys in the novel call Dr No 'the Chinaman', he is described by Ian Fleming as 'the son of a German Methodist missionary and a Chinese girl of good fortune', born in Peking. His name – Julius No – comes from 'Julius' after his father and 'No' because he has rejected everything his father stood for. Fu Manchu's origins – it eventually transpired – may have been equally mixed race, a recurring feature in Yellow Peril literature. Ian Fleming's villains – like Rohmer's – always have physical characteristics which to him signal 'evil' or 'megalomaniac'. Fans of Sax Rohmer enjoyed *his* super-villain so much that they invented a moustache for him that was never once mentioned in the novels: the James Bond films echoed the process by inventing a white cat on the lap of Ernst Stavro Blofeld. As if an absence of earlobes and a weight of thirty stone were not enough. According to the autobiography of Bond producer Cubby Broccoli, in the original treatment of *Dr No*, the parallels with Fu Manchu were *too* close. He quotes screenwriter Richard Maibaum in support of this:

> When Wolf [Mankowitz] and I began working on the script, we decided that Fleming's Dr No was the most ludicrous character in the world. He was just Fu Manchu with two steel hooks. It was 1961 and we felt that audiences wouldn't stand for that kind of stuff any more. So, bright boys that we were, we decided that there would be no Dr No. There would be a villain who always had a marmoset monkey sitting on his shoulder, and the *monkey* would be Dr No. . . . Cubby was outraged, in his usual good-natured way . . . 'No monkey, d'you hear?'

In fact, the original treatment dated 7 September 1961 did not turn Dr No into a monkey – Broccoli's memory was playing tricks – but it did feature a capuchin monkey called Li Ying with links to the Doctor. The creature belongs to a shipping agent called Buckfield, who *disguises* himself – with help from a claw hand and face mask – as the late Dr No. Buckfield aims to destroy the locks on the Panama Canal, and is backed by Cuba. On Crab Key, James Bond discovers in a Chinese cemetery, near Dr No's grave, a huge black statue of a monkey. After the usual chase and explosion, the story ends with the monkey Li Ying jumping onto Bond's shoulder, 'gibbering ironically'. Richard Maibaum and Wolf Mankowitz were trying hard – too hard, it transpired – to ring changes to clichés inherited from Sax Rohmer (Dr Fu Manchu had a pet marmoset, which sat on his shoulder). 'We felt that audiences wouldn't stand that kind of stuff any more.' But Cubby Broccoli knew better. The second draft of the treatment, dated 28 September 1961, dropped the monkey and reinstated the devil doctor in person.

Harry Alan Towers – the 'Englishman from a theatrical family', as Elizabeth Sax Rohmer remembered him – was a maverick film producer, who shared a press agent with Lord Lucan and who was making films in Europe and South America while on the run from the American authorities for alleged involvement in a call-girl racket. 'Flamboyant' did not begin to describe him. His cycle of lowish-budget Fu Manchu films was presold, partly on Sax

Rohmer's name in the title, partly on the names of the leading characters, on the correct assumption that audiences would still recognize them. The cycle began with *The Face of Fu Manchu* (1965) and was followed, returns rapidly diminishing, by *The Brides of Fu Manchu* and *The Vengeance of Fu Manchu* (both 1966), *The Blood of Fu Manchu* (1968) and *The Castle of Fu Manchu* (1969). Towers was also canny enough to feature the name 'Fu Manchu' in each of the titles. Rohmer himself had not been so canny. His second and third novels were called in Britain, *The Devil Doctor* (1916) and *The Si-Fan Mysteries* (1917): in America, they were retitled *The Return of Dr Fu-Manchu* and *The Hand of Fu Manchu*. He never made the same mistake again. The 1960s films were European co-productions (with a substantial contribution from Constantin Film of Frankfurt, playing to the West German Fu Manchu cult) and they were marketed as updating the characters 'from the Boy's Own Paper to the James Bond era'. 'A showdown between Fu and 007!' Ian Fleming had in fact seriously considered Christopher Lee – his cousin by marriage – as an excellent choice to play Dr No in 1958, and actively proposed him for the part, or failing him, Noël Coward. Lee finally got his chance when he was cast as the evil Chinaman. The main characters and the period, or such period details as they could afford, were Sax Rohmer's (paperback reprints had done well in the early 1960s, with pop-orientalist covers), but the original screenplays were written by 'Peter Welbeck' – a pseudonym of Towers himself and a reference to the street near his London office. So the films were 'based on characters created by Sax Rohmer', rather than on the original stories. Each film ended with the inscrutable Christopher Lee's words in haunting voice-over: 'The world shall hear from me again.'

Robert Morley had in fact beaten Christopher Lee to it, by three years, with *The Road to Hong Kong* (1962) – last and least of the Bing Crosby and Bob Hope films, made at Shepperton Studios, near London. Not by name, but in every other way. The film began with cartoon-style credits (courtesy of Maurice Binder, the James Bond man) of the popular visual clichés of 'China': a dragon which smothers the title, chopsticks, noodles, a teapot, a conjuring trick, mah-jong and fortune cookies. A voice-over promised 'the inscrutable sinister face of mystery and intrigue', which turned out to take the rotund form of Robert Morley ('gentlemen, we bid you welcome'), with plans to dominate the world through his fiendish 'third echelon rocket' to the moon, launched from a base in the mountains above Hong Kong. Morley makes no attempt at a Chinese accent, but is clearly intended to be a parody of Dr No. The décor of his hideout

James Gillray's hand-coloured fantasy etching *The Reception of the Diplomatique . . . at the Court of Pekin*, published on 14 September 1792, just before Lord George Macartney left on his mission to China.

The last British Governor of Hong Kong, Chris Patten, receives the carefully folded Union flag outside Government House, as part of the farewell to Hong Kong, 30 June 1997.

ABOVE: Dust-jacket – with threatening golden dragon at its centre – of *The Coming China Wars* (2006), by a professor of business at the University of California, Irvine. **OPPOSITE:** Late nineteenth-century American cartoon, depicting Chinese immigration as a colossal invader-genie, dwarfing Uncle Sam.

"ONE, TWO, THREE, FOUR, RIGHT ABOUT TURN!"
Copyright: London Missionary Society, 16, New Bridge Street, E.C.

Postcard of missionaries spreading the word in China through nursery rhymes.

Travelling in Sedan Chair, Hongkong.

'Travelling in Sedan Chair, Hongkong': a postcard for European and American consumption.

Postcard of 'The Execution of the Chinese Pirates in Hong Kong', enhanced by hand-colouring: such gruesome scenes of punishment were surprisingly popular.

Postcard entitled 'Slow Death', making a spectacle of execution in wooden cages.

CITÉ. – Femme assise   CITY. – Woman sitting down

ABOVE: Friedrich Wilhelm Keyl's portrait of the accurately named 'Looty' (1861), the Summer Palace Pekingese dog presented to Queen Victoria. **OPPOSITE:** Late nineteenth-century studio portrait of a Chinese girl, with decorative props, circulated among foreigners as a postcard.

MADAME TUSSAUD & SONS'
EXHIBITION,
BAZAAR, BAKER STREET, PORTMAN SQUARE.

The Author of the Chinese War!
The Destroyer of £2,500,000. of British Property, and his Small Footed Wife, the only Figures of the kind ever Exhibited in this Country.

COMMISSIONER LIN,
And his Favourite Consort,
Modelled from Life, by the Celebrated LAMB-QUA, of Canton, with the Magnificent Dresses actually worn by them, and the various Ornaments, &c.

Giving a perfect idea of the *Countenance, Costume, and Ornaments* of those singular people the Chinese, of whom so little is known ; lately brought to this Country by a Gentleman, a resident of Canton Eighteen Years, and to whom reference can be given.

C

Madame Tussaud leaflet promoting the arrival of the waxwork of 'Lin Zexu' (Commissioner Lin Tse-Hsu), the man who tried to ban the opium trade in 1839–40, and his 'favourite consort'.

is described as 'early egg foo yong'. He is, we are led to believe, a 'mathematical genius'. Morley: 'Personal sentimentality has no place in our movement. . . . I'll rebuild the world according to my own image after my own specification.'

Presumably on the strength of his performance in *The Road to Hong Kong*, three years later – at the same time as *The Face of Fu Manchu* – Morley was cast as 'the Emperor of China' of 800 years ago, complete with long moustache, bushy eyebrows, extended fingernails, elaborately embroidered robes, golden head-dress and, again, English accent and impeccable manners, in *Genghis Khan* (1965): 'Fear? The Chinese Empire knows no such word . . . the Great Wall merely ensures that civilization shall know it is there. . . . *It is to keep people in.*' Temujin (Omar Sharif) refers to the Emperor as 'a peacock' – Morley hands a small fan to a servant because 'it has grown heavy', he has a change of embroidered robe for every scene, and in all seriousness says things like 'although divine I'm also human' – and although revered he is presented throughout as petulant, devious and decadent. He particularly enjoys sub-Confucian aphorisms, Charlie Chan-style, such as 'better to light one candle than to curse the darkness'. The Emperor dies when a spectacular firework display over the walls of Peking ('the ingenuity of the Chinese mind') turns into an almighty explosion. It is then explained that Genghis Khan and his horde represent the star that 'burns brighter as the sun of China fades'. In other words, Omar Sharif wins and Robert Morley loses.

Dr No, The Face of Fu Manchu, The Road to Hong Kong – even *Genghis Khan* – were calculated to appeal to American audiences at a time of high anxiety about China. In the period between the Korean War (1950–53) and the Vietnam War (1959–75), when the United States had cut off contact, they embodied popular attitudes to 'the Bamboo Curtain' and the stark contrast between the civilizations of ancient and contemporary China. Long gone were the days when China was a gallant ally against Japan in the Second World War. The Fu Manchu paperback revival happened at precisely this time.

Where 'campy cult' versions of the Yellow Peril were concerned, there was also the knowing Sixties craze in Britain, school of *The Goons* (especially Spike Milligan) via *Beyond the Fringe* to *Monty Python's Flying Circus* (especially Michael Palin, with his later *Ripping Yarns* fascination), revisiting the Imperial adventure stories of the 1920s and 1930s in a partly affectionate, partly satirical, partly critical way. The Bonzo Dog Doo-Dah Band, Sergeant Pepper, I Was Lord Kitchener's Valet, The Red Baron, *Carry on up the Khyber*,

'Up the Khyber' by Pink Floyd, Charles Wood's scripts for *Help!*, *How I Won the War* and *The Charge of the Light Brigade*, the *Telegoons* and a new version of *The Moonstone* and updated versions of clubland heroes *The Saint* and *The Four Just Men* on television – all had tried, in their different ways, to exorcise the popular attitudes embodied in the paperback heroes of yesterday, while being curiously nostalgic about them at the same time, in a very British way. In *Help!* – a mix of James Bond, *The Moonstone* and the Goons – the villain Clang, representing 'the mystic East', would dearly love to become a world dominator like Fu Manchu, but British technology is constantly getting the better of him: the *Goldfinger*-style laser won't work because his assistant can't find the right British wall-plug to fit it; he travels around in an electric Harrods milk-float rather than an Aston Martin DB5, scattering tin-tacks on the road; a bomb fails to detonate because it is 'useless ex-Army rubbish' and the scientist's Webley revolver misfires at a key moment ('British, you see. Useless! Now, if I had a . . .'). In-jokes about Empire were superimposed on nostalgia for when Britain *could* still make it. A substantial chunk of British, or maybe English, popular culture at the time was obsessed with the Imperial past.

In a similar vein, just before I visited Mrs Sax Rohmer I had chanced to read 'The Fu Manchusical' (1969) by D. R. Bensen, a burlesque of the (then as now) current Broadway habit of adapting old books or 'musicalizing' well-known, presold, plays. In this case, it satirized Sax Rohmer's taste for audacious melodrama and hyperbole. The musical is set in a smart Mayfair drawing room some time in the 1920s, as the guests in evening dress await the arrival of Sir Denis Nayland Smith. The opening chorus goes:

> *He's swum the Nile and half the Brahma-Putra;*
> *He knows the man who wrote the Kama Sutra.*
> *Dacoits and Thugs to him are scarce a menace –*
> *He treats them coolly as a game of tennis.*

When Smith finally arrives, he tells his associate Dr Petrie about a funny thing that happened to him on the way to the party:

SMITH: Let me tell you, as I crossed the Park minutes ago, on my way here, I was closely followed by a most curious wasp, and managed to drive the creature off only by the nimblest of work with this stick.

PETRIE: But surely, Smith, on a warm spring day in the Park a wasp is not uncommon?

SMITH: Blood-red, hairy, the size of a pigeon? No, no, Petrie . . . I fancy I
can tell Fu Manchu's handiwork when I see it.

Smith then helpfully informs the assembled company about who exactly Fu
Manchu is – in a Gilbert and Sullivan-style song:

> Picture a person tall and feline,
> Powerful, skeleton-lean;
> A brow like Shakespeare, a face like Satan;
> Eyes of the true cat-green.
> Add to this a positive giant's
> Intellect and command of science
> And there you have the most incredible criminal genius the
> world has ever seen!

As the company goes into dinner, the Butler clears away the glasses,
comes forward and 'in the gloom his eyes glow a sinister and luminous
GREEN'.

All this was the cultural context for my play, the reason of my visit to Sax
Rohmer's widow. We continued to chat over tea – Assam rather than China,
I couldn't help noticing. I asked her about her husband's name, a pseudonym
which had become *the* most recognizable brand in popular fiction between the
wars. I knew that he had been christened Arthur Henry Ward in February 1883,
by his Irish Catholic parents William and Margaret Mary, and had changed his
middle name to 'Sarsfield' – after the seventeenth-century Irish military com-
mander and friend of King James II, Patrick Sarsfield, from whom his alcoholic
mother had fancifully told him he was descended, along with other far-fetched
Celtic tales. He was born in Ladywood, Birmingham, and the family moved to
London when he was three. He grew up at a time when children's comics, Sunday
Schools, parish magazines, religious tracts, pamphlets and school textbooks all
actively conspired to support missionary work in pagan and decadent China, and
in the process subtly justified Britain's bullying behaviour there: the 'China' they
presented was a static land of arrogance, warlords, infanticide, bound feet, pigtails and effeminacy, a land where people spat in the street and ate cats and dogs.
Crime writer Colin Watson speculates that this force-feeding of prejudice *must*
have influenced the adolescent Arthur Ward. 'So vehement and repetitive were
Sax Rohmer's references to Asiatic plotting against "white" civilization that they
cannot be explained simply as the frills of melodramatic narration.'

So where did the name 'Sax Rohmer' come from? The first *published* reference to the name 'Sax Rohmer' was as far as I knew in 1908, when he was credited as lyricist on the music-hall song 'Bang Went the Chance of a Lifetime', and on subsequent songs. He didn't use the name on his fiction until early 1912 when, with Rose Elizabeth's strong encouragement, he plucked up the courage to publish his serial *The Sins of Séverac Bablon* in *Cassell's Magazine*. Its central character is descended from 'the Royal House of Israel', he smokes opium cigarettes which he leaves burning as 'calling cards' and his main purpose in life is to punish miserly Jews by strong-arming them into supporting 'worthy projects': 'You have earned for the Jewish people a repute it ill deserves,' he says to one victim; on another occasion, he blackmails a group of Jewish financiers who are about to lend money to the German Treasury – thus postponing the First World War! Rohmer always claimed the serial was about 'a Jewish Robin Hood'. Today, it reads very differently. When he was growing up in suburban Birmingham and London, he seems to have absorbed not just the standard church prejudices of the late-Victorian age but something more extreme.

Before 1912, therefore, he was known to readers as 'A. Sarsfield Ward' or 'Arthur Sarsfield Ward' or sometimes 'Sarsfield Ward'. But he was using the name 'Rohmer' in private, to make himself sound more exotic, when he and Rose Elizabeth met in 1905. Then, for a while, he used both names – depending on the type of song, or story, he was publishing. On legal documents, he remained 'Arthur Ward' or 'Arthur Henry Sarsfield Ward (otherwise known as Sax Rohmer)'. But *she* always called him 'Sax'.

She then handed me a curling photocopy from an article in the *New Yorker* (29 November 1947), in which Sax recalled how the name had originally been devised:

> I'd done my stint in Fleet Street, you know, and was trying a spot of freelancing. Matter of fact, that's when I took this name, Sax Rohmer. In ancient Saxon, 'Sax' means 'blade'; 'rohmer' equals 'roamer'. I substituted an 'h' for an 'a' as a gesture in the direction of phonetics; pretty obscure gesture, I guess. My real name's Arthur Sarsfield Ward and, though I was born in Birmingham, my people were all Irish. . . . It's hard to say now whether I walked or was thrown out of Fleet Street.

So the name meant 'roaming blade', 'blade-runner' or 'freelance'. A name to draw attention to itself and at the same time an esoteric joke (the 'gesture in the direction of phonetics' was a characteristically pompous Rohmerian flourish). On other occasions, as with so much else in his life, Sax Rohmer told different stories about the genesis of the name. It looked good on a book's spine. It sounded exotic, or 'Nordic', and was occasionally written with an umlaut. It was vaguely Germanic, eccentrically so at a time when many Britons, including the royal family, were beginning to shed their genuinely German names such as Battenberg. It was 'eye-catching and sonorous'. Above all, it was memorable as a brand. Later, when he became commercially successful, he would change the 'S' to a dollar sign on his written signature. But why, I asked, adopt a pseudonym at all? Arthur Ward sounded perfectly respectable to me. Why was he so keen to shed the name he was baptized with? Was he ashamed in some way of his parentage? Was the change of name something to do with a flight from Irish identity – unusual at the time, in literary circles at least, when everyone seemed determined to *celebrate* Celtic roots and the revival of Celtic folk legends? Or was it perhaps a flight from bad memories of his parents' problems? Or from the Catholicism of the family home? His Fu Manchu stories contain some suggestive references: the devil doctor himself is described, in *The Trail of Fu Manchu* (1934), as speaking with the beauty of 'John Henry Newman . . . the poet cardinal', and the 'respectful gestures' of members of the dreaded secret society the Si-Fan are said to resemble 'the Roman Catholic Sign of the Cross'. On other occasions, the organization of the Si-Fan is compared with the Jesuits.

According to Elizabeth, the early stories he wrote under his own name were not particularly successful. And it was quite common in those days to adopt a 'stage name' which would stick in people's minds. Whatever the motivation, he certainly worked hard to construct a complete new persona for himself, after he had made his name, so to speak – usually photographed in an 'oriental robe', smoking a briar pipe, surrounded by a clutter of Chinese or Egyptian ornaments. I subsequently discovered that in a *Cyclopedia of Names* he was quoted as stating categorically 'that his name is not and never has been Arthur Sarsfield Ward'. Which was *partly* true – the 'Sarsfield' was his own invention. But . . . curiouser and curiouser.

One doubly ironic consequence of adopting the name 'Rohmer' was that his books were banned in Nazi Germany in 1936, on the grounds that he was a Jew. At least that is why he *thought* they had been banned. Sax Rohmer protested in print that he was in fact 'a good Irishman' and issued a complaint through his

German literary agent. He also wrote, very revealingly, in January 1938:

> [A sense of humour] was quite lacking, I thought, in the Nazi censors who withdrew all my German editions from circulation. To this day I have not the remotest idea in what way my stories are supposed to be inimical to Nazi ideals.

It was ironic that his name should be thought Jewish, given Rohmer's casual anti-semitism in his books; ironic, too, because up until then he had been so busy hiding the fact that both his parents were Irish. And it was astonishing that he was prepared publicly to admit that his books were not 'inimical to Nazi ideals'. A while after that – when such admissions had become more of a liability – the copyright page of his books proudly announced that they had the 'honour' of being banned by the Gestapo. During the war, Rohmer expressed his disappointment at the BBC radio's shabby treatment of his work by hinting at Nazi infiltration into broadcasting circles in *Seven Sins* (1943–44).

In the Fu Manchu novels, Rohmer found the names of his characters in much more obvious, less imaginative, places. The narrator of the early books was 'Dr Petrie'. He was given no first name, like the nameless narrator in Edgar Allan Poe's Dupin detective stories (1841–44) but unlike Dr Watson of *Sherlock Holmes* fame. His surname was borrowed from the maverick archaeologist Flinders Petrie, who shared some of Nayland Smith's views on racial identity in his books about eugenics and ancient Egypt, and who was at the time dividing his energies between teaching at University College London and excavating at Memphis. Aspects of the *character* of Flinders Petrie, though, were given by Rohmer to the volcanic, driven archaeologist Sir Lionel Barton, complete with unruly hair and beard. Barton, whose study we are told resembles 'an earthquake at Sotheby's the auction rooms', behaves in unethical ways that would have appalled Flinders Petrie, and unlike Petrie he is much more interested in tombs and treasures than in humble, everyday utensils, but he does share many characteristics with the professor's *public* image: notably the stubbornness, the eccentricity and the ruthless attitude towards tomb-raiders. As someone 'who first had penetrated in Lhassa, who thrice, as a pilgrim, had entered forbidden Mecca', Sir Lionel also shares some characteristics with the explorer and writer Sir Richard Burton, another very public figure dating from Rohmer's youth, as well as with Dr Ernest Alfred Wallis Budge, specialist in Egyptian antiquities at the British Museum. Budge was a notoriously difficult and short-fused man – Flinders Petrie called him 'Bug-bear' – with a chubby pink face which became redder the more angry he became; and he boasted in his autobiography *By Nile and Tigris* (1920) about how he had managed, as an agent for the Museum between 1886 and 1913, to smuggle large quantities of antiquities out of Egypt, having done deals with traders who were known to be illicit. Sir Lionel Barton also has a touch of Sir Francis Younghusband about him, the man who found a new land route across the Gobi desert at the age of twenty-three, and who had, in December 1903, managed to turn a minor diplomatic mission about the Tibetan border into a full-scale British invasion of Tibet. Rohmer's stories involving archaeological encounters in Egypt also tended to include thinly veiled caricatures of some of the leading Egyptologists of the day – seemingly gleaned from his reading of The French scholar Gaston Maspero's popular *New Light on Ancient Egypt* (1909). In Rohmer's *Tales of Secret Egypt* (1918), for instance, the Swiss archaeologist Henri Edouard Naville was renamed 'Neville' and set to work in the 'Valley of the Sorcerers' – located near the place the real Naville had worked for many years. If ever he read the story, it must have come as something of a surprise to the eminent, austere, traditionalist, Swiss Protestant scholar, who specialized in New Kingdom religious texts! Today, such pen portraits might well be actionable. By contrast, the ever dependable policemen in the Fu Manchu stories tend to be named after solidly recognizable English, Irish or Scottish place names such as 'Weymouth', 'Kerry', 'Dunbar' and 'Fife'.

Rohmer, by his own admission, had particularly enjoyed devouring popular non-fiction books about ancient Egypt while growing up in prosaic, suburban London. Rose and Sax met on Clapham Common, South Side, which was where Dr Petrie's surgery was located in the early Fu Manchu novels. Was this connection significant? Well, replied Elizabeth, not only did they meet on the Common, but their early life together was always based in South London. A year into their marriage, they moved into a newly built, end of terrace red-brick house at 6 Danecroft Gardens (which became 51 Herne Hill in October 1913), where they lived until 1919. Rohmer wrote the first three – and the best – Fu Manchu books in this house. It was from here that his reputation as a writer was first established. A Blue Plaque commemorating the connection was unveiled there on 20 October 1985. Rohmer's fantasies of Chinatown and ancient Egypt were concocted a whole world away from foggy Limehouse and the Valley of the Kings – not surprising, really – in a front garden in suburban

South London, among a rising community of lower-middle-class suburbanites. He was born just before the first Sherlock Holmes stories were published, and grew up in the heyday of the new popular press, short story magazines, large-scale serialization, cheap printing, subscription libraries, commuter literature, a W. H. Smith bookstall on every railway station. Karl Marx had famously referred to 'rural idiocy'. Had he lived twenty or thirty years later, he might well have revised this to 'suburban idiocy'. Rohmer was a struggling journalist, writer of short stories for the magazines and music-hall lyricist when he and Elizabeth first met. He had joked in that *New Yorker* article about 'whether I walked or was thrown out of Fleet Street'. Well, Elizabeth said, he certainly ran through a lot of jobs, all of them temporary, before finally hitting his stride with the first Fu Manchu story, 'The Zayat Kiss', in October 1912. It was not until after their marriage that he began to make any real progress as a writer. Having failed the Civil Service entrance examinations, he had become – she recalled – a clerk at the London office of the Hong Kong and Shanghai Bank on 31 Lombard Street, at the age of eighteen – one of his 'fellow employees' there had been the young P. G. Wodehouse – until, he liked to brag, 'he devised a foolproof scheme for stealing from the vaults' by hypnotizing a bank employee. Then he was a clerk in a gas company and a cub reporter on a weekly paper called *Commercial Intelligence* ('for the Home Trader and Exporter'), but he had trouble distinguishing fact from fiction so that job didn't last either. As he later liked to put it, 'I cannot pretend that I had set Fleet Street on fire, but I had created a moderately high temperature in the office of the newspaper which employed me.' Maybe *deliberate* fiction was the answer. Or commercial illustration: he 'pottered idly about' various evening classes in art and submitted black-and-white drawings to various publications; one, at least, was published. He tried his hand at short stories, but they were all rejected by the magazines. In fact, 'he had a whole wall of his room papered with editorial rejections'.

Finally, his persistence paid off when, at the age of twenty, he'd had two stories accepted on the same day in 1903: 'The Mysterious Mummy' by *Pearson's Magazine* (published 24 November 1903) and 'The Leopard-Couch' by *Chambers's Journal* (published 30 January 1904). 'The Mysterious Mummy' was about a thief who hides himself in an ancient sarcophagus in the British Museum, in order – after hours – to steal an exquisite Egyptian vase by substituting an exact-looking replica of it: school of Arthur Conan Doyle's 'The Ring of Thoth' (1890), set in the Louvre. Characteristically, Ward then claimed that his fictional crime was copied some six months later by a real-life thief in the Louvre. The earliest published stories were followed by three more in *Pearson's*: 'The Green Spider' (October 1904), 'The Mystery of the Marsh Hole' (April 1905) and 'The M'Villin' (December 1906), all under the name of 'A. Sarsfield Ward'.

For the next few years, he combined freelance journalism, short stories and working on music-hall sketches and lyrics. Which took the story up to when they met; as Elizabeth recalled:

> We lived together for four years and I was the one who made him *really* start writing stories. He wrote those little comic songs, for George Robey and Little Tich and others, and I encouraged him to write for the magazines as well. We were almost starving, down to our last baked potato. His father thought he was still working at the bank! Sax hadn't the heart to tell him what he was really doing.

Elizabeth herself had come from a music-hall background, hadn't she? 'Well . . . yes.' She preferred to call it 'a theatrical family'. She had six brothers, five of whom had survived infancy.

> My youngest brother, as I expect you know, is Teddy Knox, who was the youngest member of the Crazy Gang [as in Nervo and Knox, who joined forces in 1919 for their celebrated balletic 'ladder-building' and 'slow-motion wrestling' routines]. My oldest brother managed a rep company where I worked for a time. My father was a star of the music hall – a comedian and a singer – who then became a promoter and manager. And when I met Sax I was the junior half of a juggling act with my brother Bill. Not my favourite thing!

Sometimes, Sax Rohmer was credited on his songs with the music as well as the words. *Was* he in fact musical?

> No, dear, he couldn't play a musical instrument, if that's what you mean. But we had a small piano and I helped to pick out the tunes for him. This wasn't too difficult. It was usually the same tune! A drunken musician we knew made most of the arrangements. Somehow, we kept going on very little money. I remember sending some comic songs to the *Sunday Dispatch*, songs which had been turned down by various artistes, and offering them

to the paper for half-price. They bought the lot! But Sax didn't much like talking about his work for the music hall, you know. I don't know why. Did you know that when he was writing his first Fu Manchu stories, he was ghost-writing a book with Little Tich at the same time . . . ?

I had heard a couple of Rohmer's songs on recordings of 'the golden age of the music hall' – 'Bang Went the Chance of a Lifetime' sung by George Robey, and 'The Gas Inspector' (1908) sung by Little Tich. Were any of the others recorded? 'I really don't know, dear. Did you ever see Little Tich on stage? No, of course you couldn't have, could you?' Well, I replied, I had seen a short piece of film of his acrobatic 'Big Boots Dance' – *Little Tich et ses Big Boots*, made in Paris 1900 by Clément-Maurice – where he stands in front of a backdrop of a narrow street wearing his long, flat, narrow boots, ties his laces, scoops up his top hat by leaning forward at a perilous angle, does the splits, balances his hat on his nose, sits down and brings his legs together so that his face is hidden from the camera, opens his legs and snaps them shut again, leans forward to take a bow – almost touching the stage with his forehead – then – the climax – rises on the toes of his twenty-eight-inch wooden feet (each more than half his height), making him appear a giant of seven feet tall. But I had to admit that was all I had seen. 'Well, Sax knew him well, for several years. They were close friends and associates.'

So, how did the idea for Dr Fu Manchu initially arise at about the same time as Sax Rohmer was writing his Little Tich book? Sax had apparently been commissioned by 'a magazine editor' – maybe it was *Tit-Bits*, maybe *Answers* – to write an article about 'the Asiatic colony' in Limehouse and in particular about the activities of one 'Mr King', a criminal mastermind backed by a syndicate who was thought to control Chinese gambling, much of the drug traffic and not one but all of the Tongs. 'He terrified everyone in the district.' Elizabeth remembered that while Sax was doing his research in the field, 'I sat at the bedroom window upstairs in Herne Hill watching anxiously for the lights of his cab as it returned to me.' But no information about this mysterious 'Mr King' was forthcoming. 'No one would talk about him. They quickly changed the subject.' So, to meet his deadline, Sax Rohmer wrote an 'atmosphere piece' about Limehouse instead. Then, a while later, he chose to go back, night after night, to the narrow, cobbled lanes around West India Dock Road, Pennyfields and Limehouse Causeway, and this was when Elizabeth started to become seriously anxious about his safety. Eventually, she persuaded a neighbour in Herne Hill to drive her to a dingy cellar-bar in Limehouse Causeway, where she found out what Sax had been up to. He had for some time been haunting Three Colt Street, following a tip-off from a man called Fong Wah, and eventually his patience had been rewarded. What happened next had been repeated by Sax over the years in several newspaper articles and a broadcast, gaining embellishments along the way, usually to promote a newly published Fu Manchu novel. According to one version:

> I rented a room in Limehouse for some time. Another lodger, one Ah Tsong, was a medicine man and perfumer. In those days Charlie Brown presided in the bar of the hostelry famous for its museum of Eastern curiosities, and the café in the Causeway which I have called 'Malay Jack's' in some of my stories remained a meeting-place for Chinatown notables. . . . It was returning from Jack's one misty night in November, not long before the World War stripped the enamel from our civilisation and laid bare the savagery beneath, that *I had my first glimpse of Dr Fu Manchu*. I had formulated such a character but many essential details were missing. I imagined one who controlled the Tongs – those mysterious unions whose combined memberships ran far into six figures – one who could upset governments, perhaps change the present course of civilisation. He would have Caesaresque qualities; he would be a man of great scientific culture; his personal appearance remained to be built up. . . . Then, on this important night I saw a tall and dignified Chinese gentleman alight from a car before a mean-looking house. He wore a fur-collared overcoat, and, so far as I could make out, a fur cap of the kind once associated with Kemal Atatürk. He was accompanied by an Arab girl, who was also muffled in furs. The door of the house opened. The pair went in. The car was driven away. I had but a glimpse of the driver. But Dr Fu Manchu was complete: at last he lived.

And that, more or less, was how Sax Rohmer always liked to tell the story. He had, apparently, no idea whether he had glimpsed 'Mr King' or not. He had certainly never met him. But it didn't matter any more. The curtain had been raised. He was later, in 1915, to publish a novel called *The Yellow Claw* about 'Mr King' and the drug traffic in Limehouse, which in turn was to become five years after that the first of his books to be officially turned into a film serial. But for the time being, although he had only caught a fleeting glimpse of a tall, lean and feline Chinaman, and from a distance, and through the thick fog, he had convinced himself that his face was 'the living embodiment of Satan'. 'His face?' he would say. 'Well, I needn't describe it. I have written of it often enough since.'

Rohmer had also written – often – of Fu Manchu's lovely Eurasian slave-girl Karamaneh, who was straight out of a British edition of the *One Thousand Nights and One Night*, more usually known as *The Arabian Nights* or *A Thousand and One Nights*: a current or recent British edition of 1911, to be precise, illustrated with wispy watercolours by Edmund Dulac – based on his beloved Persian and Indian miniatures. Interestingly, Rohmer could have chosen Walter Crane's earlier colour lithographs of 1874 – when Crane set *Aladdin* in a China painted in flat Japanese style – but instead he referred to Dulac as a visual expression of his erotic bedazzlement. The point was that Karamaneh belonged among the cast of characters in an Edwardian erotic fantasy of the mysterious Orient which already existed.

Was there any truth in the story? Should it be taken with a pinch of soy? Or had Sax Rohmer perhaps looped the plots of *The Yellow Claw* and *The Golden Scorpion* back into real life and told the story so often that he couldn't any longer tell the difference. He was, as Elizabeth conceded, that kind of person. In *The Yellow Claw*, Mr King's elaborate headquarters, his 'cave of the golden dragon' is located behind and beneath a ginger warehouse known as Kan-Suh Concessions, in a cul-de-sac off Limehouse Causeway. In *The Golden Scorpion* – a similar story – the elaborate headquarters of the mastermind Fo-Hi (affiliated with Mr King, 'the mystery of [whose] identity we never solved') is located in the cellars beneath the three houses left and right of Ah-Fang-Fu's 'Pidgin House', junk shop and lodging-house near the corner of Three Colt Street, with a false front door, and its cellars 'planned and masked with Chinese cunning'. These goings-on cause much anxiety in the doctor hero's Battersea apartment and consulting room, his 'humdrum suburban practice'.

Or was Rohmer's reminiscence perhaps based on the plot of his *Yellow Shadows* (1925), which fictionalized Elizabeth's drive to Limehouse and vigil in Three Colt Street – or was it vice versa? In *Yellow Shadows*, the actress Yvette Chalmers (with 'closely waving hair, which gleamed with mahogany tints'), who is appearing in a thriller at the Riviera Theatre in the West End and who is by temperament 'in a real sense Bohemian', takes a cab to Wade

Street in Limehouse from the stage door. She is hoping to visit Ah Wong and his wife Annie, who is not feeling well. The cabbie – like Elizabeth's neighbour – is a man 'who has driven me many times'. Eventually, after a 'dreadful journey' to Limehouse, which has to be abandoned at West India Dock Road, Yvette becomes lost in the thick fog and wanders alone around 'an endless maze of unlighted streets'. It is like exploring a dark continent. This involves her, unwittingly, in the murder of the mysterious millionaire and Tong leader Burma Chang (the real-life Brilliant Chang), about whom 'it seemed impossible to get a word out of any Chink in the neighbourhood'. Just so, 'Mr King'.

Rohmer's reminiscence of Mr King certainly contained one of his trademarks: behind the 'cheap-looking', dingy shopfronts lay a world of oriental splendour and decadence. Condescension leading to bedazzlement. The very innocence of the shopfronts was a giveaway. Nightlife in the area was 'mole-like, a subterranean life'. The temple of the dragon was *beneath* the warehouse. When Rohmer later reminisced about his visits to the Chinatowns of San Francisco and New York ('a more extensive colony than that in London'), he always stressed that 'one could go down from floor to floor far below street level and find . . . yellow warrens'. A literally underground culture, already a journalistic cliché. The reporter would visit Limehouse expecting all sorts of exotic adventures because he had read a popular novel, be disappointed, and then hint that the adventures must have been going on behind the scenes; that appearances were a front for mysterious goings-on. H. V. Morton, for example, in his collected articles *Nights of London* (1926) wrote:

> I am not attempting to add to the romance of Limehouse, because there is no romance there; only squalor and the pathos of poor, frightened odds and ends of humanity whose lives are spent in the bowels of ships, whose pleasures consist in being stranded for three days in London, Yokohama, or Jamaica while the ships unload. . . . The squalor of Limehouse is that strange squalor of the East which seems to conceal vicious splendour. There is an air of something unrevealed in those narrow streets of shuttered houses, each one of which appears to be hugging its own dreadful secret. . . . Limehouse exerts that spell of provocative mystery which is the gift of the ancient East to the youthful imagination of the West. . . . I repeat that Limehouse is the most overrated excitement in London, but when on the spot you can forgive most of the luscious things written about

it, for it has *atmosphere*; it is a dramatic theme that just howls for a plot: a stage that cries for a drama . . . one felt oneself on the track of Fu-Manchu.

Another trademark – not just of Rohmer but of several writers from the West End of London who ventured into the East on behalf of their impressionable readers, writers such as Jack London or journalists such as George R. Sims – was the author as intrepid, tough-minded adventurer, who has access to secret information and excitement not available to the general public. As Rohmer often said, 'I made many friends in the Chinese quarter':

Charlie Brown knew much about Limehouse: the true stories behind some of those Eastern treasures of his would make fine exciting reading. Police officers of K Division know something too: and the River Police are not wholly ignorant of Chinatown's secrets. In fact only one who has mingled with its Asiatic population can speak of Limehouse as Limehouse is. . . . At one time I rented the whole of the first floor – three rooms in all – of a house in Limehouse. My landlord was a Chinaman whom we will call John Chow. He was manager of a grocery store in the Causeway. . . . His wife was Welsh, and they had three children. John was a natural gentleman, a term which applies to the majority of Chinamen I have known . . .

Rohmer also claimed to have privileged access to Inspector Yeo, of K Division (Limehouse), who in some versions of the story originally tipped him off about the activities of 'Mr King'.

Chief Inspector Yeo, of K Division, who knew much about the district, told me that the house [outside which Rohmer saw the tall and dignified Chinaman] belonged to a certain man, but he could throw no light upon the identity of the visitors. The houseowner was a known drug trafficker: but so cunningly was he covered that although the police knew him to be in the background, even the notorious Billie Carleton case [of November 1918] failed to bring him into the limelight. Brilliant Chang, his West End manager, went to gaol. The chief went abroad . . .

He also hinted darkly that he knew more than had been made public about the master criminal behind the Billie Carleton case. She was an ex-chorus girl turned revue artiste who died of an overdose of cocaine and sleeping drugs in her Savoy Court flat, after attending the Victory Ball at the Albert Hall on 27 November 1918. Her case drew public attention to networks of suppliers, pushers and users, including a dilapidated house at the eastern end of Limehouse Causeway, where Lo Ping You and his wife Ada lived: they supplied the drugs for an opium party in a Mayfair flat. The cross-heading in *The Times* read: 'The Den of Ten Ping You'. But no 'mastermind' – if indeed there was one – was ever found. Brilliant Chang, the so-called 'Dope King' – who arrived in England in 1913, ran a successful legitimate business from the City of London and was involved in supplying cocaine to nightclub dancer Freda Kempton who died of an overdose in 1922 – became in the popular newspapers of the day synonymous with a 'yellow spider' at the centre of a drug-trafficking web. According to some police witnesses, he controlled up to 40 per cent of the London drug traffic. The press coverage of Chang owed much of its sensationalism and most of its adjectives to Sax Rohmer. Rohmer, in turn, hinted that there was a criminal mastermind *behind* Chang – Chang was just the 'West End manager' – and it was that same elusive mastermind who owned the house where he had his first glimpse of Dr Fu Manchu. Brilliant Chang couldn't have been the original of Dr Fu Manchu – although he wore a flamboyant fur collar, and had his clothes tailored in Savile Row, he was not yet in England in 1911–12 – but Rohmer's inside information was in any case about his *superior*. When he was accused of basing his novel *Dope* (1919) on the Billie Carleton case, in an exploitative way, Rohmer wrote indignantly on 22 January 1919:

> . . . actually it was on the stocks long before the Carleton case brought the matter so prominently before the public. The increasing drug habit has had my attention for some time past and knowing of the link existing between certain purveyors frequenting the nightclubs and like resorts, and Limehouse, I saw an opportunity for a dramatic and strongly contrasted novel.

In the novel itself, he had written that *Dope* 'was not inspired by . . . any cause célèbre, recent or remote'. Rohmer had been writing about 'the link' between East and West Ends and his alleged inside knowledge for nearly eight years. It was the press coverage that read like a Rohmer novel, rather than vice versa.

I knew the story of the origin of Dr Fu Manchu before I met Elizabeth and I knew that no one had yet managed to track down the Limehouse article which Sax Rohmer had been commissioned to write. Elizabeth certainly had a vivid memory of sitting at her bedroom window in Herne Hill and then going to rescue her husband. She also clearly remembered that there was a magazine commission, probably from *Tit-Bits* or *Answers*. As Elizabeth pointed out to me, Sax had 'never shown an interest in Chinatown before this'. His early 'oriental' tales were all about Egypt and the Middle East. Since boyhood, when he had first read – she explained – Sir Richard Burton's then-banned version of the *Book of the Thousand Nights and One Night* under the bedclothes, and admired its overripe, archaic style combined with Victorian colloquialisms, he had developed a passion for 'the romance of the Orient'. An eroticized place of exotic beings, haunting landscapes, remarkable happenings, glittering jewels, magic carpets, when Baghdad was the richest and most populated city in the world. Actually, I hadn't the heart to tell her that this was another highly improbable story. The ten-volume Burton version (1885; *Supplement*, in six volumes, 1886–88) was only available at the time in an expensive subscription edition under the imprint of the Kama Shastra Society: more likely it was Edward William Lane's earlier, mock-biblical translations (1840, revised 1859), which were readily available in cheap editions, as well as Lane's best-selling *Manners and Customs of the Modern Egyptians* (1836). But Rohmer had certainly never written about a Chinese character before in his fiction. *Something* triggered his interest, and led to his writing the short stories which were to turn into *The Mystery of Dr Fu-Manchu*.

When exactly did it happen? The Rohmers moved to Herne Hill early in 1910. The first Fu Manchu short story was published in October 1912. The incident took place 'one misty night in November'. Sax Rohmer was editing the material assembled for the Little Tich book at the time, and he often recalled that it was the publisher of that book, Arthur Greening, who, while they were working together, would come to his study in Herne Hill in the early hours for a chat:

> ... something in the conversation having quickened my memory, I recalled the existence of an unfinished manuscript, opened the old box in which it lay with others and read it to the publisher. He sat down there and then and wrote to Newman Flower [of *Cassell's* and *The Story-Teller* magazines]. On the following day Newman Flower rang me up, and although at this time I had abandoned all idea of becoming a fictionist, it was written, as the Arabs say, that the manuscript in the box should be brought to light, and that under Flower's auspices that Old Man of the Sea, Dr Fu Manchu, should make his bow to the public ...

All of which suggests late in 1910 or 1911, depending on when the Tich book was completed. Probably 1910. Elizabeth couldn't remember the date. But 'of course that Limehouse with its narrow streets and exotic shops has gone long ago'. This had become another journalistic cliché. Limehouse *used* to be exotic, but that was a long time ago.

It was a cliché much used by the writer Thomas Burke, for example, who even claimed to have grown up in an orphanage just down the road from Limehouse, and to have made boyhood friendships with colourful members of the Chinese community there. Actually, the orphanage was in Hertfordshire and he was born in Clapham. When he revisited Limehouse in 1917, Burke could claim on behalf of his readers that the best years had passed – and that *he* was there in the best years:

> . . . as for the word 'Chinatown', which once carried a perfume of delight, it is now empty of meaning save as indicating a district of London where Chinamen live. Today, Limehouse is without salt or savour; flat and unprofitable; and of all that it once held of colour and mystery and the macabre, one must write in the past tense . . . the times change. Chinatown is a back number and there now remains no corner to which one may take the curious visitor thirsty for exotic excitement.

It used to be 'a wicked place; yes, but colourful'. Opium had become expensive and scarce. The missionaries had done their work. The 'spirit of the commercial and controlled West' had taken over:

> Nothing remains save tradition [Burke wrote in 1919], which now and then is fanned into life by such a case as the drugged actress. Yet you may still find people who journey fearfully to Limehouse, and spend money in its shops and restaurants, and suffer their self-manufactured excitements while sojourning in its somnolent streets among the respectable sons of Canton.

Interestingly, when Sax Rohmer reminisced in print about 'Mr King', he usually accompanied his memories with some kind of caveat, such as:

> I have a great respect for the Chinese. As a nation, they possess that elusive thing – poise – which I sometimes think we are losing.

> I have never claimed Fu Manchu represents the Chinese character. All I say is Fu Manchu is Fu Manchu. He can't help that. No more can I.

Burke received many letters which assumed the stories in his popular collection *Limehouse Nights: Tales of Chinatown* (first published in 1916) to have been based on real-life experiences. Some were appalled at the stories about mixed-race relationships, others fascinated. Elsewhere, Burke had worked hard to create the impression of authenticity – even harder than Sax Rohmer. But in his final autobiography – published after his death – Burke confessed:

> At the time I did them I had no knowledge of the Chinese people, and all I knew of Limehouse and the district was what I had automatically observed without aim or purpose during my unguided wanderings in remote London. I had thus been able to write those stories with the peculiar assurance a man has who knows nothing of what he is writing or talking about.

A spirited exchange of letters in the *Daily Mail* (October 1926) – between the Revd R. J. Powell, Rector of Limehouse, and Thomas Burke – concluded with Burke stating that he was a *novelist*, not a social documentarian. He *made things up*:

> As to those Chinatown books, they are *fiction*. They are not presented as reporting or as photography. *Limehouse Nights* [and others] were never meant as fair and true pictures of the Chinese quarter. They are works of imagination, nothing else; and they succeed or fail solely as experiments in the grotesque and arabesque.

This was not the same, Burke concluded, as saying that his Chinese characters had no relation to reality: 'I would ask [the Revd Powell] to observe more closely or to refer to my friend Mr Cairns at Thames Police Court.' The Revd Powell had complained that his parish had been called 'Slimehouse', that there were 'expeditions . . . in motor coaches' to see exotic Chinatown and that the tourists, from the safety of their seat, 'thrill with the thought that at any moment they may be stabbed in the back or spirited away into an opium den': this was all the fault of 'the Limehouse school of literature'. It was all very well to claim that the image of Limehouse was *fiction*. A lot of readers evidently remained unconvinced. And Burke himself 'bid us listen at his whispering windows, determined we should hear no good of ourselves'.

Sax Rohmer headed one of his autobiographical articles of 1938 – which included a version of the 'Mr King' story – with an infamous epigraph from

Bret Harte:

> *Which I wish to remark,*
> *And my language is plain,*
> *That for ways that are dark*
> *And for tricks that are vain,*
> *The heathen Chinee is peculiar,*
> *Which the same I would rise to explain.*

Beneath this, he wrote: 'I disagree entirely with Bret Harte's conclusions':

> The Chinese are an honest race. This is why Western people regard them
> as mysterious. Few Chinese know anything about China; you and I know
> nothing. Men who have lived in Shanghai, Singapore and Hong Kong
> tell tales of Shanghai, Singapore and Hong Kong. But China has an area
> of more than 4,000,000 square miles. Men on Eastern stations (for an
> exception see Rudyard Kipling) as a rule are unsympathetic to their
> environment. Soldiers and civil servants marooned in an ocean of alien
> cultures rarely try to learn anything more than the dry facts necessary to
> their job. They make a little Great Britain in the tiny island of their ban-
> ishment, with a miniature St. James's, a miniature Ascot, and even a baby
> Court. This has seemed pathetic to outside critics of the British Empire.
> Actually, it is what has *made* the British Empire. But it has done nothing
> to enlarge our knowledge of the Eastern races.

His comments on the sources of information about China which were available
in Edwardian times – usually compiled by old China hands, or by survivors
of the 'Boxer uprising' – are surprisingly acute, as is his conclusion about
the ornamentalism of 'the Raj' and other 'Eastern stations'. However, he then
goes on, as usual, to claim special information about the Chinese inhabitants
of Limehouse.

Rohmer's last utterance on the subject, in a semi-autobiographical short
story called 'Limehouse Rhapsody' (a Thomas Burkean title), published in
December 1958 shortly before he died, takes the form of a dialogue with an
elderly Limehouse storekeeper called 'Sam King'. It reads almost like a sort
of apology:

> KING: Sometimes in your writings, Respected, you have spoken evil of
> my countrymen. Is it not true?

ROHMER: It is true, but only in a limited sense. I have portrayed some of your race, perhaps, in an unfavourable light, but never the Chinese as a whole. There are evil men in China, as there are evil men in every country. Your words, Sam, are not just.

KING: I spoke the words merely to hear your reply. In friendship, misunderstanding is impossible.

'Limehouse Rhapsody' dates from a time when Sax Rohmer seemed, in his final works, to be becoming more and more sympathetic with Fu Manchu himself – ending up with Nayland Smith and Fu Manchu *on the same side*. The devil doctor makes less use of physical violence as the series progresses – he prefers more subtle methods such as hypnotism and brainwashing – and in his final book *Emperor, Fu Manchu* (1959), he asks Smith: 'Do we, or do we not, stand on common ground' in the battle against Communism and the 'Russian pestilence'? Smith replies lamely, 'Your question is one difficult for me to answer.'

There was another thing about the genesis of Fu Manchu and Sax's taste for the East, Elizabeth said. Both she and her husband were very interested in the occult, and psychical research, as was fashionable in 'bohemian' circles during the Edwardian era, and in wider society after the carnage of the First World War. He as a 'seeker', she because she thought she had 'the gift' or 'a sixth sense': 'but I would have nothing to do with Sax's magic, as I called it. It rather scared me.' As a young couple, they attended the lectures of Annie Besant – 'whom we admired very much' – about theosophy. The family doctor, Dr R. Watson Counsell, was 'a teacher to my husband in the occult all his life'. Counsell was to write 'a restatement of alchemy' called *Apologia Alchymiae* in 1925. In addition to writing the preface – the only preface he ever wrote for someone else – Sax Rohmer thanked Dr Counsell 'for the freedom of his library' at the beginning of *The Romance of Sorcery* (1914), his only non-fiction book – mainly a collection of anecdotes about famous historical figures (Nostradamus, Dr John Dee, Count Cagliostro, Madame Blavatsky) who practised magick. Written in highflown faux-scholarly style, it contained many details which had already appeared in his fiction, and would continue to do so.

Houdini was, apparently, much impressed by *The Romance of Sorcery*. 'He wrote to Sax about it and they later became good friends.' He would send the Rohmers newspaper cuttings from all over the world showing his latest elaborate escapes – and note in the margin a message such as 'It looks hard to most people but *you* would say, "Now show me something".' Apparently, Houdini once helped Sax Rohmer when he was stuck over a plot detail about a locked-room murder in *Fire-Tongue* (serialized in 1921). He also defended Houdini against accusations – from Conan Doyle among others – that he must have used 'supernatural powers' in some of his escapology routines: he may have used 'super-normal' means, wrote Rohmer, but that was an altogether different thing. For Rohmer, Houdini's real gift was 'amazing showmanship' – 'the last of those men of genius who devoted their lives to mystifying and delighting their contemporaries . . . and he was my friend'. They agreed about the need to 'expose impostors who falsely claimed to practise "spiritualism"'.

Elizabeth had recently discovered – since Sax's death – not entirely to her surprise, that he seemed to have joined the Hermetic Order of the Golden Dawn shortly before they met; other well-known members included W. B. Yeats, Arthur Machen, Algernon Blackwood and Aleister Crowley, who had joined in 1898 ('Sax detested him for what he became'). Maybe he had been introduced to the Order by Dr Counsell, who was also an 'adept' in theosophy. Maybe Rohmer had exaggerated his involvement in the Hermetic Order, to enhance his credentials as a writer about ancient Egyptian mysteries: one of the most distinctive features of his early Fu Manchu stories was their combination of detective story, adventure novel and the occult. If Rohmer *did* join around 1904 – as Elizabeth thought he might have done – he joined when the Order was already falling apart, and splitting into factions, all of whom claimed, acrimoniously, to be the true believers. The Hermetic Order was – unusually for such secret societies – open to women and non-Freemasons, and much of its work involved instruction in alchemy, natural philosophy, Rosicrucianism, Hermeticism and the Kabbalah, prior to exams and initiation rituals at various 'levels'. If Rohmer *was* a serious member, surely Elizabeth would have known at the time rather than later? More likely, the *idea* of belonging to a secret society appealed to his overdeveloped sense of melodrama and mystery. *The Romance of Sorcery* does not seem the result of deep study; more of pop-occultism, book collecting, occasional visits to Dr Counsell's library, a pretentious writing style and an enjoyment of bizarre anecdotes. When I asked her about it, Elizabeth did not seem entirely sure whether the Order in question was The Golden Dawn or The Brotherhood of True Rosicrucians (of which Counsell definitely *was* a member). But Sax and Elizabeth were both 'bohemian' in their attitude to life when they met, she said. And these things were fashionable at the time.

She herself was happy to engage in a spot of fortune-telling and parlour magic, but felt it 'abnormal' to delve more deeply. One day early in their relationship they happened to be experimenting together at home with a ouija board, a popular pastime, and Sax asked it whether he would ever achieve success as a writer. In reply the pointer on the wooden planchette (which, by the way, dated back to around 1100 in Song dynasty China) kept leading their fingers to the letters of the alphabet spelling the word 'CHINAMAN'. 'We hadn't a clue what it meant.' And weren't they at all suspicious about the use of the word 'Chinaman' from the other side – already considered some-what derogatory to Chinese people among sinologists? 'No, dear,' she said – not quite understanding what I meant. But after the Limehouse incident, they were soon to find out exactly what the word 'Chinaman' was intended to signify. Sax Rohmer was later, starting in spring 1913, to write a series of short stories about a tall and stoop-shouldered 'psychic detective' called Moris Klaw who solves crimes and hauntings by dreams and extrasensory perception – he calls his method 'odic photography' – having stimulated his wits with a verbena spray. He also carries around an 'odically sterilized' cushion to help him reach his psychic intuitions. Klaw runs an antique shop near Wapping Old Stairs, in London's docklands, which he shares with his ravishing daughter Isis and a talkative pet parrot ('Moris Klaw! The Devil's Come for You!'). Again, a workaday shop with strange secrets within. *The Dream Detective*, a collection of nine short stories, was published as a book in 1920.

Did Sax experiment with opium as well as with the occult? He was evidently fascinated by lurid stories from the headlines about drug trafficking in Limehouse and showgirls who crossed the West–East divide: novels such as *Dope* and the so-called 'Yellow Trilogy' – *The Yellow Claw, The Golden Scorpion* and *Yellow Shadows* – were centrally concerned with the trade after it became illegal. Limehouse supplied Mayfair demand. So, did he personally experiment? 'No, dear. He did try it once but said it just made him feel sick. But he did smoke a pipe. All the time!' Rohmer's own memory of this remained a vivid one:

> Opium in my case could never be a vice. I tried a pipe many years ago, but quickly learned that my stomach was not equipped to deal with

this particular amusement. I was violently sick and have avoided opium ever since.

This could explain why the customers at Singapore Charlie's are so dramatically affected by smoking opium pipes. One puff knocks them out cold! Rohmer was also fond of describing the billowing smoke of the long opium pipe – as if it was a common or garden tobacco pipe – when in reality the resin is difficult to keep alight, let alone make billow. Fu Manchu, by contrast, boasts that 'my constitution is inured to the use of opium'. Rohmer did, however, as one of his business ideas, invent an 'oriental' perfume called 'Honan' – named, he said, after the Chinese province 'notorious at the time for the cultivation of the opium poppy' – and set up a company to develop the product. It actually reached the market, complete with bright silk tassel on the cork-and-bamboo cladding and Rohmer advertising copy. There was a launch at Barker's department store in Kensington High Street, featuring a 'real live Chinaman' in an anachronistic pigtail. Rohmer soon lost interest in this forerunner of more recent brands such as 'Opium' and 'Addict'. But for a short time the 'Honan' brand employed a mixed gang of roughly a dozen Chinese and Burmese employees under a foreman called Ah Sin: Rohmer gave him the ironic pseudonym of 'Ah Sin' because 'Ah Sin' was the 'heathen Chinee' stigmatized by Bret Harte, and the foreman was very honest indeed. He once walked a mile and a half in heavy rain to let Rohmer know that the payroll had a mistake in it – sevenpence halfpenny overpaid. Or was it 'John Chow' of Limehouse who did the walking? Or was the sum 'one shilling and threepence' overpaid to Chow 'by my secretary'? Rohmer liked to tell the story in several different versions, sometimes with reference to 'Honan', sometimes not. There was always a similar punchline, though:

> Except that he was restrained with difficulty from murdering his wife some months later, I never found anything but admirable qualities in 'Ah Sin'.

In this as in so much else, Sax Rohmer enjoyed the exotic associations more than the mundane details. I asked Elizabeth if he enjoyed the process of writing.

> No, dear, he didn't like getting down to work, but when he got an idea and decided to put it down on paper, he'd go into the study and then I would lock him in! Just to make sure. After that, he'd go into hiding for six weeks at a time. Became very nervous and intense about it!

So, like Balzac's servant, she had to trap him into starting the process, or completing his quota of work. 'He liked to write longhand, with a pencil or sometimes a pen. Didn't care for typewriters at all.' Elizabeth helped in other ways too, she claimed:

> I used to get strange short story plots from Sax at night. I've always thought they came to me when he was asleep. That's when I was awake, in the early hours of the morning when he fell into bed dead tired – this always woke me and I couldn't get back to sleep again. I'm *sure* I got those plots from him because I haven't had this experience since he died.

Another way of firing up his imagination into suitably macabre and murderous channels, she recalled, was deliberately to irritate him:

> I'd pick a fight, and sometimes even throw the crockery around – or any object that came to hand! He used to say, 'She never misses.' Typical of his dry wit. Poor Sax! He was a very *private* man, you know. Never liked giving interviews.

And although the representatives of law and order in his stories tended to have loud, assertive voices – full of exaggerated nonsense – he himself 'spoke softly, without an accent'. And, Elizabeth added, he liked to believe the best in people, which sometimes made him vulnerable to crooked literary agents, business advisers or trusted friends. The words she used about him were 'mild', 'unassuming', 'private', 'ill at ease in company', which makes the dogmatic, emphatic, bullying style of his heroes – the absolute conviction they are right, and licensed to dominate everyone else's agenda – all the more fascinating. She also called him 'fanciful'.

Then Elizabeth suddenly remembered a bizarre postscript to her Limehouse adventure involving Fong Wah – one of the go-betweens who had helped Sax to find the right vantage point in Three Cold Street. This was a 'very special story'. It transpired, she said, that her husband had gone back to see him some eight years later, in 1919, when preparing *The Golden Scorpion*, to talk about 'the China that was' and indeed the Limehouse that was. *The Golden Scorpion* features an opium den, a hidden laboratory, a luxurious tapestried oriental apartment and a secret torture chamber ('I term it The Feast of a Thousand Ants: it is performed with the aid of African driver ants, a pair of surgical scissors and a pot of honey'). All the by-then usual ingredients, in other words. Fong Wah reminisced in the small and stuffy room behind his Limehouse foodstore about the old days of the Manchu era when he was a storekeeper on the Nanking Road, Shanghai, and when he had dealings with the venerable Mandarin Governor of Hankow City. Fong Wah's store sold 'strange delicacies – at least they seemed strange in those days – such as shark's fin, edible seaweed, birds' nests and eggs buried for twenty years and preserved in earth'. He lived alone: his wife Minnie had left him, which he said was a blessing because she talked too much. At one point in the conversation, Fong Wah suddenly whistled – and his pet mongoose sprang onto his shoulder and crouched there. 'Where a European would use a cat, his Chinese equivalent goes in for a mongoose.' Fong Wah was 'a very cultured man'.

He described in graphic detail how ruthless the Governor had been, ordering public executions of river pirates in the courtyard of the prison, and spoke of how highly respected a figure the Public Executioner was. 'He painted a picture of Hankow under the old regime which, if true, would account for *any* revolution there.' At the end of the conversation, he gave Sax Rohmer a present of an antique curved sword in a shagreen scabbard wrapped in a Chinese news-paper. When he unwrapped the parcel at home, Elizabeth quickly made the obvious deduction: 'Fong Wah was trying to tell him that *he* had been the Public Executioner.' As she told me all this, in some detail, I hadn't the heart to admit that I had already read exactly the same story in Rohmer's 'Limehouse Rhapsody'. And indeed in Rohmer's article about the origins of Fu Manchu in the *Manchester Empire News*, at the end of January 1938. The story had been around for a very long time.

In the 'Limehouse Rhapsody' version, Fong Wah became 'old Sam King' and the meeting was updated to after the Second World War:

> They are cutting a sixty-foot arterial road right through Limehouse; and this is a story of the condemned Asiatic colony which London once called Chinatown; it is a story of which no mention may be found in any newspaper.

Pennyfields in Chinatown – the devil doctor's old stamping ground – has by now practically disappeared, and Sam King reminisces about how 'all my good friends go too'. Sam still has a pet mongoose on his shoulder, called Emperor, and dreams of returning to Hankow 'in the northern valley of the Yellow River, where the opium poppies grow'. His wife has 'left him', but the strong implication is that King has murdered her, to ensure her silence. But he is still worried about the image of China which Rohmer's fiction has presented:

> In much that you have written, Respected, you have conveyed to those, who know no better, an impression that the Chinese are a cruel race. I wish to explain to you that what you mistake for cruelty is in reality an indispensable weapon in the hands of justice.

Sam King goes on to outline the ways in which river pirates were deterred, in the old days, through a series of very public and very elaborate tortures: 'The Pearl of Exquisite Silence' (a device resembling a split fir-cone, placed in the mouth of the condemned); 'The Four Steps of Understanding' (the condemned man's head protruding from an iron cage, while his feet rest on four stones – one of which is removed each day); and 'The Jacket of Philosophy' or 'The Fate of Divine Desire' (which forces the condemned to contemplate his greatest forbidden pleasures as he dies). In Rohmer's earlier 1938 version of the story – presented as autobiography rather than fiction – the elaborate tortures had been a little different. 'The Four Steps of Understanding' were 'The Six Steps of Wisdom'; there was '"The Way of All Penetrating Truth" (upon which I shall not enlarge)'; and 'the horrifying "Wire Jacket" – wherein the executioner's sword played an important part'. The 'Wire Jacket' had already found its way into the early Fu Manchu stories. All were carried out by the Public Executioner, under the direction of the Mandarin. 'Ah Sin' explained: 'You know, honourable friend, that my countrymen do not fear death. *Other* unpleasant misfortunes must threaten the criminal.'

Rohmer professes to be confused by this:

> I am trying to understand your assertion that I have misrepresented your race; and in your present account of justice under the old regime, I begin to see that what might be a corrective in London would be useless in Hankow.

But he accepts the parting gift of the short, curved sword of tempered steel, 'the hilt bound with plaited catgut, the blade concealed in a shagreen scabbard'. Only then does Ah Sin/Sam King deliver his punchline:

> I have loved you, Respected, because you have tried to understand my people. Your honourable friendship has raised me in my own esteem, and the only way in which I could strive to repay it was to tell you a story. . . .

For seven years I fulfilled the honourable duties of public executioner in Hankow . . .

Fact and fiction were becoming increasingly difficult to disentangle. Elizabeth had evidently retold the story so often she could no longer tell the difference either. And yet this was still a 'very special story'. In Elizabeth's version, it was *she* who deduced that Fong Wah must have been the Public Executioner. Did she still possess the sword?

No, dear. When I worked out that he must have been the Executioner, I didn't want to have it in the house. Sax said I was being superstitious. But out it went.

It was time to leave. Elizabeth Sax Rohmer was beginning to flag, and, where I was concerned, her stories were taking on the quality of a dream. Like a scratched and faded piece of film that had been through the gate of a projector too many times. Increasingly removed from reality. I had two last questions. The first was about Sax Rohmer's attitude to the many film versions of his Fu Manchu stories, which had sometimes become considerably more extreme in their racist attitudes to Chinese people than the original stories.

He wasn't very fond of them, dear. He used to say that the best actor to play Fu Manchu would be Basil Rathbone, who could be sinister even in his pyjamas!

Did it occur to him that a *Chinese* actor could ever play the part? 'Oh, my dear. There weren't any film-stars who came from China – or none that I can remember.'

The second question related to my play, and I had been saving it up until the end in case it offended her. I knew that Sax had sometimes been criticized for his stereotyping of Chinese characters – especially in the United States. What, I wondered, did he *really* feel about those criticisms?

Oh, he would always tell reporters that he *never* claimed Fu Manchu was 'the Chinese character'. He was just one character. He'd never been to China, you know.

This was identical to Sax Rohmer's standard answer. Elizabeth gave me some copies of a fan-based American publication, *The Rohmer Review* (established

1968), and some Xeroxed newspaper and magazine articles about her late husband. She also gave me a couple of publicity photos of Sax Rohmer standing by a window, pipe in hand, and wearing what looked to me like a silk Chinese overgarment of some sort. 'No, dear, it was from Egypt: he bought it when we were on our honeymoon there. Just like that perfume flask.' Did he go around the house wearing it as if it was a dressing-gown? 'Of course not! He only wore it for the photos!' when he was presenting himself as 'Sax Rohmer' to the public. She showed me one of her treasured leather and gilt large-format editions of a Fu Manchu novel, with original watercolour illustrations in the style of Dulac, and explained that someone who claimed to be the son of an old friend of Sax's from pre-Herne Hill days had recently stolen one of them from her. 'Who can you trust? Poor Sax loved those books and he trusted everyone.' I gave her a copy of my play. We agreed the wording for the programme:

> *The Devil Doctor*, based on books by Sax Rohmer, is presented for five performances only, by courtesy of Elizabeth Sax Rohmer – sole copyrights via TV, Film, Stage and Radio. The Company would like to thank Mrs Sax Rohmer, whose generosity and understanding have made this production possible.

As I was leaving, we went through the French windows into the garden and she picked a red rose – 'a rose for you from Rose' – and laced it into my lapel. She wished me luck with the play, and hoped it might lead to other theatrical opportunities, if that's what I wanted. 'You never know.' I said that this part of Lewes seemed pleasantly quiet and suburban – rather like the location of Dr Petrie's Clapham surgery, a *very* long way away from the foggy lanes of Limehouse. By now, I was just making conversation and feeling dizzy. 'Much *too* quiet,' she said with a giggle. 'I think you mean *dull*, don't you?' Maybe I would go and walk the streets of Limehouse, to pick up atmosphere for the play. 'I shouldn't bother: it's changed beyond all recognition. There's nothing left of Sax's Limehouse.' We corresponded off and on for the next few years until she died in 1979.

A. Dor

CHAPTER TWO

Charles Dickens and Princess Puffer

O
n Friday 14 May 1869, Charles Dickens wrote to Sol Eytinge, one of his American illustrators, inviting him to join his fellow countryman the publisher and editor James T. Fields and others on a conducted tour, 'with some of the Police', to have a glimpse of the darker side of London life. They could visit lock-up houses, watch-houses and even an opium den: 'No dress coat, as it will be a phenomenon in the region. We shall visit after dinner.'

Dickens and friends in fact took *two* glimpses into the abyss in May 1869 – on the nights of 30 *and* 31 May. A while later, Fields reminisced:

> Among the most memorable of these London rambles was . . . a walk through the thieves' quarter. Two of these expeditions were made on two consecutive nights, under the protection of the police detailed for the service. On one of these nights we also visited the . . . opium-eating establishments. It was in one of the horrid opium-dens that [Dickens] gathered the incidents which he has related in the opening pages of *Edwin Drood*. In a miserable court we found the haggard old woman blowing at a kind of pipe made of an old penny ink-bottle. The identical words which Dickens puts into the mouth of this wretched creature in *Edwin Drood* we heard her croon as we leaned over the tattered bed on which she was lying. There was something hideous in the way this woman kept repeating 'Ye'll pay up according, deary, won't ye?' and the Chinamen and Lascars [East Indian sailors from the region of Bombay] made never-to-be-forgotten pictures in the scene.

Actually, according to an investigative journalist who 'was personally acquainted with the old woman and her surroundings', Fields had overdone the connections with *The Mystery of Edwin Drood* (1870): the pipe was a 'scratch' one, made out of an old flageolet with the holes stopped up and a doorknob, 'the latter serving as a bowl'; Fields had mistaken it for an inkwell, because he had read the novel. The 'opium-eating establishment' – it was, in fact, for opium-*smoking*, a key distinction – was located among the two- and three-roomed houses in New Court, Victoria Street, Shadwell – north of the old Ratcliffe Highway (renamed St George's Street, because the Highway had attracted such a bad reputation), west of Blue Gate Fields (given the prim name of Victoria Street in 1857, for the same reason) and near the burial ground of Nicholas Hawksmoor's church St George's-in-the-East, Stepney. The 'haggard old woman' – who seems to have gone by the names of 'Opium Sal' or 'Lascar Sally' – was by birth one Sarah Graham, an Englishwoman who was living in New Court with an elderly Chinese immigrant called Latau or Latou. She shared the house with 'Chinese' or 'Cheeny' Emma and her Chinese husband. The English partners or associates of the opium-masters, later known as 'Chinese Amazons', earned their 'oriental names' according to the national-ities of the people they married or assisted: 'Lascar Sally', 'Canton Kitty', 'Chinese Emma', 'Calcutta Louisa'. Sal was well known in the neighbourhood because she had, over many years, been mastering the intricate art of prepar-ing the opium for smoking – one of the attractions, at the time, of taking the trouble to visit these establishments rather than drinking or eating the drug in the privacy of one's own home.

Charles Dickens must already have known about this particular house, because he had published an article about it – 'Lazarus, Lotus-Eating' – by J. C. Parkinson in *All the Year Round*, on 12 May 1866. It describes how Parkinson follows 'Lazarus', 'a poor wretched Chinaman', from Cornhill in the City of London, via Aldgate pump – where he asks directions of a police constable – to Old Yahee's opium house, New Court, Palmer's Folly, Blue Gate Fields (locals were still calling it Blue Gate Fields long after its change of name):

'No, Sir,' says Mr Policeman, 'it wouldn't be at all safe for you to venture up New-Court alone. It ain't the Chinamen, nor yet the Lascars, nor yet the Bengalees as would hurt you; but there is an uncommon rough crew of *English* hangin' in and about there . . .'

Taking this advice, and after securing the services of a police inspector and sergeant, Parkinson arrives at Old Yahee's between eleven and midnight:

There is a little colony of Orientals in the centre of Bluegate-fields, and in the centre of this colony is the opium divan. We reach it by a narrow passage leading up to a narrow court. . . . Yahee is of great age [he is about eighty], is never free from the influence of opium, but sings, tells stories, eats, drinks, cooks, and quarrels . . . without ever rousing from the semi-comatose state you see him in now. . . . The livid, cadaverous, corpse-like visage of Yahee, the wild excited glare of the young Lascar who opens the door, the stolid sheep-like ruminations of Lazarus and the other Chinamen coiled together on the floor, the incoherent anecdotes of the Bengalee squatted on the bed, the fiery gesticulations of the mulatto and the Manilla-man who are in conversation by the fire . . . are all due to the same [thick opium] fumes.

The journalist is then shown a 'sorry little apartment' which is almost filled to capacity with a French bedstead containing half a dozen 'coloured men' across its breadth, and next to it a tray and lamp – 'the cramped little chamber is one large opium-pipe'. The opium costs four pennies a hit, and at Yahee's you get the best: they come from all parts of London to smoke it, explains a Bengali merchant seaman through an interpreter. A woman called Mother Abdallah, who looks in from next door, is the interpreter:

Mother Abdallah is a London lady who, from long association with Orientals, has mastered their habits and acquired their tongue. Cheeny (China) Emma and Lascar Sal, her neighbours, are both from home this evening, but Mother Abdallah does the honours for her male friends with much grace and propriety – a pallid wrinkled woman of forty, who prepares and sells opium in another of the two-roomed hovels in the court. She confesses to smoking it, too, for company's sake, or if a friend asks her to, as yer may say – and stoutly maintains the healthiness of the habit.

She explains that Yahee, in addition to being the landlord, 'makes up the opium as they like it'. 'He has his own way of preparin' it, which he won't tell nobody.' It is his unique selling proposition. Lazarus, meanwhile, is no longer the poor wretched beggar he was when first we met him at Cornhill a couple of hours ago:

Who knows the rapturous visions passing through his brain, or the bliss-fulness which prompts that half-expressed smile? The smallest-feeted *houris*, the most toothsome birds' nests and stewed dogs, nay, the yellow mandarin's button itself, are Lazarus's now . . .

Those who have read about the agonies of Thomas De Quincey when he was struggling to free himself from opium addiction, concludes Parkinson, 'will not wonder at the utter self-abandonment of poor Lazarus and his tribe. Mother Abdallah, Lascar Sal, Cheeny Emma, and the rest, are the only Englishwomen he has known . . .'

It is difficult to tell for certain – everyone seems to be hiding behind several aliases – but Latou was more than likely the same person as Yahee. If so, when he died in 1877, looking even more cadaverous, spare as a rib, he would have been all of ninety years old. As Parkinson observes, Yahee is a very rare advertisement for the medicinal qualities of opium-smoking. Lascar Sal was the 'haggard old woman' of Charles Dickens's later visit, who shared a house with Chinese Emma, and both were 'neighbours' (in the sense, perhaps, of sharing with Mother Abdallah, who 'does the honours' when they are away).

There are two other accounts of visits to this opium house, which appears to have become one of the regular stops on exclusive tours of 'Shadwell by night'. The first is by Colonel the Honourable Frederick Wellesley (great-nephew of the Iron Duke), who as a young happy-go-lucky Guards officer on leave in the mid-1860s decided to follow the fashion of 'slumming' with a couple of high-spirited fellow officers, accompanied by a detective: 'a little wizened man called Field, who carried no more formidable weapon than a small umbrella with a little ivory crook on a handle'.

This was the same Charles (or Charley) Frederick Field, ex-amateur actor, late of the Detective Force at Scotland Yard, now a private inquiry agent available for hire at fifteen shillings a day plus tips and expenses, whose down-to-earth charm, 'roving eye', 'well-known hand' and 'horrible sharpness' Dickens much admired, and who appeared in several of his journalistic essays sometimes under the rather obvious alias of 'Wield'. Field had also been the original of omnicompetent Inspector Bucket in *Bleak House* in 1852, the first detective to appear in a major English novel and a man who 'walks in an atmosphere of mysterious greatness'. It was to become a standard feature of real-life explorations of the East End – by journalists and tourists alike – to have an experienced detective as guide, such as Field. Field was usually flanked by 'a brace of policemen' – just in case – and prided himself on his arrangements with the underworld, like an eighteenth-century thief-taker. In his invitation to James T. Fields, Charles Dickens had mentioned that they were going to be accompanied by 'the great Detective', which strongly suggests that he too may have hired Charley Field. His 'knowledge and sagacity' would have come in handy as they explored 'the thieves' quarter'.

Field had already, in the mid-1860s, been leading tours of gawping young gentlemen through Shadwell for a while, and Wellesley was impressed by his efficiency, by the route he took and by the fact that he seemed on 'intimate terms' with so many thieves and ruffians.

> We had previously been told to put on our worst clothes, to leave our valuables behind and not to carry more than a few shillings in our pockets. . . . [After] ascending a narrow, filthy staircase, a door opened into a tiny room in which were four or five plain trestle beds. It belonged to a woman known as 'Sally the opium-smoker'. Her hair was perfectly white and she appeared to be very aged. She was lying on her bed close to the wall and by her side was a long narrow shelf on which several white mice were running about. The other beds, which were in the middle of the room, were occupied by Lascar sailors, all of them apparently fast asleep. Sally seemed delighted to see Mr Field and in no way to resent our visit. She probably knew that it meant a present of opium, for Field, having aroused one of the sailors, asked us to give him a shilling or so wherewith to procure some opium. The man soon reappeared with it, whereupon Sally and her three lodgers immediately filled the tiny brass bowls of their opium pipes and commenced to smoke. When we reached the street, Field asked us how old we imagined Sally to be, and we all guessed various ages, eighty being the lowest. We were then told that Sally was but twenty-six years old.

The second account dates from after the publication of *Edwin Drood*. It is by an eager American souvenir-hunter who wanted to share with Dickens's biographer John Forster his very own *Edwin Drood* experience:

> I went with the same inspector who accompanied Dickens to see the room of the opium-smokers, old Eliza and her Lascar or Bengalee friend. There a fancy seized me to buy the bedstead which figures so accurately in *Edwin Drood*, in narrative and picture. I gave the old woman a pound

for it, and have it now packed and ready for shipment to New York.

'Old Eliza'? Maybe he went to the wrong address or maybe not. Everyone associated with the Shadwell opium-smoking business hid behind several names. If the going rate for a good pipe was still four pennies, the bedstead was sold for the equivalent of sixty pipes, which does not sound like a good deal for Eliza unless she was desperate.

According to Virginia Berridge, a specialist in the history of narcotic use in Britain:

> . . . descriptions of opium-smoking as a domestic [i.e. British] phenomenon began only in the 1860s. In part a reflection of the greater numbers of Chinese actually settling in the country – part, too, of the general fashion for investigation of 'darkest England' and East London in particular – the early presentations of opium-smoking in the East End were notable for their calm descriptions of the practice.

They lack the melodrama, the exotic imagery and the shrillness of later accounts.

Another opium house in the square was investigated by a journalist in July 1868, shortly after it had been visited by the Prince of Wales no less. The Prince did not indulge, so the house could not put up a 'by royal appointment' sign, but he did make a joke, according to the proprietor and 'opium master' Chi Ki – also married to a 'youngish, very thin and pale-looking' English wife:

> 'Yas,' observed Chi Ki, suddenly lighting up; 'the Prince, he say, "Come smokee pipe wi' me, and bring you' lady, whens conwenince".'
>
> 'Ah, yes; but I don't believe he meant it,' said Mrs Chi Ki, dubiously. But the lame old Chinaman grinned and winked to himself knowingly, so that I should not be in the least surprised if, one of these fine days, the porter at Marlborough House is startled by a Celestial apparition.

The Chinese person in London, when he was not being referred to as 'John Chinaman' or 'Jack', was often dubbed 'a Celestial' – a supposedly jokey epithet based on a Chinese term for 'heavenly dynasty'. It satirized the sense that Chinese officials had back home that they were the elect.

The reporter for *London Society: An Illustrated Magazine of Light and Amusing Literature for the Hours of Relaxation* began his article 'East London Opium-Smokers' with a reference to *The Arabian Nights*:

[Opium] is invested with a weird and fantastic interest (for which its Oriental origin is doubtless in some degree accountable). And there hovers about it a vague fascination, such as is felt towards ghostly legend and the lore of fairyland. . . . It is the vulgar supposition that the one occupation of the lives of eastern grandees is to recline on soft cushions and indulge in the charming narcotic; that the thousand and one seductive stories contained in the 'Arabian Nights' were composed by writers whose senses were steeped in it . . .

Since princes had been so drawn to Blue Gate Fields, commonly known as 'Tiger Bay' – 'on account of the number of ferocious she-creatures [prostitutes] in petticoats that lurk there' – the reporter decides to take a look for himself. It is, he writes, 'a narrow lane . . . with courts and alleys on either side full of one-storey high hovels'. The opium house is in 'a tiny square of ill-looking little houses and an appalling odour of bad drainage'. But when Chi Ki first appears at a nearby pub, the reporter is disappointed:

Being so celebrated a character, with lords and marquises for his patrons and customers, I expected to see a man able and willing to demonstrate in his attire his native ideas of splendour. It would not have surprised me if so exalted a person as an opium master had appeared in a gown of gold-embroidered crimson silk, and with a sash and curly-toed slippers; but poor Chi Ki was very poorly clad indeed. He is a man of ostlerish cut, wearing a long jacket and a comforter wisped round his neck, and tight trousers, and an old cloth cap on his head. He is lame of a leg, too . . .

In the parlour of the dingy opium house, there is a little blinking fire where the opium cookery takes place, 'a Chinaman looking the picture of despair' and a 'large bedstead, with a bed made the wrong way on it'. Then, up the stairs to the public smoking room. The anonymous reporter must have had his notebook with him, or else a very precise memory:

It was an extremely mean and miserable little room. . . . The chief and most conspicuous article of furniture the room contained was a large four-post bed, and a bed like the one downstairs. The bed was not arranged according to the English fashion. It was rolled up bolster-wise all along the length of the bedstead, leaving the mattress bare except for a large mat of Chinese grass. The bed-hangings were of some light Chinese gauze, but very dirty, and hitched up slatternly on the hanging-rails. The walls of the room were hung with a few tawdry pictures highly coloured, and contrasting grimly with the blackened walls, all stained above with rain-leakage, and below with the filthy saliva with which the smokers had besprinkled them.

Chi Ki demonstrates 'the mysteries of his craft', and hands around a well-saturated bamboo-and-clay pipe he claims is worth £10: 'nothing but the best opium smoked in it for fourteen years'. He charges three halfpence a hit, 'a more expensive enjoyment than dram drinking':

> . . . his chief customers are the sailors who arrive at the London ports. Sometimes, I was informed, trade was so slack that not more than two or three customers would apply all day long; while at other times it was as much as Chi Ki could do, distilling and frizzling and frying, to keep the smokers going.

As for 'poor English Mrs Chi Ki':

> [She] looks as though she is being gradually smoke-dried, and by and by will present the appearance of an Egyptian mummy:
> 'I can stand a good deal of it,' said she, 'but sometimes it's awful. Sometimes two or three ships come in at once, and then we have a house-ful. Upstairs as well as down. We've had as many as fourteen smoking in this room at one time, and them that couldn't find room on the bed lay all about the floor . . .

Chi Ki must have had several aliases – it was a standard joke name, 'Cheeky', in pantomime at the time. He also sometimes went by the name of Ah Sin or George Ah Sin, and has been identified with the 'Jack Chinaman t'other side of the Court' mentioned in *Edwin Drood*, the one of whom the old crone is jealous in her trade. The prefix 'Ah' before the name of a male Chinese was a Guangdong diminutive – like putting a 'y' or an 'ey' at the end of an English first name. Sin or Sing was the usual name of the firstborn, meaning 'number one' or 'first'. So Ah Sin was 'little firstborn', 'number one son'. Calling oneself 'Ah Sin' was like signing a hotel register as 'John Smith'.

In another account of a visit to an East End opium house, published in September 1868 in *The Ragged School Union Magazine*, the proprietor is called 'Jack' as in 'John Chinaman' – the commonest term for a male Chinese in London, applied indiscriminately. The article 'In an Opium Den' has a strong moral message, and is notably less sympathetic than the *London Society* piece. The opium habit is 'becoming popular among the lower strata of society', especially in the East End of London, it begins, where 'not only do the chemists vend the drug in large quantities, there are dens where the opium is as regularly smoked as it is in China'. The practice is spreading from Asiatics to British sailors to 'men and women who desire to find in opium that oblivion from care which alcoholic liquors cannot give'. The account of the visit itself, accompanied by the police, was reprinted from an earlier article by one Albert Wolff in *Le Figaro* – who remembered the vague location of the den as around 'Whitechapel':

> The room we enter is so low that we are unable to stand upright. Lying pell-mell on a mattress placed on the ground are Chinamen, Lascars, and a few English blackguards who have imbibed a taste for opium. Some stretched at full length abandon themselves to the fumes of intoxication in its different stages, while others are only just commencing to light their pipes at a kind of night lamp, which is placed by the side of each smoker. Jack, the master of the house, jabbers a little English . . .

The police officer asks if there is an upstairs room. There appears to be no staircase. Jack fetches a ladder and leans it against the wall 'where some cats' and rats' skins are hanging'. He points to a hole in the ceiling:

> Seated on a mattress in a room lighted by a dim lamp is an old woman with dishevelled white hair, thin face, and dull-looking eyes, blowing a cloud of smoke and coughing every now and then like a person in the last stage of consumption. She casts a stupefied gaze upon us, then throws herself back, and continues to puff away at her pipe of opium. The room where she is is a small loft . . . but beyond the mattress on which the old sorceress is reclining there is not a single piece of furniture . . .

Both these articles appeared in 1868, the year before Dickens made his nocturnal visit, and the year in which the Pharmacy Act was passed – giving the subject more topicality. The purchase of opium in various forms – in grocer's shops, from travelling hawkers and in pharmacies – was widespread and legal: tinctures of opium and patent medicines were a popular way of sending the children to sleep, a practice known as 'syruping the infants'. So, on a much more limited scale, was recreational use for those who wished to emulate Coleridge and De Quincey, and try to open the doors of perception.

There had been sporadic, confused debates among medics in the first half of the century about whether opium-*eating* or *drinking* was to be treated as a vice or a disease, a question of morality or addiction, whether its effects were stimulating or calming, and whether there was a valid distinction between medical and non-medical use. There was also disagreement about whether opium shortened life or lengthened it. But following the Opium Wars in China, and the professionalization of medics and pharmacists, the debates became much more focused. Some argued for more controls at the point of sale, others for regulation of the purity of the drug, others still for restricting it to 'medical use' only – if such a definition could be sustained. There was a crescendo of talk about how dangerous opium could be – if taken in large quantities. And because opium-*smoking* was a special craft which tended to take place in establishments run by Chinese immigrants, there was an increasing emphasis in the discussion on the communities of the East End of London. The Pharmacy Act listed opium in its schedule of 'poisons' for the first time, but demoted it to the Second Schedule, which meant that only labelling restrictions would apply, nothing tougher. General dealers could still sell opium-based products, and the Pharmaceutical Society – which had responsibility for implementing the Act – in practice had very few powers. Opium had been moved to the Second Schedule because of the lobbying of pharmacists, who argued it was 'one of their chief articles of trade'. So opium remained the aspirin of Victorian England – and maybe opium was the religion of the people. Aspirin itself was to appear on the market in 1899, produced by Bayer Pharmaceuticals as a follow-up to their best-selling heroin-based cough mixture – the drug given the name because it made its users feel like heroes and heroines. The 1868 Act was the first move in the direction of official control of the trade, but that was about it. According to Virginia Berridge:

> The isolation of the Chinese community in East London, and the likelihood that an English stranger wanting to buy opium would be regarded with suspicion, made the use of the Pharmacy Act as a means of control in this area a dead letter.

Opium imports into Britain, which came mainly from Turkey rather than China, with Persia as the second-largest supplier, were unaffected.

So opium houses were certainly in the news. Charles Dickens's weekly journal *Household Words*, on 1 and 22 August 1857, had run two long feature articles on the international opium trade. The first was on the monopoly of the East India Company over the cultivation of the vast white poppy crops of Bengal, and its export – in competition since 1834 with private traffickers – of 60,000 mango-wood chests a year to China, each crammed with forty brown cakes of opium roughly the size of a human head (in total worth more than £5 million, or 'one sixth of the entire revenue of our vast Indian empire'). The second described the various middlemen who surreptitiously arranged the import of the drug ('illegal and contraband') in narrow, fast-moving craft called 'scrambling dragons' along the southeast coast of China. The opium was exchanged for silk, China tea and especially silver:

> The Chinese rarely *eat* opium; they generally smoke it, and are very particular concerning its quality. . . . The prepared opium is smoked in pipes, as we smoke tobacco. The Chinese believe that the effects of the drug – the exhilarating effects, at any rate – are more apparent by inhaling the fumes than by chewing the solid itself. . . . There are smoking-shops by hundreds in the towns within moderate distance of the Coast; and these shops, we are told, are kept open day and night, each being furnished with a number of couches formed of bamboo-canes and covered with mats and rattans; a sort of wooden stool serves as a bolster or pillow; and in the centre of the shop is a lamp that serves for many smokers . . .

After a brief account of the Opium Wars, the article summarized 'the arguments on both sides of the opium question'. On the one hand, there were those who denounced the trade as immoral and dangerous ('opium-smoking is not an ancient habit in China; it is comparatively modern, and therefore more easily eradicated') and who gave the Chinese government credit for sincerity in their ineffectual attempts to ban it; these people were prepared to accept that some forms of business in the Empire *could* be morally wrong. On the other, there were those who claimed that 'opium-smoking is deemed by medical men not so pernicious as opium-*eating*' and in any case less dangerous than alcohol; that highly coloured accounts of the evils of opium were usually written by 'men who have neither tasted nor smoked it themselves'; that the East India

Company made *at least* £5 million a year from the trade – far too great a sacrifice to demand of the Company; there could be no question of compensating them adequately: the moral issue was beside the point.

Enter *Edwin Drood*. John Forster wrote in his *Life of Dickens* (1872–74) about the unfinished novel that

> Not a line was wanting to the reality, in the most minute local details, of places the most widely contrasted; and we saw with equal vividness the lazy cathedral town and the lurid opium-eater's den.

Dickens had blended his personal experiences of May 1869 and maybe later, his own knowledge of laudanum which he drank as a painkiller to help him sleep, and his reading of editions of periodicals, to create the celebrated opening chapter of the book. We know that he must have read the articles in *Household Words* and *All the Year Round*. He may also have read the exposés in *London Society* and *The Ragged School Union Magazine*: there are some strong similarities between them and chapters 1, 14 and 23 of *Edwin Drood*, which have led commentators to cite the articles as 'an important influence on the depiction of Princess Puffer's den and on her esoteric knowledge of opium-smoking'. What we do not know is whether, when he visited the opium den in Shadwell, he had already decided to give his central character Jasper the opium habit, so he was checking his facts, or whether it was the visit that put the idea into his head. Or indeed whether the article in *All the Year Round* originally suggested the location to him. We do know that he had started writing by June 1869. We also know that he held strong views about Chinese culture, having written sardonic articles about a Chinese junk moored on the Thames at Blackwall, in the East End (1848), and about a freelance 'Chinese exhibition' (1851) – evidently sharing the prejudices of most mid-Victorian politicians and businessmen. And he was delighted to report in 1860 his son's plan to join the victorious British troops in China.

Edwin Drood begins with John (or Jack) Jasper, the moody young organist and choirmaster at drowsy Cloisterham Cathedral, having an opium dream out of *The Arabian Nights* and Coleridge's 'Kubla Khan' (written in 1797; published in 1816). The tower of the cathedral becomes a scene of oriental torture; deep England has become orientalized:

> What is the spike that intervenes, and who has set it up? Maybe, it is set up on the Sultan's orders for the impaling of a horde of Turkish robbers, one

by one. It is so, for cymbals clash, and the Sultan goes by to his palace in long procession. Ten thousand scimitars flash in the sunlight, and thrice ten thousand dancing-girls strew flowers. Then, follow white elephants caparisoned in countless gorgeous colours and infinite in number and writhing attendants. Still, the Cathedral Tower rises in the background, where it cannot be, and still no writhing figure is on the grim spike. Stay! Is the spike so low a thing as the rusty spike on the top of a post of an old bedstead that has tumbled all awry?

He is, it transpires, in 'the meanest and closest of small rooms', in complete contrast with his expansive dream:

> Through the ragged window-curtain, the light of early day steals in from a miserable court. He lies, dressed, across a large unseemly bed, upon a bedstead that has indeed given way under the weight upon it. Lying, also dressed and also across the bed, not longwise, are a Chinaman, a Lascar, and a haggard woman. The two first are in a sleep or stupor; the last is blowing at a kind of pipe, to kindle it.

The woman asks in a rattling whisper if he would like another pipe. He rises unsteadily from the bed, places the pipe on the hearthstone, and notices that the hostess 'has opium-smoked herself into a strange likeness of the Chinaman'. As with the 'oriental names' in the journal reports – like 'smoke-dried' Mrs Chi Ki and the 'self-abandonment' of Mother Abdallah and Cheeny Emma – there is the suggestion, no more than that, that the old crone shares her bed as well as her opium pipe with those Asian sailors lying across the bedstead. This would later, taking the cue from *Edwin Drood*, become a more marked feature of exposés of opium dens. Already, in 1862, in his *London Labour and the London Poor*, Henry Mayhew had referred to rumours among prostitutes that

> the disease communicated by the Malays, Lascars and Orientals generally, is said to be the most frightful form of lues to be met with in Europe. It goes by the name of the Dry ——, and is much dreaded by *all* the women in the neighbourhood of the docks.

What visions can Princess Puffer have, wonders Jasper under the influence of the opium. In a sudden fit of violence, he pounces on the Chinaman, grabs him by the throat, and asks him the same question. Then he leaves some money on the table, stumbles down the broken stairs and bids 'good morning' to the rat-ridden doorkeeper.

Jasper does not visit the opium house for over six months. Probably, he has been indulging back home in Cloisterham. When he returns there, he first checks into a 'hybrid hotel' behind Aldersgate Street:

> Eastward and still eastward through the stale streets he takes his way, until he reaches his destination: a miserable court, specially miserably among many such. He ascends a broken staircase, opens a door, looks into a dark stifling room, and says: 'Are you alone here?'
>
> 'Alone, deary, worse luck for me and better for you,' replies a croaking voice.

She is surprised that Jasper has managed to stay away, alive, for so long from the poor old soul with the *real* recipe for mixing opium. As he inhales from the pipe, she gently encourages him to talk about the potency of opium and its way of taking him on a journey of the mind, as a relief, and how the journey happens 'before the changes of colours and the great landscapes and glittering procession began'. Before orientalism. She has learned the secret of how to make him talk when under the influence, though he is not on this occasion giving much away. Finally, he gets up, 'chilled and shaking', and leaves the court by its entrance, this time followed at a cautious distance by the 'woman of haggard appearance'. She follows him to the hotel behind Aldersgate Street, where he changes his clothes, and thence that evening to Cloisterham. In the course of a conversation in the cathedral precincts there, Dick Datchery, a lodger – possibly a detective – intrigued by such a person coming to Cloisterham, learns that she is known in the trade as 'Hopeum Puffer' or 'Er Royal Highness the Princess Puffer' and that she lives among the 'Jacks. And Chaynermen. And hother Knifers.'

The following morning, at the seven o'clock service, she sits behind a pillar in the cathedral, 'as ugly and withered as one of the fantastic carvings on the under brackets of the stall seats', shaking her fists at the choirmaster. And there *Edwin Drood* abruptly ends, with a strong image of Albion's hypocritical attitude towards opium: the revenge of the opium-master, in the heart of England, no less.

Shortly after the first instalment of *Edwin Drood* was published, at the beginning of April 1870, Dickens received a letter from the seventy-eight-year-old

Sir John Bowring complaining about inaccuracies in the description of the finer points of opium-smoking. Bowring – famous for his short fuse, his accounts of various missions abroad, his hymn-writing and his translations of esoteric poetry – had been the Governor of Hong Kong and Plenipotentiary to China who in 1856 had responded to the boarding of a British-registered ship in the Pearl River by the Chinese police by ordering the Royal Navy to bombard and occupy the forts guarding Canton. This action, initially controversial back home, ignited the Second Opium War. Prime Minister Palmerston spoke hyperbolically of

> an insolent barbarian [who] has violated the British flag, broken the engagement of treaties, offered rewards for the heads of British subjects in that part of China and planned their destruction by murder, assassination and poison.

No matter that the Chinese policemen were probably smugglers in disguise. So Bowring knew a thing or two about opium, and Dickens appears to have consulted him in the past about matters Chinese. Bowring had enclosed with his letter about *Edwin Drood* a sketch of a traditional opium pipe 'and the manner of its employment'.

Dickens replied from Gad's Hill on 5 May 1870. He was evidently rattled:

> I send you my cordial thanks for your note, and the very curious drawing accompanying it. I ought to tell you, perhaps, that the opium-smoking I have described, I saw (exactly as I described it, penny ink-bottle and all) down in Shadwell this last autumn [presumably a return visit, after May 1869, or else Dickens's memory was playing tricks]. A couple of the Inspectors of Lodging-Houses knew the woman and took me to her . . .

Sir John, with uncharacteristic restraint, beat a tactical retreat:

> No doubt the Chinaman [sic] whom he described had accommodated himself to English usage, and that our great and faithful dramatist here or elsewhere most correctly pourtrayed [sic] a piece of actual life.

Accurate or not, Charles Dickens's description of an opium den – and Luke Fildes's illustrations of 'In the Court' and 'Sleeping It Off' (which Dickens 'recognized as the very portrait of the place') – had a profound influence on the ways in which such dwellings were to be described by novelists, storytellers and journalists in the future, and on the public debate about opium-smoking: the dark alleyway, the miserable court, the *Arabian Nights* fantasy, the collapsed bedstead, 'a Chinaman, a Lascar, and a haggard woman', Jack Chinaman, the woman who has 'a strange likeness of the Chinaman', the contrast between London's dockland East End and sleepy cathedral town. Within two years, Gustave Doré had made 'An Opium Den in the East End of London', illustrating the journalist Blanchard Jerrold's *London: A Pilgrimage* (1872), inspired by Fildes and depicting the den which Dickens visited in 1869 – and the dominant *visual* image was set in place as well. The early pre-*Edwin Drood* descriptions of visits to opium houses had certainly emphasized how mean and dingy the establishments were, but had also noted how calm and unthreatening they were. *Edwin Drood* added mystery, melodrama and a memorable iconography.

Estimates of how many opium houses there actually *were* in the East End during the 1870s tended to vary – but *The Friend of China*, house journal of the Quaker-founded Anglo-Oriental Society for the Suppression of the Opium Trade, which had a vested interest in inflating the number in its crusade to stamp out the India–China contraband, reckoned there were almost half a dozen 'of these loathsome places'. *Edwin Drood* created the impression there were a lot more than that. Dickens's unfinished novel also fixed the idea of the 'den'. Most investigations at the time concluded that the 'den' did not in fact exist – but that social clubs, or rooms in boarding-houses, did exist as places of relaxation where gambling and smoking routinely took place. One writer in the 1870s who, after smoking five pipes (perhaps to keep up with Jasper), hallucinated a giant centipede crawling up his leg, said that he would definitely be returning, but

> As for the so-called 'dens', they seemed to me simply poorly fitted social clubs, and certainly as free from anything visibly objectionable as, to say the least of it, public-houses of the same class.

It soon became a journalistic commonplace to visit a 'den' with lurid thoughts of *Edwin Drood* in mind – only to be disappointed by the more mundane reality. American essayist James Platt, for example, in *The Gentleman's Magazine* of 1895, made a point of contrasting his own investigations into 'Chinese London and the Opium Dens' with Dickens's by-then canonical description. He concludes that Dickens never stayed long enough fully to understand what was really going on. Then he writes movingly of what happened to 'the particular den' in New Court – which Platt knew well – the one described by Dickens, which has been demolished to make way for a schoolboys' playground:

> It was worth going to, if only to see a Chinaman and an Englishwoman so sincerely attached to one another as were the old couple who kept it. They might without impropriety have been called Darby and Joan.

The man of the house – Platt calls him 'Johnny' – was evicted, his equipment and effects dispersed, much of it 'purchased by Americans and others interested in curious relics'; after that, 'he never settled down again, but wandered from lodging to lodging'. He died at the age of sixty-four, 'due to the rupture of a blood-vessel accelerated by destitution'. These were the kinds of people demonized by writers about opium dens. Another problem in writing about 'dens' was that when prurient visitors from the smarter West End looked in, the Chinese tended to put on a show for them.

Dickens had placed Princess Puffer's den in a court just beyond the end of the churchyard of St George's-in-the-East, Stepney. The Revd Harry Jones, Rector of St George's, also reckoned that Dickens and disciples had given the neighbourhood too bad a name, in a reminiscence written some twenty years before Platt's article:

> Even in Courts of worst repute, none of us have ever met with any rudeness, and some of the places which ought by all their associates to be dens of disorder exhibit a few exceptionally remarkable phases of neatness. [These included] a notorious, I might say infamous Court. It had furnished Dickens with a scene. The reader of *Edwin Drood* may recollect the spot to which Jasper betook himself for his opium-smokes. This was the place. The old crone who received him, well-known as 'Lascar Sal' [lived there until quite recently]. And I know the 'John Chinaman' of whom she was jealous as a rival in her deadly trade. He had a ground floor in the same Court. . . . But in this Court of evil fame we have been ever welcome when paying a kindly visit or attending the sick . . .

If 'slummers', journalists and novelists sometimes met with 'affronts or insults' when gawping at these courts, then it was almost certainly the fault of the visitor:

[They] exist only in the imagination of those who know nothing about the matter, or they are invited by the visitor himself. If he sniffs about censoriously, and asks impertinent questions, or gives himself airs in any way, he is likely to meet with a rebuff, which the offended party does not know how to convey in the shape of polished sarcasm.

The Revd Jones agreed that 'it was right to demolish this "Court of evil fame" – whatever its fame among Dickens buffs' – 'being in a grievously dilapidated state'. But the inhabitants, and their working environment, had been sensationalized and demonized.

Joseph Salter, evangelical Missionary to the Asiatics in England – especially those of Blue Gate Fields – and author of *The Asiatic in England* (1873), agreed about the demolition, but then had a rather less charitable view of the opium-masters:

Here is [an opium house] in the extreme corner, kept by an extraordinary-looking Chinese, decrepit with old age, so singular in appearance, that a newspaper correspondent, in describing his visit here, and holding, perhaps, the opinions of Darwin, thought he might be the connecting link between the human and the brute, and endeavoured to show that this waif from the Celestial Empire was closely related to the chimpanzee. That he only had animal developments is sadly true, but of how many more may this be said, who have not yet fled for refuge to lay hold on Jesus, the sinner's only hope.

This man, 'the chimpanzee-looking opium-smoker', turns out to be none other than Latau or 'L–t—', Lascar Sally's partner. So the intrepid Salter sets out to convert Princess Puffer herself, armed with various tracts and scriptures and a strong reading voice:

Her eyes used to sparkle with a strange brightness as we spoke of the gospel story, and from many a token we had hope that even poor Lascar Sally would find her place before the throne.

Then he turns to Chinese Emma, who shared Sally's lodgings as well as assisting in another opium house. 'Although sunken far in depravity, Emma still possessed a sense of right.' Of her own accord, she leaves her den of iniquity and goes to an asylum run by nuns: 'in which the efforts of a Sister in Christ

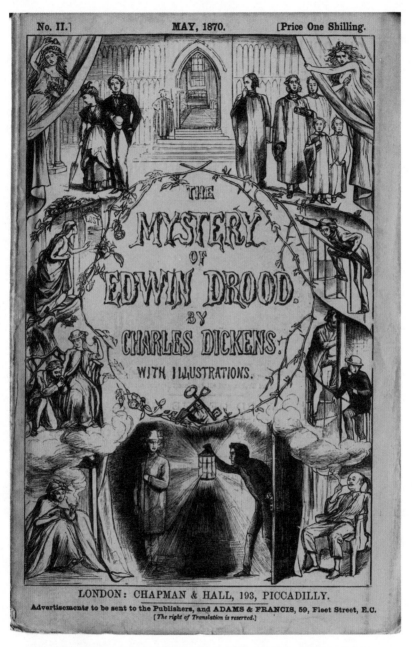

THE
MYSTERY
OF
EDWIN DROOD.
BY
CHARLES DICKENS.
WITH ILLUSTRATIONS.

LONDON: CHAPMAN & HALL, 193, PICCADILLY.
Advertisements to be sent to the Publishers, and ADAMS & FRANCIS, 59, Fleet Street, E.C.
[*The right of Translation is reserved.*]

Cover, by Charles Allston Collins, of Charles Dickens's incomplete serial *The Mystery of Edwin Drood* (issue of May 1870), with opium-den scenes at bottom left and right. OVERLEAF: D. W. Griffith's film *Broken Blossoms* (1919), showing a 'scarlet house of sin' in Limehouse, where Chinese, Malays and Lascars share 'the lilied pipe' with Mayfair women.

Colonial postcard of a Chinese opium den, a popular subject in Britain during the nineteenth-century debate about the dope trade.

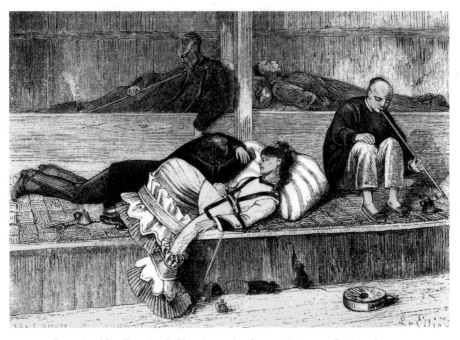

Exposés of San Francisco's Chinatown also favoured images of opium dens: a print of *c.* 1880. **OPPOSITE:** The Harbour Master's office at 74 Narrow Street, Limehouse, in 1905. The early Fu Manchu stories are centred on the Thames, the great artery of Empire.

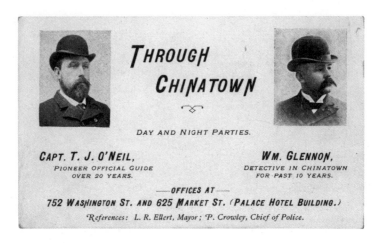

Business card advertising day-and-night conducted tours, for visitors to San Francisco's Chinatown, *c.* 1895.

Cartoon by Low of two journalists eagerly, and unsuccessfully, seeking adventure in a prosaic Limehouse, 1932. **OPPOSITE:** Title page of the article 'The Cockney John Chinaman', from *The English Illustrated Magazine* (July 1900): the phrase had recently entered the English language. **OVERLEAF:** Sword dancer performing on a street in San Francisco's Chinatown, photographed by Arnold Genthe between 1896 and 1906.

THE COCKNEY JOHN CHINAMAN.

By GEORGE A. WADE.

THERE are some strange colonies of foreigners in the East End of London, as most people know, but it is doubtful if there is any stranger one than that in the little street which is given over to the Chinese who have made their home home of the Chinese, can Limehouse Causeway be considered as even a third-rate street. If you pass through the City and eastwards to Aldgate, then along that thoroughfare of nations, the Commercial Road, till you come, far down it, to the

GENERAL VIEW OF THE CAUSEWAY.

The woman in the picture is English, but married to a Chinaman.

in that corner of the Metropolis which lies close to the entrance to the West India Docks.

"Limehouse Causeway" has an imposing sound as the name of a street, and one thinks instinctively of several other "Causeways" and "Broadways" whose fame has passed far beyond London. But in no sense, except that of its being the broad street known as West India Dock Road, you will then soon arrive in sight, on the right hand as you go down it, of a narrow, somewhat dirty-looking street, which cuts away from the main road at an oblique angle. This is Limehouse Causeway, the Chinese quarter of England.

Once in the Causeway itself, evidences of its inhabitants and their characteristics

were effaced by the puerilities of Rome . . . and Mary's intercession was substituted for a Saviour's love and sacrifice'. A few weeks in such a place was enough to bring Emma 'back to her old position'. But all was not lost. After Salter has prayed for 'better success another time', and distributed his tracts, she begins to see the light. Which just went to show that 'thanks to the vital power of the Gospel we preach, there is hope for the lowest of our race'. In general, Joseph Salter had no problems with Dickens's description of the opium den. In fact, for him the den was more than a Gothic nightmare – it was a terrestrial version of hell itself:

> We are about to enter Satan's stronghold, and shall observe how shamelessness has its premium and admirers, and honesty, truth, and self-respect are trampled in the dust. The locality is by the river-side, and in a turning in High-street, Shadwell, with other smaller turnings running out of it. Here disease and death, decked in gaudy tinselled robes, allure the victim to the grave. . . . We are now in the Oriental quarter; there are several houses here devoted to Asiatics, presided over by Chinese, Malays and Indians, according to the country of the Asiatic seeking companionship. Each of the proprietors is assisted by an English mistress, some of whom have lived so long in this element, that they use the Oriental vernacular. . . . Let us enter the first house in this colony of evil spirits. It is a house of three rooms and is kept by a stalwart Chinese, aided by Emma.

Interestingly, several of the Asiatics residing in Blue Gate Fields had at one time in their lives worked for music halls as jugglers, conjurors, acrobats, and in two cases for 'the Chinese Junk' which had been moored in the Thames at the time of the Great Exhibition in 1851. One of these was 'Awa, a native of Macao'. He arrived at the docks in 1851, as a sea-cook, then worked in a Whitechapel tea shop; after that, he went to Liverpool with 'the famous Chinese junk' after its London exhibition had closed, and passed the following year at a tea shop in Coventry; from there, he became part of a Chinese knife-throwing act on the halls, but essentially walked out – with many wounds on his fingers and neck to show for it – because his boss refused to pay him what he was owed; then he turned to conjuring. His *pièce de résistance* was 'the amputation-feat which secured the greatest applause from the public'. Salter was more interested in real miracles, but he was still fascinated:

The Chinese bared his arm, first having sent the sharp chopper into a block, and then, taking the weapon, made a furious blow at his arm; and then he exhibited his limb, with the chopper fixed and the red fluid flowing copiously down, and the people were astonished, and said, 'Look at the blood'. But it was not blood at all – it was only red ochre the people were looking at, and the instrument was not the same that he stuck in the block; he had dexterously changed that for another, which had a gap suited to fit his arm, the gap being covered with a thin skin containing ochre. . . . We might have learnt more of his tricks, but had no use for them; so we allowed him to retain the secret, and gave him a Chinese Testament. The truths of the Gospel were repeatedly set before Awa and his companions.

Most journalists who witnessed what Salter called 'the sickening scenes' in opium houses – 'too forbidding and appalling for any but a sturdy Christianity and an earnest love to penetrate' – tended to be disappointed rather than revolted. The journalist George R. Sims, in his collection *Living London* (1901–3), was a characteristic example. Sims was as much of a celebrity in *his* day as Dickens had been to the previous generation: his articles on 'how the poor live' and 'humble London' in 1882–83 had provoked a Royal Commission; he wrote ''Twas Christmas Day in the Workhouse' and other popular ballads/ songs; and he founded the 'George R. Sims Hair Restorer Company Ltd.' in 1897, with its patent ointment 'Tatcho'. Sims deliberately set out to challenge the 'picturesqueness' of earlier investigative essays, which had piled on the exoticism for the benefit of the credulous 'stay-at-home public'. His descriptions of Limehouse stress that the docklands area is among the most congested, impoverished, low-wage areas of London – with the highest levels of child mortality. He was, on the other hand, credited with being the first to apply the word 'Chinatown' – borrowed from the United States – to the Limehouse dockland area.

Sims was well known for using various media – songs, ballads, plays – to put over his social ideas. In 1905, he was to publish a short story which set out to challenge the popular stereotype of the opium-smoking, shiftless Chinaman. It was called 'Li Ting of London', and concerned a quiet, hardworking entre-preneurial Chinese who checks into a boarding-house in Limehouse Causeway one summer afternoon, even though 'he was no sailor'. He progresses from giving away handbills outside a tea shop in nearby Walworth (where he is given the affectionate nickname 'Ching-a-Ring') to becoming a rag-and-bone man, to running a bric-a-brac shop. He marries his Walworth business partner's daughter, becomes a naturalized British subject, and moves into the property business. Then, just as he is making a success of his life, he disappears back to China. It transpires that he is really the son of a Prince who fled to London from 'a conspiracy against his life' because he had been a ringleader of the Boxers ('The Boxers are patriots, mother,' said Miss Ting quietly, 'I've read all about them'). He has been summoned by an old mandarin, who 'cannot bear the rule of the Dowager Empress and the Emperor who was a puppet in her hands' and wants the Prince to lead a 'great revolution'. This plan goes wrong, Li Ting is imprisoned in the Imperial Palace, escapes and returns to London. 'The Tings now have a very profitable curiosity shop in the neighbourhood of Westminster, where they are well-known.' Sims deliberately made the story as lacking in 'picturesqueness' and mystery as he could.

But as the public debate about opium – among medics, politicians, clerics, lobbyists and journalists – came into focus around questions of addiction, recreational use and disease, and gathered momentum, the practice of opium-smoking began to be associated more and more with a single alien minority, the Chinese. And they were presented as a problem. If the opium habit had, as it was argued by missionaries, been an impediment to the spread of Christianity in mainland China, it had also encouraged the spread of vicious practices among 'helpless slaves' in docklands Britain. The Quaker monthly *Friend of China* used off-putting descriptions of opium dens to show 'the domestic retribution likely to be incurred through encouragement of the Indo-Chinese trade'. There was, of course, a large measure of double-think in this, and the writers were well aware of it. The British had encouraged the opium trade, one side-effect of which was the 'poppy culture' in East London, which was spreading to Europeans. But by drawing attention to that culture, and the 'oriental' colony which sustained it, propagandists could now criticize both the Chinese *and* the trade. So, amid articles about opium-growing in China, production and consumption, the patent medicines which contained the most 'powerful poisons', 'the physical ruin and moral degradation of multitudes of Chinese' and hindrances to the spread of Christianity – which take up the bulk of the journal – in August 1883 *The Friend of China* reprinted a letter from the Wesleyan missionary in Canton, George Piercy, to the *Methodist Recorder* about the danger of contamination:

Many are aware that this drug for a long time has been used *non*-medically, in many parts of the country, to the great injury, physically and morally, of individuals, but not that it is *smoked* by any except by some of the Chinese in London. With great pain of mind, I now must say evidence clearly and strongly shows that we really have a new habit, prolific of evil, springing up amongst us. But where? . . . In our great metropolis. . . . It is coming closer to us with a rapidity and spring undreamt of even by those who have dreaded its stealthy and unseen step . . .

Alarms have been sounded by our cousins across the Atlantic which ought to have rung through the land. . . . Does not it demand equally careful study at the hands of Englishmen when in our metropolis for years past there have been six or eight *schools for opium-smoking*, the presiding spirits in each being hardened opium-sodden Chinamen, confirmed smokers themselves, and earning their livelihood by teaching others also. Writers of fiction and caterers for popular papers, too, have given the public information of these places, and sometimes in a way calculated rather to minister to the spirit of prurient curiosity than to repress it.

'Schools for opium-smoking' were just the thing cunning, inscrutable Chinamen *would* think of. 'It begins with the Chinese, but does not end with them!' Opium is 'the evil they have brought', but it is spreading – not only with English folk visiting such 'schools of opium vice', but even in West End hotels, where '*opium is ordered of the waiters*', and over the counter in public houses. 'Let the evil be dealt with at once . . .'

Arguments against the recreational use of opium were becoming hopelessly entangled with racial stereotypes, and all too easy to exploit when jobs in the docks became scarce, when young male Chinese married or lived with white women, and when feelings about the 'morally indefensible' India–China trade began to run high. An inspector for the London County Council, an ex-policeman, visited the Asiatic Sailors' Home in Limehouse, West India Dock Road, in 1904 and saw

oriental cunning and cruelty . . . hall-marked on every countenance. . . . Until my visit, I had always considered some of the Jewish inhabitants of Whitechapel to be the worst type of humanity I had ever seen.

What's more, the inhabitants of one of the 'dens' were 'jabbering in an incoherent manner' *which the inspector could not understand.*

By the 1880s, the public arguments about opium were beginning to stress – as the Revd Piercy's letter shows – that a vice which had been incubated by Chinese opium-masters in the East End was in danger of spreading to the local English population and, beyond them, to degenerate white middle-class citizens. It was one thing to take opium – medicinally – in the privacy of one's own home; quite another to take the drug socially or recreationally. What if the collateral damage of the Opium Wars – in the form of addicts and adepts – took revenge by *deliberately* turning respectable English folk into addicts themselves? What if the slaves came to haunt the masters? The more lurid the image of the 'opium den', the stronger the association between racial anxieties and the anti-opiumist cause. As academic John Seed has justly summarized, in his article 'Limehouse Blues' (2006):

> There is much more to be said about this – about how the Victorian opium den was transformed into a broader space for the interplay of sexuality, Empire and drugs; about anxieties surrounding inter-racial sex; about some kind of historically-specific crisis of masculinity . . . and about how these intersected with fears and frustrations about unemployment, low wages and housing shortages in working-class districts like Limehouse and Poplar.

The respectable choirmaster Jasper's opium dreams were derived from Thomas De Quincey's *Confessions of an English Opium Eater* (1821, revised 1845), which had made the powerful and lasting connection between a drug grown in oriental earth and the oriental dream-imagery which resulted from drinking it. For, although the title was 'Opium Eater', it was really about the drinking of laudanum, a cocktail of purple drops dissolved in alcohol. 'Confessions' in the title was a nod towards Jean-Jacques Rousseau. And 'English' because, as De Quincey wrote, earlier published accounts had come from travellers' tales about Turkey and Persia and 'numerous pictures of Turkish opium-eaters'. 'Eating' was the Turkish preference. For him, as for the poet Coleridge, the 'Orient' encompassed China and India, the Near East or 'the Bible Lands', North Africa and even Eastern Europe – and a 'predisposition' to its generalized imagery, from books and artefacts, 'must always have existed in my mind'. This meaning of 'Orient' was relatively recent: an eighteenth-century philosopher would have thought of the Orient as the Levant – Syria, Lebanon and Jordan – rather than China or India. For De Quincey, the 'predisposition' seems to have come from *The Arabian Nights*, travellers' tales, book illustrations, readings about 'mystical tortures', 'Kubla Khan' (including Coleridge's preface of 1816, where he wrote about the oriental imaginings which came to him after taking 'an anodyne'), classical accounts of processions in ancient Rome, some recent acquisitions by the British Museum, Coleridge's description of Piranesi's *Prisons* (which he thought were called *Dreams*) – and the fashionable *Chinoiserie* of his youth: fanciful screens, panels and wallpapers featuring pagodas, dragons, parakeets and crocodiles, chairs in the Nile style with carved sphinxes and gryphons' feet, fireplaces with sculpted fire-breathing dragons. The Royal Pavilion in Brighton was full of them. But De Quincey turned these objects of delight and desire into images of deep anxiety:

> I know not whether others share in my feelings on this point; but I have often thought that if I were compelled to forgo England and to live in China, and among Chinese manners and modes of life and scenery, I should go mad. The causes of my horror lie deep . . .

De Quincey recalled these 'awful images and associations' as something to do with 'ancient, monumental, cruel and elaborate religions'; with great antiquity, stasis, and lack of resource and development in the modern era; with strange and unpronounceable names; and above all a sense of a vast empire – 'of eternity and infinity' – with never-ending tracts of land, 'the part of the earth most swarming with human life . . . Man is a *weed* in those regions', a land of endless reproduction, a breeding-ground for inhumanity. He associated these with 'all oriental names or images'. And, he said, they *terrified* him. They invaded his inner life. A contagion. They amounted to a 'barrier of utter abhorrence, and want of sympathy, placed between us by feelings deeper than I can analyse. I could sooner live with lunatics or brute animals'. For some very deep-seated reason, he was prone to morbid fantasies about 'Asiatic scenery' when orienting the streets of London, between Oxford Circus and Euston Road: the immensity and impersonality of the metropolis, its tawdriness and teeming multitudes, had given him a lifelong fear of London since he was seventeen years old, a panic-stricken and penniless lad from the provinces, victim of moneylenders, frantically trying to find the teenaged prostitute Ann who had been friendly to him.

De Quincey's famous description of an opium dream conflated the 'usages and appearances' of China, Hindustan and Egypt, pleasure-dome and torture garden, in a psychedelic fantasy of *Chinoiserie* gone to the bad. It was the antithesis of his Lake District hearth and home:

> I was stared at, hooted at, grinned at, chattered at, by monkeys, by paroquets, by cockatoos. I ran into pagodas: and was fixed, for centuries, at the summit, or in secret rooms. . . . I came suddenly upon Isis and Osiris. I had done a deed, they said, which the ibis and the crocodile trembled at. I was buried, for a thousand years, in stone coffins, with mummies and sphinxes, in narrow chambers at the heart of eternal pyramids. I was kissed, with cancerous kisses, by crocodiles, and laid, with all unutterable slimy things, amongst reeds and Nilotic mud. I thus give the reader some slight abstraction of my oriental dreams, which always filled me with such amazement at the monstrous scenery.

But this amazement and ecstasy morphed into 'hatred and abomination', especially of the 'cursed crocodile'.

Usually, his waking dreams began – like Jasper's – with 'vast processions . . . friezes of never-ending stones . . . spectacles of more than earthly splendour'. Sometimes, these were followed by 'descents into chasms and sunless abysses, depths below depths' and drowned cities. Then came the wide landscapes and expanses of water made up of 'innumerable faces, upturned to the heavens'. And childhood memories orientalized. Such fantasies did not have much impact on the debate about opium at the time – the 1820s: that would come later, during the two Opium Wars. And later still, they would profoundly influence the drug scene of the twentieth century – the recreational smoking, the doors of perception, the oriental iconography – where they would eventually shed their deviant image and become part of the attraction.

In fact, many years later, De Quincey himself would write a series of ferocious, apoplectic articles, justifying – in brutal terms, even by the standards of the day – British intervention in China, 'our vilest oriental enemy', culminating in the pamphlet *China: A Revised Reprint* (1857), explaining the '*justice* of our British pretensions and attitude', to coincide with the Second Opium War. De Quincey's grounds for armed intervention 'with exemplary vigour' – he advocated an army of 14,000 strong marching on Peking and 'firing at the tiger' – included, in no particular order, China's 'vile population', its lack of 'true civilization', 'its incurable savagery in the moral sense', its monkey-like talent for mimicry – the Jesuits, apparently, taught the Chinese all they knew about 'mathematics and erudite sciences', from the 1640s onwards – its ingratitude for British help with developing the tea trade, its 'roll-call of murder' using a putrescent tribe of 'hole and corner assassins', its taste for elaborate tortures, its shilly-shallying diplomacy, its turpitude in banning opium imports (De Quincey, for obvious reasons, wanted the trade to become respectable), and above all the prevention of any acts of revenge on Britain which the Chinese, with a 'government universally capable of murder', might well be planning and which were likely to 'spring forward with a tiger's bound' at any moment. So China should be taught a lesson, by force. Tinkering with the coastal ports would not have the desired impact on central government. The only solution, ultimately, was to invade, and then incorporate China into the British Empire. All Britain was asking was for China, in future:

1. not to swindle . . .
2. not to patronise murder
3. to keep a better tongue in her head . . .

De Quincey's son Horace had embarked for China as an army lieutenant on active service, in December 1841, and died – apparently of malaria – near Canton on 27 August 1842, and this seems to have intensified his pathological loathing of all things and people Chinese. But it has to be said that his loathing did not need very much intensifying in the first place.

Recent scholarship has concentrated on this aspect of De Quincey's work – known as 'The Infection of Thomas De Quincey' – rather than on his aesthetic contribution as a Romantic dreamer, or on his legacy in the oriental imagery of twentieth-century drug culture. It has been claimed that the Victorian stereotype of the Chinaman – as vengeful, cunning, cowardly, devious, inscrutable and effeminate: beyond redemption – came into focus, or was at least synthesized, in *China*. But the broader question is: why did the eighteenth-century enthusiasm, the sinophilia of Enlightenment *philosophes* and the fashion for *Chinoiserie* – when China was associated with sophistication and style, and when imported Chinese porcelain, silks, wallpaper and tea were *haute culture* – turn into such dark imaginings?

One clue lies in De Quincey's repeated assertion that, despite the best efforts of 'the leaders of civilization', the British, to open up trade with China and energize Chinese entrepreneurship, the Chinese response was to 'call us in all proclamations by scurrilous names'. For him it all went back to 1793 and the very first diplomatic contact between the court of St James's and the Manchu dynasty: Lord George Macartney's 'pacific' mission to the court of the Chinese Emperor at Peking, financed by the East India Company. There had been talk of such an embassy for a number of years before that, but Company officials at Canton had always warned that the Chinese court would simply view such an initiative as 'an acknowledgement of inferiority', and Macartney only agreed to lead it on condition that he be made an earl when he came back – which he was. The mission, timed to coincide with the Qianlong Emperor's eighty-third birthday, had several objectives: to find more openings for trade, beyond Canton; to establish a permanent British embassy in Peking; to challenge the 'misrepresentation of the national character' which British businessmen in China had complained about; and 'to create a desire in China for British products'. With this last objective in mind, Macartney had arrived bearing £15,610-worth of gifts for the Emperor. Prominent among them were a mechanical planetarium and an accompanying map of the globe, but they also included:

> measuring instruments, chemical and electrical instruments, window and plate glass, carpets, Birmingham goods, Sheffield goods, copper ware and pottery – some of the finest examples of the late Mr Wedgwood's art.

It was a little-known fact that Mr Wedgwood's system of factory production for ceramics had originally been inspired by the Chinese version of the division of labour at Jingdezhen, as outlined by the Jesuit historian Jean-Baptiste Du Halde in his *Description of the Empire of China* (published in English in 1738). So, where the Macartney mission was concerned, carrying Wedgwood pots to Peking really *was* like carrying coals to Newcastle. All this, and a carriage as well. When these novelties and manufactured goods were presented to the aged Emperor, in the spectacular surroundings of his vast Summer Palace at Jehol, north of Peking, his reply took the form of a poem – written with exquisite coldness, and massively condescending:

> *Formerly Portugal presented tribute,*
> *Now England is paying homage . . .*
> *My ancestors' merit must have reached their distant shores.*
> *Though their tribute is commonplace, my heart approves sincerely.*

Curios and the boasted ingenuity of their devices I prize not.
Though what they bring is meagre, yet,
In my kindness to them from afar I make generous return
Wanting to preserve my good health and power.

This was to be distilled into a crisp edict to King George III, which was in fact written *before* Macartney even arrived on Chinese soil, and handed to him as he left. It acknowledged the desire of Britain 'to partake of the benefits of our civilization', and rejected the requests to set up an embassy and extend trade – on the grounds that these made it seem as though Britain and China were equals, which of course they were not. As to the presents: 'Our Celestial Empire possesses all things in abundance, I set no value on objects strange or ingenious, and have no use for your country's manufactures.' Why should the country which produced the finest porcelain in the world be improved by pieces of heavy pottery? The map of the globe was derided, because China was not shown as in the middle of it. The planetarium was treated as a nursery toy.

On meeting the Emperor, Macartney had been expected to take part in the ceremony of the *koutou* – three separate prostrations, each with the forehead touching the ground three times – as the normal mark of respect for the Son of Heaven. This he refused to do, only agreeing to go down on one knee and bow his head – as he would to his own King. The mission, of nearly a hundred strong, was ordered to leave Peking after forty-seven days.

It had been a disastrous encounter. De Quincey described it, over and over again, as a national humiliation – a mixture, on the part of the Chinese, of superstitious politeness and 'monstrous arrogance':

Does the ambassador dine at some imperial table – the Emperor has been feeding the barbarian. Do some of the court mandarins dine with the ambassador – then the Emperor has deigned to restore happiness to the barbarians, by sending those who represent his person to speak words of hope and consolation. Does the ambassador convey presents from his own sovereign to the Emperor – the people of Peking are officially informed that the barbarians are bringing their tribute. Does the Emperor make presents to the ambassador – in that case, His Majesty has been furnishing the means of livelihood to barbarians exhausted by pestilence and the failure of crops . . .

For De Quincey, the last straw came when one of the Emperor's officials intimated that 'the Emperor was as truly Lord of the British Isles as of Peking'. According to the historian Piers Brendon:

> Mutual misunderstanding aggravated interracial contempt. The British were disgusted by the Chinese diet, which included snakes, tortoises, dogs, cats, bats, new-born rats (known as 'honey peepers') and raw monkey brains, but believed that they would readily buy tweed. The Chinese thought the British looked like devils, stank like corpses and probably had webbed feet. They also reckoned that a ban on the export of rhubarb from Canton could bring England to a halt via an epidemic of constipation.

When the Summer Palace was sacked, after the Second Opium War, British troops found some of Macartney's unwanted gifts and brought them back home again.

The encounter was satirized in a celebrated hand-coloured etching by James Gillray, *The Reception of the Diplomatique and His Suite at the Court of Pekin*, which showed the British diplomat naively hoping that the impassive Chinese court, including an obese, smoking Emperor sitting on a cushion, would be impressed by a selection of children's toys made in Birmingham – a rocking-horse, a magic lantern, a windmill, some balls and shuttlecocks, a balloon, a model coach and a bird in a cage. Interestingly, this etching was published on 14 September 1792, a week *before* Macartney left for China: it accurately predicted the reaction of the Emperor of such an ancient civilization to the ill-considered gifts. Macartney approaches the Emperor down on one bended knee (as he actually did), while several of his colleagues try to perform a farcical *koutou*. Gillray was satirizing the ignorance of the British as much as, if not more than, the impassivity of the Chinese. True to form, several published accounts of the mission by members of the team confirmed the deep resentment and sense of hurt felt after the event. As Macartney's valet Aeneas Anderson recalled: 'We entered Pekin like Paupers, remained in it like Prisoners, and departed from it like Vagrants.' Taken together with the influential volume of drawings by the official draughtsman William Alexander, these accounts also included much to think about. On the one hand, the mission provided first-hand visual evidence of Chinese architecture and design – its splendid palaces and gardens, its magnificent court – for the first time, which enhanced admiration for the style and would inspire some of the finest Regency decorative artists. Sir William Chambers in his *Chinese Designs* (1757) had expressed the hope that one day soon there would be an end to 'the extravagancies which daily appear under the name "Chinese", though most of them are mere inventions'. On the other hand, it seemed to establish that behind the whimsical fantasies of *Chinoiserie* lay a rotting Manchu state, 'the tyranny of a handful of Tartars over more than 300 millions of Chinese', involving much misery and barbarity. As Macartney wrote:

> The Empire of China is an old, crazy, First rate man-of-war, which a fortunate succession of able and vigilant officers has contrived to keep afloat for these one hundred and fifty years past, and to overawe their neighbours merely by her bulk and appearance, but whenever an inefficient man happens to have the command upon deck, adieu to the discipline and safety of the ship. She may, perhaps, not sink outright; she may drift some time as a wreck, and will then be dashed to pieces on the shore; but she can never be rebuilt on the old bottom.

If Britain did not wish to over-extend herself in China – and there was little appetite for this – she could either give up the Canton trade altogether, or learn to play by China's rules and hope that trade would gradually expand. Since China seemed to be uninterested in 'British products' – she was *not* after all just an extension of the India market, a dumping ground – and insisted on being paid in silver rather than imports of manufactured goods, and since there was no question of pulling out of Canton completely, the only option for the time being was to try and understand China better – its difference and its sheer size – and to encourage a substitute for silver in the form of Indian opium. Either that, or use force. In 1816, another mission was attempted, under Lord Amherst, this time to the Jiaqing Emperor. Again, the ambassador refused to kowtow. A letter from the Prince Regent which began, 'Sir, my brother', caused deep offence in the Chinese court. The mission was summarily expelled from Peking for displaying 'irreverent arrogance'. The stage was set for the Opium Wars.

The Macartney mission – and the tensions it so spectacularly embodied – confirmed 'China' as part of the imaginative geography of the Orient, and provided the dark setting for 'Kubla Khan' (written in the late 1790s) and De Quincey's opium dreams. Soon, even the camp extravaganza of *Chinoiserie* would go out of fashion, travelling from high style to common cliché, as De

Quincey's oriental fantasies were to do. In 1864, the writer and civil servant George Otto Trevelyan linked De Quincey's two great obsessions when he wrote that the popular view was that opium served the useful purpose 'of soothing John Chinaman into a temporary forgetfulness' of the disasters that had befallen this country, 'deluding his soul with visions of a Paradise where the puppy-dogs and rats run about ready-roasted; where the birds' nests are all edible . . . and the women all [have] short feet'. By the time Oscar Wilde wrote *The Picture of Dorian Gray* (magazine version June 1890, toned-down and padded-out book version April 1891), the Dickens-inspired description of opium dens – and of outcast London in general – had also turned into the clichés of journalism. As social commentator Charles Booth concluded of *East London*, volume one of his *Life and Labour of the People of London* (1889), published the year before *Dorian Gray*:

> East London lay hidden from view behind a curtain on which were painted terrible pictures: – Starving children, suffering women, overworked men; horrors of drunkenness and vice; monsters and demons of inhumanity; giants of disease and despair. Did these pictures truly represent what lay behind or did they bear to the facts a relation similar to that which the pictures outside a booth at some country fair bear to the performance or show within? [The writers of this book] have tried to lift this curtain and to see for themselves the world it hid.

East London examined underlying tendencies such as the decline of the docks and the ways in which its inhabitants are being 'played off, one against the other', the low wages, the casualization of labour, the changing social patterns of life in docklands, the many *connections* between East and West Ends – 'all the necessities and most of the luxuries of our elaborate civilization pass familiarly through the dock labourer's hands, or under his feet' – and the use of foreign labour to drive down wages. Booth could well have added among his 'terrible pictures' of East London dingy opium dens, and among his 'demons of inhumanity' inscrutable Chinamen and their British wives. Wilde knew all about such exposés: he had written regularly for the *Pall Mall Gazette* between 1885 and 1889, when its editor W. T. Stead was busy producing shock-horror investigations – the 'new journalism' – into child prostitution (*The Maiden Tribute of Modern Babylon*, summer 1885) and the Whitechapel murders (autumn 1888), which combined salacious detail with moral indignation. In

April 1891, Wilde complained to Arthur Conan Doyle about the kinds of sensationalist journalism – school of Stead – which were 'written by the Prurient for the Philistine'. In the same year, he had made a similar complaint in his essay *The Soul of Man under Socialism* (published between the two versions of *Dorian Gray*) in which he also revealed how knowledgeable he was about 'outcast London' writings, which had become legion.

The description of Dorian's journey to 'dreadful places near the docks' – which was added to the 1891 version, as an outward and visible sign of 'the terrible pleasures of a double life' – uses deliberately artificial language and the clichés of the Gothic, which helped Wilde to avoid a 'tedious *document humain*', Emile Zola-style. The inhabitants of the East End are 'puppets' and 'marionettes' – 'grotesque things', 'automatons'. The setting is foggy, dimly lit, labyrinthine, with narrow passages and devious ways like stage-designs – it looks on the surface 'as if it had come out of a country booth', just like the images criticized in *East London*. The night after his murder of Basil Hallward, shortly after he has endured an aristocratic dinner party in his honour and is feeling particularly jaded, Dorian Gray returns to the library of his Mayfair house, staring at his large Florentine cabinet of ebony, ivory and blue lapis as if it 'held something that he longed for and yet almost loathed'. Then the mad craving comes over him:

> A triangular drawer passed out slowly. His fingers moved instinctively towards it, dipped in, and closed on something. It was a small Chinese box of black-and-gold-dust lacquer, elaborately wrought, the sides patterned with curved waves, and the silken cords hung with round crystals and tasselled in plaited metal threads. He opened it. Inside was a green paste, waxy in lustre, the odour curiously heavy and persistent.

Actually, opium in its raw, waxy state is brown. But this must be opium: the 'Chinese box' gives the game away. Thus primed, Dorian Gray disguises himself just like the slummers, social explorers and voyeurs Wilde had been reading about, and hails a cab in Bond Street. Dorian Gray is already familiar with the alleyways and rookeries of the East End. Earlier, we have been told 'he would creep out of the house, go down to dreadful places near Blue Gate Fields, and stay there, day after day, until he was driven away'. But this time he has the craving for opium 'in a den of horror where the memory of old sins could be destroyed by the madness of sins that were new'. Not at home, but in the social space of a den. At this point, the journalistic clichés – describing 'the sordid shame of the great city' – which could be the title of one of Stead's exposés – are piled on thick and fast. 'A large misshapen cloud', 'streets like the black web of some sprawling spider', 'the mist thickened':

> Most of the windows were dark, but now and then fantastic shadows were silhouetted against some lamp-lit blind. He watched them curiously. They moved like monstrous marionettes, and made gestures like live things. He hated them. . . . As they turned a corner, a woman yelled something at them from an open door, and two men ran after the hansom for about a hundred yards. The driver beat at them with his whip.

Dorian soon reaches a dark lane where 'over the low roofs and jagged chimney-stacks of the houses rose the black masts of ships. Wreaths of white mist clung like ghostly sails to the yards.' There, Dorian pays the cabbie off and walks for seven or eight minutes until he reaches the small shabby house: Daly's bar and opium den. He knows the 'peculiar knock' already. It is not his first time. A 'squat misshapen figure' opens the door, and, through a tattered green curtain, there is 'a long, low room which looked as if it had once been a third-rate dancing saloon'.

> Some Malays were crouching by a little charcoal stove, playing with bone counters, and showing their white teeth as they chattered. In one corner, with his head buried in his arms, a sailor sprawled over a table, and by the tawdrily-painted bar that ran across one complete side stood two haggard women [shades of Dickens's 'haggard woman'], mocking an old man who was brushing the sleeves of his coat with an expression of disgust. 'He thinks he's got red ants on him,' laughed one of them . . .

Dorian hurries up 'a little staircase, leading to a darkened chamber'; the thick odour of opium greets him. He 'looked around at the grotesque things that lay in such fantastic postures on the ragged mattresses. The twisted limbs, the gaping mouths, the staring lustreless eyes'. Back in the bar, a 'half-caste, in ragged turban and a shabby ulster, grinned a hideous greeting'. One of the women smiles 'a crooked smile, like a Malay crease [kris]', like Princess Puffer, too, who had 'smoked herself into a strange likeness of the Chinaman'. She rakes Dorian's money off the counter 'with greedy fingers'. He darts through a dim archway to another 'ill-famed place' he has visited before. As Wilde has made clear, in the chapter preceding the murder of Basil Hallward, Dorian Gray is searching 'for sensations that would be at once new and delightful, and possess that element of strangeness that is so essential to romance' – searching for

> that vivid life that lurks in all grotesques, and that lends to Gothic art its enduring vitality, this art being, one might fancy, especially the art of those whose minds have been troubled with the malady of reverie.

Dorian Gray's visit to the opium den – and to the docks of the East End – is one of these sensations, made up of the clichés of Gothic art which Gray confuses with reality. Those critics at the time who called the novel 'stupid and vulgar', and who complained that the subject was straight out of a cheap novel, were being more perceptive than they realized. The point was that the vulgarity was deliberate – the opium den as artificial construct, a conscious manipulation of elements that had become commonplace in literature.

Dorian Gray was originally commissioned at the same dinner with the American publisher J. M. Stoddart that resulted in Arthur Conan Doyle's *The Sign of the Four* (1890). Both Wilde and Conan Doyle wrote about the abyss of East London in the artful language of the Gothic, which some have confused with lazy drafting: imaginary cartography, made up of readymade impressions, was actually one of their literary strengths.

The Sherlock Holmes story 'The Man with the Twisted Lip', one of the first half-dozen Holmes short stories to appear in the year after *The Sign of the Four*, was first issued in *The Strand* in December 1891. It opens with a description of one Isa Whitney, respected brother of the late Principal of a Theological College and one of Dr Watson's patients, who is addicted to opium-smoking. He first experimented with the drug, we are told, while at college, 'for having read De Quincey's description of his dreams and sensations, he had drenched his tobacco with laudanum in an attempt to produce the same effects'. Watson is asked, late one evening, by Whitney's wife Kate, to rescue Isa from the 'opium den' he regularly uses, called the Bar of Gold in Upper Swandam Lane 'in the farthest east of the City'. He leaves his 'armchair and cheery sitting room', speeds eastward in a hansom cab and reaches

> a vile alley lurking behind the high wharves which line the north side of the river to the east of London bridge. Between a slop-shop and a gin-shop, approached by a steep flight of steps leading down to a black gap like the mouth of a cave, I found the den . . .

Then Dr Watson enters a long, low room, thick with the brown smoke of opium and terraced with wooden bunks:

> Through the gloom, one could dimly catch a glimpse of bodies lying in strange fantastic poses, bowed shoulders, bent knees, heads thrown back, and chins pointing upward, with here and there a dark, lack-lustre eye turned upon the newcomer. Out of the black shadows there glimmered little red circles of light, now bright, now faint, as the burning poison waxed or waned in the bowls of the metal pipes. The most lay silent, but some muttered to themselves . . . each mumbling out his own thoughts, and paying little heed to the words of his neighbour. At the farther end was a small brazier of burning charcoal . . .

This 'low den' is managed by a Lascar, aided by a Dane, with a 'sallow Malay attendant' distributing the filled pipes, and it includes among its facilities a trapdoor at the back of the building 'near the corner of Paul's Wharf' which opens to the Thames below. Sherlock Holmes, disguised as a very thin, very wrinkled old man, has beaten Watson to it, and is busy working on a difficult case – that of one Neville St Clair, a businessman in the City (or so everyone thinks) who has disappeared. It transpires that St Clair, like Whitney – and like Jasper in *Edwin Drood* – is leading a double life, but in a different way. He *really* earns his living as a beggar-man with a 'horrible scar' on his upper lip and bright red hair, in Threadneedle Street, in the heart of the City, and uses the second floor of the opium den – which he rents from the Lascar – to change clothes and apply his makeup.

The plot of 'The Man with the Twisted Lip' may have been based on a *Tit-Bits* article of January 1891 about 'the day in the life of a beggar'. But its setting probably came from nearer home: an article in *The Strand*, June 1891, by Coulson Kernahan – the man who copy-edited the 1891 version of *Dorian Gray* – called 'A Night in an Opium Den'. Some of the details do seem to recall *Dorian Gray*: the 'strange fantastic poses'; the steep flight of steps; the charcoal stove. But these were by now obligatory in descriptions of opium dens. Kernahan's article begins:

> Yes, I have smoked opium in Ratcliffe Highway, and in the den which was visited by Charles Dickens, and through the pipe which had the honour of making that distinguished novelist sick.

There follows the description of a meeting with the proprietor of the den, 'a Chinaman named Chang' who has a fixed grin on his face, despite the fact that he has recently had his pigtail cut off while he was asleep and who has vowed 'a terrible vengeance upon the perpetrators' of this deadly insult. Chang leads the way 'up the most villainous treacherous staircase which it has ever been my lot to ascend', and into the den itself.

> 'Den' was an appropriate name for the reeking hole to which he conducted us. It was dirty and dark, being lit only by a smoking lamp on the mantel-shelf, and was not much larger than a full-sized cupboard. The walls, which were a dingy yellow (not unlike the 'whites' of the smokers' eyes) were quite bare, with the exception of the one facing the door, on which, incongruously enough, was plastered a coarsely-coloured and hideous print of the Crucifixion. The furniture consisted of three raised mattresses, with small tables on which were placed pipes, lamps, and opium.

Two smokers are curled up on those mattresses, one with his eyes turned up to the ceiling, the other immobile and staring. Two other smokers are friendly Chinamen and a third is 'a partly naked Malay of decidedly evil aspect', coiled up in a dark corner like a snake in a zoo. A pretty young Englishwoman enters the scene, and carefully appraises the author's clothes while Chang prepares the pipes.

> Yes, I had lovely dreams, and I have no doubt that by the aid of imagination, and a skilful manipulation of De Quincey, I could concoct a fancy picture of opium-smoking and its effects. . . . I can just recall a sensation of sailing, as on a cloud, amid regions of blue and buoyant ether; of seeing, through vistas of purple and gold, a scene of sunny seas and shining shores where, it seemed to me, I beheld the fabled 'Blessed Isles' stretching league beyond league afar . . .

Then the author wakes up with a splitting headache, to discover that his boots, hat and umbrella have been stolen, 'with a taste in my mouth which can only be likened to a cross between onions and bad tobacco'.

This visit takes place in Ratcliffe Highway (which hadn't been called that for years). Conan Doyle's opium den is located in the fictitious Swandam Lane, backing onto a corner of Paul's Wharf opposite St Paul's Cathedral, which is also 'in the farthest east of the City' and 'to the east of London Wharf', off Lower Thames Street. Conan Doyle must have meant slightly west of London Bridge, off Upper Thames Street. Several of the commentaries, and guides, locate the den in Limehouse, but, wherever exactly Swandam Lane is supposed to be, it is a long way – several miles – *west* of Limehouse. Sax Rohmer gleaned details from 'The Man with the Twisted Lip' for his *Mystery of Dr Fu-Manchu*: the opium-den setting, Holmes's disguise, which was later adapted by Nayland Smith and Dr Petrie; the trapdoor at the rear of the building 'which could tell some strange tales of what has passed through it upon the moonless nights'; the 'old briar pipe' which Holmes smokes – a whole 'ounce of shag' – while solving the puzzle through the night, which became Nayland Smith's briar pipe and rough-cut shag. Rohmer's opium den, too, was located 'off the old Ratcliffe Highway'. Oscar Wilde's opium den, in *The Picture of Dorian Gray*, is located 'near Blue Gate Fields', linked to the Ratcliffe Highway, scene of Princess Puffer's den in *Edwin Drood*. Again, it hadn't been called that for many years, since it disappeared from the maps when Wilde was three years old. In his day, even its successor Victoria Street had been demolished – to make way for the East London Railway – and rebuilt over the underground tunnel. By the time he wrote *Dorian Gray*, the modern docks had been built on the riverside. But Wilde preferred the earlier location of *Edwin Drood*.

And yet, as with 'The Man with the Twisted Lip', most commentators automatically locate Wilde's opium den in Limehouse, which was a mile or so to the *east* of the Shadwell–Ratcliffe Highway area, in docklands. By the same token, some have referred to *Chinese* opium dens in 'Twisted Lip' and *Dorian Gray*. Again, Wilde mentions 'some Malays' and Conan Doyle a Lascar and a 'Malay attendant', but neither of them mentions a Chinese person. Their vision of the East End predated the knee-jerk popular association between 'opium den' and 'Chinaman'. In the second collection of Sherlock Holmes stories, *The Memoirs* (1894), there was to be a story called 'The Yellow Face' (published in *The Strand*, February 1893). Conan Doyle originally wanted it to be called 'The Livid Face', perhaps to avoid the by-then obvious associations. It was *not* about a Chinese villain. Elizabeth Sax Rohmer, when talking with me, even referred to her late husband's *Limehouse* as 'like a scene from Charles Dickens'. But Dickens's opium den, too, was in Blue Gate Fields, in *Shadwell*, and predated Chinese settlement in Limehouse.

When James Platt wrote his amused article on Limehouse for *The Gentleman's Magazine* in 1895 he concluded:

> [This house], which appears to have been the only one known to Dickens, was really outside the boundary of what I call Chinese London. By this term I understand a single long narrow street with Chinese boarding houses and shops on both sides of the way. This street constitutes the quartier. . . . It exists by and for the Chinese firemen, seamen, stewards, cooks and carpenters who serve on board the steamers plying between China and the old port of London.

This little community was 'a drop of water in the ocean compared with the vast Chinese settlements which are to be found in the United States', but it existed and it was becoming increasingly identifiable. Blue Gate Fields, and the Ratcliffe Highway, were 'outside the boundary'. The 'long narrow street' was Limehouse Causeway.

Joseph Salter, too, at the end of *The Asiatic in England*, noted that the opium dens of Blue Gate Fields and Ratcliffe were now closed for business:

> The masters of the opium-smoking dens and other houses that lived by Oriental ruin were gone; the voices from the open doors of these lairs and dens gave evidence of the occupants seeking a livelihood by some other means.

The voices were no longer Chinese. All except old Latou, who went right back to Dickens's time and who was 'the last survivor': he ended his days in the workhouse. Salter attributed the closure of the dens to the success of his – and others' – missionary work among Chinese congregations. In fact, the social geography of London had shifted. By April 1908, *What's On* felt able to provide some tips for 'the casual seeker' who intended to spend an entertaining afternoon wandering around Limehouse looking for its sweet-and-sour soul. By then, it was beginning to appear on the tourist map. But the map was not easy to navigate:

> The Chinaman has not been encouraged in London. We look at him with suspicion, accuse him of all the vices in creation and distrust him generally. This is partly British prejudice, no doubt, but we have heard much of the Chinese quarters in New York and other American cities, and the

reports of Chinese ways that were so freely aired when we imported 'John' to the [mines in the] Transvaal were all distinctly unfavourable to that gentleman's moral character. Nevertheless, London now has a Chinatown of sorts, albeit one that is severely limited in extent and exceedingly difficult to find.

Difficult, partly because the Chinese seamen who live around the West India Dock Road 'affect European garb for the most part and are not so easily spotted as one would expect'; and partly because 'John . . . certainly keeps himself apart from the "follin debbils" whom he instinctively mistrusts even as they in their turn mistrust him'. But once the tourist has managed to *find* Chinatown, he or she would do well to note the recommendations of *What's On*: dress for slumming; find someone who can direct you to Limehouse Causeway; find a restaurant where the sign is in English; order chop suey ('uncommonly good it was and well worth the sixpence we paid for it'), followed by tea ('not in the least reminiscent of the "China" tea served in popular restaurants'); then find a bilingual Chinese sailor who is willing to direct you to an opium den ('"Hip joint" is the cant phrase'), preferably a spacious premises with sumptuous furnishings 'up to the modern standard of taste', where 'well-dressed Occidentals, men and women, come in the evening from the West End'. Not one of the shabby upper rooms with 'cunningly contrived emergency exits' where Chinese people like to gather for a social smoke. *What's On* was happy to discuss these freely, 'withholding only actual addresses'. Like music halls, opium dens were apparently becoming part of a respectable night out for middle-class patrons.

In response to a question about 'Chinatown' and where exactly it was, in *Notes & Queries* (April 1896), readers were directed to Platt's article in *The Gentleman's Magazine*. The answer was Limehouse. Platt contributed his own article to *Notes & Queries* in July 1900, the same month and year as, according to the *Oxford English Dictionary*, the phrase 'Yellow Peril' had its first serious usage in the English language, in a sensational newspaper article about the 'hordes' of Boxers besieging the Legation in Peking and a 'massacre' of British men, women and children on 5 July. The massacre turned out not to have happened: *The Times* had erroneously printed an obituary of its own correspondent! This first English usage – 'the Yellow Peril in its most serious form' – also ran in the *Daily News* of 21 July 1900, and according to the *OED* it launched a phrase which denoted 'a supposed danger of a destructive invasion of Europe by Asia'. Actually, two years before, in July 1898, *The Spectator* had speculated about 'a Japanese military caste controlling China and organizing a native army and navy', and referred to this possibility as 'the Yellow Peril'. The context implied that the phrase was already in common use. Platt's article was responding to a *Daily Mail* piece of 27 June 1900 which, under the headline 'London's Chinatown', had included an illustration of 'a London opium den': he felt that 'the present juncture, when all eyes are turned upon China', was an excellent moment to set the record straight. There were many misunderstandings, Platt wrote, about 'these opium and gambling houses', and as a seasoned journalist who had often written about the subject over the years, he was particularly well placed to respond:

> These opium dens have been several times more or less (generally less) successfully portrayed in works of fiction, from *Edwin Drood* to Sherlock Holmes, but always with sole reference to smoking, and not to any other aspect of life in Limehouse.

In fact, he continued, the opium houses were mainly used for playing cards, for eating, for reading books about Chinese history, for strumming stringed instruments, and generally for socializing:

> The opium shops are really Chinese boarding-houses, with a floating population drawn from the Steamers plying between China and the port of London. . . . Those whose ideas of such places are solely derived from reading novels will find far less of the sensational and far more of the milk of human kindness, in the daily life of their inmates, than would seem credible to anyone who does not reflect that, after all, these men are simply honest shopkeepers, and their customers honest sailors . . .

It was, indeed, quite possible for a pedestrian to walk around the quarter 'without any suspicion that he was within the boundaries of a Chinatown'.

What was surprising, Platt believed, was that no novelist had yet written truly *memorable* stories about 'the London Chinatown' and its inhabitants, based on personal observation. The obsession with 'gentlemen going there to smoke' had distorted the picture:

No novelist has divined what eccentric local colour might be brought into a story along with those quaint gaming tables, covered with Canton matting, and always surrounded by a polyglot-crowd, which are as characteristic of the opium dens as the pipe itself.

He would not have long to wait. But the memorable stories which *did* come along were even more far-fetched than the literary tradition from which they grew.

PRICE & REYNOLDS'
SIXPENNY SERIES.

Nº 210.

SOMEBODY'S GOT TO GO THROUGH IT!

GEO. ROBEY

HEAD OF THE ROYAL ACADEMY OF MIRTH.

By permission of JAMES UPTON LTD., Baskerville Printing Works, Birmingham.

WORDS BY
SAX ROHMER
MUSIC BY
ALF. GLOVER

SUNG BY

GEORGE ROBEY.

LONDON:

W. PAXTON,
95, New Oxford Street, W.C.

PRICE & REYNOLDS,
41, Berners Street, W.

AGENT FOR AUSTRALIA. E. W. COLE. MELBOURNE. SYDNEY & ADELAIDE.

CHAPTER THREE

At the Sign of the Swinging Cymbal

As his widow confided, Sax Rohmer never much liked to talk about his work in the music hall, writing sketches and comic songs (and occasionally music), combining this as he did with freelance journalism, and submitting short stories and illustrations to fiction magazines under the name 'A. Sarsfield Ward'. He always downplayed the significance of this portfolio phase in his life between 1905 and 1912, saying that the music hall just helped to 'pay the rent', or that it was a temporary stop-gap while he developed his *real* craft as a 'fictionist'. In fact, it played a key part in his formation as a writer of thrillers.

During his interview given to the *New Yorker* on 29 November 1947, some forty years after the events it described, he let his guard slip and joked about his creative relationship with one particular music-hall star:

'... between times I wrote a hell of a lot of comic songs for George Robey, the comedian.' . . .

In a jagged baritone, he sang '"Of monarchs who e'en have merry been / the something I have reckoned / For never was seen a King or Queen / as potty as Charles the Second". Now . . . wait a minute . . . "Wenches and wine" – no – ah, yes – "The something is fine in wenches and wine / Whatever their age or shade is / And none can surpass our play with the glass / Or out-tickle us with the ladies".'

Mr Rohmer beamed and had just announced 'Refrain' when a handsome blonde lady broke in upon us.

'My wife,' said Mr Rohmer.

'Used to do a turn myself in variety,' said Mrs Rohmer. 'Got a long way from that since I married Sax . . .'

Rohmer did indeed write many comic songs for 'George Robey, the comedian' and others, but what he omitted to mention was that his first published book was written in collaboration with Robey. It consisted of a series of essays and stories about George Robey's personal interests and beliefs – very different from his celebrated anti-establishment stage persona, mocking hypocrisy, 'bigots and little 'ots'. Although almost entirely written by Rohmer, it was later attributed by biographers to Robey. Called *Pause!* (the paperback cover featured an image of a man's hand, palm forward), it was published by Arthur Greening and Co. in 1910. 'It was George Robey who introduced me to the publisher . . .' Oddly, the book did not have either Robey's or Rohmer's name anywhere in or on it. Even in a pre-branding age, this was eccentric, especially for a celebrity biography. But a 'preparatory note', bylined 'Herne Hill February 13 1910', indicated the shape of things to come. It laboured very hard to emulate in prose the humorous profundity, the absurd solemnity and faux-pretentiousness of Robey's stage act:

> Of that hour when, standing in a solitude margined about by London's millions, he first opened the locked door, to yield a glimpse of the treasury of his mind, I shall not speak here. But of those later occasions when, carried on by the restless tide of a busy thoroughfare, speeding through deserted streets and silent highways, seated, amid volumes ancient and rare, with pottery of Japan, Gods of Egypt, peeping from the Athenian shadows, he talked and I wrote or he wrote while I was silent – be it said that they afforded me an unique prospect of that tumultuous mind . . .

The note went on to claim that books in at least six different languages had been used as sources, 'and even the ancient hieroglyphic writings have been assiduously scanned, that the old wisdom might bear witness of the now'. 'Such a collection of papers – essays – term them as you please – has probably never before been offered to the public.'

The book – divided into 'Hypotheses', 'Theorems' and 'Parables' – explored in the first section the appreciation of beauty ('he that hath eyes'), the passage of time ('a single grain of sand . . . under the shadow of the Great Pyramid of Cheops'), the making of things ('the primeval man to first utilize a stone implement, very conceivably did so at the instance of a monkey . . .'), idolatry ('cats were sacred in the cities by the Nile and cats are still sacred in Mayfair'), celebrity ('the attitude of certain cliques toward certain temporarily notorious "celebrities" is akin to idolatry in its lowest and basest form'), Zoroastrian sun worship, and human sacrifice by the Aztecs on the altar of Quetzalcoatl (a monologue – resembling a music-hall recitation or parlour ballad about conquistador Juan Martinez as 'the obsidian knife' hovers over him). The second section takes the form of a series of fantasies about an exotic Greek dancing-girl in the ancient world, a visit to the British Museum's round Reading Room, an actress 'of the fast set' found dead in the locked study of an Egyptologist and specialist in 'esoteric medicine' who is researching – with help from *The Book of the Dead* – the 'sending back' of corrupt souls to the underworld, and a magic bronze mirror which reveals a hallucination of an ancient room from Cleopatra's time 'such as I knew of . . . in the canvases of the great English artist Alma Tadema'. Finally, a series of 'Parables' about, among other things, London cyclists intruding on a peaceful country scene and being punished for it by 'the spirit of nature' – school of Kenneth Grahame and the Pan interlude in the recently published *Wind in the Willows* (1908). *Pause!* is a very strange brew indeed.

Rohmer never mentioned the book in interviews, but its style – including a lot of pseudo-scholarship ('Nefer – the poet's licence is claimed for this reading') – its fashionable references to research into the occult ('the innate love of the occult common to us all'), its lower-middle-class social attitudes (socialism was scary, trades unions were probably subversive, shirkers too often asked for handouts, the *status quo* had to be protected against instability, intellectuals didn't know enough about the university of life) and its stories (a locked-room mystery, a timidly erotic orientalist fantasy about a dancing-girl) all point towards Rohmer's more mature fiction. Three passages were in this respect particularly prescient:

> They were Londoners, and, whilst their presence stilled the newly awakened voice and brought him back to the prosaic realities, he knew that *he* was a Londoner too and thought of a stuffy office, with the occasional waft of fetid air from an underground kitchen. That was his life; and this – but a fleeting dream. Why could he not forget the real, and live in the vision?

> A black marble floor, wherein is mirrored a couch having feet shaped as those of a leopard – having the skin of a leopard cast across it, and, upon the skin, silken soft cushions, wrought by Greek cunning, in patterns of

gorgeous schemes. . . . See, now, mirrored in the marble, a small bare foot peeps from the edge of the couch. . . . From the reflection turn, then, to the reality and look upon the slim ankle, encircled by a gold band. Follow the perfect lines gleaming, vaguely sinuous, through the purple haze of the cloudy raiment. . . . The moulding of that pliant form is flawless – each curve soft as the texture of the creamy skin. . . . The whole woman a lovely allurement.

And, of a visit to the British Museum's Reading Room, where 'extracts from several [books] that have received especial encomium from the Intellectual Public' stimulate convoluted thoughts about contemporary fiction and drama:

Who shall accuse us [the great modern public] of harbouring sensation-mongers? Who shall cry that we heap honours upon the heads of the unworthy who pander to our depraved tastes? . . . Future ages shall decide if this has been a period of literary degeneracy – of unusual mediocrity . . .

Robey was to publish, also with Greening and Co. and also in paperback, an unrevealing and often inaccurate 'naughtibiography' at around the same time – called *My Life up Till Now*. Strangely enough, it makes no reference to its sister publication *Pause!*, though it does advertise other music-hall titles. But *My Life* gives a brief glimpse of Robey's double-edged attitude to his own songs:

If you think music hall 'art' is easy, just you read some of the songs and decide for yourselves whether they do not require an extraordinary amount of inventive elaboration . . . to make them effective.

This must say something about his relationship with songwriters such as Rohmer.

Sax Rohmer worked closely – but not exclusively – with Robey between 1908 and 1911, and then again in 1922. They kept in touch between times. He was fascinated by the comedian's large collection of blue-and-white Chinese porcelain, and by his interest in amateur Egyptology. One of Rohmer's most treasured possessions was a 'beautifully bound, rare edition of *The Book of the Dead*':

. . . it reached me [he recalled in 1938] by registered mail one day with a note: 'Dear Sax, I picked this up for you while I was prowling round Manchester – George Robey.' George of the eyebrows is a keen Egyptologist, as I am myself. It is a study that grips you oddly . . .

Eventually, George Robey's huge black eyebrows would become so well known with the public that they alone were all that was needed on his promotional material – postcards, programmes, sheet-music covers. Like Charlie Chaplin's tramp silhouette, they were his trademark. Robey's act was built around a gallery of character sketches – usually involving a look of pained surprise on his face, and feigned annoyance that the audience wasn't taking him seriously enough – like a bishop shocked by his congregation – rather than tunes. What songs there were, as often as not – in Robey's words – 'came from the pen of Sax Rohmer, who was later to attain his eminence as a novelist'.

One of the first collaborations between Rohmer and Robey was on the song 'Shakespeare: Waggish Will of Avon' in 1908. This was also among the first appearances in print of the author's pseudonym: 'Written by Sax Rohmer. Composed by Henry E. Pether. Sung by George Robey.' The cover of the sheet music featured a cartoon of a harassed-looking Shakespeare, sleeves rolled up, struggling with the washing-up in a hot-water tub while a cat looks on. In the sketch, Robey would point to his capacious forehead and say: 'You people sometimes complain of a headache. Many come up, look at me, and conceive what I suffer when *I* get one!' Then he would introduce the song, which grew seamlessly out of the sketch:

> *All hail, friends; give me speech.*
> *This clamour doth surprise me.*
> *I am great William Shakespeare,*
> *But no doubt you recognise me.*
> *Gaze on this gleaming pate,*
> *And note my noble seeming;*
> *Look well into these lustrous eyes,*
> *Where genius lies gleaming!*
>
> Refrain: *High, high, high, upon*
> *The scroll of fame engraven,*
> *My name's Shakespeare:*
> *Waggish Will of Avon.*

In July of the same year, Rohmer had published the words and music of the song 'Bang Went the Chance of a Lifetime', which, together with 'Archibald, Certainly Not!' and 'I Stopped – I Looked – I Listened', was among Robey's best-known numbers at the time. He even recorded it. Rohmer always claimed that it was inspired by a real-life experience, when a barber – while cutting his hair – offered him an old painting for £5, saying that the ornate, gilded frame alone had to be worth at least that much. Rohmer turned down the offer. The barber then took the painting to Christie's for a valuation and they auctioned it as a genuine George Romney portrait of Emma Hamilton – for £60,000. Bang went the chance of a lifetime. It made a good story, anyway.

Returning one morn from a ball
In a mellowish mood, and reflective,
I saw a strange light, in a bank; I said 'Ha!
I will play Sherlock Holmes the detective.'
A half-open window I spied,
And inside I proceeded to slip;
Then a burglar I saw forcing wide the safe-door,
So I grabbed him in muscular grip!

Refrain: *But he slipped, and he bunked; he was wiry and thin;*
And the safe was wide open – and bung full of tin!
I drew a deep breath – then two coppers rushed in
And bang went the chance of a lifetime!

And so on. The narrator manages *nearly* to shoot his wealthy aunt, the Dowager Duchess of Diddle, 'whilst gunning the moors on the twelfth', but narrowly misses. He meets a sweet, winsome girl, they fall in love, but his wife gets to hear about it and bang goes another chance of a lifetime.

Eight months later, Rohmer tried to repeat his success with 'Bang' by providing the words for the similar – if more sour – 'It's a Lie!', music composed by George Robey himself:

Once I stayed with the Mayor of Beerhampton-on-Booze,
And he showed me a relic historic.
'Twas a barrel all studded with rusty old nails;
It was 'what ho!' in terms metaphoric.
It was there, so the Mayor's wife most kindly explained,

That the witches were formerly put.
So we all had a try what it felt like; then I
Gave the barrel a push with my foot.

Refrain: *I admit that the barrel rolled right down the hill;*
I admit that I pushed it – why shouldn't I?
If I liked to proclaim that I wasn't to blame,
I could say someone else pushed it – couldn't I?
That with nails it was lined, of the long, rusty kind,
Is a fact which I wouldn't deny;
But to say that I knew the Mayor's wife was inside,
It's a lie! a lie!

The final verse was about the death of a well-heeled uncle (another wealthy relative), after a good supper ('But to say I shoved rat-poison into his beer, / It's a lie! a lie!').

In 1910, Rohmer wrote two more songs for Robey – 'Wow-Wow', and 'Somebody's Got to Go Through It!', which was included in the comedian's first anthology of *Jokes, Jibes and Jingles*, published the year after *Pause!*. 'Wow-Wow' (music by Alfred Glover, the composer of 'Archibald, Certainly Not!') was a saucy seaside postcard of a song – an example of what Robey called 'honest vulgarity' – as distinct from smut. In the one verse, two young lovers – Horace and Pansy – lose their way in a dark wood and miss the last train home. Horace suggests to his girlfriend:

'Let's be babes in the wood'
And the dicky-birds said, 'Wow-wow!'

'Somebody's Got to Go Through It!' (again composed by Alfred Glover) is a much tougher song, almost harking back to the rough-and-tumble days of the free and easies of the 1840s. It tells of a short-fused, beer-drinking man of few words, who when he has been slighted has to punch *someone* – whether or not the victim is the guilty party – and usually it is 'a little man': in verse one, it is someone who drinks his beer; then it's the rent-collector; then a 'fair youth' who seems to be dallying with his wife. The final verse is full of topical allusion:

I sit in the House! I do, straight, no kid!
'Hard work,' I said, 'doesn't suit me;

I'll represent *Labour, not do it!'*
And now I'm Jaggs – M.P.! . . .

Refrain: *I'm not here to argue, I've no time for words!*
I do a thing well when I *do it!*
I've mentioned no names, Mr Asquith – nor do
I know why our friend Winston is hiding from view!
And although, my dear Lloyd George, I don't say it's you,
Still somebody's got to go through it!

Again, although the lyrics were specially written to accompany George Robey's sketches – and to play to the presumed attitudes and enthusiasms of music-hall audiences in the more 'respectable' houses – amid the standard gags about little men against the establishment, saintly mothers and ridiculous wives, sweet courting couples and disastrous marriages, they may still reveal some of Sax Rohmer's own concerns at the time. The cliché of Shakespeare's gleaming pate (Fu Manchu was to have 'a brow like Shakespeare'); 'Sherlock Holmes the detective'; finding a formula to get rich quick; popular historical legends (the punishment of witches); sadistic tortures (the barrel studded with long rusty nails); the naughty-but-nice innuendos about sex; scorn for the emerging Labour Party, which was hanging from the coat-tails of the Liberals at the time and had only adopted its name in 1900 as the 'Labour Representative Committee' ('I'll *represent* Labour, not do it!'); narrative and melodrama rather than pathos. And the misunderstandings/use of archaic words. In *Pause!*, 'margined about by London's millions'; in *It's a Lie!*, 'It was "what ho!" in terms metaphoric.' How much of this was Rohmer, how much Robey, how much canny market research is difficult to judge. Henpecked husbands, battleaxe wives, wealthy relatives, flighty young women at the seaside, pompous mayors, eggheads of various descriptions, the one that got away, were all stock characters and situations – of songs as well as seaside postcards. George Orwell was to write a celebrated essay about them.

Music-hall performers reflected – and maybe shaped – the attitudes of their audiences. Writers and intellectuals began to take music hall seriously and to write about the good old days. Sickert painted at the Bedford and Gatti's Hungerford Palace from the late 1880s onwards. The beer-stained and smoke-filled auditoria of the Victorian era were making way for stages and proscenium arches; 'stars' with their 'turns' were now a big part of the attraction;

audiences were more organized and better disciplined. There was less ad-libbing. London's West End halls catered for increasingly middle-class audiences, with ticket prices to match; suburban halls provided an undemanding evening out for lower-middle-class/upper-working-class audiences. Big syndicates like Moss Empires and Stoll were establishing chains of halls. Yet performers still did and spoke in public what 'society' did and said in private. And audiences still joined in, which they could not in legitimate theatres, creating 'a sense of community'.

By 1912, it has been estimated that there were some forty-eight music halls in the London area alone – considerably fewer than there had been in the mid-Victorian heyday, before fire and licensing regulations and safety curtains were introduced; but they were larger and better equipped – they could seat 70,000 people per performance, many of them offering 'twice nightly'. Plus there were nearly 200 halls in the regions. Between the 1890s and the First World War, big profits could be made from the halls, hence the chains. In the years 1908–12, when Sax Rohmer was at his most active as a writer of lyrics, music hall, pantomime and their more respectable cousins musical comedy, musical theatre and variety were *the* media of escapist entertainment for the mass audience. Soon after that, 3.5 million people would become regular filmgoers, daily.

Performers who could make the transition from the small Victorian halls into the more comfortable Edwardian variety theatres, adapting their signature acts to cater more for their family audience, could make more money than ever – up to £500 a week, a colossal sum – singing their greatest hits or doing their specialities over and over again. That was a plus, for the fortunate ones. But the minus, for George Robey at any rate, was that the halls were becoming too 'refained': 'refainement could well be the death of them,' he wrote; but at least the money was good. Actually, he had always been a bit 'refained' himself, and fond of social climbing: one fellow comedian called him 'a toffee-nosed twat'.

The going rate for songwriting was one guinea for words and music, and there was no radio, film or television to boost the royalties: just live performance, early phonographs, mechanical musical instruments and sheet-music sales for use in front parlours (there had been an astonishing growth in the domestic possession of pianos). Often – as with Rohmer and Robey – for that sum, the songs would become the exclusive property of an individual artiste, part of their unique selling proposition. No one else could sing them. Another of Robey's writers was Joe Tabrar, the man who later claimed to have created up to 10,000 songs over a sixty-year career – even though he couldn't actually read or write. His best-known song was 'Daddy Wouldn't Buy Me a Bow-Wow', for which he supplied the words and music. Tabrar left an account of what it was like to be a small-time lyricist in London in this period, which has been paraphrased:

> Like most [of the songwriters] he lived ... south of Waterloo Bridge, which was Music Hall land. There he would sit in his favourite pub surrounded by the small fry of lyric writers, all wanting him to put melodies to their words. ... Conceiving the idea of collaborating with [a well-known lyric writer of the day], the two men met in Tabrar's usual house-of-call one Sunday morning. There was the usual crowd of needy songwriters and Tabrar suggested that they should walk over to his house. Before they left he turned to the songwriters and said, 'Now boys, you know where to go. Just as usual.' ... [At home, in the back room, the lyric writer later discovered] seated round the table were all those writers who had been with Tabrar in the pub, all devouring baked potatoes, of which an immense dish was set on the table. It was Tabrar's weekly treat to them ...

Thomas Burke, during one of his meandering *Nights in Town*, subtitled *A London Autobiography* (1915), was to lament the anonymity and neglect of music-hall songwriters:

> That seems to me one of the greatest tragedies of the vaudeville world: that a man should compose a song that puts a girdle round about the globe ... a song that, like 'Tipperary,' is now the slogan of an Empire; that a man should create such a thing and live and die without one in ten thousand of his singers knowing even his name. ... We know the names of hundreds of finicky little poets and novelists and pianists; but their work never shook a nation one inch, or cheered them in sickness and despair. Of the men who really captured and interpreted the national soul we know nothing and care less; and how much they get for their copyrights is a matter that even themselves do not seem to take with sufficient seriousness.

If that could be said of 'It's a Long, Long Way to Tipperary' (1912), what price 'Bang Went the Chance of a Lifetime'? The key to shaking a nation was *catchiness*. As Felix McGlennon, a lyricist and songwriter himself, had written in *The Era* in March 1894: 'I will sacrifice everything – rhyme, reason, sense, sentiment, to catchiness. There is . . . a great art in making rubbish acceptable.' It looked easy but it wasn't. In the weekly newspaper *Answers*, for 6 May 1911, an article – quite possibly written by Sax Rohmer himself – explained how 'the ditty industry is not delightful', and not nearly as straightforward as it might appear. The headline was 'The Sorrows of Song-Selling', and the article was by an anonymous investigator.

> Full of the knowledge that 'Ta-ra-ra [Boom-de-ay]' and the rest had earned £20,000 or thereabouts for the author and publisher, I sat down to earn – well half that, to begin with, for an effusion on similar lines.

So the investigator tries his hand at some 'catchy choruses and nonsensical nothings'. The first performer he tries offers him five shillings for the best of them. 'Did he mean for the loan of it?' No, for its outright purchase. 'Don't want it, sonny. Got a basketful of them.' Another performer – more of a star – has 'millions of songs – millions was his own enumeration – and couldn't take another to save his life'. He offers 'half a dollar' for the best song.

> I learned quite a lot about singing rights, sole and part, publishing shares and the paraphernalia finally of song launching. And it dawned upon me that herein lay Business, with a capital 'B'. Song writing is one thing, and song *selling* quite another. There's a lot in 'placing'.

Eventually, the *Answers* investigator actually manages to sell one, 'but frankly I am not hopeful of a fortune out of that or any other song which I may write'.

In Sax Rohmer's collection of stories *The Exploits of Captain O'Hagan* (1916), the dashing Irish captain's first exploit involves forcing a music-publisher at gunpoint to purchase nine pieces of music written by the fragrant Pamela Crichton, a newsagent's daughter. She has informed O'Hagan that 'they won't give me a chance' and that the publisher Paul Ritzmann *has* offered to publish one of her pieces, but 'for nothing'. O'Hagan discovers that it is in fact 'an elusive melody, which haunted the ear, which spelt popularity'. It could even be catchy. There's just one thing:

'Four sharps,' he criticised, 'are bad in a composition designed for general popularity. Would it lose by transposition into a more simple key?'

'I think not,' said Pamela.

So the excitable and slightly mad Captain the Honourable Bernard O'Hagan, VC, DSO, marches round to Ritzmann's office in London's Berners Street – dressed in a satin-lined cape, and staring through his monocle, he is mistaken at first for 'a gentleman of title interested in a new musical comedy for the "Gaiety"' – and forces Ritzmann to sign agreement forms and royalty forms for 10 per cent plus ten guineas advance on each of the nine pieces. The curly-haired Pamela swoons with gratitude, and asks what the Captain seeks in return:

> Never, for a moment, did he presume upon that superiority of blood which is so real in his eyes, nor upon the service he had done this news-agent's daughter. . . . He kissed her hand in his astonishing, cavalier way, tactfully ignoring her sweet confusion, clapped her rather patronisingly on the back – and swung out of the shop.

End of exploit the first. The story is by today's standards disturbingly anti-semitic – it pits the swashbuckling and chivalrous captain, who is supposed to represent 'the grand Monsieur', against 'the Semitic presence' of the bejew-elled Mr Paul Ritzmann – but is interesting for the wish-fulfilment of making a young and hardworking songwriter's dreams come true, through the agency of a good angel. Bribery – and in this case 'a pistol pointed at this bald skull' – are evidently needed to get Pamela's music published. The story seems based on bitter personal experience.

Another source of income for lyricists and songwriters was pantomime, which since the 1880s had evolved into its recognizably modern form, out of the old-style 'harlequinade' in the *commedia dell'arte* tradition: the princi-pal boy played by a girl, the pantomime dame played by a man, the demon king, spectacular transformation scenes, elaborate ballet interludes, topical allusions – affectionate rather than subversive on the whole – all-join-in patri-otic choruses; and, by the Edwardian era, music-hall comedians adapting their favourite stand-up routines, especially useful in front of a backdrop during complicated scene-changes. It has been said of pantomime that the financial health of the late-Victorian theatre depended on it. George Robey worked the Christmas season – forty pantomimes in all – in large provincial cities, usually as Widow Twankey (in *Aladdin*) or Dame Trot (in *Jack and the Beanstalk*). In fact, he played Widow Twankey so often that the Stoll Film Corporation was to make a short silent film of his performance, now lost. He/she was a figure of misrule rather than misogyny, parody rather than bitterness, and loved all the more for it.

Whereas today we tend to associate *Aladdin and His Wonderful Lamp* with Persia and the Middle East – thanks to various film versions of *The Thief of Baghdad* and the Walt Disney feature derived from them – in the Victorian and Edwardian periods it was usually set in a fairytale, topsy-turvy China. In this, *Aladdin* was following – from a considerable distance it has to be said – Antoine Galland's eighteenth-century translation of *The Book of the Thousand Nights and One Night* where the story takes place in Western China and North Africa. Sir Richard Burton, at first not sure whether *Aladdin* was genuine or not, added the story to his *Supplemental Nights* in 1886–88. Successive versions of *Aladdin* (as play and as pantomime), from the 1780s onwards, came to reflect popular attitudes towards China – from benign and bedazzled *Chinoiserie* in the eighteenth century, via condescending veneration, to outright contempt in the late nineteenth.

In October 1901, a correspondent in *The Times* asked, 'Have not pantomime librettists familiarised holiday audiences for years past with the manners and customs of Pekin through the medium of our old friend *Aladdin*?' It was a good question. These 'manners and customs' included an indolent young Aladdin finding the lamp (in the original he was just 'naughty'), a cruel and sadistic 'off-with-his-head' Emperor, a wicked wizard who uses fiendish Chinese cunning and magic, a fragrant, veiled Princess Badroulbadour from the perfumed world of *The Arabian Nights*, a magic palace all of gold and silver, and of course the formidable Widow Twankey with her Chinese laundry (quite a recent invention: before that, she tended to run some kind of a shop). Plus assorted walk-ons with funny names, silly voices and subnormal reactions: obsequious *and* treacherous. Widow Twankey was originally called Widow Souchong, and she, too, took her name (or rather he took her name) from a type of China tea grown in the Tuan Ky district of the Manchu Empire (Tuan Ky: Twankey – get it?). Other characters were named after kinds of tea, as well: Pekoe, Sou-chong, Bohea, Congou, Oo-long, Hy-son – names which the audience could be expected to recognize from their domestic lives. Other names were more obviously jokey: they might well include Cheekee Creecha, the maid of all work, and Saw-See, the maid of no work. There would be gags about the inability of Chinese people to pronounce consonants ('l' for 'r'), lots of pidgin English, cracked China, rascally and over-bureaucratic mandarins, obsequious kowtowing, the Lord High Executioner, the eating of cats and dogs, and laundries as women's work. There would be nonsense songs, a Westernized oriental gentleman who uses ridiculous malapropisms, some topical references to the effortless superiority of the British and the 'Boxer uprising'. And there would probably be the tune of 'Chopsticks'. Originally called 'The Chop Waltz' (1877), because it was intended as an exercise for children to use their index fingers – like the act of chopping, nothing at all to do with China – the tune had long been associated with the oriental eating utensil instead.

Costumes would range from baggy blue trousers and a black tunic (for the underlings) to brightly coloured dressing-gowns with embroidered dragons, sequins and mirrors, and head-dresses (for the mandarins and emperors). No peacock feathers, though – there was a strange superstition among pantomime folk about having these on stage. The senior characters would sport long, thin moustaches and goatees, and bald caps, with the emperors wearing long talon-like fingernails in metal sheaths. All the actors in yellowface would have their eyebrows hidden with glue and makeup, and their elongated eyes outlined in Indian ink. And they would all have long pigtails. The backdrops would belong to a willow-patterned world; the props would include Chinese chairs, fans, lanterns and banners. The popular visual imagery of China, as *The Times* correspondent suggested, came from pantomime and music hall in pre-cinema days; together with comics, press and book illustrations. Reminiscences by visitors to China sometimes noted that this was how they actually *saw* Peking when first they arrived. Then they discovered that the pantomimes were *really* about England in fancy dress.

Meanwhile, a series of expensive, escapist, glossy and visually spectacular musical comedies with oriental themes and settings – and with more scantily clad dancing-girls than the previous generation could manage – was proving excellent box-office around Shaftesbury Avenue and Coventry Street in the West End of London. These were partly spin-offs from pantomime and music hall (luxurious all-the-year-round versions, which in turn fed back into the halls), partly an attempt to repeat on a grander scale, with the latest mechanical inventions, the success of Gilbert and Sullivan's *The Mikado* (1885: 672 performances in its first production), only without the satire on British institutions.

The 'sex and shopping' craze seems to have begun with *The Shop Girl* (1894, set in the Japanese department of a fashionable Kensington High Street store, maybe Barker's), followed by *The Geisha* (1896, set in a Japanese teahouse with Marie Lloyd as O Mimosa San: it ran for 760 performances), *San Toy* (1899, set in China, with its hit song 'Rhoda and Her Pagoda': 768 performances), *A Chinese Honeymoon* (1901, with its hit song 'Martha Spanks the Grand Pianner': 1,075 performances over three years), *The Cingalee* (1904: 365 performances), *See See* (1906, in which two of the principals performed a duet dressed as Ming vases), *The New Aladdin* (1906), and the non-musical *Kismet* (which opened with much brouhaha from Broadway in 1911, and ran for 330 performances). In the same year as *Kismet*, Max Reinhardt opened a play without words, the modernist *Sumurun*, also adapted from the *Thousand and One Nights*, at the Coliseum. *The Times* critic (20 February 1911) was besotted:

> The like of this marvel has surely never been seen in London before! It presents harmonies of colours that are now suave and tender, now ablaze and dazzling – the quiet hues of an old Persian rug and the glitter of gems. . . . Then it tells a dramatic story of love and jealousy, revenge and death with most eloquent silence. . . . Sumurun's eyes twinkled like stars through the faint mist of her veil, [then] they grew soft and she paused straight and slender like a palm tree against the noon.

'Saki' (H. H. Munro) even wrote a short story involving *Sumurun* called 'The Peace Offering' (1911), in which a country-house play is directed 'in the Sumurun manner' with 'weird music, and exotic skippings and flying leaps and lots of drapery and undrapery, particularly undrapery'. In Saki's version, this all proves too ambitious for the am-dram contributors. In the early 1950s Sax Rohmer was to launch his final series of five adventure novels, which featured Sumuru – a powerful woman pledged to 'purge the world of ugliness and destroy the rule of brute force' by forcibly placing women in positions of power ('women were designed – to be not men's mistresses but their masters'). The ferociously sexy Sumuru has a pet barracuda called Satan. Maybe Rohmer had fond memories of *Sumurun*, dating from when he worked in the business.

Historian John M. MacKenzie, in his study of *Propaganda and Empire* (1984), has observed of all these spectaculars:

In plays and musical comedies the Orient provided an unrivalled opportunity to portray not only spectacle in setting and costumes, but also peculiar people with ... odd laws and customs, and characters who were slippery, grasping, and even more interestingly lascivious. The Orient, after all, had become a source of anxiety and strain, a place of complex trading relations and periodic warfare. ... The plays and musical comedies sought to define the position of their British audiences in that ever-extending and infinitely complicated oriental relationship by portraying the foibles of Eastern peoples, their iniquities, their mindless autocracies and their general inadequacy ... the audiences could be titillated with a heady atmosphere of perfumed lust, repulsive yet attractive.

The punchline was usually 'British is best'.

In *San Toy*, for example, the mandarin Yen Hew – the eponymous girl's father – becomes a fervent admirer of the British way of life, thanks to the dashing Captain Bobbie Preston, son of the British Consul in China:

So we'll imitate the styles of the blessed British Isles
Though the reason isn't easy to divine –
Ah! But they do it in the West, so of course it must be best
And I mean to introduce it into China.

The most successful of them all was *Chu Chin Chow* (1916). A spectacular blend of musical comedy and pantomime, it ran for five years and 2,238 performances, with 2.8 million tickets sold, and was subsequently filmed twice, in 1923 and 1934. It was written by the Australian-born actor Oscar Asche, who had played Hajj the Beggar in *Kismet*, and who between times had managed an Australian tour of *Antony and Cleopatra*, complete with more dancing-girls than Shakespeare happened to mention and gigantic Egyptian temple sets. *Chu Chin Chow*, a reworking of *Ali Baba* – which this time had the robber chief Abu Hasan stealing the identity of a Shanghai merchant called Chu Chin Chow, 'with his camel loads of silks and spices' – managed somehow to combine the old Baghdad of *The Arabian Nights* with elaborate stage *Chinoiserie*. There was even a camel, and a donkey, wandering around the stage. The merchant, with shaven head, wispy beard and fingernail extensions, announces himself with the words:

I am Chu Chin Chow from China,
Of Shanghai China.
No celestial blood is finer
In Shanghai, China.

The 1934 film, produced by Michael Balcon, had George Robey as a scratchy, layout Ali Baba and Austrian actor Fritz Kortner as Abu Hasan/ Chu Chin Chow. Robey's performance included several of his catchphrases ('I stop, I look, I listen'; 'well, I meantersay'), elaborate insults to petty bureaucrats ('thou itch, thou scab, thou boil, thou bloodsucker . . .'), saucy innuendo ('before you call me that, remember we are all sons of the self-same mother'), a jokey theme-tune played on a penny-whistle, and some larger-than-life burlesque costumes (a huge turban with a wayward feather protruding from it). Fritz Kortner's acting style, on the other hand, was unrestrained expressionism, and as the merchant mandarin Chu Chin Chow – in a long false moustache, black skullcap, mandarin robe and elaborate head-dress – he became the demon king, relishing elaborate tortures to Anna May Wong as the servant-girl Zahrat: 'Your body's still too young for death. . . . Show my angel the *paradise* that awaits her' – as she is led to the great wooden wheel that opens the cave. Abu Hasan is like a wicked child: when he is Chu, he is like . . . well, Fu Manchu. The other ingredients of pop-orientalism – half-naked slave-girls in a 'slave bazaar' scene, a perfumed harem and a Chinese fan dance, plus a water-dance at the foot of a huge art deco staircase with shell motif – relieved the tension of the main plot, as in a pantomime. In general with such entertainments, shiny bright colours were associated with 'decadence' and effeminacy, dark colours with seriousness and masculinity. Lady Herbert Tree, noting how little the pretty chorus girls were wearing in the original stage show, observed – in a celebrated line – that *Chu Chin Chow* was 'more navel than military'. Or was it Beerbohm Tree, who rented out His Majesty's Theatre for the production, murmuring, 'Hmm, more navel than millinery', as Oscar Asche recalled? Whichever it was, *Chu Chin Chow* was the sort of success that encouraged urban myths. It proved particularly popular with exhausted servicemen on leave from the trenches of the First World War; 'The Robber's March' accompanied British troops into Germany.

The unprecedented success of *Chu Chin Chow* led directly to yet another *Aladdin*, this time at Drury Lane no less, in Christmas 1917. Reviewing this production, the *Pall Mall Gazette* applauded 'the final and complete divorce from the rough-and-ready music-hall element. . . . *Aladdin* is as *Aladdin* should be, a piece of conscientious *Chinoiserie* always.' Just the thing to take your mind off the trenches of Flanders . . . After the show, though, audiences and cast had an immediate reminder of them – as actress Stella Patrick Campbell wrote – with the 'long grey line of motor ambulances waiting for the wounded at Charing Cross – what a sight it was to pass, almost every night, coming home from the theatre'. Siegfried Sassoon, in his poem '"Blighters"' (1917), was squeamish about the very idea of escaping into music-hall land:

> *I'd like to see a Tank come down the stalls*
> *Lurching to ragtime tunes, or 'Home Sweet Home',*
> *And there'd be no more jokes in Music-halls,*
> *To mock the riddled corpses round Bapaume.*

Chu Chin Chow was called a 'stock theatrical joke'. One critic suggested that its real contribution to the war effort was to encourage soldiers to go 'gladly . . . back to the trenches'. But there was no gainsaying the show's phenomenal success, and its impact. It may even have given Puccini the idea for *Turandot* (1926). It also led to some serious merchandizing in the high street of perfume, Chinese food (restaurants called 'Chu Chin Chow') and clothing. Pots, as featured in the 'Mean Street' scene, were on sale in the theatre foyer, courtesy of Wedgwood. Sax Rohmer's 'Honan' perfume dates from this time.

The theatrical craze for oriental extravaganzas coincided with the spread of 'oriental departments' to large stores in the suburbs of London as well as in the West End. Liberty's in Regent Street had been specializing in 'oriental' goods – and especially Chinese ornamental products – since 1895: Oscar Wilde famously shopped there, and the store had many connections with the 'Aesthetic' taste for interior design. But in the Edwardian period, shops such as Whiteley's in Westbourne Grove – lower down the market – began to advertise in their catalogues cheap Chinese blackwood furniture, strips or squares of Chinese embroidery for use as cushion-covers and antimacassars, and blue-and-white ceramic plant-pots, vases, plates and ginger jars. These were sometimes marketed as 'memories of old China', of 'mandarins and pagodas'. The fashionable strips of embroidery, according to Liberty's, could well have been cut from genuine 'dragon or mandarin robes'. With the crushing of the 'Boxer uprising' of 1900 and the overthrow of the Manchus in 1911, such promotions managed to be topical as well as nostalgic: nostalgic for the Imperial Manchu dynasty and nostalgic for the golden age of connoisseurship for things Chinese in the eighteenth century. Contemporary China seemed to have little appeal.

The early years of the twentieth century also saw Chinese food, served in a few restaurants in the West End, beginning to lose its 'capacity to intrigue or to shock'. The first one opened in Central London in 1908, followed by the Tanhua Lou in Piccadilly. There had been foodstores and a few eating places catering for the small local Chinese population in Liverpool and London since the mid-nineteenth century, but these had seldom been visited by Western customers. Investigative journalists, as we have seen (p. 90), tended to treat them with suspicion or scorn. Sax Rohmer continued to do this until at least the 1930s, as did articles in the popular press. From 1919 onwards, though, the numbers of 'dining rooms' in Pennyfields and Limehouse Causeway began to rise, catering for a slightly more international clientele. The cuisine had been properly introduced to British tastes at the 1884 Health Exhibition in South Kensington, where one of the exhibits was a fully operational 'Chinese Restaurant and Tea House, owned by Cooks from Peking and Canton', with the menus written in French. The organizers pointed out that 'the English idea of the Chinese Tea-House and Chinese Restaurant has nothing corresponding to it in China': if the *genuine* article were to be shipped over intact, 'English sight-seers would neither eat in it nor sit in it'. So the choice of dishes – and the ambience – would be tastefully adapted to South Kensington. The idea was to show that Chinese cooking *could* be as sophisticated as French. So the menu included:

> Saucisson de Frankfort . . .
> Bird's Nest Soup . . .
> Biche de Mer à la Matelote Chinoise . . .
> Shark's Fins à la Bagration . . .
> Boule de Riz.
> Shaohsing Wine.
> Noisettes de Lotus à l'Olea Fragrance . . .
> Vermicelli Chinoise à la Milanaise.

Punch complained that this 'Chinese Dinner' was only by the wildest stretch of the imagination Chinese. Even the *waiters* were Swiss, German or French.

This might of course be just as well because the Shaohsing wine, which *was* Chinese, tasted of 'a mixture of hock, the traditional flavour of furniture polish, and chocolate cream'. Others argued, more seriously, that the Chinese diet could be better for overall health than the meat-based Western one, and that there were distinctions to be drawn between South China (rice and fish) and North China (cereals and pulses). In the Edwardian period, as the historian J. A. G. Roberts has pointed out, 'ignorance of, and prejudice against, Chinese food was still the dominant mind-set in Britain, but a few Westerners . . . had begun to voice their appreciation of it'. Or at least of a customized version. Most concurred with Hilaire Belloc's little verse:

> *Birds in their little nests agree*
> *With Chinamen but not with me!*

So, Chinese restaurants, and food, were adapted to suit South Kensington and West End tastes. But those strips of embroidery sold in Liberty's could well have been actually looted from forbidden places and smuggled over. At around the same time, the fashion for Pekingese lapdogs – Pekingese pugs or 'sleeve dogs' – began to spread as well, especially among the British upper classes. Their pedigree went back to the looting of the Summer Palace in 1860, when five of these revered 'Palace dogs' had been discovered in royal apartments and shipped back to England. One of them had been duly presented to Queen Victoria by Lieutenant John Hart Dunne of the 99th Regiment, been given the insensitive name of 'Looty', and had her portrait hung at the Royal Academy in 1862. These miniature guardian lions were revered in China because, it was said, they were a worldly representation of the god Fo, protector of all faith, and embodied the Emperor himself in animal form. Although they were not supposed to leave the Palace grounds, enough of them were smuggled out to establish the breed in Britain. One specimen, called Ah Cum, which left China in 1896 in a cage of deer, was stuffed and presented to the South Kensington Museum (now the V&A) in 1906 as an outstanding example of the breed. By 1921 it was estimated that over 30 per cent of all registered pedigree toy dogs were Pekingese, which had overtaken the Pomeranian as the most popular. A published guide to the care and grooming of Pekingeses – said to have been written by the Empress Dowager Cixi herself as part of *Pearls Dropped from the Lips of Her Imperial Majesty Tsu Hsi, Dowager Empress of the Flowery Land* (1909) – was, in its English version, a strange mixture of practical handbook and popular stereotyping: the dogs were apparently partial to biting 'foreign devils' and venerating their ancestors; their ears should ideally be 'sails set like a war junk'; and their favourite supper was curlews' livers. In short, the Imperial Palace dog behaved suspiciously like his/her original Chinese masters and mistresses. By 1914, following the overthrow of the age-old regime, this identification was to become even more explicit. The novelists Agnes and Egerton Castle wrote at length about Loki, their much-adored Pekingese, and how he stood for all the right values – against the modern world of suffragettes, socialism and nasty revolutions in China:

> Loki will not believe that the Manchu masters have fallen in China (of course it is not from *us* that he has heard these distressing rumours), so he still demands as his right the best silk eiderdowns to lie upon, satin for his cushions, grilled kidney for his breakfast, freshly poured water in his bowl every time he wants to drink. . . . He sits up and waves his paws with imperious gesture; or else rolls over on his back and puts them together in an attitude of prayer.

Such a creature deserved nothing less than an 'Imperial bride', 'bred in the secret sinister splendours of a Manchu palace'. The Castles even took Loki on shopping trips to London – Liberty's, no doubt – though not to the theatre. If they had, the London Hippodrome would certainly have been the place to go.

The Hippodrome, which had opened in 1900, came to specialize in oriental spectaculars. It evolved from a circus-cum-music hall into a musical-comedy house. Its first proprietor, Edward Moss, explained in 1911 the ways in which, with productions now costing so much, his theatre could hope to make any profit:

> In connection with the London Hippodrome it has been our view not to restrict expenses in any way where we have had an opportunity to produce a spectacle which should warrant an elaborate *mise en scène*.

For the Christmas season of 1921–22, the Hippodrome hosted an elaborate Julian Wylie production of *Jack and the Beanstalk*, with George Robey as Dame Trot – on a rare London appearance in pantomime. The principal boy, Jack, was played by Clarice Mayne – later to become the Rohmers' sister-in-law. Towards the end of the run, Robey started rehearsing a new revue, co-written by Sax Rohmer, producer Julian Wylie and Julian's brother Lauri. The revue was a 'musical adventure' called *Round in Fifty*, an updated version of Jules Verne's *Around the World in Eighty Days* (1873) in which Phileas Fogg's dissolute nephew Phil bets that he can beat his uncle's record by thirty days. Robey, in his *Looking Back on Life* (1933), judged it to be 'altogether I think . . . the best revue I ever took part in'. After a try-out week at the beginning of March at the Empire Cardiff, it opened in London's West End on 16 March 1922.

Round in Fifty begins at the Gridiron Club, London, where Phil – the only surviving relative of Phileas Fogg – learns that in order to secure his large inheritance, he must attempt the round-the-world journey: 'Same route! no aeroplane!' It will be covered by journalist Jill Carey, working for newspaper proprietor Lord Southcliffe (a satirical reference to press baron Lord Northcliffe). Jill, we learn, is well qualified for this because she has reached

> such inaccessible places as Moscow, where she interviewed Lenin; Pekin, where she dined with the new President of the Chinese Republic; and Llasa, where she was received by the Grand Lama.

The chef at the Gridiron Club happens to be Harold, grandson of Passepartout. Passepartout – played of course by George Robey – will accompany Phil. Hot on their heels are Chief Inspector Tutt and his assistant Tippett, who suspect Phil of a bank robbery, and who pursue the adventurers round the world – including Hong Kong: cue jokes about Fu Manchu and overpopulation – in a series of ingenious disguises.

One big innovation in *Round in Fifty*, Robey recalled, was the use of 'the cinematograph' for a motorboat sequence and the final road race to London. This was Sax Rohmer's idea. It was also used in a scene in Burma, where 'cinema film [was] thrown on from the front flooding the air with hundreds of snakes', making Passepartout's hair stand on end by another special effect. Slides were projected to show telegrams, maps and newspaper headlines, letting the audience know where the intrepid adventurers had reached. Sax Rohmer had in fact spotted the potential of film much earlier. In his short story 'The Green Spider' (October 1904), issued only eleven months after his first publication 'The Mysterious Mummy', the hideous 'green spider – only with a body twice the size of a football' turns out on closer inspection to have been an illusion, projected by 'a magic lantern with cinematograph attached'. Instead of being the killer of Professor Brayme-Skepeley in his bacteriological laboratory, the projected and enlarged creation – which looks like 'an unclassified aptera' – is the means of his escape and disappearance. This use of film as evidence deliberately planted at the scene of the crime – film as a way of *deceiving* the eye – may well have been a first in detective fiction. Later, of course, Rohmer would have many more connections with the world of film, through adaptations of his novels.

Robey's published reminiscences of the show – as with so much else about his life – were highly unreliable: 'My part was that of old Fogg's spend-thrift son Phil (you will remember he was the valet, Passepartout, in the novel).' Wrong on three counts! *Round in Fifty* was not only a great success with audiences (it ran for 471 performances), it also says a great deal about Rohmer's suburban 'take' on spectacular musical comedies in the West End and the kinds of material their audiences would enjoy: among them, references to Sherlock Holmes again; quick-change routines; crude Chinese stereotypes in dialogue and song; the assumption that London is the centre not just of the Empire but of the universe; the overt racism presented as a joke; the willow-patterned romanticism of dance routines; the understanding of the potential of film; the deliberately corny integration of Robey's well-known patter into the story. Again, England in fancy dress.

At around the same time as *Round in Fifty*, Rohmer worked on a musical adaptation of the Captain Kettle stories by J. Cutcliffe Hyne about a pugnacious, bearded sea-captain, which had in the 1890s been 'more popular than Sherlock Holmes'. Nelson Keys was to play the title role, and Rohmer was to collaborate on the book and lyrics, but it was never completed. Nor was a musical play for the Adelphi Theatre called *London's Sweetheart*, 'with W. H. Berry as chief comedian'. Rohmer made one last attempt at a spectacular musical comedy in the late 1940s, when his book sales had taken a dip. Michael Martin-Harvey had drafted the book and lyrics of a show based loosely on Hans Christian Andersen's fairytale 'The Chinese Nightingale'. Because the theme was 'Chinese', Sax Rohmer was brought in for a complete rewrite. The music had been composed by Kennedy Russell. The story, about a girl who wins the heart of the Emperor of China by her singing, was set in and around the Imperial Palace in the seventh century. The Japanese envoy Kamatari was the villain. Rohmer called it 'an operetta, of which I am part-author'. *The Nightingale*, a musical romance produced by Jack Hulbert with 'delicolour lighting', opened in July 1947 at the Prince's Theatre (now the Shaftesbury) and closed six weeks later. Mimi Benzell of the Metropolitan Opera was praised for her performance as the songbird, but apart from that the notices were terrible. W. A. Darlington, in the *Daily Telegraph*, wrote that the music was 'a distinct cut above the lyrics of Michael Martin-Harvey and Sax Rohmer'. The *Daily Mail* went further. *The Nightingale*, it announced, had 'claptrap words and indifferent music'. Sax Rohmer never again ventured into the world of musical comedies.

Although his songs and scripts for George Robey attracted the most interest, back in the years 1908–12 Rohmer wrote lyrics and occasionally music for several other music-hall performers – and some songs on spec as well. For Will Bentley, he wrote the words of 'Vain Regrets' (1908): 'I am strangely unlucky by nature / My life is one long vain regret' goes the song, while each of the verses explains in a contrived way how lucky he *really* is. The roof falls in 'with an earthquake in the tropics' while he has a winning hand at cards: the others die, but he survives. He meets a rabid dog, which has bitten ten people to death, and escapes unharmed – but he *should* have let the dog into the house and locked the door because

> *My rich Uncle Ned, whose heir I shall be*
> *Was alone in the house at the time!*

The refrain was that the singer has regrets, but worse things could have happened to him. The music was by the prolific arranger and composer Henry Pether, who also wrote the mock-tragic 'Waiting at the Church (My Wife Won't Let Me)' (1907), his greatest, most catchy hit.

For the buxom, strong-voiced, Australian-born singer Florrie Forde, Rohmer wrote and composed 'Tom Took Tickets for Two' (1909), with the chorus:

> *So Tom took tickets for two, to take*
> *Topsy to Tooting to tea.*
> *Topsy tickled his fancy there, under*
> *The shade of a crab-apple tree.*
> *And then Tom said 'Topsy, let us married be!'*
> *Tops said 'Yes!' and they were, you see.*
> *Tom took tickets for two, but he's now*
> *Taking tickets for three!*

TOP: Publicity photograph of Sax Rohmer, in his robe, used on several of his publications and given to the author by Mrs Rohmer in summer 1971. With Rohmer's signature, from the early 1930s; by then, he liked to turn the 'S' into a dollar sign. **ABOVE:** Rose Elizabeth Sax Rohmer, photographed in 1976 for the *Sunday Times*, beside her late husband's desk in their living room.

Memorandum from

CHUNG LING SOO

MARVELLOUS CHINESE CONJURER

WORLD'S TOUR

19

PLEASE ADDRESS
YOUR NEXT TO

DIRECTION
MAURICE E. BANDMAN

Headed notepaper of Chung Ling Soo (or rather William Ellsworth Robinson), the best-known of the many Edwardian 'Chinese' conjurors.

Photogravure of Little Tich as King Ki-Ki of Ko-Ki, with (inset) jokey Chinese pictograms, both from *Little Tich: A Book of Travels (and Wanderings)*, ghost-written by Sax Rohmer in 1911. **OVERLEAF:** Sheet-music cover of 'Orange Blossom: A Chinese Tale' (1921) by Sax Rohmer, a monologue performed by Bransby Williams, who wrote 'it gave me the chance of a Chinese study'.

Musical Monologues

RECITATIONS WITH MUSICAL ACCOMPANIMENTS   (No. 237)

ORANGE BLOSSOM

A CHINESE TALE

BY

SAX ROHMER

索士老馬

PERFORMED
BY

BRANSBY WILLIAMS

164

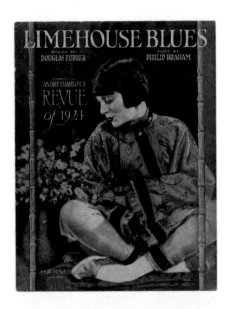

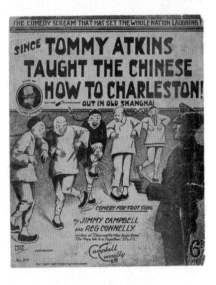

CLOCKWISE FROM TOP LEFT: British dance-band music from the 1920s with a 'Chinese' flavour: the 'Chong Fox-Trot'. Sheet-music cover of 'Limehouse Blues', a very popular hit originally sung by Gertrude Lawrence in a 1924 revue; it soon became a jazz standard. Cover of 'Since Tommy Atkins Taught the Chinese How to Charleston!', a comedy fox-trot dating from the mid-1920s. Original poster design for the first production of *Chu Chin Chow* (1916), which ran at His Majesty's Theatre in London for five years, and proved particularly popular with servicemen on leave from the trenches of the First World War.

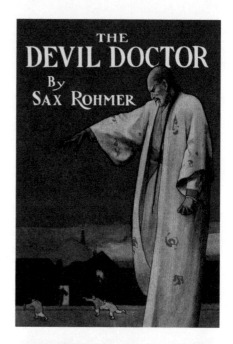

CLOCKWISE FROM TOP LEFT: Dust-jacket of *The Golden Scorpion* (American reprint, 1928). *The Devil Doctor* (first British edition, 1916). *Tales of Chinatown* (American paperback reprint, 1950). *Yellow Shadows* (first British edition, 1925).

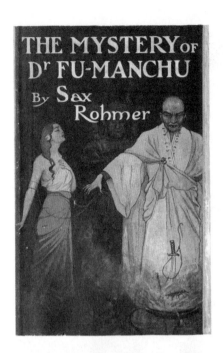

CLOCKWISE FROM TOP LEFT: *The Mystery of Dr Fu-Manchu* (first British edition, 1913), the earliest book illustration of the devil doctor. *The Insidious Dr Fu-Manchu* (first American edition of *The Mystery*, 1913). *The Hand of Fu Manchu* (American reprint of *The Si-Fan Mysteries*, the third in the series, 1920s). *The Mystery of Dr Fu-Manchu* (British reprint, 1977) – note the resemblance to Chairman Mao.

'In her . . . I share the sorrow of Shakespeare's *King Lear*': *Daughter of Fu Manchu* (American edition, 1931).

The punchline is:

His case was sad – but it's sadder yet
Since Topsy's turned into a suffragette!

And the moral of the tale is:

Oh boys, beware what you do or say:
Poor Adam was had that way.
And so was Tom, for he found, you see,
That a woman's weak spot is a crab-apple tree.

Florrie Forde had become famous for conducting sing-alongs with her jewelled cane, and among the songs she made famous were 'Down at the Old Bull and Bush', a revival of 'Has Anybody Here Seen Kelly?' (1909) and 'Hold Your Hand Out, Naughty Boy' (1914). The troops were to march to her familiar anthems 'Pack Up Your Troubles' (1915, originally written as an entry for a competition) and 'It's a Long, Long Way to Tipperary', which she performed at the start of the war within hours of receiving the sheet music, immediately recognizing its potential. The song came to symbolize the naivety of the early optimistic phase of the war in 1914, when everyone hoped it would be over by Christmas. And, as J. B. Priestley was to note, it also showed how 'as soon as the English go to the music halls, they love the Irish'. Forde was among the first celebrities to put her own diet on the market, with herself as its advertisement.

'Has anybody here seen Kelly – K-E-double L-Y?' was first sung by Nora Bayes in the American impresario Lew Fields's revue *The Jolly Bachelors* (1909). The following year, the sequel to the song and the answer to the question – written by Sax Rohmer, music by T. W. Thurban – was featured in Fields's follow-up, *The Midnight Sons*, and sung by 'the queen of song' Maud Lambert: 'Kelly's Gone to Kingdom Come'. Lambert had achieved a moment of fame in 1904 by recording the song 'Two Little Sausages' for Thomas Edison. On the sheet music, the 'Kelly' sequel was hyped as 'a bigger hit than *Has anybody here . . . ?*', which soon proved to be very wishful thinking. The song's publication in the United States may have been the first use of the name 'Sax Rohmer' over there.

There is an Irish gentleman who's caused a great commotion
But where he is at present no one has the slightest notion.

> *The boy that I'm referring to was born in Balla-Shelley*
> *Pat O'Hara Connemara, Palestine O'Guggenheim,*
> *Li Hung Dooley Ballyhooley J. Columbus Kelly.*

And then the chorus:

> *Kelly's gone to Kingdom Come, Kingdom Come, Kingdom Come!*
> *Bought an aeroplane, by gum.*
> *Oh my!*
> *Tried to do what others did.*
> *Now he's below where the dead ones go and he never said goodbye.*

Kelly has the ambition to fly across the Channel and then the Irish Sea, but he disappears in the attempt. Mrs Kelly goes to London and consults Sherlock Holmes:

> *I rather guess you want his new address?*
> *I think I made a note of it – somewhere.*
> *Yes, yes.*

But the body cannot be found anywhere. The song finishes with the funeral service, and a confused parson who 'instead of Hymn 163' leads the congregation in yet another chorus. In the original, Kelly hailed from 'County Cork in the Emerald Isle': in the sequel, he seems to have become more multicultural – to judge by the names – a mix of Irish, Jewish, Chinese and American. Maybe Florrie Forde could have done something with the song. Probably not.

Rohmer in fact went into partnership with the prolific composer T. W. (or Tommy) Thurban in 1908–10 – they wrote at least five songs together, and the composer lived near Herne Hill – until he thought he had discovered that one of the songs for which he'd written the words *and* the tune had been published under Thurban's name, at which point they had a blazing row and went their separate ways. One of the last songs they worked on together was 'The Camel's Parade: A Desert Arabesque (Introducing the Original Bedouin Melody The Mizmoune)' (1910). Since 1890, when Caroline Norton's 'The Arab's Farewell to His Horse' (1833) had been turned into a very popular song, various 'Arabesques' had tried to repeat the formula. 'The Camel's Parade' begins with a camel-driver humming a prayer before departure, followed by a loud shout of 'Hi-You', then:

Allah: o'er the Desert speeding to City great and fair –
On the Caravan ere long departing with myrrh and spices rare
Show'r thy blessings, Allah, then shall each heart be glad.
Be ye, Lord, with our Caravan bound for Old Baghdad.

'The Camel's Parade' is at times more like a 'musical monologue' than a song, and Rohmer was in fact better known at the time for the monologues he wrote (including the piano accompaniment) – he called them 'poems' – for the barnstorming, roaring actor Bransby Williams. Williams had originally intended to use his voice as a missionary but instead made his name at the London music hall in Shoreditch, in the East End. He had, since 1897, come to specialize in larger-than-life Dickens impersonations on music-hall stages. Standing alone, with the help of many quick changes of costume – he once played thirty-seven different characters in a week – this protean performer would become in short order Mr Pickwick, Sam Weller, Scrooge, Fagin, Bill Sikes, Micawber, Uriah Heep and even Little Nell. His routine inspired the young Charlie Chaplin to imitate him, and to a lifetime love of reading the novels of Charles Dickens. When Williams's act went through a fallow patch, his melodramatic monologue with music 'The Green Eye of the Yellow God', written by J. Milton Hayes (1911), helped revive his fortunes:

There's a one-eyed yellow idol to the north of Khatmandu,
There's a little marble cross below the town,
There's a broken-hearted woman tends the grave of Mad Carew,
And the Yellow God for ever gazes down . . .

The monologue of love and death set in the Himalayas tells of how 'Mad Carew' tries impetuously to impress the Colonel's daughter by stealing 'the green eye of the little yellow god', but for his sacrilege on the night of the regimental ball he ends up with a knife in his heart. It is a robustly melodramatic mix of Kipling and *The Moonstone* – which must have seemed old-fashioned, even at the time – but it proved extremely popular, and much parodied. Stories and novels about Englishmen stealing objects sacked from temples – jewels, sculptures, treasures of various descriptions – and being punished for it by Indian priests or Chinese mandarins, were one consequence. The assumption of the parodists was that the audience knew the original by heart. One of Williams's personal favourites was an early parody by louche, shabby-genteel comedian Billy Bennett – who specialized in nonsense send-ups of dramatic monologues, using gibberish – called 'The Green Tie of the Little Yellow Dog', in which Mad Carew attaches his tie to the tail of his girlfriend's dog, and the dog – in revenge – plants the girlfriend's false teeth in his bed. Bennett would perform it in a stained dinner-jacket, his hair plastered down, wearing a large sergeant-major's moustache. He was billed as 'almost a gentleman', as well, and apparently adopted an 'air of brisk commonsense':

> There's a cock-eyed yellow poodle to the north of Gonga-pooch,
> There's a little hot-cross-bun that's turning green,
> There's a double-jointed wop-wop doing tricks in who-flung-dung,
> And you're a better man than I am, Gunga-Din.

'Gonga-pooch', by the way, was thought to be a Hindustani colloquialism for 'arsehole'.

Billy Bennett later added a related monologue to his repertoire – set in Limehouse rather than 'north of Khatmandu'. It was parody, in part of the Limehouse tales of Thomas Burke, in part of Sax Rohmer's stories:

> In the street of a thousand lanterns
> To the East of Limehouse Reach
> Lived a bland Chinee, who loved the sea
> For he was a son of the beach.
> At his pub called the Thousand Bung-holes
> He would serve up dope and hashish
> To a motley group who drank hair soup
> That was flavoured with Chinese moustaches.
> He'd a wife called Who-flung-poo . . .

The couple's niece, called Way-Way, meets and falls for a Chinese man from over the seas called Hugh Pi Kan – 'a conjuring man' – but Uncle Wun Lung, in a fury at the dishonour to his family, stabs both her and him:

> All is silent in Limehouse Causeway
> There is nothing but peasoup fog
> It's so thick you can't see the lamp-posts.
> That's tough luck on a limping dog . . .

This recitation either led to – or was inspired by – a much coarser version which was still popular in the armed forces in the Second World War, on their way to Singapore and Burma:

> *On the street of a thousand arseholes*
> *'Neath the sign of the swinging tit*
> *Stood a beautiful Chinese maiden*
> *Her name was Oo [or Hu] Flung Shit.*

This would sometimes be accompanied by rough jokes about the widespread belief that the labial plane of a Chinese vagina was horizontal rather than verti-cal . . . In the forces' version, the beautiful Chinese maiden meets the libidinous Won-Hung-Low, with very predictable and increasingly obscene results. *This* version became so well known in Britain that the brash signature tune of the weekly BBC radio programme *Pick of the Pops* from 1961–67 was called 'At the Sign of the Swinging Cymbal'. It was composed in 1950 by Brian Fahey.

Another Billy Bennett parody – again of Thomas Burke's *Limehouse Nights* and Rohmer's 'Yellow Trilogy' stories – was 'Limehouse Liz', about a naive farmer's daughter who comes to London, meets a stranger on the Thames Embankment one night, goes to the bad and finds herself on the streets:

> *Then she drifted down to Chinatown –*
> *And you all know where that is –*
> *Where slitty-eyed Chinks take forty winks.*
> *And she's known as Limehouse Liz.*

There, she 'lives on dope and tarry rope', after the one-eyed One Lung Chew has 'given her a packet'. In Sax Rohmer's stories set in Limehouse, the elab-orate oriental apartments of Fo-Hi, or of Mr King, tend to include, sitting in an ornate niche, 'a yellow leering idol green-eyed and complacent' (whatever *that* may have meant).

Sax Rohmer wrote two musical monologues specially for Bransby Williams – as follow-ups to 'The Green Eye' – 'The Pigtail of Li Fang Fu' (1919) and the more popular 'Orange Blossom: A Chinese Tale' (1921). 'The Pigtail of Li Fang Fu' opens in 'Green Eye' style, all stops out:

> *In a deep and a midnight gully, by the street where the goldsmiths are,*
> *'Neath the Mosque of Mohammed Ali, at the back of the Scent Bazaar,*

Was the House of a Hundred Raptures, the Tomb of a Thousand Sighs;
Where the sleepers lay in that living death which the opium-smoker
dies . . .

There, muttering his mounted drill to himself – dementedly – is the 'wreck of a splendid man', the grey-haired Captain Dan. He catches sight of Li Fang Fu's daughter 'as sweet as a lotus, with the grace of a willow bough', and notices through an opium haze that her 'ivory shoulders bare' are being scarred by her father's whip. Captain Dan, in a frenzy, grabs the whip, lashes Li Fang Fu and cuts off his pigtail. ('Note: a Southern Chinaman regards his pigtail with superstitious reverence.') There is the sound of a gong. 'Like fiends of an opium vision, they closed in a fight for life.' Li Fang Fu is about to stab the Captain, when he is shot dead. The narrator returns to the Tomb of a Thousand Sighs a while later to find out what happened next:

. . . within sat the golden idol, and he leered as he leered of old!
And I thought that his eyes were moving, in a sinister, vile grimace.
When suddenly, there at his feet I saw a staring and well-known face!

It is none other than Captain Dan, dead, with the pigtail of Li Fang Fu wound around his neck.

'Orange Blossom: A Chinese Tale', which became a regular in Bransby Williams's act, is narrated by little Orange Blossom's husband, who is reminiscing with his old and trusted friend Wu Chang:

Alas! Wu Chang, much water's flown from Honan
To the Yellow Sea since you and I were playmates –
Playmates in the valley where the opium poppies grow.

The husband has been away in Honan, and he has entrusted his wife to Wu Chang's care. But Wu Chang abused that trust – so he must die, just as Orange Blossom has died, both poisoned by the same cup of 'the famous Pekoe':

'Twas so with her, at dawn, as 'tis with you tonight.
Go! sleep in hell – in HELL! my friend, Wu Chang!

Bransby Williams was featured on the cover of the sheet music in an embroidered mandarin robe, with a fan, stooping and glancing sidelong in a suitably inscrutable manner. So successful was his performance that Rohmer in the early 1920s 'submitted a Fu Manchu melodrama for my reading. It was a great show. Unfortunately, I was so booked that I had no chance of doing it.' Which was a pity, he said, because 'in Rohmer's play were all the effects used in the lighting of [Edgar Wallace's very successful] *The Ringer* of the future'.

Bransby Williams and his daughter – a neighbour of the Rohmers – became friends with Sax and Elizabeth. Unlike most surviving music-hall stars of his era, he successfully adapted his act for television, though the writer of 'The Green Eye' refused to let him broadcast the piece. Harry Relph – or 'Little Tich' as he came to be known – became even closer, for several years, as Elizabeth Sax Rohmer had told me. 'Little Tich had few intimates,' recalled Sax in 1938, he kept his private life entirely separate from his professional career. But Sax nevertheless became one of the few who developed a close association 'with that inimitable droll'. The four-foot-six-inch-tall Relph is the reason why even today the word 'Tich' is applied in playgrounds to anyone who is diminutive. Having first become a music-hall star in Chicago, New York and Paris (where in 1896–97 he got to know Toulouse-Lautrec, who was exactly the same height), Little Tich had been topping the bill in England since 1890. For a time, he was the highest-paid performer of his kind in the world. His act consisted of a series of minuscule 'characters' – including King Ki-Ki of Ko-Ki, a parody in drag of Loie Fuller's 'Serpentine' dances of 1899, a Chinese General, a Gas Inspector – where words and gestures became mixed up, with some quick changes in the wings and, as the climax, his 'Big Boots Dance' in his long, flat, wooden shoes. Audiences would shout 'Boots! Big Boots!' at him until in the end he became thoroughly fed up with it. He had an infectious Punch-like grin, a taunting look on his face, and came over to the audience like an infuriated gnome. The *Manchester Guardian* wrote of his 'diminutive proportions, his infantile costume and a peculiarly bland smile rivalling that of the Heathen Chinese'. His success had less to do with songs or patter than

> the comic intensity of his characterisations, the finesse of his 'business', the impish, quicksilver energy with which he darts around the stage, as if continually improvising, as if at play.

It was his 'characters' rather than his songs that made his name. In fact, several critics noted how weak his songs tended to be. But in the period 1908–11 it was Sax Rohmer who provided many of his songs and his patter – including 'The Gas Inspector', with music by Thurban, which was recorded. As Rohmer wrote: 'Tich did not deal [so much] in innuendo but relied upon a sort of lunatic logic to secure his effects. His material was most difficult to write.'

The publisher Arthur Greening, who had published *Pause!* the year before, approached Rohmer in 1911 to edit and ghost-write – in partnership with Tich – an illustrated book of memories and backstage stories. It would credit 'Little Tich' on the title page, so again it would not use Rohmer's – or Ward's – name: his second book, like his first, would be anonymous. But it was the first time the name 'Sax Rohmer' had appeared *in* a book rather than on sheet music, and the text made his contribution clear enough. *Little Tich: A Book of Travels (and Wanderings)* (1911) consists of a series of showbiz anecdotes about Tich's career – his upbringing in Kent, in and around The Blacksmith's Arms pub; how he was given his name; early performances in blackface with a tin whistle; experiences on the stage in Chicago and Paris; his love of playing the cello; jobs he would have liked to have done (a liftman and a steeplejack); all interspersed with digressions (the 'wanderings' of the title), comic sketches, photographs and drawings of some of his 'character studies' – and jokes. Samples: 'I don't mean salaam the door'; 'I couldn't very well expect a *big* part, could I?'

The text is studded with a series of references to conversations with 'my friend' or 'my esteemed contemporary', 'the Abbé Sax Rohmer' – so, Tich's relationship with his ghost-writer becomes part of the story. The Abbé compliments Tich on his new songs ('he had written them'). He offers advice on how to write well ('I'm remarkably gifted with my pen, you know'). He recommends modesty, which clearly *isn't* his strongest suit. He provides scripts and lyrics for Tich's 'character studies'; there are jokes about how little money scriptwriters make. He helps with the translation of a 'Roman tablet (not of soap)'. And the Abbé tends to over-write, in a faux-scholarly style:

> That, in the words of my friend the Abbé, is a chunk of concentrated jubilation.

> My first character song was *The Lamplighter*. Then came *The Police Inspector*, and then came *The Chinese General*. Since then I have lost count. Many of my more recent characters have been from the pen of the Abbé Sax Rohmer. This ascetic has provided me with a number of remarkable theses. . . . I will not particularise, as his excessive modesty might be wounded.

At the end of the book, Tich consults the Abbé Sax Rohmer about how to bring the piece to a sensible conclusion:

> He kindly (but idiotically) sent me a *list* of suggestions, including *I Dance in a Harem* ('I don't! I didn't! I wouldn't!') and *I am Betrothed to a Fiji Princess* ('I deny it!').

Eventually, Tich settles on a joke about 'My Chinese Correspondent', in which mock-Chinese pictograms written on the page are interspersed with Tich's increasingly exasperated responses.

The chapter on 'My Impression of the Great Pyramid' brings all these themes together: the wordplay, the pomposity, the surreal misadventures, the repartee between Tich and the Abbé. Tich is passing through the Suez Canal, watching 'the ships of the desert (I refer to camels)', when he engages a chatty Old Gentleman in conversation:

> 'What's your impression of the Great Pyramid?' asks the Old Gentleman.
>
> I said to myself: 'One day, unhappy man, you intend to write a book. Now is the time to try your hand at descriptive stuff!' . . .
>
> 'My impression, sir, is a most impressive impression. It impressed its impression upon me with great impressiveness! When first I saw that tall, star-shaped cylinder . . .'
>
> '. . . Your account of your visit, sir, is most preposterous and ridiculous!'
>
> 'I've given no *account* of my visit! . . . I gave you my *impression* of the Great Pyramid. That was what you asked me, I believe? Very well. I have done my best. I dare say I've gone a bit wrong at times; but that's only natural – as I've never been there.'

Which brings him back to 'my learned friend the Abbé', who of course had never been – at that stage in his life – to the Great Pyramid either. Or to China.

According to Tich's daughter Mary, this 'paperback of 1911' – the only memoir the intensely private man ever authorized – was later 'virtually disowned' by Little Tich. Did it give too much away? Or too little? Or had the gag about learning to over-write become stale? Tich, who was a very clever man, may have become ashamed of it. At the time, the book initially sold well, though neither Tich nor Rohmer collected any royalties because – Elizabeth was to recall – Greening went into receivership. Maybe *that* was why Tich disowned it. According to Rohmer, *Little Tich* had been a book wherein facts and fancies were so nicely mixed that few could distinguish one from another. . . . P. G. Wodehouse thought highly of this queer effort, as he told me some years later. I was unable to agree with him.

Little Tich topped the bill, but further down the programme there would usually be a conjuror or an acrobat or both. While Rohmer was busy writing his lyrics, there were several 'Chinese' magicians touring the halls. By far the most successful of these was 'Chung Ling Soo', who first appeared at the Alhambra (a 'Palace of Varieties' since 1884, now the Odeon Leicester Square) in London in May 1900, with his petite wife and assistant Miss Suee Seen. In fact, he was William Ellsworth Robinson from New York, with his wife Olive or Dot. Robinson had adopted various stage personae on his way up the variety ladder: Achmed Ben Ali, Nana Sahib, Abdul Khan, Robinson the Man of Mystery, Hop Sing Loo and finally, at the age of thirty-nine, Chung Ling Soo, 'The Marvellous Chinese Conjuror'. In the process, since leaving 'Robinson' behind, he had shaved off his big moustache and part of his hair to raise his hairline, and gained a 'pigtail'. Everyone in the audience was convinced that he really *was* Chinese – he performed in complete silence, was an excellent mime, and 'in every gesture and movement he was convincing'. In February 1907, he was even beaten up by fourteen disgruntled dockers in Hull, because they thought he must be a 'coolie labourer' working for lower wages than they were prepared to accept. This tension between British dockworkers, their union representatives and casual Chinese workers was a major issue at the time.

Robinson had modelled his act on that of a Mongolian magician who was successful on the American vaudeville circuit with traditional Chinese magic tricks – producing a goldfish bowl from under his robe, and pigeons or ducks from under a tablecloth or shawl; fire-eating; juggling with eight linked metal rings; throwing multicoloured silk fabrics around the stage; turning shreds of paper into a single large sheet. *He* was originally called Chee Ling Qua, with his daughter Chee Toy (billed as 'the only small-footed Chinese woman singing coon songs', which was surely no more than the truth), but they soon changed their names to Ching Ling Foo and San Toy. The success of Chung Ling Soo in London, building on this act and making it considerably more glitzy and spectacular – including Fee Lung, a Chinese acrobat who could swing by his pigtail from a suspended bar – led, predictably, to many imitators. According to historian of conjuring Sidney W. Clarke, writing in 1928, 'soon

Yankee Chinamen, English Chinamen and Chinamen of all nationalities but Chinese were as thick as pebbles on the beach'. And that does not include one of the very few *genuinely* Chinese acts touring the British halls at the time, who were originally known as 'Tschin Maa and his Seven Holy Grave Watchers and Necromancers', but who changed *their* name to the less memorable 'The High Priest Tschin Maa and his Chunchusen Magicians'.

In January 1905, the Mongolian Ching Ling Foo (appearing at the Empire Leicester Square, the other 'Palace of Varieties' there) went head-to-head with the American Chung Ling Soo (filling the huge Hippodrome nearby) and challenged him to prove he *was* 'a Chinaman after all' in front of a witness from the Chinese Legation in London. Chung responded, through an interpreter of course, by claiming that he was not only Chinese, he had been 'honoured by the Empress Dowager' in person, so he would not demean himself by undergoing any nationality test. Instead, he drove down the Strand, with Suee Seen, in a large red open-top Daimler, under a huge Chinese umbrella, surrounded by crowds of well-wishers. The *Weekly Despatch* asked the inevitable question: 'Did Foo Fool Soo? And Can Soo Sue Foo?' What mattered was that Soo had ousted Foo. He was the better showman, by far.

Chung Ling Soo added 'DEFYING THE BULLETS' to his act in 1904. The silken curtains 'bearing the sacred green dragon of the Manchus' would open, to reveal two ranks of Chinese warriors in 'antique armour of brass and leather'. They would stand in two diagonal lines, as Soo – in a mandarin robe and elaborate head-dress – was carried in on a throne 'presented to him by the Dowager Empress of China' and 'made of solid ebony'. A small Chinese assistant would then step forward to the front of the stage and say: 'Mr Soo now show how he escaped from Boxer bandits in Chinese way.' So this was to be a *reversal* of the Boxers' deeply held belief that they were 'protected' from the bullets of the foreign devils. 'Now pliz,' continued the assistant, 'two gentlemen from audience. . . ?' The chosen volunteers would go up onto the stage and examine a pair of muzzle-loading guns, and two lead bullets in a cup presented to them by Suee Seen, which they would mark with their initials. Soo would carefully load the guns, hand them with great ceremony to two warriors and smile at the audience before giving a 'Chinese handshake' (clasping his hands together above his head). Then Suee would hand him an earthenware plate, which he would hold at arm's length. As he 'straightened himself to his full height', he would nod to the warriors and they would shoot, firing-squad style. Chung Ling Soo would catch the initialled bullets in his plate. Except that on the night of Saturday 23 March 1918 at the Wood Green Empire in North London – when he had been performing this stunt with the same guns for about fourteen years – something went seriously wrong and Soo was shot. A bullet went through his right lung. He died in the cottage hospital a few hours later. The newspapers were full of wild speculation: Was it murder? Some kind of Chinese revenge killing, perhaps by the Tongs? Was it suicide? Was he *really* a Chinaman – or was he a Scotsman, a Yorkshireman, a Lancastrian, an American, or *who* was he? The Sax Rohmers, with their many personal connections in the world of showbusiness, probably knew Chung Ling Soo. They would certainly have known *of* him.

One thing is for sure, though: Fu Manchu was born in the Edwardian music hall. He is an indestructible pantomime villain, complete with impossible Chinese name: 'Manchu' is not a surname but the name of a people and dynasty; 'Fu' means many things, including 'radiant' or 'eternal', and in Chinese it would be written last. As author Leslie Charteris was to write – and he should know since he was part-Chinese himself – '"Fu Manchu" is impossible to duplicate in Chinese'. Fu Manchu has a performing marmoset on his shoulder, a long plain yellow silken robe, close-shaven skull, 'muffled gong' to signal his arrival and surreal sense of the dramatic. He claps his hands when the next 'act' is to appear. He uses trapdoors and elaborate magic tricks. In the *Si-Fan Mysteries*, for example, in the house of hashish next to the Café de l'Egypte near Frith Street in Soho, he makes a characteristically theatrical entrance:

> . . . a trapdoor, which was slowly rising, inch by inch . . . inch by inch . . .
> the head appearing in the opening . . .
> 'By God! It's Dr Fu-Manchu!'

Fu Manchu is surrounded by curtains and tapestries with golden dragons embroidered onto them. He is a master of illusion, disguise, makeup and the quick-change routine, and a first-rate escapologist. Like Chung Ling Soo, he can DEFY THE BULLETS, which he does at the end of several stories. He is often associated with old-time magic and the occult. He uses as his assistants a small army of dacoits, Thugs and zombies. His props include an arsenal of rare poisons in bubbling glassware, rare fungi and bacilli, exotic brightly coloured insects with lots of legs ('my deadly ministers'), and such fiendish torture devices as 'The Zayat Kiss', 'The Coughing Horror' or 'The Cat with

Poisoned Claws', which he likes to present in detail to the victim (and the reader) in advance – just like producing a goldfish bowl from under a robe, or sawing a body in half.

Sax Rohmer's other villains are just as colourful, and just as theatrical. Yu'an Hee See (alias Mr King, also known as 'The White Slaver') from *Yu'an Hee See Laughs* (1932) speaks in a falsetto voice, and when he laughs he sounds like a squeaking bat: this is because his throat has been shot away. His speciality is commandeering U-boats, to assist in his own personal variations on the *Lusitania* disaster. Sin-Sin Wa (*Dope*) is ostensibly a one-eyed Chinaman, with a one-eyed talking raven perched permanently on his shoulder. In fact, of course, Sin-Sin has two eyes: he is just trying to fool the police. Mr de Trepniak (*Grey Face*, 1924) is a red-haired albino, with a face 'like Nero' and a pathological fear of death; he refuses to possess any object which will outlast him. In these and other cases, Rohmer piles on the bizarre characteristics with surreal abandon. His Chinese villains are visually distinctive, difficult to take seriously – and at the end of their stories, the supporting acts are always caught by the police, but the star turn manages to escape by the stage door.

Fu Manchu's exploits, like those of his compatriots, are described in a pedantic style, complete with lengthy and over-written parentheses, which was evidently learned during Rohmer's apprentice years working for Robey, Tich and others. George Robey's stage act, as we've seen, was famous for its pompous use of euphemism, as was Tich's:

. . . a coarsening of the auricular appendage. In other words, a thick ear (Robey)

. . . a thick voice inquired, brutally, why the sanguinary hell he had had his blood-stained slumbers disturbed in this gay manner, and who was the vermilion blighter responsible (Rohmer: *The Yellow Claw*)

. . . and said I might expeditiously migrate, in other words, buzz off (Robey)

Thrice to redouble the lure of My Lady Nicotine would be but loosely to estimate the seductiveness of the Spirit of the Poppy (Rohmer: *Dope*)

Watching George Robey and Tich – as well as earning a modest living by writing for them both – seems to have had a permanent effect on Sax Rohmer's prose style and indeed on his attitude to the mystery story. 'It is me – or rather it is I!' says Nayland Smith in a particularly tense scene, during a Fu Manchu story. He used archaic 'poetic' words, or compressed his sentences – as if composing a lyric to fit the tune – in both genres: examples from the early Fu Manchu novels (among many) include nights which are 'beetlesque', music which is 'luresome', shadows 'cloisteresque', a room 'prosy', a narrator 'palsied by horror', a villain who 'shadowly raised his hand', a place where 'the Thames tided slumberously seaward' or where 'the reach was lonely of rowers', a mansion 'which now sufficed Lord Southey' and a spot of 'intertwining serpentinely'. His convoluted style and pompous phrasing – never using a single adjective when two will do – read at times like a George Robey routine, with an auto-didactic straining for effect.

Above all, the Fu Manchu novels have their spiritual home in the 'air and sentiment' of the music halls. Economist J. A. Hobson famously wrote in 1901:

> [The music hall] is the only 'popular' art of the present day, its words and melodies pass by quick magic from the Empire or the Alhambra over the length and breadth of the land, re-echoed in a thousand provincial halls, clubs and drinking saloons, until the remotest village is familiar with air and sentiment. By such a process of artistic suggestion the fervour of Jingoism has been widely fed . . .

Hobson was writing about the Boer War (1899–1902). In the ensuing years, others wrote of the halls as 'the only popular art of the day' – strongly reflecting and even enhancing Imperial attitudes: some (such as the humourist Max Beerbohm) thought this was amusing; others (such as the socialist H. M. Hyndman) thought such 'rampant chauvinism' was dangerous; others still sensed a conspiracy among songwriters, singers and managers to put over Tory ideas. All were agreed that the halls were a crucible of popular attitudes, and that in the Edwardian period 'the fervour of Jingoism' – carried by 'quick magic' – became less defensive, more offensive. Even in the make-believe, glittering world of 'oriental' musical comedy, Imperial villains became externalized on the stage, to be jeered at and diminished. Chinese good guys became good by becoming British.

The same kind of 'quick magic' operated with the Fu Manchu novels. It is clear from the narrator Dr Petrie's descriptions of the devil doctor that he has no facial hair: 'He wore a plain yellow robe, of a hue almost identical with that of his smooth, hairless countenance'; 'I looked up at his face – his wicked hairless face'. And yet filmmakers – and successive generations of readers – invented a pantomime-length moustache for him, to the point where a 'Fu Manchu moustache' is one of the books' most lasting legacies. The moustache is never once mentioned in the novels. It is as if in embellishing and re-echoing their favourite villain, readers have 'completed' his pantomime credentials.

In his novel *The Yellow Claw*, Rohmer described how the dishonest butler Soames (whose 'failing courage' has been 'somewhat restored by a second Scottish stimulant' in a public house), having been released by his Chinese captors from a Limehouse opium den – 'the catacombs of Ho-Pin' – for an hour or two, wanders into 'a brilliantly lighted music-hall', where he samples 'the first house . . . in a plush-covered tip-up seat in the back row of the stalls'. Rohmer's description is unusually precise:

> The programme was not of sufficient interest wholly to distract his mind, and during the performance of a very tragic comedian, Soames found his thoughts wandering far from the stage. . . . The comedian finished, and the orchestra noisily chorded him off. . . . The new performer, number seven on the programme, proved to be a speciality dancer, and all the lights were lowered in the front of the house in order to allow for lime effects. . . . Should he avail himself of this darkness to make his escape? . . . The dance proceeded, terminated, and was followed by a second. The fascination of the lady's performance consisted in the problem which she set her audience: at the present rate of disrobing, how many more dances could she perform without incurring official interference?

And Rohmer did include the occasional theatrical in-joke in his Fu Manchu stories. In the second collection, *The Devil Doctor*, Dr Petrie – on his way to Cragmire Tower near Glastonbury – suddenly remembers the words of a song about a Fen-Man:

> *Far from all brother man, in the weird of the fen,*
> *With God's creatures I bide, 'mid the birds that I ken . . .*

Although he did not say so, the words are from one of Sax Rohmer's own songs.

Arthur Greening, himself an ex-music-hall entertainer, published Rohmer's first two books of showbusiness anecdotes, as follow-ups to *Dan*

Leno: Hys Booke, which Greening had published in 1899. Greening's greatest publishing success was Baroness Orczy's *The Scarlet Pimpernel*, which came out in January 1905. His business was based for a time in Cecil Court off Charing Cross Road, then a centre of the fledgling British film industry – known in the trade as 'flicker alley'. It was George Robey who first introduced Rohmer to him. And it was the same Arthur Greening – with his publishing list divided into music-hall tie-ins and adventure novels – who immediately spotted the potential of the first Fu Manchu stories, and helped to find a publisher for them, his own company having failed. Sax Rohmer later recalled:

> We used to return by train [from Greening's office] and head for a coffee stall just outside the station [in West Dulwich]. After sausage and mash and a cup of 'dirty', we would feel so monstrously renewed that almost invariably we would find ourselves in my study [in Herne Hill] – where we would often remain until daylight was not far off. It was one of these nights, or rather mornings that . . . I recalled the existence of an unfinished manuscript . . . and read it to the publisher.

CHAPTER FOUR

'A Little Amusement . . .'

S hortly after leaving school, in his late teens, the young Arthur Ward – presumably obeying his father's wishes – worked as a bank clerk in the City of London. He never revealed which bank it was, but Elizabeth Sax Rohmer was certain that 'one of his fellow employees was the future humourist P. G. Wodehouse' – in which case, it was the Hong Kong and Shanghai Bank at 31 Lombard Street, some time between 1900 and 1903. Wodehouse certainly did work as a junior clerk at the HKSB between July 1900 and September 1902, and later wrote that he was 'the most inefficient clerk whose trouser seat ever polished the surface of a high stool'. Both would have had to wear to work a frock coat, wing collar and bowler hat; they would have sat at a high desk, balancing ledgers by hand with pen and ink, and their lives would have been expected to resemble that of Mr Pooter, the diarist of a Nobody, in the late 1880s. Unlike Mr Pooter, though, Wodehouse was recorded as late for work on twenty days in 1900, a figure exceeded only by two of his fifty-six contemporaries. Was Arthur Ward one of them? Impossible to say, for a trawl through the archives of today's HKSB has yielded no reference to a Ward or a Furey (his mother's maiden name) working there at the time.

Perhaps Arthur Ward was not recorded because of the short period he worked for the bank, or because of the very junior position he held? In any case, Ward never used his bank experience as material for his later fiction – although he certainly did use Hong Kong and China. All he ever said about it was that his daily ledger duties bore no relationship with either reason or reality, that he devised a foolproof method of robbing the vaults – which he tested one day after hours by hypnotizing a 'foxy-looking' bank messenger with protruding eyes named Gedge – and that 'the customers were nearly all stockbrokers'.

By all accounts, Wodehouse behaved like an overgrown public schoolboy at this time, doodling on his ledgers and generally playing pranks. Ward – as the son of a clerk rather than of a Hong Kong magistrate – would have had to express his boredom in less privileged ways. But both young clerks dreamed of becoming professional writers. Neither had the ambition to serve for two years at the London headquarters, then off to the Far East as maybe an assistant manager if they were lucky. In 1908, Wodehouse fictionalized the bank as the 'New Asiatic Bank' in his serial *The New Fold* (which became an early book about his monocled dandy, *Psmith in the City*, 1910): the hero of *The New Fold*, Mike Jackson, spends his working hours 'reading a surreptitious novel behind a plate of ledgers'. 'Surreptitious reading' probably describes Arthur Ward as well – though the books, in his case, would have had a more pop-occult flavour.

While working at the bank, both clerks would send off articles, jokes and stories to the small-print penny weeklies such as *Tit-Bits* and *Answers* and especially the London evening paper *The Globe*, which would recycle news from the day before, in the form of snippets, funny columns, diary entries and 'odds and ends', most of these printed under an anonymous byline. Also 'turnovers', which were short pieces beginning with an eye-catching headline and column on the front page, followed by a continuation on an inside page. Wodehouse was later to call them 'thousand-word articles of unparalleled dullness. You dug these out of reference books and got a guinea for them.' He reckoned that he published 'some 62 articles, jokes and stories' during his time as a clerk at HKSB, mainly written in the evenings. His literary career began with 'fifteen shillings from one periodical for "Men Who Have Missed Their Own Weddings" and later a guinea from the same magazine for "Single Day Marriages"': both appeared in *Tit-Bits*, the first on 21 November 1900. The penny weeklies, together with an assortment of fiction magazines such as *Pearson's* and *The Strand*, were part of the huge expansion of print journalism for urban readers and commuters which had begun in the late nineteenth century: the aspiring, salary-earning middle class, who believed in self-help and wanted some light reading. Rohmer wrote of this period in his life:

> I believe [P. G. Wodehouse] was contributing humorous material to *The Globe*, and I was doing 'Turnovers' for the same paper. It would be interesting to know the names of those who contributed to the old *Globe*. The first original piece of mine to be printed was a *Globe* 'turnover'.

That would have been before the end of November 1903, when he had his first short story accepted.

Wodehouse also sent off short stories to the weeklies, and even managed to write a full-length novel during his second year at the bank. He could, he recalled, 'have papered the walls of a good-sized banqueting hall' with rejection slips. Interestingly, Ward said much the same thing, in suspiciously similar language: he claimed to have papered an entire wall of his bedroom with multi-coloured rejection slips. Did the two junior clerks perhaps discuss and joke about their literary ambitions? Wodehouse left the bank on 9 September 1902, when he was already earning as much from his writing as from his clerical salary. Within ten weeks he was employed on the staff of *The Globe*, where he had previously freelanced. Ward left a year later, when he had no other regular source of income. It had, apparently, been 'quietly suggested' to him that he leave the bank's employ. Clerical work clearly did not suit his daydreaming temperament and 'intense distaste for banking'. For a time, he kept up the pretence to his father that he still had a steady job at the bank. Then, after a stint as clerk in a gas company, he became a journalist proper on the weekly *Commercial Intelligence*. For once, *his* family connections proved useful to him: 'My mother's family', he recalled, 'were friends with T. P. O'Connor, the famous Irish editor, who opened the way for me in journalism.' T.P. was MP for the Liverpool Scotland constituency, an Irish nationalist who had founded the *Star* and the *Sun* newspapers. Rohmer was to remember 'his rich brogue uttering words of worldly wisdom' and called him 'my old friend T. P. O'Connor [who] was my guide, philosopher and friend in those disturbed days'.

After his brief tenure at *Commercial Intelligence*, at the same time as he was writing lyrics for music-hall performers, we know that Ward/Rohmer was contributing anonymously to the weeklies *Tit-Bits* and *Answers* as well as to *The Globe* – while he was a 'free lance' and up to the beginning of the Great War, when he volunteered for the Artists' Rifles. *Tit-Bits* and *Answers* provide intriguing insights into the world of popular journalism he inhabited while he was honing his craft – and into the attitudes of his readers. *Tit-Bits*, published every Thursday for Saturday, price one penny, had been founded by George Newnes – his first publication – in October 1881 to give, as he put it, 'wholesome and harmless entertainment to crowds of hardworking people, craving for a little fun and amusement. It is quite humble and unpretentious.' One of its early regular contributors was Alfred Harmsworth (later Lord

Northcliffe), who in 1888 entered newspaper publishing by launching a direct competitor in a very similar format, but with more contributions from readers, called *Answers*. This was the start of his empire, which by 1894 included the *Daily Mail*. *Tit-Bits* was aimed squarely at readers who did not have much time to read: 'it is impossible', said its first editorial, 'to even glance at any large number of the immense variety of books and papers which have gone on accumulating', and it would be the business of *Tit-Bits* 'to find out from this immense field of literature the best things that have been said or written, and weekly to place them before the public for one penny'. It claimed to sell between 400,000 and 600,000 copies a week, on average, during Newnes's time as editor (1881–1910). Kate Jackson, the magazine's historian, has neatly summarized its miscellaneous contents:

> A sixteen-page patchwork of advice, humorous anecdotes, romantic fiction, statistical information, historical explanation, advertisement, legal detail, quips and queries, and reader correspondence. Competitions were a central feature. . . . It could be argued that *Tit-Bits* had closer connections with music hall entertainment than with the more structured environment of the nineteenth century theatre. Mr Newnes fine-tuned his individual act, he resembled one of the great entertainers of the variety style of entertainment . . .

Newnes moved up the social scale, a little, in January 1891 by launching the very successful *Strand Magazine*, which was also advertised extensively in *Tit-Bits*: its first issue sold 300,000 copies. He responded directly to the naysayers among London's cultural elite:

> Oh, you may call it cheap journalism; you may say it combined lottery with literature, but I will tell you this, that it guided an enormous class of superficial readers, who craved for light reading, and would have read so-called sporting papers if they had not read *Tit-Bits*, into a wholesome vein which may have led them to higher forms of literature.

'Wholesome' is an interesting word to use, in this context. It is worth looking in more detail at some of the 'light reading' supplied by *Tit-Bits* – especially in Sax Rohmer's areas of interest – during the time he contributed to it.

Tit-Bits of 1910 featured 'a great humorous serial by P. G. Wodehouse' – *The Intrusion of Jimmy* (also called *A Gentleman of Leisure*) – from June onwards. Highlights of the year included The Great Japanese Exhibition which opened at the White City in West London in May. There was a series of articles about 'the oriental splendour of its stalls and stands' and the 'twelve large tableaux reproducing the principal events in the history of our ally' which

> forcibly remind one that fifty years ago Japan was an isolated country having little intercourse with the outside world – then she determined to throw open her doors and adopt Western Civilisation . . .

The Formosa Village exhibit, 'inhabited by aborigines from this island, and who a few years ago were head-hunters', just went to show how far Japan had progressed. These aboriginal inhabitants, called the Ainu, proved a big attraction. They were noted for their unusual hirsute growth. Wodehouse referred to them as 'Hairy Ainus'. Then there were the 180 'crack jugglers, magicians and dancers of Japan [who] have taken up their abode at the White City'. One of the magicians delighted the audience by 'making live birds and chickens appear in the most extraordinary places'. It was Japanese people as *display*, and the more exotic the better. Articles on 'Dr Jekylls in real life – odd cases of dual personality' and 'Curious blood tonics in Northern China . . . made of tiger bones ground to a powder and mixed with Chinese wine' shared the crowded column inches with 'the Peckham coon':

> A young gentleman from Peckham, in a minstrel suit and a face that appeared to have been rubbed in a pickle jar, appeared and began to sing in his quavering voice, until the audience could hold their sides no longer.

New developments in 'the cinematograph' were regularly noted throughout the year: 'a perambulatory fiction palace on wheels'; 'my first animated picture by an actor'; 'producing picture plays'. An extract from the memoirs of Mr Maspero, the great French archaeologist, described how he once tried to pass an ancient Egyptian mummy through the French Customs: in the end, after much head-scratching, they apparently classified it as 'dried fish'.

In July 1910 there was the 1,500th issue, with a special cover, including tributes from Conan Doyle, Rudyard Kipling and J. M. Barrie. 'The Adventure of the Speckled Band' (1892), a reissued Sherlock Holmes story, was featured over two weeks to coincide with 'the play [version] now at the Adelphi Theatre', together with 'Humorous Suggestions in Murder Mysteries': the suggestions included photographing the victim's eyes at the moment of death to reveal the identity of the murderer; dreams which could guide the police to the scene of the crime; and handwriting to reveal hidden aspects of a villain's character. 'The Speckled Band' was followed in September by another Sherlock Holmes story, 'Silver Blaze' (1892). September also saw the headline 'My Three Best Stories: George Robey Confesses to a Particular Weakness for the Following Yarns', one of them being about a 'shipwrecked Hebrew' who, when a sail is at last sighted, complains that he 'hasn't got no [sales] catalogue' with him: this was the start of a series featuring selections of jokes by well-known music-hall comedians. The year finished, on New Year's Eve, with a long two-column exposé of 'Drug Maniacs in Society: Amazing Revelations of a West-End Clubman':

> Public attention has again been directed to the growth of the drug habit, not only among people in society, but among the middle classes as well . . . for the professional man, morphia is the common prescription; the actor likes cocaine; the soldier tries strychnia or atropine; while many women take chlorodyne . . .

The article then turned its attention towards opium:

> Opium has many devotees in East London, and other parts of the country. It is sometimes openly sold in shops, but hundreds of people use it without knowing. It is compounded in advertised specifics [even for children] which are warranted to cure various ills, and by its alluring properties gains a hold on the purchaser, who desires never to be without it.

In fact, *Tit-Bits* had ushered in 1910 with an unsigned article headlined 'The Opium Dens of London'. Mrs Elizabeth Sax Rohmer thought that Sax's article on 'the Asiatic colony' in Chinatown and the mysterious 'Mr King' might have been commissioned by 'a magazine editor' in early 1911, and that he might have returned to the location that autumn. The *Tit-Bits* article was dated 1 January 1910 – there is nothing in the magazine for 1911 on this theme. So the commission, or the visit, could well have happened in late 1909 rather than 1911. 'The practice of opium-smoking', began the article melodramatically, 'is on the increase in London', and in response to this the London County Council had recently taken powers under new regulations to revoke a lodging-house's licence if the 'house in question was used as an opium-den':

The Chinese always have smoked opium, and probably always will. They are inured to it by heredity, but when white men abuse the poppy goddess the results are serious.

What had hastened the LCC's action was the fact 'that a certain class of criminal is now frequenting the Chinese lodging-houses in Limehouse'. Professional syndicates, and even the Chicago 'mob', had recently moved in on the turf:

Practically every American criminal known to the police either sends to Limehouse for his opium or smokes in one or two 'joints' in that district.

In the absence of any hard evidence to support this – apart from the opinions of the head of the detective department in New York City; one of the criminologist Cesare Lombroso's disciples in Italy; and the chaplain of San Quentin Prison in California: these three generalized as 'every authority on criminology' – the article then outlined exactly what was involved in the business of opium-smoking.

A good pipe costs from £3 to £5. The lay-out, consisting of a tray, little dishes, sponges, an oil lamp, and yen-hoks or elaborated darning needles, costs £1 more, so the opium habit is expensive.

After explaining about the extraction, cooking and smoking of the drug, the final paragraphs focus on the question of addiction:

... the smoker inhales the smoke, usually swallowing most of it, then cooks another pill, or, as they say in India, makes another tackey. To acquire a regular habit a man must smoke consistently for three months. Opium does not induce immediate sleep, as has been so often stated. On the contrary, it buoys up the smoker for a certain time ...

'The Opium Dens of London' seems to contain several giveaway 'Sax Rohmer' characteristics: the assertion as undisputed fact that 'the Chinese always have smoked opium'; the reference to 'the poppy goddess'; the rhetorical announcement that the mob has moved in – with prestigious names, or rather 'every authority on criminology' to 'prove' it; the very detailed account of how to smoke opium, including prices, which suggests inside knowledge – as well as padding the article out to the required word length. It has to be said, though, that these tricks were by no means exclusive to Sax Rohmer! But this piece *could* have been the occasion for Rohmer's visit as a researcher to Limehouse, and for his consequent interest in Chinatown – in fact, the start of his successful career as a novelist. If it was, then his interest in Chinatown and Chinese characters dates originally from late 1909 – the commission – with a return visit in 1910 rather than 1911. He had much longer to reflect on Fu Manchu, and have his manuscript stories ready for Greening, than his widow remembered.

Tit-Bits for early 1911 was full of reactions to the 'Houndsditch Murders', which had taken place in the eastern fringe of the City of London on 16 December 1910 – when two police sergeants and a constable had been shot during a bungled raid on a jeweller's shop at 119 Houndsditch – and the subsequent Siege of Sidney Street, in Stepney fifteen minutes away, on 2 and 3 January 1911, when a group of exiled Latvian anarchists – desperate to raise funds in their struggle against the Tsar of Russia, and possibly with connections to the Bolsheviks – were besieged by 200 police officers who had surrounded the area, supported by Scots Guards from the Tower of London under the personal direction of the Home Secretary Winston Churchill clutching his Purdey shotgun. When the house eventually caught fire, Churchill had prevented four men from entering the cordoned-off area and putting it out: 'I thought it better to let the house burn than spend good British lives in rescuing those ferocious rascals.' Most of the survivors were acquitted, and all the blame was attached to the dead anarchists. But there were shock-horror headlines about foreign anarchists and revolutionists on the streets of London, and calls for tighter restrictions on immigration.

Tit-Bits also began the year with a series of articles about 'a mysterious murder on Clapham Common'. In the early hours of New Year's Day, according to *The Globe*, 'a foreigner, apparently a Jew', had been found dead 'with his head battered in': in his pocket was an address off Commercial Road in Stepney. 'The police investigations soon shifted from Clapham to the East End,' and direct connections were being made with the anarchists of Sidney Street and the 'Houndsditch Murders'. 'Anarchist Terror', screamed the *Globe* headline. 'The Clapham Murderer, Link with Houndsditch and Stepney?' Could the victim have been some kind of Polish spy? Or something even more sinister. The most mysterious aspect of the case was the markings on his cheeks, like a letter 'S' or a 'Z': 'That they were intended as a deliberate design is agreed by all who have seen them. What was their meaning?' In the same issue of

The Globe, 11 January 1911, it was reported that mainland Chinese politics had become particularly tense: 'The masterful old woman who directed the affairs of the [Chinese] Empire is dead, and there is no longer any authority in the Forbidden City.' The main concern of *Tit-Bits* was how the Clapham Common murder raised questions about 'the secret societies of the Continent' and how they were operating in London. The mysterious 'S' mark on each cheek – 'a Sign of Four in real life' – could well be a reference to 'the oldest of all secret societies, the Chinese Tien Ti (or Hung) League whose members were numbered by the millions and scattered over the whole globe'. It was an established fact, a subsequent article stated, that 'in every other country where Celestials are settled, including our own', the secret symbol of the Triads was recognized by those in the know. So the murder on Clapham Common *could* have been the work of a *Chinese* secret society – a Tong, or something even more esoteric. Ward/Rohmer may well have registered this thought, or may even have worked on the story. His *Mystery of Dr Fu-Manchu*, the first book in the series, opens in a surgery on Clapham Common, his equivalent of Baker Street, and its sequel, *The Devil Doctor* opens with a fiendish attempt by a secret society to poison Nayland Smith with the aid of a cat in a tree – also on Clapham Common.

In *Tit-Bits*, such concerns seemed to chime with a more general article on 21 January – side by side with the Clapham murder coverage – headlined 'How Undesirables Enter England'. The answer was that they arrived clandestinely by ship without any permission, thus easily evading the Aliens Act.

> The ranks of Chinese residents in this country are steadily recruited in the same way. Of late years, many 'sailors' from the Celestial Empire have married English girls and settled in our large ports.

On arrival in England, 'laundries "run" by their compatriots absorb some of them'. Although,

> Six or seven years ago, an attempt was made to establish Chinese laundries in London, with the result that the promoters got such a fright from hostile crowds that the enterprise faded away . . .

This again was a Tit-Bit probably gleaned from *The Globe*, which on 6 January had summarized newspaper coverage of the Clapham murder by linking it with 'The Aliens Act of 1905: Loopholes for Anarchists'. It was *Tit-Bits*, though, which effortlessly moved from Latvian or Polish anarchists to *Chinese* immigrants. A week later, it was further reported that in 'certain districts of Liverpool' where 'foreigners – mostly Chinamen – have settled down to carry on certain nefarious practices', policemen have to use 'considerable heaviness' dealing with them because the aliens have no hesitation in 'using a knife when cornered'.

Surprisingly, *Tit-Bits* did not run with *The Globe*'s story of 24 January, which had Sir Arthur Conan Doyle, 'the most famous detective novelist in the world', being requested by Scotland Yard to assist the police in 'tracking down criminals in the East End of London'. Or with the very characteristic headline of 28 January: 'The Plague in China: Great Loss to Europeans'. Then, in February's *Tit-Bits*, yet another speculation about the murder on Clapham Common shared the page with a piece about 'the curse of the Meux mummy': this ancient corpse (2,250 years old) had been generously bequeathed to the British Museum by Lady Meux, but 'does not seem to be able to rest completely unless he is doing somebody a bad turn' – including several members of the benefactress's family, who came to sticky ends. 'Now some people are wondering', the article concluded with a certain logic, 'what is going to happen to the Director of the British Museum if they accept the bequest.' The 11 March issue contained a large advertisement for 'The Sherlock Holmes Reminiscence' 'The Adventure of the Red Circle' in the latest issue of its sister publication *The Strand Magazine*. This advertisement cleverly played to readers' prejudices, while relating them to recent events in Houndsditch and Sidney Street:

> People imagine that the mysteries of London, the shadows of a great city which are sometimes never lifted, only happen in the East End and in the dubious districts of Soho. The recent Houndsditch tragedy goes to prove this. But the characters who played out this strangely sinister drama frequented every part of London . . .

So, readers could not reassure themselves that dark mysteries only happened *over there*, among the people of the abyss, who were not likely to subscribe to *Tit-Bits*: they also happened in the West End and even in commuter territory, the suburbs.

A week later, on 18 March, there was a leading article on 'Character Reading from Foreheads and Eyes', which compared Bismarck and the mandarin Li Hung Chang from a phrenological point of view. Li, who had died in

1901, was one of the leading Chinese statesmen of the late Manchu Empire – well known in British diplomatic circles, and in the press. He had worked with General 'Chinese' Gordon to quash the Taiping Rebellion. In 1896, he had toured the capital cities of Europe, with much pomp and ceremony: in London, he had ridden through the West End on Bank Holiday Monday, in an elaborate coach, wearing a senior mandarin's yellow jacket, and laid a wreath on Gordon's tomb in St Paul's. In many ways, he was more highly regarded in Britain than back home in China, and he influenced the depiction of mandarins in popular fiction. The article explored 'genius for intrigue': it was, apparently, something to do with the two characters' 'eye-brows that project so sharply as to cause the hair of the brows to bristle outwards'. One conclusion was that 'green eyes, though often fascinating, are dangerous, for they are the tokens of deceit and coquetry'. Fu Manchu was, of course, to have cat-green eyes.

The issue for 18 April included George Robey on the joys of collecting old china and studying Egyptian antiquities, and the particular fun he had performing 'my Shakespeare skit'. This piece could also have been written by Rohmer, as could a subsequent profile of Little Tich (5 August). Rohmer's Little Tich book had recently been issued, and here was an opportunity to promote it. Further reprinted adventures of Sherlock Holmes, throughout the year, competed for the readers' attention with 'White Slavery in Tea Shops: Girls Working Sixteen Hours a Day for Ten Shillings a Week', all to present a cosy picture of 'Merrie England', and some real-life 'Locked Room Mysteries'. In the issue for 21 October, an essay on 'The Real Sherlock Holmes – Sir Joseph Bell' was printed side by side with 'Making Pets of Spiders': many famous people, including Beethoven and Paganini – readers might care to note – had 'formed real friendships with spiders'. So maybe the creatures were not so frightening after all. Sax Rohmer later claimed 'the honour of having popularized venomous insects as instruments of villainy' and prided himself on having once made the acquaintance, in Panama, of

> a gigantic black spider – its body was the size of a hen's egg, and its legs nearly of the thickness of a man's fingers and . . . it fell with an audible plop.

But the scoop of the autumn appeared in the 26 October issue, when 'a Tit-Bits Man' somehow managed to gain an exclusive interview with Dr Sun Yat Sen, 'leader of the Chinese Revolution', on one of his visits to London.

The article began by reminding readers about the dramatic daylight kidnapping of Sun Yat Sen by members of the Chinese Legation, representing the Manchu dynasty, and forced imprisonment in 49–51 Portland Place for eleven days in October 1896. The plan had apparently been either to poison him, or to 'convey him home as a dangerous lunatic . . . to be beheaded without trial'. The kidnapping had revealed just how far the Manchu net stretched overseas from China, and his release was effected only after the personal intervention of Foreign Secretary and Prime Minister Lord Salisbury. The newspaper headlines at the time – 'A Chinaman Kidnapped in London', 'Alleged Kidnapping at the Chinese Legation', 'Outrage in the Heart of Fashionable London' – had helped to turn Dr Sun into a global celebrity, and since then he had paid several secret visits to London, gathering sympathizers and money – despite a reward of £50,000 having been put on his head, dead or alive, by the Manchu regime.

The interview takes place – secretly – in an old set of chambers in Gray's Inn:

> It was difficult to imagine that this soft-spoken Chinaman, who dressed like a European, spoke excellent English, and indulged at times in humorous remarks, was the powerful revolutionary who swayed millions of his countrymen.

Dr Sun Yat Sen begins by explaining the purpose of the revolution of 1911, in terms which *Tit-Bits* readers would understand:

> We are fighting against the Manchu dynasty, which is thoroughly hated for its years of bad government and misrule. The number of Manchus is between half a million and a million. The Chinamen number 400,000,000 yet the Manchus get half the official posts of any value. . . . And there is no proper government in China. All is oppression, and corruption is universal.

He continues by describing how provincial governors extort money on their own account 'from the masses' as well as from rich people who are not favourably disposed towards them, or who lack influence at the Imperial court. They do this with the support of local magistrates. The victims are tortured for three days 'to confess the guilt they know not' and then they are beheaded – without appeal – and their property seized. 'Beheading saves prison expense, and effectively silences the accused.' The entire procedure is arbitrary, and deeply corrupt. The three days' torture is presented 'for the soothing of official conscience' as a chance for the prisoner to find witnesses to prove his innocence. In fact, the victim is not allowed any contact at all with the outside world.

> The tortures inflicted on the accused prisoner during the three days . . . are as brutal as the most horrible tortures ever known in the most barbaric ages. Every possible species of mechanical instrument for causing excruciating pain is brought into use. A favourite form of torture is to tie a man down near a heated stove and gradually roast him . . .

Do you wonder, asks Dr Sun, 'that bitter hatred of the dynasty and of the Imperial officials prevails in every province of the empire . . . ?' He hoped in conclusion that 'the Bible and education' would be the means by which the blessings of the rule of law – and the advantages of civilization – would be conveyed 'to our unhappy fellow-countrymen'. Dr Sun had apparently been baptized by missionaries in 1884. The personalization of the conflict – Dr Sun versus the evil Manchus – the reminder about the kidnapping on the streets of London, the gloating emphasis on elaborate tortures and the conclusion about 'the Bible' – all were characteristic of the *Tit-Bits* house-style. In one of the early Fu Manchu stories, Sax Rohmer has the devil doctor say to the eminent British brain surgeon who removes a bullet from his head: 'Virtually, Sir Baldwin, you stand in China; and in China we know how to exact obedience.' Actually, Sir Baldwin is standing in London. This was a direct reference to the sinister greeting Dr Sun said he received as he entered the Chinese Legation in Portland Place: 'Here is China for you; you are now in China.'

The *Tit-Bits* article was not a detailed analysis of the course of the 1911 revolution, and its relationship with the heavy-handed Western response to the 'Boxer uprising' of 1900. Nor was it a presentation of Dr Sun's three guiding principles of 'nationalism, democracy and the people's livelihood', and the development since 1896 of the 'Young China' movement. It was, instead, a genial conversation with a 'soft-spoken Chinaman, who dressed like a European', which played, through anecdotes, to the readers' preconceptions about the cruelty of the Manchu regime: Dr Sun was evidently keen to present himself as a peaceful reformer – 'the Bible and education' – rather than a violent revolutionary, and *Tit-Bits* was just as keen to present him as 'civilizing' his own government. This could prove a double-edged argument. At the time of the kidnapping, in October 1896, several newspapers – including the

Daily Mail, the *Sun* and the *Evening News* – had quoted the first verse of Bret Harte's 1870 poem 'Plain Language from Truthful James', or 'The Heathen Chinee', to express the lessons they drew from the incident:

> *Which I wish to remark –*
> *And my language is plain,*
> *That for ways that are dark,*
> *And for tricks that are vain,*
> *The heathen Chinee is peculiar –*
> *Which the same I would rise to explain.*

The *Sun* went on:

> There is no doubt about it. The story of Sun Yat Sen . . . is as brilliant a specimen of the ways and tricks of the Aborigines of the Celestial Empire as has been discussed since Bret Harte sang of the oriental card-player.

The poem, whatever its intentions, had become entangled in anti-Chinese rhetoric during the 1870s, and the phrase 'heathen Chinee' had taken on a life of its own. Just so the rhetoric about the Manchus in 1896, during the kidnapping and since. The popular newspapers had extended their criticism of the Manchu dynasty to the Chinese people as a whole. The publicity in 1896 certainly helped Dr Sun's cause, and turned him into a celebrity as well as an internationally respected statesman, but it also played to deeply rooted prejudice about 'the Chinese' in general. The interview could be read in a similar way.

As if to reinforce the point, this scoop was followed in *Tit-Bits* on 2 December by another major article on 'What I Think of the Chinese' by the Revd E. J. Hardy, late Chaplain to the Forces in Hong Kong. Since China was very much in the news, the editor evidently assumed his readers were ready for this. The article began at full throttle:

> Napoleon said that when China was moved the face of Europe would be changed. Yet, as the Chinese are naturally peaceful, we think that the Yellow Peril is a commercial one. The peril is that China will manufacture things cheaper than Europeans can and dismiss us from trade in the Far East. How can we, with our high standards of comfort, strikes, and unrest generally, compete with the Chinese, combining, as they do, the native industry of the most civilised people with the passive patience of

the North American Indians? ... With this, rather than with armies and navies, they will conquer.

The Revd Hardy went on to describe his perceptions of 'the Chinese', based on his experience as a chaplain and his reading: the 'Celestials' are, apparently, resourceful, polite, skilled at manual occupations, very industrious and patient; they enjoy making money and they are conservative by nature, 'which is why they have put up for so long with their wretched government'. On the less positive side, they put 'business before sentiment', they have a 'dread of change', they are cruel to animals and to suffering humans and they have a tendency to over-complicate their organizations – at national and local levels: 'even beggars and thieves have guilds'. Sometimes, on the surface, what appears to be politeness turns out to be the Chinese fear of 'ridicule and disgrace'. Where culture was concerned, 'One has only to watch their storytellers in the streets to see that the Chinese are natural orators. They are also very clever conjurors.'

Such generalized perceptions – not surprisingly – match those of the standard texts on the 'national character' of the Chinese which were available at the time, such as the popular and influential *Chinese Characteristics*, originally published in 1890 and often reprinted since, by Arthur H. Smith, 'twenty-two years a [Protestant] missionary of the American Board in China'. Smith's list of positive Chinese characteristics (as he saw them) was similar to the Revd Hardy's: 'the practice of politeness ... brought to a pitch of perfection', 'patience and perseverance', 'staying qualities', 'industry', 'conservatism', 'endurance of physical pain', 'absence of nerves'. The negatives, the other side of the coin, were also similar:

> There are two quite different aspects in which the politeness of the Chinese, and of oriental people in general, may be viewed: the one of appreciation, the other of criticism.

In *Chinese Characteristics*, the criticism predominated: there was 'superfluous ceremony' and 'face talk ... external decorum as a mere external veneer'; 'disregard of time ... to the foreigner "time is money" ... but in China everyone has an abundance of time, and very few have any money'; 'an attitude of procrastination'; 'an absence of public spirit among the people'; 'intellectual turbidity', 'a blind and obstinate adherence to the warp of the past'; 'an indifference to the sufferings of others which is probably not to be matched in any other civilized country'; 'an absolute and generally sanctioned licence in lying and dissimulation . . . ignoring, concealing and misrepresentation'; 'a chronic suspicion which prevails in China', embodied in the lofty walls around their cities and in the Great Wall around their country.

One problem, wrote Smith, was that 'many Chinese unconsciously adopt towards foreigners an air of amused interest, combined with depreciation'; this is because they find it particularly challenging *to learn the English language.* 'One never feels sure that one has been told the *whole* of anything.' This in turn led to an irritating, ever-present, uncertainty about whether one was dealing with deviousness or simple-mindedness: it had to be one of the two.

Smith constructed out of his 'characteristics' a series of prescriptions about how the West should best deal with 'the Chinese' in future: all of them (even the positives) subtly or not-so-subtly assumed the superiority of the West, and his list of 'defects' were ones which could be remedied by the spread of Protestantism and a different kind of work ethic. The Chinese were industrious and skilful, but they needed *Christian* guidance and through it an assurance – by 'irrefragable object lessons' – that 'foreigners are the sincere well-wishers of the Chinese'.

> What China needs is righteousness, and in order to attain it, it is absolutely necessary that she have a knowledge of God and a new conception of man, as well as of the relation of man to God. . . . The manifold needs of China we find, then, to be a single imperative need. It will be met permanently, completely, only by Christian civilisation.

Without this 'light of righteousness', the Chinese 'absence of nerves' could well have dire consequences for the West:

> What the bearing of this pregnant proposition may be on the future impact of this race with our own – an impact likely to be more violent as the years go by – one shall not venture to conjecture. We have come to believe, at least in general, in the survival of the most fit. Which is the best adapted to survive in the struggles of the twentieth century, the 'nervous' European, or the tireless, all-pervading, and phlegmatic Chinese?

A Christian China was much less frightening than the other kind. By the same token, if the modern-day 'impediments to population growth' were to be removed, the Chinese people would doubtless inhabit the earth:

If a people with such physical endowments as the Chinese were to be preserved from the effects of war, famines, pestilence, and opium, and if they were to pay some attention to the laws of physiology and of hygiene, and to be uniformly nourished with suitable food, there is some reason to think that they alone would be adequate to occupy the principal part of the planet and more.

In reply to the potential criticism that it was wrong to think of 'the Chinese' as an undifferentiated mass of people, and to make sweeping generalizations about them, Smith offered: 'The people and languages of India are many and various, while the people of China, with some exceptions not materially affecting the issue, are one and the same.'

The Revd Hardy, for his article for *Tit-Bits*, had evidently been reading and inwardly digesting his *Chinese Characteristics*. He had probably also studied the other standard, best-selling text of the time, J. Dyer Ball's *Things Chinese, Being Notes on Various Subjects Connected with China* (first edition 1892), which owed much to Smith. *Things Chinese* summed up the difference between East and West in one word, 'Topsy-turvydom' – 'back to front', or in today's terms, 'otherness'. Ball had been born in Canton in 1847, the son of a missionary doctor, and had become 'Protector of the Chinese in Hong Kong' for HM Civil Service. His book was intended, promisingly, as an antidote to the many 'books and pamphlets which, amidst interesting and sprightly narratives of stirring events, contain a mass of crude and undignified second-hand information of the people they scarcely know'. J. Dyer Ball knew better. *Things Chinese* was organized alphabetically from 'Abacus' to 'Zoology' – with the length of individual entries having more to do with the presumed interests of English-language readers than with an understanding of Chinese people and society: Opium (nine pages), Porcelain and Pottery (twenty-three pages), Secret Societies (thirteen pages), Silk (fourteen pages), Tea (thirteen pages), Trade (fourteen pages) – as compared with Astrology (fifteen lines), Confucius (two pages), Feng Shui (two pages), Philosophy (two pages), Woman, the Status of (four pages). Chinese people are referred to throughout by the generic name of 'John Chinaman', with the implication that they have no individual identities. How *can* one distinguish one Chinese from another? Ball asks. Think of 'the analogous case of a shepherd knowing each sheep under his care'. In any case, the Chinese tend to think *we* all look the same too: with red faces, tight clothes and too much facial hair.

Ball's tone of voice is that of a Victorian official, sitting in the armchair of his club after a good luncheon. Who are *we* to turn up our noses at 'hundred-year-old eggs' when we eat semi-putrid game birds? 'Geomancy' or 'Feng Shui' is briskly dismissed as 'this farrago of nonsense . . . these insane vapourings . . . this pseudo science'. And don't ever expect a traditional handshake: handshaking, in the Western sense, was fortunately 'not in vogue in China, as it would be extremely unpleasant to feel the long talons gripping one's hand'. Maybe more outdoor sports would be beneficial: under 'Sports', Ball advises:

> It would be a good day for the inhabitants of certain districts of China if sportsmen would follow the example of a few of their number and go tiger shooting.

Where the civil service entrance examinations were concerned, it was not unknown for Chinese candidates to *die from over-excitement*. The Manchu dynasty, which had 'occupied the throne of the whole of China' since 1644 but which had recently been showing signs of decay, was compared to 'the incursion of the Huns in Europe' and to their relations 'the Mongols under Genghis Khan': by continuing the tradition of calling the Manchu people 'Tartars', Ball created around them an aura of unpleasantness and aggression; he also argued that China itself was under alien control – one reason why the country tended to be so very obstructive.

Again, the good qualities of 'the Chinese people' included, for Ball, 'honour to parents', 'never-tiring industry', 'politeness – the prime virtue', 'honorifics', 'etiquette', benevolence, thrift, stoicism and placidity. These were more than cancelled out, though, by 'ancestor worship', 'a fatal want of veracity', treachery, cunning, lack of public spirit, corruption, distrustfulness, indifference to human life, incompetence in political economy and cluelessness with modern, as distinct from ancient, technology. The Chinese did not even have a recognizable religion of their own, such as 'Mohammedanism' (Islam) and Hinduism were: instead, they were prey to mumbo-jumbo such as geomancy and ancestor worship. 'Dislike of change' he was not sure whether to place among the positives or negatives. And where 'this mighty empire' was concerned, he veered between 'cowardly' and 'warlike'. 'What', he asked rhetorically under 'Riots', are the causes that turn 'the law-abiding Chinaman into a demon of destruction'? Such paradoxes were summed up in the key entry on 'Topsy-turvydom' (four pages): 'It is the unexpected that one must expect.'

There were also some entries which would have come as a surprise to readers of *Tit-Bits*. Under 'Mandarin', for example:

> ... with the rhythmic flow of the word and with its foreign flavour, a certain *soupçon* of the poetic and the mysterious is imported into it, so that the distant Westerner is apt, when reading about mandarins, to picture in his mind's eye some highly exalted and privileged class, the members of which are born to the purple, and dwell amidst all kinds of pleasure surrounded by affluence and luxury and ministered to by the poor down-trodden populace. A better appreciation of what mandarin means would doubtless have resulted had the terms used been 'officers of government', or 'civil and military officials'.

Or under 'Opium':

> When the liking of it began [in the mid-nineteenth century, beyond its ingestion 'for medicinal purposes'], the English, to their shame, be it said, continued to bring the fatal drug to administer to the depraved tastes of the Chinese, whose rulers made piteous attempts to prevent its intro-duction. And the feeling of dislike to the English and, through them, to the hated and despised foreigner in general, partially due to this cause, is not confined solely to the upper classes, as anyone may find who knows the language and mixes with the people; for it is not an infrequent ques-tion: *Why do you foreigners bring opium to China?* And the only reply that can be given is: 'There are bad people ... in any nation as well as good; and if you Chinese would not smoke it, they would not bring it.'

So the existence of 'Chinese opium dens in the United States and in London' was yet another paradox – returning to England 'the destructive vice of opium-smoking' which English traders had done so much to encourage on mainland China in the first place.

Ball, as an ex-civil servant of long standing, distanced himself from those popular writers who peddled 'second-hand information of the people they scarcely know'. And yet, both *Things Chinese* and *Chinese Characteristics* – and the Revd Hardy's article in *Tit-Bits* seemingly derived from them – were full of equally sweeping generalizations about 'national characteristics' or 'race' – the terms seemed almost interchangeable – often based on visual impres-sions rather than personal interactions. In fairness to Smith, at the beginning of *Chinese Characteristics* he cautioned against using the word 'Chinaman' which was already (by 1890) beginning to gain a derogatory connotation as an insult implying wiliness or artfulness. It had a contemptuous flavour to it, especially when abbreviated to 'Chink':

> It is a matter of surprise, and even more of regret, that this barbarous compound [Chinaman] seems to have rooted itself in the English language, to the exclusion of the proper word *Chinese*. We do not know a foreign periodical in China in which natives of that country are not constantly called 'Chinaman', nor of a single writer in the Empire who consistently avoids the use of the term.

But Smith, as we have seen (p. 203), was still fond of submerging any regional or individual differences into the single word 'Chinese' – and he, too, favoured the concept of inscrutable.

One root of the problem was that the sources of these endlessly repeated generalizations were the old China hands – from the Civil Service, Customs and Excise, the business community, the clergy and even the Missions – who tended while they were in China to keep themselves to themselves, sheltered in their settlements and protected by extra-territorial rights. For those who did not speak the language, there was no easy and informal way of getting to know Chinese society. But that was not about to stop them. Their big complaint was that the Chinese found it so challenging to *learn the English language*. Their 'fantasies' were the dominant way of writing about China in popular non-fiction – and thus is fiction – back home in the 1890s and 1900s. The article 'What I Think of the Chinese' simply distilled them for readers of *Tit-Bits* at a time when Chinese domestic politics was back in the headlines.

Tit-Bits finished 1911 with a Christmas parody of boys' adventure stories about the 'Boxer uprising' transposed to that year's revolution. Several of these stories had featured British boy-wonders who rescued Christians – European and 'native' – from their hiding-places in the basements of the Legations, and then carried important messages, in the nick of time, to the multinational relief expedition which was marching towards Peking. In G. A. Henty's work *With the Allies to Pekin*, the boy-wonder Rex Bateman also manages to dismantle two mortars and cope with an angry tiger – as well as the fanatical forces of 'the secret society' – on his eventful journey to the Allied army. These young heroes tended to be disguised – skin dyed with berries, fake pigtail and loose peasant clothing – to 'speak Chinese' and to have a friendship with a close 'native' companion.

The *Tit-Bits* Christmas parody was called 'How I Led the Chinese Rebels to Victory' – supposed to be written by 'All-round Arthur, the Boy-Bobs', an all-conquering Boy Hero, this time – like the Boxers – fighting *against* the Manchus. The yacht *Yellow Cloud*, flying the golden dragon, under Arthur's command defeats two Chinese battleships – with well-placed broadsides – and 'three days later I reached Hankow at the head of ten thousand rebels, faced by six times that number of royal troops'. Having routed the Manchu forces with ease, Arthur's rebel army then reaches the green pagoda of Hanking, which is packed with 200 tons of 'dragonite, the most powerful explosive known to Science' that has been attached 'with all the cunning of the Celestial mind' to a huge bell on the turret of the pagoda. Arthur manages to disconnect the mechanism connecting bell to explosives and cries to the rebels: 'On to Pekin. Another victory and the tyranny of ages is ended!'

But only 200 of his followers now remain: the rest have deserted. And they are surrounded by the royal troops. 'Twenty men against tens of thousands!' Finally, just two men and All-round Arthur are left . . . and the foe falter. Yet another bullet strikes him, to add to his many wounds. When he wakes to consciousness, he is given the good news in tremulous tones: 'You give muchee socks to Chinamen. Manchu monarchy bustee up.' Arthur's job has been done.

'How I Led the Chinese to Victory' sent up boys' fiction about the Boxers at the same time as celebrating it: the laughter was not directed at Arthur, his dash and daring and his mission on behalf of the British Empire, just at ludicrous penny-dreadful exaggerations and conventions. Actually, children's comics and magazines of the Edwardian period were in some ways very similar to this *Tit-Bits* parody. There were serials in *Chums*, the official journal of the Boy Scouts, and elsewhere about young heroes working for the Chinese Customs Service or on the high seas, helping to establish the legitimacy of British trading interests against secret societies, pirates or protection racketeers. The Manchu Empress Dowager in the early 1900s was often seen as the evil genius preventing the 'real' China from emerging, the decent one. Back home, the *Chums* 'Commissioner' – protected by a clergyman – experienced on behalf of readers the 'Terrors of the Opium Den' hidden behind the innocent -looking 'front' of a barbershop in the East End of London. In the weekly

Magnet, 'the Greyfriars Chinee' called Wun Lung arrived as a new boy in the Remove, complete with conjuring tricks, jiu-jitsu skills and eccentric dietary preferences ('What you tinkee of dogee?'): he doesn't understand the rules of cricket, is ineffective as a form captain (until helped by the Brits) and spends too much time with a mysterious Chinese sailor at the gates, who turns out to be an opium pusher. Wun Lung's uncle, an elderly mandarin, comes to rescue his nephew from the foreign devils, but in the end he sees the benefit of staying at Greyfriars and playing by the rules. Chinese 'master criminals' and wizard mandarins, with fiendish plots to undermine England – sometimes taking revenge on the 'barbarians' after the 'Boxer uprising' – began to outnumber other minority groups in boys' magazines at this time. Much later, some of the early Fu Manchu stories were to be serialized in *Chums* in 1923–25 'in response to requests from readers'. The *Girls' Own Annual* of 1909–10 help-fully distilled all these Edwardian tendencies for young readers into its own definition of the Yellow Peril:

> This enormous mass of humanity shows a marked tendency to spread out in all directions and overflow into the other countries of the world. It is this readiness of the Chinese to settle in the midst of other nations, and the evils which may follow in its train, which constitute 'the Yellow Peril'.

These were the kinds of story of which George Orwell later famously wrote that 'the year is 1910' – always 1910 somehow – and 'at the outposts of Empire the monocled Englishmen are holding the niggers at bay'.

Tit-Bits began 1912 with an advertisement for a boys' story published by Newnes called *Britain Invaded*, and a poem called 'Ten Little Manchus', after the then-popular nursery rhyme 'Ten Little Nigger Boys':

> *Ten little Manchus, going out to dine,*
> *Cook slipped the prussic, and then there were nine;*
> *Nine little Manchus, headed for a fête,*
> *Met a bunch of rebels, and then there were eight . . .*
> *Three little Manchus, in an awful stew –*
> *Boiling oil composed it – and then there were two;*
> *Two little Manchus, both upon the run,*
> *Couldn't reach the fortress, and then there was one;*

One little Manchu, age not far from nine,
Writing out a message, meaning 'I resign'.

The last couplet was a reference to the young Emperor Pu-Yi, who was in fact five years old at the time, but that would not have rhymed with 'resign'.

The contents of *Answers: The Popular Journal for Home and Train* in the same period were similar: Sexton Blake stories (instead of Sherlock Holmes); popular criminology (poison, drugs, how to read clues, locked-room mysteries, memoirs of prison warder X); reviews of recently published memoirs; articles about clever animal criminals such as the 'pickpocket monkey with spidery arms' and the trained snake; features by suffragettes and anti-suffragettes; predictions about German rearmament and shipbuilding and a possible forthcoming attack on England; warnings about 'the "moving" penny dreadfuls' at the Picture Palace and their dire effects on 'children and weak-minded people of all ages'; questions about 'Why Banks Fail – when speculation and peculation bring disaster . . . the bank that speculates is lost'; serialization of *The Invaders: A Story of the Coming War*. Plus some rib-tickling Chinese names, sent in by a reader from Melbourne, Australia:

> Ah Tack is a carpenter; Sam Ling is a fish-hawker; Ah Leek a vendor of vegetables; and Wah Sing a popular Chinese laundryman. Ah Tick's establishment has the prudent notice over the counter 'Cash on Delivery' . . .

To match *Tit-Bits*' 'What I Think of the Chinese', there had been in December 1908 'Queer Tales from China: A Few Startling Things about the "Flowery Land"'. It was unsigned.

> To the ordinary Briton, China is a land of contradictions and mysteries. It bristles with surprises. The phlegmatic nature of its natives is in marked contrast to their inherent cruelty.

There followed a long list of 'the refinements of torture', including:

> . . . the cage in which a man was placed so that his head protruded at the top, while his toes only touched the ground sufficiently to prevent dislocation of the neck. His hands were bound behind him, so that he could not relieve himself, and he was left to be jeered at by the public until hunger and exhaustion put an end to his sufferings.

Other 'refinements' included the bastinado – beating with a split bamboo – death by water-drops, being tied to a beam by the thumbs and big toes, and the 'cangue' or wooden stocks. Then came some comments about the innate conservatism of Chinese people: 'machinery for the most part is despised', 'the wheelbarrow' is still a passenger conveyance, and ferries usually consist of 'canoes towed by a number of swimmers'. Under the cross-head 'Providing for the Future', there was a detailed description of a Chinese funeral, with hired mourners, beggars and streetboys in outlandish costumes, and the burning of paper money at the grave – all of which appeared 'almost as a mockery to the visitor'. The conclusion to these 'Queer Tales' was that China is indeed a land of 'topsy-turvydom'.

> In a country where women are held so cheaply, it is a remarkable fact that for the last decade one of the sex – the late Dowager-Empress – was the predominant power in its destiny.

Like *Tit-Bits*, *Answers* covered 'the Jap-anglicans' at the White City Exhibition in May 1910. Even before the show opened, there were early reports of 'the band of wiry little almond-eyed men – the rank and file of the Japanese workmen' constructing the pavilions. Then, an interview about the English stage 'through the eyes of Udagawa, the Beerbohm Tree of Japan', which referred to 'the little brown men from the land of the Rising Sun'. Udagawa, it emerged, had much to learn from English theatre. Then, from 24 December 1910, a series called 'The East End after Dark: An Amazing Description of a Personal Visit to London's Crime Centre' by the Special Commissioner for *Answers*, accompanied by a guide who was billed as 'one of the worst criminals in the history of the metropolis' and who certainly knew his stuff. First, Whitechapel, scene of 'the unsolved Ripper murders', with revelations about Eastern European traders and street corner 'hooligans'. And then, on 31 December:

> We made for the Limehouse district and the payment of 5 shillings each secured us admission, without too many questions being asked, to a low opium den kept by a Chinaman. . . . The den into which we have penetrated is not one visited by the society woman seeking a new sensation, but an ordinary low den where they would have no compunction in robbing you of all you possessed, and then flinging you into the street to finish your drug-laden sleep.

The reeking atmosphere, continued the Special Commissioner, was nauseating, but there was undoubtedly 'an indefinable fascination, a luring, seductive something which one cannot explain'.

> . . . one of the Chinamen, with a smile that only the Celestial can assume, offered me a pipe which he had already prepared . . . I stretched out my hand to seize it. But my guide, with a lusty lunge, sent the Chinaman sprawling to the floor . . .

After this cliff-hanging end to the article and the year, the next article in the series, on 7 January, described what happened next:

> 'Quick,' said my guide, as the Chinaman . . . whom he had knocked down, showed signs of resenting the liberty. 'These folks are very clannish, and we shall be in the middle of a fight in no time.' There was no sign of excitement about him, but his eyes glinted dangerously He had the air and look of a man with a sublime confidence in his own powers. We hurried along a passage . . . wished the proprietor a civil 'good night' without referring to the occurrence upstairs, and regained the street.

The whole series consists of visits to shady places, described with lots of adjectives, where . . . nothing really happens. In this case, the only dramatic incident is caused by the journalist himself – the punching of the 'Chinaman'. The article is similar to the visits to opium dens in Sax Rohmer's fiction, with the lantern-jawed guide standing in for Nayland Smith. Maybe *this* was the article he was commissioned to research in Limehouse, rather than the *Tit-Bits* article of the previous January. December 1910 rather than January 1910. Or both. The attitudes to the Chinese inhabitants certainly bear a strong family resemblance.

In the wake of the Siege of Sidney Street, on 14 January and 21 January 1911 *Answers*, like *Tit-Bits*, covered 'The Aliens Act Farce: The Way the Wily Foreigner Wriggles into Britain' and related the Act to 'Aliens in London – the discovery of an arsenal for preparing bombs in Whitechapel. . . . Anarchist outrages planned . . . at "murder clubs"'. Then, on 28 January, its focus shifted from the East End of London to Cardiff, where 'only five months ago . . . there was as fine a fight as ever the heart of an Irishman could desire'. It involved two members of the Chinese community 'attacked by others of their countrymen', which led to forty further Chinese getting involved and then to a full-scale riot.

This was followed, in April, by a characteristically bizarre 'Chat from Across the Seas' about 'a place called the City of the Dead, in Canton', which consisted of 194 small houses with a corpse placed in each plus cardboard effigies of servants and 'two handsome paper females to guide the spirit on the way to heaven'. Then, following the piece about Cardiff, a series of three full-page articles headed 'China in England' by the *Answers* Special Commissioner – protected this time by 'the uncrowned queen among the Asiatics', a 'half-caste Chinese' called Mrs Emily Hoare who acts as a kind of 'consul for the Chinese community'. The first article promised readers 'revelations of life among the yellow men of Liverpool', which would 'read like the pages of a fascinating novel' and take them on a journey 'where no journalists have ever been before'. It begins:

> . . . a few minutes' walk from the great docks of Liverpool lies Chinatown, in the vicinity of Price Street, unquestionably the lowest quarter of the town where, in addition to the yellow men themselves, dwell, for brief periods, the scum of all nations.
>
> A zone of peril! And yet, on behalf of the hundreds of thousands of readers of *Answers*, I have just been through all this area of danger so that you might see exactly how the Chinamen, about whom there has recently been such an outcry, live.

The Special Commissioner's guide quickly proves invaluable:

> Her slightest word is law; her merest gesture a command which must be obeyed. Fearlessly she walks in the most dangerous quarters, and the uplifting of her hand will quell a riot in which the participants are men who would plunge a knife between another's shoulders without the slightest compunction.

The article then describes the celebration of the 'Chinese Good Friday' – 'strange-looking creatures, whose faces seemed to haunt one's dreams uncannily for nights afterwards, were moving to and fro' – and the ceremony of respect to the dead in Anfield Cemetery. Chinese funerals and burials seemed particularly fascinating to popular journalists at this time. Why had the intrepid *Answers* Commissioner 'come to be living among the Chinese of Liverpool'? It was because of a riot in Birkenhead which had taken place a short while before, following an allegation that a Chinese 'had proffered an insult to a white girl'. An infuriated mob had attacked Chinese homes with sticks, stones and bottles, and there had been a 'free fight which seems to have resembled the one I saw at Tonypandy during the Welsh coal strike riots'. One problem was that 'the number of Chinamen resident in Liverpool is probably two hundred . . . and there are only two Chinese women!'

The second article, on 13 May, starts with a rant about the Aliens Act of 1905 and how easy it is for a Chinese sailor to desert from a ship docking in Liverpool:

> In my wanderings to and fro, the centre of dozens of pairs of Chinese eyes, I saw white women with their half-caste babies, and I reflected sorrowfully that these infants must combine the worst vices of both nations. The poorer women who live in the slums which the Chinaman invades are in daily danger from morally degenerate yellow faces, but it is only fair to say that, so far as Liverpool is concerned, much of the trouble is caused by the local girls themselves, who behave in such a manner as to invite insult. That there is a remedy is apparent, and that remedy is to exclude the Chinese from British soil altogether.

But readers could rest assured that there is some hope. For those who settle, 'even if the yellow face is a blot on Liverpool, efforts are being made to reclaim him', in particular by the Christian Institute for Seamen on Paradise Street. The Commissioner then visits, with his guide, a boarding-house crammed full of sailors; the headquarters of the Tong-Yu-Tong and an informal opium room ('in front of one of the walls was a horrible-looking idol'); a grocery store and the house of a girl from Poplar who is very happily married to a Chinese: she concedes that 'when a Chinaman is cruel he doesn't go in for half measures', but adds that she has *never* had personal experience of this. Finally, in the third article, the writer catches sight of a man recovering from long bouts of opium-smoking – 'a Chinaman, whose face was as repulsive as anything I have seen in a long time'. He is having 'a paroxysm of terror'.

> Naturally, there was much in my visit to Liverpool that cannot be described in a paper like *Answers*. Some of the things I investigated ought to receive the attention of the police, and the city cleared of the large number of residents who make very considerable sums of money catering to the most vitiated tastes of the Oriental mind . . .

Again, nothing actually happens. Just rhetoric about race and gender, lots of adjectives and hints of melodrama and a rant about immigration. The assumption throughout is that the suburban readers of *Answers* will never venture into Chinatown to check for themselves. Everything is described as bizarre or sinister, stroking their prejudices. And yet, all the intrepid journalist really sees is a ceremony of respect for ancestors, a Christian Institute, a boarding-house, a mutual benefit society, a grocery store, a happily married couple ('for the statement of this young woman I can, of course, accept no responsibility') and a man suffering from a bad trip. Even the illustrations are humdrum: some chopsticks, a toothpick, some joss-sticks, a 'mystic' phial of liquid to clear the head, the store where they were purchased. Overlaid on this is an opinion-piece on the Aliens Act and how it ought to be tightened up. Plus some strong views about 'John Chinaman' and opium, and about impressionable young white working-class girls. Chinese immigration to Britain should be stopped; recreational opium-smoking should not be criminalized, though, so long as it was confined to Chinese people in Chinese ghettos: opium was not yet perceived by this Commissioner to be part of a 'drug problem'.

'China in England' was followed by a review article on 24 August on the question 'Is the Anglo-Saxon Race decaying – unpleasant facts which tend to prove that Britain has passed her prime'. It is centred on a new book called *Racial Decay* by the Irish-Australian Octavius Beale: a heady mix of a declining birth rate, too much self-flattery, decadent vices, idiocy in the young and assorted other evidences that Britain has been, over the past thirty years, 'mentally, morally and physically unsound to the core'. These have led to a 'rude awakening':

> In a few years it will be manifest to the world, as it is already to the greatest thinkers of all nations, that the British Empire cannot continue as an Anglo-Saxon organisation. Its dominion and power will have ceased.

Racial Decay was a contribution to the 'degeneration' debate which had been fashionable since the *fin de siècle*. Beale, a piano manufacturer, was a champion of the Australian anti-abortion lobby and a convinced racialist. Finally, at Christmas, the year 1911 finished as it began, with an article 'In the Underworld of London':

Space does not permit me to do more than briskly mention the Chinamen who keep opium dens in Limehouse; and the frequenters of swell West End gambling clubs.

Such was the background to Sax Rohmer's formation as a popular journalist, which he combined with his work as a lyricist for the music hall. The proprietor-editors of *Tit-Bits* and *Answers* prided themselves on knowing, and interacting with, their middle-class audience: competitions, correspondence columns, prizes, stories submitted by readers, insurance schemes, treasure hunts, advertising stunts, agony columns, cooperative philanthropy, legal and medical questions answered – all were intended to create and exploit the common interests of 'an enormous class of superficial readers' in inclusive ways which nevertheless excluded everyone else. A community of print. George Newnes claimed that

> *Tit-Bits* fed not on current political crises, but on *everyday life*. *Tit-Bits* thrives best when the world moves on smoothly, and when people have to seek amongst its pages for that interest which is denied to them on the perusal of commonplace current events.

The interpretation of 'everyday life' – and the means by which 'interest' was to be stimulated – were to be carried over, in exaggerated form, into Rohmer's novels. He knew fairly intimately his readers, and their attitudes, too.

The Edwardian era – notably the years from 1906 to 1912 – was a period of high anxiety about the Chinese in Britain and the rising dragon in the East. The anxieties took many forms. There was the fear of physical unfitness among the British population, the result among other pressures of urbanization and industrialization – leading, as we have seen, to 'racial degeneracy'. The 'science' of eugenics, derived from Social Darwinism, was very concerned about the relative capacities of different races. If 'Britain has passed her prime', what then? Admiral Lord Fisher, First Sea Lord, who as a boy had been a midshipman on the China Station, speculated:

> When by-and-by the Chinese know their power, they have only to walk slowly westwards, and, like the locusts in Egypt, no pharaohs in Europe with all their mighty boats will stop them. They won't wait to fire guns or bombs. They'll just all walk along and smother Europe.

In October 1900, a correspondent to *The Times* from the Conservative Junior Constitutional Club, Piccadilly, wrote of the dangers of colonies of Chinese 'silently forming and wakening in our very midst'. Such anxieties were inflamed by the territorial ambitions in China of Japan, Russia, Germany and France, and maybe even the United States. The British position was still, in Prime Minister and Foreign Secretary Lord Salisbury's words, 'no partition of territory . . . only a partition of preponderance'. But there could be a repeat of the scramble for Africa. The instability of the Manchu dynasty was an unpredictable factor in this. China lay outside the official 'family' of the Empire, so Britain was not responsible for her. Yet it was important, as far as possible, to maintain control of the China trade though the Treaty Ports and beyond. If the 'awakening giant' were to wake up, or if there *were* to be an open door policy, all sorts of unforeseen consequences might follow. J. A. Hobson, in his book *Imperialism: A Study* (1902), had tried to raise the tone of the debate by suggesting that the important issue was to 'understand the active or latent forces of the subject race and to develop and direct them'. China as a society had been underrated and misunderstood, he wrote. There was a 'genuine spirit of equality' there, as well as a 'reverence for things of the mind' and an 'extraordinary capacity of steady labour'. It was a big mistake to see China as 'stagnant' – a superior civilization in ancient times which had reached a 'stationary' point in the modern world. On the contrary:

> . . . hitherto backward nations are taking the place analogous to that which unskilled workers have held in each one of the civilised nations. Such an event opens a new stage in world history.

But this conclusion only increased anxieties about cheap goods from Asia flooding the market; and Chinese labour undercutting the wages of British workers, being prepared to accept worse conditions, and ignoring trades unions. On Ernest Shackleton's expedition to the South Pole in 1908–9, the most patient and hardworking of the pack-ponies was called 'Chinaman'.

Since the General Election of January 1906, when the Conservatives had lost to the Liberal and Labour opposition over the government-sanctioned importation and employment of some 20,000 Chinese labourers to offset the shortage of black workers in the goldmines of the Transvaal – during the aftermath of the Boer War – the issue of 'coolie labour' had become seriously politicized. During the election campaign, there had been a parade of some fifty unemployed members of the Dockers' Union dressed up as 'Chinamen'. With pigtails made out of oakum, 'a yellow countenance', and wearing yellow, loose-fitting coats and chains, they were flogged by 'slave-drivers' down the streets of the Liverpool constituency of Toxteth. What the neighbouring Chinese inhabitants made of this – and of the chants of 'Chinese slavery' and 'pigtail' – has not been recorded. There were similar parades in London. G. K. Chesterton reacted to them:

> . . . the popular joke against the Chinese labourers was simply that they were Chinese; it was an objection to an alien type; the popular papers were full of jibes about pigtails and yellow faces. It seemed that the Liberal politicians were raising an intellectual objection to a doubtful document of State; while it seemed that the Radical populace were merely roaring with idiotic laughter at the sight of a Chinaman's clothes . . .

Since then, the debate had been about the interpretation of the Conservatives' Aliens Act of 1905, which restricted the entry of immigrants to eight nominated ports – where aliens who could not support themselves, who had 'loathsome or infectious' diseases, or who had been convicted of a felony, were liable to be sent back home by the authorities. After the election of 1906, the Liberal Home Secretary Herbert Gladstone recommended that, if immigrants could convince the authorities that they were fleeing from persecution of some kind, they should be allowed in – a new argument at the time. This led to complaints in sections of the press about 'soft' interpretations of the Act of 1905: hence the comment pieces in *Tit-Bits* and *Answers*. Some journalists argued for similar restrictions to those contained in the American Exclusion Act of 1882 and the 'White Australia' policy of 1901. Claude Blake, the Special Commissioner of the *Sunday Chronicle*, was one of them:

> Is Great Britain going to profit from the bitter experience of America and Australia, by the experience of all white communities cursed by the influx of the yellow men? Or is she going to wait and deal with the scourge after half a million or so of Chinamen have settled in these islands to contaminate the white race?

When thirty-two Chinese were detained, under the terms of the Aliens Act, at London's Royal Albert Docks in November 1906, there was a furious press debate. Conservative writers accused the Liberals of making a farce of the Act by letting in too many immigrants. Trades unionists wrote articles about 'England for the English'. The debate culminated in open attacks by seamen's leaders on the employment of Chinese sailors in the merchant marine in Liverpool and Cardiff, during the transport workers' strike of 1911 – resulting in three nights of rioting in Cardiff during the summer heatwave, with the burning of all thirty or so Chinese laundries in the city, the stoning of Chinese sailors and the smashing of windows in the Chinese quarter. Not only did Chinese sailors seem to be undercutting the union men, the laundries were taking work away from their wives and widows.

Similar confrontations had happened in London's docklands as well. In May 1908, there were clashes in East India Dock Road between a picket of British seamen – from the Sailors' and Firemen's Union of Great Britain and Ireland, located at No. 77 – led by Joseph Havelock Wilson MP, President of the Union – and some Chinese sailors who were trying to sign on for work on the steamship *Zambesi* at the Board of Trade offices in the same building. One issue was 'the signing of Asiatics whilst there are any unemployed left'. Another was the attempt by the Master of the *Zambesi* to escort the Chinese sailors to Surrey Docks, where the steamship was moored, and thence to Cardiff – where they might, it was thought, be able to sign on with less trouble. But at Surrey Docks there was a gathering of some 300 angry seamen and labourers who forced the Master to back down. An all-white crew was registered instead. Then, the Master of *another* steamship, the *Strathness* out of Cardiff, tried to escort a Chinese crew to the Board of Trade offices, with a view to signing *them* on. His attempts to reach the offices were blocked by a furious crowd. This led, three days later, to Wilson addressing a mass meeting outside the Board of Trade offices and to a question in the House of Commons. Winston Churchill, newly arrived at the Board of Trade, replied that 'Chinese boarding-house-keepers would not be allowed access to Board of Trade premises for the purpose of supplying crews of Chinamen': if they attempted this, there could well be legal proceedings under sections of the Merchant Shipping Act of 1894 which, it seemed, were being ignored. When the applicants to the *Zambesi* and the *Strathness* had tried to return to their lodgings in Pennyfields, they met 'a crowd numbering about 1000'. There were scuffles, and as reported by the *East End News*, 'several of the Chinamen tested the quality of British muscle'. The crowd was apparently indignant about the extent of police protection given to the Chinese. As 'ratepayers', they claimed the right to express strong views about Asiatic sailors, and accused the police of 'taking sides'.

A month later, on 19 June, someone signing himself 'E.J.T.' wrote to the *East End News* about 'scenes that are disgusting' where the Chinese in Limehouse were concerned: he was particularly aerated about 'English women associating with them'; fireworks being set off at all hours of the night; and the fact that 'this band of foreign riff raff' did not even recognize the Christian Sabbath.

> We cried aloud in England when the Chinaman was in South Africa. Why should we say nothing when they, on our own shores, seem to be prospering better than our own?

'E.J.T.' had another, more irate, go on 8 September: 'What's being done to prevent them from continuing the things they practise?' The fireworks, the 'lounging on steps', the cracking of nuts and spitting out the shells, the smelly refuse lying outside their restaurants – plus their incomprehensible habit of 'setting upon one another with hammers and choppers' for no apparent reason. *And* the fact that they still did not recognize the Christian Sabbath. The Borough Council should *do* something about all this. Four days later, one 'W.H.D.' agreed about 'the annoyance of these undesirable creatures' and wondered why it was taking such 'a lot of time to arouse Robert [the constabulary] from his slumber', over at Poplar Police Station.

In April 1909, the *East London Observer* reported under the headline 'Chinese in East London' that 'Chinese labour was growing in favour with steamer owners', because of the 'economy effected in wage bills', the 'scale of provisions' and the fact that there was 'less likelihood of claims arising from injury'. It was hoped that the language test stipulations in the Merchant Shipping Act (so that crews could understand orders given in English) would help to counter this 'lowering of standards' – but 'the framers of the test reckoned without the Chinaman'. For 'the Chinaman' had found ways round it – by asserting he was from Hong Kong or Singapore (which were exempt), by getting an English-speaker to sign on in his place – difficult to detect because 'all Chinamen, to English eyes, look very much alike' – and by taking lessons in how to answer the questions by rote. Winston Churchill was, apparently, arguing for a more rigorous test, and for certificates including photographs, thumbprints and details of the sailor's place of origin. The absence of such measures, concluded the article, could well lead to a general reduction in wages and a 'lowering of conditions'.

The *East End News*, in May 1910, reported a 'Murderous Fracas' which resulted in the stabbing to death of Ah Fang (or Ing), a ship's steward, and the serious wounding of another steward, Me Tonk (or Lee Fong – the reporter was vague about the names, as were his colleagues), outside a lodging-house at 5 Pennyfields. The two men had been 'talking to two young women'; and one Scandinavian sailor, and two Russians, who happened to be passing by, took strong exception to this. One of them yelled 'rotten Chinaman', and there was much 'foul language'. The policeman in charge of the case was Divisional Detective Inspector Albert Yeo, of K Division. It transpired that one of the young women was Catherine O'Shea, well known in the neighbourhood, whose nickname was 'Buy me chocolates'. The hapless Ah Fang's nickname was, apparently, 'Kiss me on my birthday'. At Poplar Coroner's Court, the surviving victim was very reluctant to identify Miss O'Shea in public as one of the young women, and witnesses from the Scandinavian Sailors' Home, in their evidence about the offending sailors, had evidently been intimidated by someone. So the proceedings were stilted, to say the least. But Yeo eventually achieved a verdict of wilful murder against the Scandinavian.

Assaults seem also to have triggered the most serious riot to have happened at this time in Limehouse Causeway and East India Dock Road, on a Saturday night in April 1912. One was on Ny Yong, proprietor of a lodging-house in Limehouse Causeway, who had been chased, stabbed with a knife and hit with an iron bar; the other was on Chang Sing, who was riding a bicycle when hit hard with another piece of iron. These led to a full-scale riot, the distribution of 120 iron bars and 'wild scenes in Limehouse Causeway for several hours'. Both the *East London Advertiser* and the *East End News* reported that 'something approaching pandemonium prevailed', as rival gangs of Chinamen set about each other with 'revolvers, knives and hammers'. A particularly sinister detail was that 'one of the rioters' was using a curious-looking weapon – a short length of iron bar, wrapped in a red cloth – which the police officer stated was 'well known among the Boxers'. Some lodging-houses in the Causeway were wrecked, and two others in Pennyfields (including No. 5, 'where some time ago a Chinaman was done to death by foreign sailors'). There were rumours that agents provocateurs had travelled to London from Liverpool – members of a secret society known as 'The White Lily', which 'in strength . . .

is said to far exceed that of the Masonic Order the wide world over' – specially 'to silence informers', and that the ensuing riot 'arose out of a dispute between two rival organizations': the Nautical Progress Society and the White Lily.

Two lodgers in Pennyfields were charged at Thames Police Court with cutting and wounding Ny Yong, three others were charged with the felonious wounding of Chang Sing, and eleven others with disorderly conduct. Some promised to go to sea at once, in which case the charges would be dropped. A representative of the Commissioner of Police explained that 'for some time there has been unrest among the Chinese in the East End'. The *Advertiser's* response was to comment that this was worrying not so much because of the Chinese rioters as because of 'the [British] public who went about risking a crack on the head with a hatchet'. The *News* reported on 30 April that the leaders of the two factions had 'figuratively speaking, buried the hatchet'.

Posters of 'coolies' put up by Liberal and Labour candidates in the 1906 election – and cartoons in the press – had helped to disseminate racial stereotypes in the name of delivering the Chinese from exploitation: G. K. Chesterton's 'popular joke'. Educationalist Graham Wallas shrewdly observed in his study of *Human Nature in Politics* (1908):

> Anyone . . . who saw much of the politics in the winter of 1905–1906 must have noticed that the pictures of Chinamen on the hoardings aroused among very many of the voters an immediate hatred of the Mongolian racial type.

This 'non-rational' reaction, he added, was a classic case of unintended consequences. It also showed that the anxieties of politicians and political economists about the map of the world were as nothing compared with anxieties about the Chinese at home – *beyond* the labour issue. In fact, where Chinese overseas trade was concerned, one side-effect of the Liberal election victory of 1906 was that there was a substantial majority in Parliament against the India–China opium trade, for the first time: in May 1906, the House of Commons finally accepted that the trade was 'morally indefensible'. This coincided with pressure from the anti-opium movement within China, which saw the trade as a very unfortunate symbol of Chinese backwardness and impotence. The following year saw the Anglo-China opium agreement – leading to its consolidation in 1911. The trade was in decline anyway, which may have eased the consciences of waverers.

But at home in Britain the question of what was 'morally indefensible' did not seem so clear-cut. The articles in *Tit-Bits* and *Answers* are characteristic of the rhetoric and hyperbole of many newspaper pieces, and not just in the popular press: a cocktail of sexual jealousy (Chinese communities being predominantly male), religious bigotry (references to 'horrible-looking' idols, funerary customs and the refusal to assimilate), accusations of indecency (five or more to a bed in boarding-houses), exposés behind the scenes (innocent-looking laundries and boarding-houses as 'fronts' for opium dens), white slavery (underage girls being seduced and sold into prostitution), bizarre dietary preferences (usually dogs, cats and rats) and scapegoating (unemployment in the merchant marine, untidy streets, smelly refuse). All of which made the 'problem', in some circles, seem increasingly urgent. And, as these newspaper reports emphasized, the Chinese community was easily identifiable. The coverage of Liverpool was at times particularly sour – where Irish politicians and community leaders, the aristocrats of immigration, fanned the flames. Here, the Chinese became – in Edward Said's phrase – 'the victims of victims'. One Royal Commission (1903), one Commission of Inquiry in Liverpool (1907) and an official report into the relationship between Chinese men and English girls, following a complaint from a London County Council school headmistress (1911), patiently explained that Chinese communities tended to be tight-knit and law-abiding; that gambling (admittedly illegal) was a small-scale problem and relatively harmless; that marriages between Chinese men and white women were usually a success – rather than embodying 'the vices of the two racial stocks'; that laundries and boarding-houses were subject to periodic inspections; and that the numbers of immigrants had been grossly inflated by politicians and the press. The uncertain and tentative tone of these reports suggested that they were not sure where the opposition to Chinese immigration was coming from nor why it was happening: they had difficulty in formulating Chinese communities as 'a problem'.

Census returns for this period can provide only a rough estimate. They do, however, provide a useful guide to tendencies even if not rock-hard facts. According to census returns, the numbers of 'Chinese' who were living in the whole of England and Wales were 78 in 1851, 665 in 1881 and 545 in 1901. In other words, at precisely the time when press reports began to complain about the growing numbers of Chinese they were in fact going down. Even in 1911, the totals were 1,319 in the whole of England and Wales – or 0.5 per cent of the 'total number of foreigners' – 247 of them living in London. This, at a time *before* the Aliens Restriction Act of 1914 – which restricted immigration in time of war or national danger, extended to peacetime in 1919 when 'limited controls' were exercised over Chinese immigration to Britain. Even in the late 1920s, Chinese constituted just over 1 per cent of 'the total number of foreigners'.

Where London was concerned, the East End, and in particular the boroughs of Stepney and Poplar – Limehouse was split between the two boroughs – were from 1881 (the first year these data were collected) through to 1911, and beyond, the most concentrated area of primary settlement for Chinese immigrants. The next largest concentration was in Marylebone and St Pancras. Chinese numbers were very small in other working-class areas along the river. The community in East London was predominantly male, and around 1911 significantly so. In 1901, the census revealed that over 60 per cent of *all* Chinese men living in England and Wales were 'seamen, merchant service, boatmen', 27 per cent in 'laundry and washing services' and 2 per cent in domestic service. By 1911, 49 per cent worked as merchant seamen, 36 per cent in laundry and washing services. By the early 1920s, with the decline of the docks, the figure for 'laundry and washing' had overtaken the figure for seamen, and in turn it would soon be overtaken by the restaurant trade. These proportions seem to have been roughly matched in Stepney and Poplar. In 1901, 82 per cent of the Chinese in London were single and between the ages of twenty and thirty five, but by 1911 the figure for the same age group had fallen to 50 per cent. According to sociologist Ng Kwee Choo, most of the Chinese living in East London – as defined by the census returns – 'originated from Kwangtung Province [Guangdong, in mainland China], with a sprinkling from Chekiang, Malaya, Singapore and Fukien'.

So at the turn of the twentieth century, when the Limehouse area had recently been labelled as 'Chinatown', and when Chinatown consisted of three streets – Pennyfields, Limehouse Causeway and West India Dock Road – the census recorded forty-six Chinese-born people living there, three-quarters of them able-bodied men, predominantly from Kwangtung. It was a far cry from an extensive and densely populated 'Chinatown' area like those of San Francisco and New York. And on census day 1911, just 480 Chinese were recorded out of a total of 15,246 'foreign sea men' in England and Wales, vastly outnumbered by Lascars – also of Asian origin. This was what all the fuss was about. These were the people singled out for so much press attention.

Kelly's Directory of trades and shops in Chinatown tells a similar story, although the definition of 'Chinese' needs to be treated with caution – as does the listing of Limehouse businesses and lodging-houses with apparently Chinese names – but it is a guide. In 1897, the *Directory* shows no Chinese businesses at all in Pennyfields, two in Limehouse Causeway and none in West India Dock Road. By 1910, the equivalent figures are two in Pennyfields, five in Limehouse Causeway and two in West India Dock Road; by 1919, the equivalents are eight in Pennyfields, eight in Limehouse Causeway and four in West India Dock Road; and by 1928, nine in Pennyfields, ten in Limehouse Causeway and none in West India Dock Road. Businesses ebb and flow between these years, with the most established (four of them appearing four times 1919–28) located in Limehouse Causeway. Very few Chinese businesses were ever listed in West India Dock Road –instead there were a number of established institutions with which the Chinese community would have come into contact one way or another: the Strangers' Lodging House for Asiatics (which changed its name to the Asiatic and Overseas Home in 1928), the Police Station, the National Sailors' and Firemen's Union and the British and Foreign Sailors' Society. Interestingly, a single Chinese interpreter set himself up in business near the union in 1910 and was still at the same address in 1919. The *Directory* shows clearly the rise of Chinese restaurants between 1919 and 1928, steep in the 1920s, with confectioners appearing in 1926–28. Lodging-houses and laundries are scarcely listed – most laundry, to judge by the *Directory*, seems to have been taken in at home, in private houses. Only 'official' lodging-houses were listed. According to yet another report by the London County Council on *Licensing Seamen's Lodging Houses*, in 1912 there were four in Pennyfields, one in Limehouse Causeway and four in West India Dock Road – some of them quite substantial. Very few were listed in *Kelly's*. The local newspapers had estimated in 1909 that there were some twenty licensed and unlicensed lodging-houses in the area: including one at 5 Pennyfields (proprietor Charles King – who may have owned more than one), one at 9 Limehouse Causeway (proprietor Ah Tack) and one unlicensed one at 5 Limehouse Causeway (in a house which, according to *Kelly's*, would become a Chinese grocer's). There are no references to the Chi Kung Tong (known as 'the Chinese Masonic Hall') or to Chinese 'joss-houses' or places of worship. Apart from tobacconists (the largest number), chandlers and grocers – and the occasional confectioner and butcher – the kinds of trades and crafts which operated around the Causeway and Pennyfields – coopers, tinplaters, coal hauliers, publicans and beer retailers, wharf offices and harbour administrators – were not Chinese-owned or run, and probably not open to the Chinese. An employment exchange appears on the scene in 1923. Throughout the period 1897–1928, the Chinese business community in Limehouse was considerably outnumbered by businessfolk with Eastern European roots and by Scandinavians.

But the media of the day – encouraged by some local and national politicians playing to the gallery in the knowledge that the Chinese they were criticizing could not vote – still reported floods of immigrants entering Britain on ships, not even able to speak the rudiments of the language; and, where the settled Chinese communities were concerned, gambling parlours and opium dens, white doves becoming broken blossoms, uneatable food, and benefit societies as secret conspiracies. It was all too easy to project anxieties onto the Chinese in Liverpool, Cardiff and – in fiction – especially London. As the Chinese writer 'Lao She' (Shu Qingchun), who spent four years teaching at the University of London (1924–29) and visited the *real* Limehouse several times, wearily noted in his novel about 'a sojourn in London', *Mr Ma and Son: Two Chinese in London* (published in China, 1929):

> If there were twenty Chinese living in Chinatown, their accounts would say 5,000; moreover every one of those 5,000 yellow devils would certainly smoke opium, smuggle arms, murder people then stuff the corpses under beds and rape women regardless of age.

Not least because readers of most of English newspapers and magazines, it was assumed, were unlikely to go and see for themselves. The campaigning journalist Walter Besant, in his collection *East London* (1901), decided to do just that:

> Compared with the Chinese colony in New York, part of which I once visited . . . that of London is a small thing and of no importance. Yet it is curious. There are not, I believe, more than a hundred Chinese, or thereabouts, in all; they occupy a few houses [around Pennyfields]; there are one or two small shops kept by Chinamen; it is not considered quite safe to visit the place . . .

Besant went into a curio shop, a social club where a little gambling with dominoes was taking place. He was surprised that 'nobody took the least notice of the stranger who stood at the door'. Then he crossed the road into another house, where there was an 'opium den':

> Greatly to my disappointment, because when one goes to an opium den for the first time one expects a creeping of the flesh at least, the place was neither dreadful nor horrible. . . . Half a dozen men were waiting their turn. One of them had a musical instrument. Except for the smell of the place, which was overwhelming, the musical instrument was the only horror of the opium den. When I think of it I seem to remember a thousand fingernails scratching a window . . .

Otherwise, Limehouse was a surprisingly ordinary sort of place, with Chinese and other nationalities going about their business and keeping themselves to themselves.

But that, as Walter Besant hinted, was no longer the point. In October 1912, *The Story-Teller* magazine published 'The Zayat Kiss' by Sax Rohmer, the first of ten short stories which would run until 1 July 1913 and together form *The Mystery of Dr Fu-Manchu* – despite a recommendation to 'reject' by the publisher's referee. Soon, readers would be sharing Dr Petrie's worst imaginings:

> I saw the tide of Limehouse Reach, the Thames lapping about the green-coated timbers of a dock pier: and rising – falling – sometimes disclosing to the pallid light a rigid hand, sometimes a horribly bloated face.

TALES OF CHINATOWN

SAX ROHMER

CHAPTER FIVE

'The Yellow Peril Incarnate in One Man'

he Mystery of Dr Fu-Manchu started life in October 1912 as a series
of interconnected short stories, many of which were eccentric variations on the locked-room mystery which went right back to Poe's 'The
Murders in the Rue Morgue' (1841) and which had recently become popular
among readers of detective stories with Gaston Leroux's *The Mystery of the
Yellow Room* (1908) and Jacques Futrelle's short story 'The Problem of Cell
13' (1907). The first story, 'The Zayat Kiss', also introduced readers to Nayland
Smith – ex-District Commissioner, 'late of Mandalay' – his friend and the narrator Dr Petrie and, in Smith's classic description, to Dr Fu Manchu himself.
Petrie has asked Smith the question, 'What perverted genius controls this awful
secret movement?' Smith replies:

> Imagine a person, tall, lean and feline, high-shouldered, with a brow like
> Shakespeare and a face like Satan, a close-shaven skull, and long, mag-
> netic eyes of the true cat-green. Invest him with all the cruel cunning of
> an entire Eastern race, accumulated in one giant intellect, with all the
> resources of science past and present, with all the resources, if you will,
> of a wealthy government – which, however, already has denied all know-
> ledge of his existence. Imagine that awful being, and you have a mental
> picture of Dr Fu-Manchu, the yellow peril incarnate in one man.

In the final short story of this first series, 'The Knocking on the Door'
(July 1913), the description was partially reprised by Dr Petrie, as he waited
anxiously in suburban Dulwich Village for news of the dreaded Fu Manchu:

> Between my mind and the chapter upon which I was at work a certain
> sentence persistently intruded itself. It was as though an unseen hand
> held the written page closely before my eyes. This was the sentence:

'Imagine a person, tall, lean and feline ... one giant intellect ...
Dr Fu-Manchu.'

Fu-Manchu as Smith had described him to me on that night which
now seemed so remotely distant – the night upon which I had learned of
the existence of the wonderful and evil being born of that secret quickening which stirred in the womb of the yellow races.

Sax Rohmer was so pleased with this description that he repeated much
of it yet again, word for word, in the opening story of the sequel, called 'The
Wire Jacket' (June 1915):

My thoughts were centred upon the unforgettable figure of the murderous
Chinaman. These words, exactly as Smith had used them, seemed once
again to sound in my ears:
    'Imagine a person . . .'

This time round, the description omitted the sub-clause about 'all the resources
. . . of a wealthy government, which, however, already has denied all knowledge of his existence'. Extracts from the passage reappeared in future novels
at regular intervals thereafter.

It was like a signature tune, or a piece of the liturgy perhaps, moving
through the early Fu Manchu stories, reassuring readers that their favourite
turn was about to begin – and just as the way in which it is introduced shows
Rohmer's writing at its laziest ('persistently intruded', 'seemed so remotely
distant', 'that secret quickening'), the passage also shows Rohmer at his best:
Rohmer the journalist and music-hall lyricist. At last he had written a catchy
lyric. There is a terrible beauty about it. As the critic D. J. Enright has observed:

A brief examination of the passage shows how effective it is, in its way,
and also how effective a writer Rohmer was, in his way. We note the
highbrow (and alliterative) references to Shakespeare and Satan, the
conventionally sinister adjectives 'feline' (backed up by 'long, magnetic
eyes'), the unexpected 'high-shouldered', the shuddering allusions to
'cruel cunning', the menacing talk of 'giant intellect' and 'the resources
of science', the term 'yellow peril' (originally inside quotation marks as
if to admit to its vulgar journalistic origin while pointing to some dreadful truth in it), and the rather grand touch, 'incarnate in one man'. The

reader enjoys the agreeable feeling that what he has embarked on is a cut above the common-or-garden thriller – Shakespeare and Satan! – but still well within his expectations.

It is worth looking at this passage much more closely to understand the roots of Sax Rohmer's fiction. He always claimed that it described what he saw through the Limehouse fog when he glimpsed 'Mr King'. But it clearly had literary antecedents. And it is distilled essence of popular orientalism.

'Imagine a person . . .'

Sax Rohmer was always intrigued by the idea that the most wildly romantic adventure stories could be retold using everyday London locations. This sense of *incongruity*, combined with the conviction that his own experience of Limehouse – and of the occult – was special to him, runs through all his early works. Behind the Limehouse shopfront, within a stone's throw of the Strand ('Oh, my God!' Dr Petrie groaned, 'can this be England?'), in a London taxi, or even on Clapham Common, the Yellow Peril may strike at any time. 'Into my humdrum suburban life,' writes Petrie, 'Nayland Smith had brought fantasy of the wildest.' Dr Petrie is an amateur writer even before Smith contacts him, and he readily agrees to join the struggle, 'for unfortunately, my professional duties were not onerous' (just like Dr Conan Doyle's and Dr Watson's). Smith plays on Petrie's frustrated romanticism:

> 'Mysterious enough for you?' he laughed, and glanced at my unfinished MS. 'A story, eh? From which I gather that the district is beastly healthy – what, Petrie? Well, I can put some material in your way that, if sheer uncanny mystery is a marketable commodity, ought to make you independent of influenza and broken legs and shattered nerves and all the rest.'

This prompts one of Petrie's characteristically bland reactions:

> Today we may seek for romance and fail to find it: unsought, it lies in wait for us at the most prosaic corners of life's highway. Into the heart of a weird mystery the cab bore me. . . . The drive that night, though it

divided the drably commonplace from the wildly bizarre – though it was the bridge between the ordinary and the outré – has left no impression on my mind.

Arthur Ward always tried to shroud his early years in mystery, as we have seen (p. 61). He evidently had a highly romanticized notion of what bohemian life in London for an all-purpose freelance would be like, and in his disappointment his use of the word 'prosaic' took on special meaning. His dilettante interest in *The Romance of Sorcery* was just one of his responses to the 'prosaic' side of London life he encountered in his freelance years: the fictional works abound in references to Dr Dee, Nostradamus, Cagliostro and the ancient Egyptian sorcerers. When Rohmer is discussing cryptography, he refers to Poe's essay; when he is describing the effects of opium, he quotes De Quincey – but his involvement in all these subjects was essentially on the level of popular adventure stories or of a *Tit-Bits* turnover.

He was the sort of man who couldn't go to the shops in Herne Hill without returning some hours later with a string of colourful anecdotes about his exploits: a born embroiderer of the everyday. The crime writer Julian Symons wrote of him, 'He was one of those engaging, maddening characters who half-believe their own fantasies.' The Fu Manchu stories are full of portentous 'asides' from Petrie about his journeys through London, usually eastward. Here he is, travelling by taxi along the Whitechapel Road:

> Poles, Russians, Serbs, Roumanians, Jews of Hungary, and Italians of Whitechapel mingled in the throng. Near East and Far East rubbed shoulders. Pidjin English contested with Yiddish for the ownership of some tawdry article offered by an auctioneer whose nationality defied conjecture, save that always some branch of his ancestry had drawn nourishment from the soil of Eternal Judea. . . . And the fine drizzling rain fell upon all alike, pattering upon the hood of the taxi-cab, trickling down the front windows. . . . Sometimes a yellow face showed close to one of the streaming windows; sometimes a black-eyed, pallid face, but never a face wholly sane and healthy. This was an underworld where squalor and vice went hand in hand through the beautiless streets, a melting-pot of the world's outcasts; this was the shadowland, which last night had swallowed up Nayland Smith.

The mantle of dusk had closed about the squalid activity of the East End streets as we neared our destination. Aliens of every shade of colour were in the glare of the lamps upon the main road about us now, emerging from burrow-like alleys. In the short space of the drive we had passed from the light world of the West into the dubious underworld of the East.

Crime writer Colin Watson singled out this passage as a classic example of Rohmer's technique:

The vehemence of this prose is interesting. It is occasioned by nothing in the story itself, and indeed seems unrelated to experience of any kind. Why should street activity in a particular area be described as 'squalid' as if rendered so by a mere compass bearing? Why are alleys inhabited by 'aliens' specifically 'burrow-like'? And what has geography got to do with the distinction between 'world' and 'underworld'? Even the verb 'emerge', with all its suggestion of secret and evil purpose, would seem a curious choice. . . . But nothing happens. Rohmer's narrative rolls on elsewhere. The readers have not been thrilled; they simply have been prompted to feel superior.

Rohmer was writing from the suburbs about a London viewed through a car windscreen – a new experience in 1912 for most of his readers. He was also writing for readers who – like as not – had never seen a real Chinese person, and who were unlikely to venture as far east as the Whitechapel Road.

Countless exposés in the press had warned them of 'the abyss', the dark pit of the East. He was reinforcing the clichés currently fed to *Tit-Bits* readers. To them, London *was* the Empire. *The Mystery of Dr Fu-Manchu* was first serialized in the year Greenwich Mean Time was established. On a wider geographical canvas, what if a mighty power threatened to redraw the map of the world, so that instead of Greenwich at its centre, Europe appeared an insignificant peninsula to a great Eurasian continent? What if, instead of measuring 'the Far East' and 'the Middle East' by their distance from London, the earth was measured from the Middle Kingdom? It didn't bear thinking about. The world Rohmer was conjuring for his readers came from his overactive imagination, his frustrations, and from his/their deep suburban prejudices. He assumed that they would be reading about it, probably feeling uneasy and jaded, 'in the home and on the train'. His geography was the geography of inexperience. And the *seriousness* of his prose – which gave a certain zest to his highly improbable stories – full of eccentricities, was like the seriousness of someone who really wants his tall stories to be believed.

Just occasionally, Dr Petrie stands apart from this humourlessness and reflects on it:

> That sense of fantasy, which claimed me often enough in those days of our struggle with the titanic genius . . . now had me fast in its grip again. I was an actor in one of those dream-scenes of the grim Fu-Manchu drama.

After his thirteen-year disappearance, Fu Manchu returned in 1930 having abandoned his Limehouse roots: from then on, his adventures would be set on the Riviera, in Haiti, New York, Venice – and finally, with *Emperor Fu Manchu* – Rohmer's last book – in Mao's China. With the exception of *Emperor*, Rohmer never set stories in locations he had not either visited or researched in detail: *Emperor* has Nayland Smith and Fu Manchu wandering around the People's Republic in ridiculous ways. But it is clear from *Brood of the Witch-Queen* (1918; written shortly after Rohmer had visited the Meidum Pyramid) and from *The Day the World Ended* (1930; written in 1928, after his visit to Baden-Baden) that he was only interested in presenting an aggressively cavalier version of what he had seen. Like Little Tich, he was giving his inimitable *impression* of those exotic locales, with an eye on bizarre details. No wonder he decided to abandon his career as an investigative journalist . . .

'. . . tall, lean . . .'

The clichéd Chinese figure in printed illustrations and cartoons tended to be short and squat, Buddha-like. 'The burly mandarin of caricature', with a proneness to obesity. But Dr Fu Manchu is tall and lean. This character came not from images of China so much as from the super-villains of recent British literature. These were the heirs of the scowling villains of the Gothic novel and the Byronic hero-villain, together with the mysterious conspiracies of French *romans-feuilletons*. The immediate inspiration for the craze was Professor Moriarty, who had appeared in 'The Final Problem', in December 1893, subsequently collected in *The Memoirs of Sherlock Holmes*. Although this was the only story in which he actually appeared, it was Moriarty who was always considered Holmes's greatest nemesis. It was as if the reading public had to invent a foe to match Holmes's powers. In popular mythology – through William Gillette's play *Sherlock Holmes* (1899) and silent films – Moriarty moved centre stage. But Conan Doyle was not really interested in him. In 'The Final Problem', Holmes tells Watson that the story of how to find the evidence against Moriarty could prove to be the greatest Holmes story of all: but Doyle never actually wrote it. He is introduced by Holmes in suitable suggestive and theatrical fashion:

> 'You have probably never heard of Professor Moriarty?' said he.
> 'Never.'
> 'Aye, there's the genius and the wonder of the thing!' he cried. 'The man pervades London, and no-one has heard of him. That's what puts him on a pinnacle in the records of crime.'

By the time Dr Watson provides a *physical* description, courtesy of Holmes, we have learned that Moriarty is 'the Napoleon of crime', a philosopher, an abstract thinker, a gifted organizer, in short that he has 'a brain of the first order':

> He is extremely tall and thin, his forehead domes out in a white curve, and his two eyes are deeply sunken in his head. He is clean-shaven, pale and ascetic-looking, retaining something of the professor in his features . . . his face protrudes forward, and is forever slowly oscillating from side to side in a curiously reptilian fashion.

Sax Rohmer had often referred to Sherlock Holmes in his music-hall lyrics: Sherlock Holmes equals Great Detective. He derived the plots of several of the Fu Manchu stories from Conan Doyle – notably 'The Speckled Band' (an incident involving an 'Australian death-adder' secreted inside a wooden cane at Abel Slattin's house); 'The Naval Treaty' (1893) (the stealing of plans for an aero-torpedo from the American inventor Frank Norris West); *The Hound of the Baskervilles* (1901) (a desolate moor with 'hungry mire', complete with strange cry in the night) and *The Sign of the Four* (a clue concerning *Andaman Second*, a passenger ship leaving Tilbury). Not to mention the central relationship between Nayland Smith and Dr Petrie, by means of which Smith's high-handed arrogance is mediated through a more conventional turn of mind, just like the relationship between Holmes and the narrator Watson. It has been said that Holmes would be insufferable without Watson. Just so, or even more so, Nayland Smith and Dr Petrie, the main difference being that Smith is no match for Fu Manchu's intellect, and knows it; he has to make do with pluck and a stiff upper lip. American radio adaptations tended to relocate Dr Petrie's surgery from Clapham to Baker Street. P. G. Wodehouse, Rohmer's ex-colleague as a bank clerk, made the connection too in *Cocktail Time* (1958), published the year before Rohmer's death:

> Professor Moriarty, Doctor Fu Manchu and The Ace of Spades, to name but three. And every one of them the sort of chap who would drop cobras down your chimney or lace your beer with little-known Asiatic poisons as soon as look at you . . .

Two years after Moriarty, the Australian novelist Guy Boothby's serial featuring Dr Nikola helped to launch *The Windsor Magazine*, a competitor of *The Strand*. Dr Nikola has been called 'the first real master-villain'. He was introduced in *A Bid for Fortune* (1895) – later retitled *Enter, Dr Nikola!* – then continued his increasingly popular adventures in four more full-length novels (1896–1901) in which he became more and more prominent by public demand. Early covers featured a striking portrait of the pallid and saturnine Doctor, staring out at the reader through dark eyes, dressed in his white cravat and fur coat, with a feline familiar sitting on his shoulder. Readers were introduced to Nikola, in the first instalment of the serial, at a small dinner party at the Imperial Restaurant on the Thames Embankment, a version of the Savoy:

> In stature he was slightly above the ordinary, his shoulders were broad, his limbs perfectly shaped and plainly muscular, but very slim. His head, which was magnificently set upon his shoulders, was adorned with a pro-fusion of glossy black hair; his face was destitute of beard or moustache, and was of oval shape and handsome moulding; while his skin was of a dark olive hue, a colour which harmonised well with his piercing black eyes and pearly teeth. . . . In age he might have been anything from eight-and-twenty to forty; in reality he was thirty-three.

Nikola is charming, cosmopolitan, courteous – and he speaks exemplary English. In addition to being a master criminal, he is a first-rate chess-player, an accomplished mesmerist, a thought-reader, a theosophist and a practitioner of necromancy. The first two novels are centred on his elaborate plot to possess a sacred Chinese relic – resembling an 'executioner's symbol of office' – which will win him control over some Tibetan magical sects. His adventures involve sinister Chinamen, secret societies, exotic places recently made famous by theosophy – and a diabolical reputation that extends from 'Chinese mothers nursing their almond-eyed spawn in Pekin' to 'the Sultan of Borneo . . . they all know Dr Nikola and his cat and, take my word for it, they fear him'. If readers, as well as writers, had a sneaking sympathy with the rascals, this was reflected in the villains of popular fiction becoming progressively more colourful than the fine, upstanding, bluff heroes.

It may have been memories of the music hall, as well as literary ante-cedents, that led to Rohmer's tall and thin. 'Chang Yu Sing the Chinese Giant' claimed to be nearly eight feet tall (he was in fact seven foot nine). 'The magic giant could be viewed daily' at the Egyptian Hall in Piccadilly, and elsewhere, dressed in jewels, gold, embroidered silk and panther skin. Some newspapers claimed 'he stood eight feet four inches tall, and could reach to twelve feet'. A showbusiness legend, he went on tour in Europe and America, and retired to Bournemouth in 1890 to run a seaside oriental tearoom. His act consisted of standing onstage during a short lecture on 'Chinese giants', followed by the playing of polka music during which he would shake hands with the audience, Western-style. Then there would be a recital of Chang's celebrated 'Ode on the Crystal Palace', praising the Great Exhibition and all it stood for, which he performed for decades afterwards.

The association between 'the Chinese Giant' and the Great Exhibition was interesting, because China had not in fact officially contributed – the 'Chinese Pavilion' was entirely assembled by the East India Company. Notoriously, however, a Chinese in embroidered satin robe, carrying a fan, managed to gate-crash the Grand Opening Procession, kiss the Duke of Wellington – much to the old boy's confusion – and prostrate himself before Queen Victoria (who handled the situation, it was said, 'with superb tact but an ill-controlled smile'). At a time when the issue of whether senior British officials should kowtow to the Emperor was still in the news, this had real symbolic significance. No one knew who this Chinese was – China had not, of course, sent an official repre-sentative – but everyone was sure that 'he *must* be someone of consequence, probably a Mandarin', otherwise he would not *be* there. So he was placed next to the Archbishop of Canterbury. Actually, he was a member of the crew of the 'famous Chinese junk', moored 'hard by the Temple-stairs' in the heart of London, and his surprise appearance – probably a publicity stunt for the junk's attractions – was all about *display*, the display of the exotic 'other'. When Christopher Lee was making the film *The Face of Fu Manchu* in 1965, he discussed with Mrs Sax Rohmer, on the set in Dublin, how her late husband had envisioned the devil doctor. She particularly recalled the unusual height of 'Mr King', which reassured the six-foot-five Lee that he was right for the part.

'. . . and feline . . .'

Dr Fu Manchu has a pet marmoset perched on his shoulder, 'with a dreadful yellow face', a creature that has a 'chattering whistle' and keeps grimacing. Dr Nikola's enormous cat Appolyon – 'black as the pit of Tophet' and named after a dark angel – may have been on Sax Rohmer's mind, but so was the history of the cat in ancient times and especially in New Kingdom Egypt (from the mid-sixteenth century BC onwards). In *The Green Eyes of Bâst* (1920), Rohmer wrote of Nahémah, a woman who has the nasty habit of transmuting into a cat during the modern equivalent of 'the gothic month of Phanoi', which was dedicated to the Egyptian cat-goddess Bâst. She is 'controlled or influenced' by the deity. The book opens with a newspaperman being watched through his window by a pair of enormous catlike eyes; but a search of the grounds reveals only the footprints of a pair of high-heeled shoes. It transpires that the cat-woman seeks revenge on the whole Coverly dynasty for the usual complicated reasons. The theme of ancient Egyptian sorcery in a contemporary setting – which may or may not be explained away: it usually is – evidently appealed to Rohmer's imagination; he devoted several novels and short stories to it, including *Brood of the Witch-Queen* and *She Who Sleeps* (1928). His researches for *The Romance of Sorcery* led him to the cat-headed goddess Bâst or Bastet, to the cult of the cat, mummified sacrifice, and the sculptures of domestic cats – cats had only relatively recently been domesticated – which were the living form of the cat-goddess. (Did he but know it, there was in fact an earlier, *Chinese* origin for feline domestication, but that discovery was not yet available to him.) They also revealed to him black cats as 'familiars' and symbols of Satan in the Middle Ages, and to the English witch trials of 1566–1684 – some of which involved cats which went 'by the name of Sathan'. The archaeological excavations by Egyptologists of the cult centre at Bubastis in the late nine-teenth–early twentieth centuries led to the arrival in British ports of boatloads of mummified cats (sometimes as ballast) and their display in public museums. One 1890 cargo – of mummified cats intended as fertilizer – weighed nineteen tons: one of them was retrieved from its fate and is still in the British Museum. So, to Rohmer, 'feline' had connotations of ancient magic, medieval mystery, and cunning. Fu Manchu's marmoset, by the way, occasions one of his more amusing references to Sherlock Holmes, when Nayland Smith observes in all seriousness: 'They were the footprints of a small ape . . . !'

'. . . a brow like Shakespeare and a face like Satan . . .'

We have seen how Sax Rohmer contributed to George Robey's Shakespeare skit – 'Waggish Will of Avon' – in which Shakespeare's 'enormously broad and towering forehead' becomes the excuse for a series of gags (p. 141). Fu Manchu's brow is described as 'dome-like': according to the fashionable science of craniometry – as well as music-hall sketches – this connoted super-ior intelligence and the brain of a 'mental giant'.

Sax Rohmer's readers would have known that Shakespeare equals genius, and that 'Milton's Satan' equals fallen angel, fine poetry and a kind of nobility: a defiant challenge to an unbeatable force of light. And if they knew *one thing* about *Paradise Lost* (1667) – whether they had actually read it or not – it was William Blake's famous reaction to it: Milton was 'of the Devil's party without knowing'.

'Milton's Satan' was the patron saint – so to speak – of literature's super-villains, which is why commentators on Rohmer have invariably associated the 'Satan' reference with *Paradise Lost*. But it just as likely refers to Dante's *Divine Comedy* and in particular to the last canto of the *Inferno*. Rohmer often associated the words 'Dante' and 'hell', 'Dante' and 'Hades' – as in 'I felt like another Dante emerging from the Hades', or 'like a glimpse of the Inferno seen by some Chinese Dante' – almost like a reflex in the Fu Manchu stories. A particularly suggestive example occurs in *The Trail of Fu Manchu* to describe the devil doctor:

> [His coat], tunic fashion, was buttoned to his neck – a lean sinewy neck supporting a head which might have been that of Dante. The brow was even finer than the traditional portraits of Shakespeare. . . . [The face]

was that of a man of indeterminable age, heavily lined, but lighted by a pair of such long, narrow, brilliant green eyes that one's thoughts flashed to Satan – Lucifer, Son of the Morning: an angel, but a fallen angel.

The phrenological reference to Dante – *did* he have a specially large head? – followed by the comparison with 'Lucifer, Son of the Morning' – seems to have put into Rohmer's mind, by association, an image from Dante's *Inferno*. The last canto of the *Inferno*, set in the lowest circle of hell, describes the 'three faces' of Satan:

> *The one in front, this one was vermilion . . .*
> *The right one seemed between white and yellow;*
> *the left was such to look upon as those*
> *who come from where the Nile descends.*

The fashionable reading of this passage, in the nineteenth and early twentieth centuries, was a racial one: the left face was black (representing Africa); the front face was red or blushing (representing Europe); and the right face was yellow (representing Asia). This in fact had much more to do with nineteenth-century racial theories than with *The Divine Comedy* – where the three faces were more likely to be an anti-Trinity – but it was certainly current in Sax Rohmer's time. So one of the faces of Satan was thought to be yellow.

'. . . long, magnetic eyes of the true cat-green . . .'

Dr Petrie first encounters Dr Fu Manchu, in Singapore Charlie's opium den:

> He had a great, high brow, crowned with sparse, neutral-coloured hair. Of his face, as it looked out at me over the dirty table, I despair of writing convincingly. It was that of an archangel of evil, and it was wholly dominated by the most uncanny eyes that ever reflected a human soul, for they were narrow and long, very slightly oblique, and of a brilliant green. But their unique horror lay in a certain filminess (it made me think of the membrana nictitans in a bird) which, obscuring them as I threw wide the door, seemed to lift as I actually passed the threshold, revealing the eyes in all their brilliant iridescence.

From then on, Fu Manchu's eyes are invariably described as 'brilliant green', 'reptilian' and possessing a 'viridescence which hitherto I had supposed possible only in the eye of the cat'. According to the *Tit-Bits* article on 'Character Reading from Foreheads and Eyes', green eyes could be 'fascinating', but they were also 'dangerous' because they were tokens of deceit. But the green eyes and the 'sparse, neutral-coloured hair' of the devil doctor are interesting for other reasons as well. According to Pamela Kyle Crossley, a scholar specializing in the history of the Qing dynasty and author of *The Manchus* (1997), Fu Manchu

> was clearly not Chinese – the early stories described him as having 'bright green eyes and neutral-coloured hair' . . . not a stereotypical 'Chinese'. Rather, Fu Manchu in these stories represents a stereotypical combination of 'Tartar' savagery with the cosmopolitan heartlessness of the new global criminal class. . . . When Hollywood decided to bring Fu Manchu to the screen the character was recast as strictly Chinese . . .

From *The Mask of Fu Manchu* (1932) onwards, the devil doctor still has eyes 'which were green as the eyes of a leopard', but in other ways his dependence on an elixir of youth seems to have changed his appearance. 'The indescribable evil of [the face]' is from now on increasingly likened to 'that of Seti the First, the mighty pharaoh who lies in the Cairo Museum', or to Buddha, as well as to Shakespeare and Satan and sometimes Dante. Where Nayland Smith is concerned (in *The Mystery*), 'all my efforts thus far have not availed me to trace the genealogy of the man called Dr Fu-Manchu'. *Is* he meant to be entirely Chinese? Yellow Peril villains often combined Japanese (warlike) with Chinese (clever) blood, or mixed other races with the Chinese. And why does the elixir diminish his Chinese characteristics, while enhancing his nobility in Rohmer's eyes?

'. . . all the cruel cunning of an entire Eastern race . . .'

Standard texts such as Arthur H. Smith's *Chinese Characteristics* routinely listed 'absence of sympathy' and 'refined cruelty' as defining features of 'the Chinese character' (or rather, the lack of it). Smith wrote that the Chinese 'display indifference to the sufferings of others, which is probably not to be matched in any civilized country'; and after listing various extreme punishments for adultery and theft, added ominously that 'we have no space even to mention the dreadful tortures . . . in the name of justice'. His characteristic conclusion was that 'physical force cannot safely be abandoned until some moral force is at hand adequate to take its place'. The answer was Protestant Christianity. The European tradition of circulating sets of pictures illustrating Chinese punishments and tortures – for example, engravings of naked oriental women roasting on spits – had been around for at least two centuries, but was reinvigorated at the turn of the century.

A recent study of the changing significance of Chinese torture in the imagery of the West has concluded:

> During the nineteenth century, the historiography that equated cruel punishments with historical backwardness . . . turn[ed] China into a museum of all that Europe had left behind, a Pandora's box of leftover images blending moral denunciations with realistic reports, fictive fantasies with picturesque imaginings. Out of these fancies and fears, Western observers produced an image of a torturing China that, among other consequences, gave the imperialist West the justification it sought to prove that it had to act in China, carving it up just as the executioner cut up his victims.

So, at the time when the tormented body vanished from public view in the West – with the ending of public torture and execution – it reappeared, through the printed word, prints and then photographs, 'in that now quintessentially Oriental place, China'. In this oriental aesthetic of horror, the most widely publicized tortures included the *bastinado* (the bamboo rod), the *canque* (the wooden stocks), flaying with bamboo and whip, water dripping onto the victim's head (waterboarding), roasting over a fire, and – the most severe legal penalty the Manchu dynasty could impose – *lingali*, or 'the death of a thousand cuts' or 'the lingering death'. As the study points out, eyewitness accounts of these – and second-hand retellings – tended to fall prey to the growing fashion for sinophobia, and so to misrepresent what actually happened because it was *incomprehensible*. The death of a thousand cuts, for example, was *really* about whether the body remained whole in death as in life, and in practice the coup de grâce – a dagger in the heart – was always administered after a few gashes. It was, in the hierarchy of punishments, worse than decapitation, which in turn was worse than strangulation. The punishment was finally abolished in April

1905, in an attempt to align Chinese practices more closely with 'international standards'.

But this aspect of 'the Chinese character' gained fresh credence following sensational tales of atrocities against Europeans – and especially against missionaries – during the 'Boxer uprising' of 1900, and following the publication the year before of Octave Mirbeau's *Le Jardin des Supplices* (Torture Garden), which added an explicitly erotic dimension. Many of the Boxer atrocities proved to have been exaggerated – or in the case of the 'Pekin massacre' of July 1900 entirely fabricated – but many were not (an estimated 200 'foreign devils' killed and 30,000 'secondary devils' or Chinese Christians), and they had wide circulation through popular exposés and hastily compiled memoirs by survivors from the British Legation: the Boxer slogan 'Preserve the dynasty, destroy the foreigners' sent shivers down the spines of British middle-class readers, even if in the event many thousands more Chinese than Europeans had been killed. Mirbeau's novel – about a frustrated, sadomasochistic English girl called Miss Clara, who leads the French narrator through an exquisite pleasure garden, where 'torture is mingled with horticulture, blood with flowers', in the heart of a Canton prison – was intended as a satire, in time-honoured fashion, on bourgeois morality back home and on contemporary scandals in North Africa. She feels drawn to Eastern mysticism and sexuality – as well as to cruelty. 'Clara confided to me that she felt increasingly disgusted by Europe. She couldn't tolerate its rigid customs . . . Only in China did she feel happy and free.'

So, Mirbeau's satire was received as yet another sadistic projection onto China – more extreme than its predecessors – with aesthetic shock-value for urban readers who sometimes secretly craved 'images of the body in pain, just as they craved images of the body in pleasure'. But it was the tortures above all else which found their way into popular culture, not least in the fiction of Sax Rohmer. To the existing repertoire, *The Torture Garden* added the bell (or 'the swing'), where the incessant reverberations slowly kill the victim (added by Hollywood to *The Mask of Fu Manchu*, 1932); and the rat torture, where the rodent – 'deprived of nourishment for a couple of days' – is attached to a large pot on the victim's back and has only one direction to go. Described in lovingly sadistic detail as 'a prodigious invention' by the prolix roly-poly executioner in *The Torture Garden*, it was soon to be adopted by Fu Manchu. He, characteristically, called his variation 'The Six Gates of Joyful Wisdom' (in *The Devil Doctor*), and added the refinement of six separate compartments into which 'Cantonese rats, the most ravenous in the world' are introduced in stages: the first is the Gate of Joyous Hope, the second is the Gate of Mirthful Doubt, the third the Gate of True Rapture – and so on up to the Gate Celestial – which no victim ever reaches. Nayland Smith prefers the other option offered to him – a samurai sword 'of very great age' through his neck, wielded by his best friend Dr Petrie. As well as some peculiarly elaborate assassination techniques, which go well beyond the need to avoid detection, Dr Fu Manchu also has in his repertoire 'flaying alive', 'my wire jackets' (a tourniquet of wire netting screwed tightly) and 'my files' (whatever they were), usually described with vague rhetorical adjectives – like Joseph Conrad's 'unspeakable rites' in *Heart of Darkness* (1899).

'. . . with all the resources of science past and present . . .'

In the late nineteenth century, the standard popular view – in books such as Smith's *Chinese Characteristics* and J. Dyer Ball's *Things Chinese* – was that pre-modern China had once been a very inventive society, but that a mixture of 'intellectual turbidity', 'conservatism', isolation from the West and a lack of European influence had frozen the country into the static, complacent state it was in today. The Chinese had invented gunpowder – even before the Battle of Hastings – printing and bookshops, world-beating ceramics and other handi-crafts, innovative irrigation systems; and their age-old entrance examinations into the civil service were – in principle anyway – about talent rather than aris-tocracy or money. But something had gone seriously wrong round about the time of the European Renaissance. The Chinese had lost interest in advances in science and technology, perhaps because of their religious teachings, and so they had never experienced an industrial revolution. When British trade missions, in the wake of Macartney, showed off the latest Western goods in the nineteenth century, they were treated as 'toys' rather than as symbols of progress. If eighteenth-century writers sometimes tended to accentuate the positive where China was concerned – partly for domestic political reasons – their nineteenth-century successors went the other way. The West had the technological lead and China had a lot of catching up to do. How could a place that had invented gunpowder waste it on fireworks? asked Ball.

The key words in Rohmer's description of Dr Fu Manchu are 'science past and present'. Science past, everyone would expect. The Great Wall, blue-and-white ceramics, the quality of China's medieval navy – all these were well known. But what about the present? Nayland Smith provides one answer, towards the end of *The Mystery*:

> Dr Fu-Manchu was the ultimate expression of Chinese cunning; a phenomenon such as occurs but once in many generations. He was a superman of incredible genius who, had he willed, could have revolutionised science . . .

He is undoubtedly 'the greatest fungologist the world had ever known; a poisoner to whom the Borgias were as children'. 'His knowledge of venomous insects has probably never been paralleled in the history of the world.' He has developed a 'poisonous gas, in many respects identical with chlorine, but having unique properties'. He knows all about 'the anaesthetic properties of the lycoperdon, or common puff-ball'; he has distilled 'from the venom of a kind of swamp adder' an amber-hued preparation that 'produces madness', and amnesia and artificial catalepsy, 'but not always death – a drug not to be found in the British a pharmacopeia'; he has discovered 'an unclassified species of jatropha [orchid] belonging to the Curcas family', which has a poisonous hollow thorn and is called the Flower of Silence; and he has even 'solved the secret of the Golden Elixir'. But all this is dedicated to promoting his evil empire, and destroying opponents of it; 'the weapons wherewith he visited death upon whomsoever opposed the establishment of a potential Yellow Empire'. When he requires up-to-date scientists, inventors, cartographers, aviators, explorers, engineers, surgeons and physicians to further his plans, he has to kidnap them from London or try and steal their ideas, in his distinctive version of the brain drain. But when it comes to 'my menagerie . . . scorpions, pythons, hamadryads, my fungi and my tiny allies the bacilli . . . and you must not forget my black spiders', he is second to none. His Sacred Baboon (cynocephalus hamadryas) from Abyssinia, with its ferocious temperament, gleaming fangs and long hairy arms – school of Edgar Allan Poe's 'Rue Morgue' – proves particularly useful when strangling people, but tends to turn on those Burmans 'who had educated him'. Nayland Smith is constantly trying to protect eminent scientists from Dr Fu Manchu and his army of dacoits. So, following the clichés about Chinese science, the devil doctor has not seen the need to adapt to the progressive industrial world. His laboratory is like a pre-Renaissance alchemist's cell. He prefers the occult to Euclidean geometry. But in his own fields of research, as Nayland Smith concludes, 'We're children to that Chinese doctor . . . to that weird product of a weird people who are as old in evil as the pyramids are old in mystery.'

Smith is full of admiration for the doctor's mastery of ancient Chinese wisdom, and his research into toxicology. There is, however, a note of anxiety running through the Fu Manchu stories – hence 'past and present'. The doctor keeps making a mockery of 'our boasted modern security'; he moves through the modern metropolis – like Professor Moriarty – with the confidence of a spider in his web; he usually outwits the bombastic Nayland Smith. So he is in no way fazed by modernity. What if such a man *did* choose to 'revolutionize science'. What then?

It has been said of Sax Rohmer that he racialized the anxieties of more Modernist writers. In *The Golden Scorpion*, for example, he writes of a 'dreadful sudden menace, not of men and guns but of brains and capital'. Dr Fu Manchu in *The Devil Doctor* reflects that 'the East has grown in spirit, while the West has been building machinery . . .' The Foreign Secretary and Prime Minister Lord Salisbury had famously spoken, in May 1898, of 'living nations' expanding at the expense of 'dying nations', of 'great countries of enormous power' and countries which were 'weaker, poorer, less provided with leading men or institutions in which they can trust': he had been specifically referring to the scrambles for territory in Northern China when he made his influential speech. But what if the coordinates of 'living' and 'dying' were to be reversed? What if 'leading men' *did* appear? This was the paradox at the heart of Britain's attempts to 'modernize' China. The Chinese intelligentsia clearly had the ability to cope with modern science and technology. It was just that, for complex reasons, they had chosen not to. In fiction, contemporary scientific expertise in China was displaced into drugs and poisons and destructive technologies. But what if distant historical examples of 'genius' *were* to adjust to the world of modern science – without the moral and social conscience of the West? What if a new Kublai Khan – armed with modern science and technology – were to unite the nations of the East?

'... with all the resources, if you will, of a wealthy government – which, however, already has denied all knowledge of his existence ...'

The Mystery of Dr Fu-Manchu seems to have been partly written in 1911, the year a revolution in China ended the Manchu dynasty and the Confucian social order. Its serialization began the following year when Dr Sun Yat Sen's Chinese Republic was founded. With an 'impossible' Chinese name meaning 'the esteemed Manchu', it might be assumed that Dr Fu Manchu represented the dispossessed ancien regime and was bringing a rearguard action to 'the heart of London'. There are occasional hints in the early stories that he speaks in some underground way for the overthrown Manchu dynasty, and that in his youth he administered the province of Honan under the Empress Dowager. The kidnapping of Dr Sun Yat Sen in Portland Place, in broad daylight, by Manchu-sponsored officials had clearly made a strong impression on Sax Rohmer. Either that, or Dr Fu Manchu could perhaps be a renegade member of the dynasty, who was in sympathy with the ideas of Dr Sun's 'Young China'. The popular press in England was not yet quite sure what to make of the fledgling Chinese Republic, which hoped to remake itself as a nation independent of the Imperial and territorial ambitions of Britain, Germany, France, Russia and Japan. Where might this lead?

When Nayland Smith blunders into Dr Petrie's humdrum Clapham surgery at the beginning of *The Mystery of Dr Fu-Manchu*, his explanation of the fiend's motives is confused, to say the least: Fu Manchu is 'not the emissary of an Eastern power', his 'mission among men' is rather to destroy assorted orientalists who know 'the key to the secret of Tongking', or 'the truth about Mongolia', or 'the importance of the Tibetan frontiers' – all of them particularly well-informed men 'who would arouse the West to a sense of the awakening of the East'. Fu Manchu is also intent on overthrowing the Indian Empire. Smith is not even sure at this stage whether his adversary is 'a fanatic' or 'a duly appointed agent' working for some organization or other. He *is* sure, though, that he personally has travelled all the way from Burma 'not in the interests of the British government merely, but in the interests of the entire white race'; that the victory of Fu Manchu 'might mean the turning of the balance which a wise providence had adjusted between the white and yellow races'. This has something to do with 'the backing of a political group whose wealth is enormous', and Fu Manchu's mission in Europe is to *pave the way*. 'Do you follow me?' he asks Petrie, as well he might. During a subsequent argument with the Revd J. D. Eltham – the 'Fighting Missionary', the man who 'with a garrison of a dozen cripples and a German doctor held the hospital at Nan-Yang against two hundred Boxers' – Smith tries hard to discourage Eltham from returning to the scene of his former triumphs:

> China to-day is not the China of '98. It is a huge secret machine, and Ho-Nan one of its most important wheels. . . . The class of missionary work which you favour, sir, is injurious to international peace. At the present moment, Ho-Nan is a barrel of gunpowder; you would be the lighted match. . . . The phantom Yellow Peril to-day materialises under the very eyes of the Western world.

Eltham scoffs at this, but Smith is insistent. It implies that Fu Manchu is in some way associated with 'Young China'. He is 'the agent of an advanced political group' and of 'the futuristic group in China', in 'the advance guard of the Yellow Peril' – which, incidentally, makes him sound like an avant-garde performance artist as well. But when the two men meet, Fu Manchu derides this thesis, with studied aristocratic cool:

> You have presumed to meddle with a world change. Poor spiders – caught in the wheels of the inevitable! You have linked my name with the futility of the Young China Movement – the name of Fu-Manchu! Mr Smith, you are an incompetent meddler . . .

Eventually, while taking stock of all this confusion in *The Mystery*, Dr Petrie ponderously grapples with the key question: who exactly *was* Dr Fu Manchu?

> Let me confess that my final answer must be postponed. I can only indi-cate . . . the trend of my reasoning:
>
> What group can we isolate and label as responsible for the overthrow of the Manchus? The casual student of modern Chinese history will reply: 'Young China'. This is unsatisfactory. What do we mean by Young China? In my own hearing Fu-Manchu had disclaimed, with scorn, asso-ciation with the whole of that movement. . . . Amid such turmoils as this

we invariably look for, and invariably find, a Third Party. In my opinion, Dr Fu-Manchu was one of the leaders of such a party.

In the next two Fu Manchu books, this Third Party is identified with 'The Sacred Order of the White Peacock'. The Doctor's peacock goes astray just before his initiation ceremony, causing much loss of face and giving Smith and Petrie the temporary advantage. As a symbol of rank, according to Ball's *Things Chinese*, the peacock historically represented the *third rank* of the civil service, after the crane and the pheasant. But in Rohmer's universe it represents the very tops: 'the greatest man in China' is to attend the ceremony. It is identified with 'The Seven', and then with the 'murderous cosmopolitan group known as the Si-Fan'. We learn that 'the mandarin Yen-Sun-Yat' was *once* a member of The Seven, before he became a traitor – presumably a scurrilous reference to Dr Sun Yat Sen. And that 'there is a giant conspiracy' centred on the province of Honan; 'a great secret society [which] means that China, which has slumbered for so many generations, now stirs in that age-long sleep'. The society deals 'in wholesale murder, aimed at upsetting the balance of the world'. Dr Fu Manchu is a 'high official', 'a sort of delegate' in this giant conspiracy, but is junior in rank to the mandarin Ki-Ming, 'master of the unholy arts of the Lamas of Rache-Chûran'. After his time as administrator of Honan, Fu Manchu was himself initiated into 'Tibetan mysteries', and 'Si-Fan' is in fact one among other Chinese words for 'Tibet'. The Si-Fan dreams 'of Europe and America under Chinese rule'. Then again, Dr Fu Manchu predictably has some 'giant, incredible scheme of [his] own'. He seems to be working from both inside and outside the organization, using gambling and drug trafficking as need arises, and he is not above deceiving the other senior officials of the Si-Fan. He is both a member of an international criminal organization *and* a man with political ambitions.

So although he is prepared to make use of existing secret organizations to further his aims, he is also and predominantly a freelance operator – destabilizing the great powers, causing maximum disruption through his suicide cult of Indian/Burmese dacoits, constantly moving his headquarters around so he cannot be captured, communicating with Nayland Smith in very public ways. The Osama Bin Laden of his day. After the first three novels, the action was to shift, as we have seen (p. 234), from England to a global stage. Limehouse and opium dens made way for cosmopolitan conspiracies: 'Poor infants, who transfer your prayers from angels to aeroplanes! *Bringing everyone's home in the firing line . . .'* The narrative of each book takes place roughly at the time of first publication (i.e. in the 'present'), and Rohmer gradually infused more political background into the cycle, to keep pace with current events. So, Dr Fu Manchu promotes himself from small-time Limehouse crook to member of the Si-Fan to head of the Council of Seven who believes that Russia has been 'stolen by fools' (1931, *Daughter of Fu Manchu*); then he becomes self-styled controller of the balance of power in Europe against the new dictatorships (1940, *The Drums of Fu Manchu*), via manipulator of 'gold reserves, exacerbating the financial crises of the 1930s' (*President Fu Manchu*, 1936, in which *he* can't become President, of course, but his candidate can), and eventually potential world dominator, armed with various weapons of mass destruction concocted in a cavern beneath Haiti – still underground after all these years (*The Island of Fu Manchu*, 1941). In *The Drums*, he comments of Rudolf Adlon (a.k.a. Adolf Hitler), whom he seeks to control, 'whatever his failings, the man was fearless'. And of his own motives:

> My power rests in the East, but my hand is stretched out to the West. I shall restore the lost grandeur of China. . . . When you have reduced to ashes your palaces and your temples . . . I shall set back the clock. . . . Your Western world is locked in a stupid clash of arms. . . . Shadows of Russia, that deformed colossus, frighten the children of Europe. . . . German hordes over-run Europe.

Europe is unstable: China could become stable again. But in *The Island*, Fu Manchu helps the Allies against the Axis powers, to further his aims: 'When your civilization, as you are pleased to term it, has exterminated itself . . . *I shall stir.'* By *Shadow of Fu Manchu* (1948), his 'mission is to save the world from the leprosy of Communism' – to which Sir Denis Nayland Smith can only reply: 'I appreciate your aims. I don't like your methods' – and by the end of Sax Rohmer's life, he 'fights for the same goal as Free China' against the tyranny of Chairman Mao: 'Communist fools . . . ignorant, power-mad demagogues. . . . My methods in achieving [my] ideals are beyond your understanding.'

He talks autumnally of 'the traditions to which I have always adhered' and 'the selflessness of my motives', and Sir Denis even develops a grudging admiration for him. Fu Manchu is, after all, 'always an aristocrat', the Confucian ideal of a gentleman. He always keeps his word, though as Smith often discovers, his *exact* words need to be scrutinized with great care. He represents 'the lost grandeur of China' in the modern world. Rohmer tried hard, from *The Drums* onwards, to suggest that 'Hitler and Stalin were babies and sucklings compared to Dr Fu Manchu', and that in unnamed mysterious ways the *real* conflict centred on the devil doctor. But this became increasingly difficult to sustain:

> In a moment of perhaps psychic clarity I saw [Nayland Smith] against a different background: I saw the bloody horror of Poland, the sullen sorrow of Czechoslovakia, that grand defiance of Finland which I had known, and I saw guns blazing around once peaceful Norwegian fjords. An enemy pounded at the gates of civilisation, but Nayland Smith was here [in New York], and therefore here, and not in Europe the danger lay . . .

Clearly, Rohmer adjusted Fu Manchu's political motives to changing times. There was a big change in the scale of his operations between 1917 and *The Si-Fan Mysteries* and the next novel, in 1931, *Daughter of Fu Manchu* – by which time Hollywood had contributed to his public mythology, and American readers had vastly increased the sales of the books. It was in the late 1920s that the editor of *Collier's* paid a visit to Calvin Coolidge in the White House, and was pleased to discover that the President had been avidly reading, in *Collier's*, 'the current Sax Rohmer mystery; he just could not wait each week to learn whether the hero would foil Fu Manchu and how'.

At the beginning of his career of crime, Fu Manchu aims to harness traditional Chinese greatness to modern science and technology; by the end, he is reacting *against* the modernization of China and talking more about reviving the ancient values of the culture and the principles of Confucius. Rohmer kept mysterious the *precise* allegiances of his villain as they shaded into international crime – like the villains in the James Bond novels. Whether this was because he was being canny, or because his grasp of politics and geography was shaky, is not clear. But Fu Manchu is always serious. Unlike most adventure formulae, the series never deteriorated into self-parody. Sax Rohmer evidently became weary of his creation towards the end – and it shows – but he never once laughed at him. He was not that kind of writer.

'. . . the yellow peril incarnate in one man . . .'

In early editions of *The Mystery of Dr Fu-Manchu*, the phrase 'yellow peril' was sometimes presented in quotation marks, as if to acknowledge that it had been around as a slogan for some time – in journalism, popular culture and even politics. As we have seen (p. 134), *The Spectator* had used the phrase in July 1898. But some have in the past credited the Irish-West Indian novelist Matthew Phipps Shiel with originating it in the English language. In fact, the phrase itself seems to have dated from three years before Shiel's *The Yellow Danger*, when Kaiser Wilhelm II, grandson of Queen Victoria, roughly sketched and gave detailed instructions to an artist to produce on his behalf an allegorized image of 'die Gelbe Gefahr'. It showed a group of warrior women – including Britannia – standing on a rocky promontory overlooking a vast European valley beneath a shining Christian cross, being rallied by a Germanic-looking archangel Michael with a flaming sword. On the other side of the valley was a huge, threatening statue of Buddha, a 'heathen idol' seated on clouds of fire and smoke. Its printed caption, in various languages, was 'Nations of Europe, join in the defence of your faith and your homes'. The image was also signed in facsimile with the Kaiser's own handwritten prescription: 'Nations of Europe, defend your holiest possessions!' This certainly popularized a phrase which German journalists had begun using towards the end of the Sino-Japanese War, when China suffered a humiliating defeat in April 1895. The Kaiser's version dated from September of that year. He sent it in print and postcard form to 'all and sundry', and made sure it was stocked on German steamships going to the Far East. It was reproduced in Britain by journalist W. T. Stead in the Christmas 1895 issue of his monthly *Review of Reviews*.

The Kaiser appears to have become obsessed with promoting the thought behind this image, although his biographers are not agreed on how seriously he took it. He wrote to the Tsar that Russia's historic mission was to help protect Europe from the Yellow Peril, and after the defeat of Russia by Japan in 1905 added, 'Remember my picture – it's coming true!' Even on the eve of the First World War, he was still reiterating that 'the coming antagonism is between the Asiatics and the Eastern peoples'. There was much debate, though, in the British press about whether the Kaiser's Yellow Peril image was *really* about Germany's ambition to lead, or even to dominate, Europe. Sometimes the Buddha figure was interpreted as representing Japan, sometimes 'orientals' lumped together, more usually China – or even Chinese 'hordes' under Japanese military leadership. After the 'Boxer uprising', the Chinese tended to be seen, in European and especially British political culture, more and more as 'demons', rather than as sedate citizens (as they had been by late eighteenth-century philosophers) or badly behaved children (as they had been by mid-nineteenth-century businesspeople). In July 1900, responding to the 'Boxer uprising', W. T. Stead printed another version of the image in his *Review of Reviews*, this time a Dutch variant: in it, Confucius replaced the archangel Michael, a Western battleship with a Christian cross on its mast replaced the seated Buddha, and the warrior women became a selection of Asian troops. The caption read: 'People of Asia, defend your sacred gods!' It satirically reversed the Kaiser's battle-lines.

According to historian Michael Keevak's *Becoming Yellow* (2011), the chromatically inaccurate colour 'yellow' had only been applied with any consistency to East Asian people from the beginning of the nineteenth century. Before that, they tended to be categorized by European commentators as 'white' or sometimes as 'grey'. Only when East Asians were absorbed into the new racial category of 'Mongolian' did the concept of 'yellow' begin to gain widespread currency. And it was only when 'yellow' came to be perceived as a 'peril' – crossing European linguistic boundaries in the process, for the first time – that 'yellow skin would be agreed upon' as a description. In other words, 'yellow' was as much about anxiety among 'whites' as about description of an ethnic group. One of the first to write 'with absolute certainty' of 'yellow' as a racial category was Comte Arthur de Gobineau in his infamous *Essai sur l'inégalité des races humaines* (On the Inequality of Human Races) (1853–55). Mid-nineteenth-century European anthropologists had adopted an evolutionary model of 'civilizations', and tended to group them in a hierarchy of categories – savagery at the bottom of the scale, barbarism in the middle and 'civilization' (meaning Northern European societies or 'us') at the apogee. China was in the middle category. Barbaric. For Gobineau, who presented the hierarchy of 'civilizations' in racial terms, the physiological distinctions between 'white, yellow and black' were fixed, permanent and 'clearly marked' – rather than evolutionary – as was the 'immense superiority' of the white, and the inequalities between the three main races. Generalizations about 'the Chinese character' which other commentators had noted or were soon to note – 'steady conservatism', 'formalism', 'unrivalled stability', 'inability to imagine another system', 'inclination to apathy', 'lack of invention' – were to Gobineau as natural and unchangeable as their 'yellow colour, wide face and slanting eyes'. In his history of the rise and fall of civilizations, Gobineau attributed such 'civilization' as had once existed in the Celestial Empire to 'an Aryan colony in India' which must have brought 'the light of civilization' with them to the benighted 'native Chinese'. By 1880, Gobineau was warning his colleagues about the dangers of an 'Oriental movement into Europe', and how this could push Western Europe back into the Dark Ages. His last work, published posthumously, was an epic account of a battle royal between the 'whites' and the 'yellows'. In short, although sweeping generalizations about 'the Chinese' as a mass had been around for a while – and were to have a long shelf life – it took the racial theorists of the mid-nineteenth century to set the scene for 'yellow' as a *threat*.

This threat took four main forms. First, there was the *military* threat, if the vast numbers of Chinese people were to become a fighting force – as Japan had succeeded in doing, to everyone's surprise, against China and Russia, and as the Boxers had shown when they rushed fearlessly against modern weapons: the Chinese were bound to count in the wider world, sooner or later. Then there was the related *economic* threat, if the Chinese digested the lessons of modern industry and capitalism: the world would surely be deluged with their products and the dominance of foreign businessfolk in China would soon evaporate. Third, there was the threat of Chinese *immigration* and of 'hordes' of Chinese – that loaded word was originally applied to Central Asia – spilling over into the cities of Europe. And finally, the *racial* threat – the social degeneration that was thought to exist in 'Chinatowns' and to be spread through partnerships and intermarriage. All four were distilled into the catchphrase 'the Yellow Peril'. Its urgency was new; the anxiety was not.

We have seen how 'the opium den' and 'Chinatown' turned into fully fledged popular myths in Britain, during the late nineteenth century, and how Sax Rohmer fed off them. Chinese immigrants had been the small-time villains of popular fiction, and the butts of vaudeville jokes, since the 1850s. Critic William F. Wu's study of *The Yellow Peril: Chinese Americans in American Fiction, 1850–1940* (1982) examines the roots of these stereotypes in the American context. There was the fear of a flood of cheap labour – especially strong among Irish immigrants – arriving from war-torn China, after the building of the transcontinental railroad. It has been said of Irish and Chinese labourers in America – especially on the West Coast – that together they were, historically, the original American 'urban proletariat', and that there were very significant tensions between them at the bottom of the economic pile. Then, there was the threat to 'Americanization' of people who were not Christian, who talked funny, who ate strange food, wore pigtails, were visibly different and on the whole had no wish to assimilate with the mainstream even if they were permitted to. Then, after the Chinese Exclusion Act of 1882, itself mostly the result of stereotyping and demagoguery in California, the focus shifted to myths of 'Chinatown', where East Asians had gathered for self-protection – mainly in San Francisco and New York: urban ghettos as the shock troops of mass immigration; Tong wars, secret societies, opium, gambling and prostitution; a colourful exterior masking a sordid interior; a hidden, underground culture. The kinds of myth we have seen developing in Britain at around the same time. So the industrious Chinese (miners, railroad navvies, domestic servants, launderers, cooks) were remade as a threat, and the Yellow Peril became 'the overwhelmingly dominant theme in American fiction about the Chinese Americans' from 1850 right through to 1940. At first, this was about labour disputes between the Irish and Chinese communities; then about American 'nativism' and white supremacy. The very word 'coolie' came to connote servitude, low pay and stupidity. Wu concludes that it took the character of Fu Manchu to distil much of this into a single character – a *leader* – and to spread what had been a fairly marginal form of literature to the wider American readership and to cinema goers for the first time. Fu Manchu proved particularly popular in the United States. Many thought 'Sax Rohmer' must *be* an American. Even the earliest Fu Manchu stories – with their Limehouse settings – were immediately successful in America. The second and third collections appeared there first, several months before their British publication. All of Sax Rohmer's 'Chinatown' stories and novels were published simultaneously or soon afterwards in the States, between 1913 and the late 1940s: his stories without Chinese characters were not.

Equivalent studies of the image of Chinese people in American *drama*, such as the theatre historian Dave Williams's *Misreading the Chinese Character: Images of the Chinese in Euroamerican Drama to 1925* (2000), have come to similar conclusions. Williams plots four main phases in the representation of the Yellow Peril on the stage. First, round the time of the Opium Wars, plays set in China about belligerent Westerners routing the inept and cowardly natives – such as *Mose in China, or Life Among the Foo-Foos* (1850).

The word 'Fu' has many meanings, but in this play it just means one thing: 'foo is outsiders and outsiders is foo-foos'. Then, between the gold rush of 1848 and the Exclusion Act of 1882, frontier melodramas and anti-Chinese polemics, usually set in California and often emphasizing the rivalry between working-class Irishmen and more recent Chinese immigrants with cod 'Chinese' names who are represented in stereotypical ways (drunkenness, lust, clumsiness, stupidity, economic dependency). Also at this time, the presentation of genuinely Chinese performers as 'curiosities' in freak-shows back East: in April 1850, for example, P. T. Barnum promised that a Chinese woman 'is now prepared to exhibit her charming self, her curious retinue and her fairy feet (only two and a half inches long) to an admiring and novelty-loving public' – the equivalent of the 'curiosities' on display at the time of the Great Exhibition in London. After the Exclusion Act, there were comedies set in New York's or San Francisco's Chinatown – often about intermarriage – or else idealizations of Chinese women such as the very popular (and originally British) *San Toy*, set in a never-never-land of China, in which audiences 'no longer insulated themselves from the Chinese by claiming superiority over them, but rather by placing them on a pedestal'. Sometimes, such idealizations were intended as a comment on American modernity; sometimes they were expressions of fashion and style, with an emphasis on production design and the central character as a quaint, pretty doll. The characters' names now began to be derived from actual Chinese nomenclature – or at least to *sound* plausible. The settings were 'upper-class and royal', rather than working-class California. As Williams observes, 'the Chinese had moved from inferiority to superiority in Euroamerican perception without ever passing through equality and common humanity'. His conclusion, too, is that the image which distilled and 'quickly and thoroughly superseded' all previous stereotypes of the Chinese – the image which successfully *embodied* the Yellow Peril for Euroamericans, at least until the 1960s – was that of Fu Manchu.

Historian Krystyn R. Moon has similarly studied vaudeville in *Yellowface: Creating the Chinese in American Popular Music and Performance, 1850s–1920s* (2005). In the 1850s and 1860s, in California, the 'John Chinaman' character – with singers making no attempt to *look* Chinese – fed off the jokes and melodies of black minstrelsy, with very little reference to Chinese music and a lot of reheated gags (first used about African-Americans and European immigrants) about why the Chinese should go home. Musical versions of Bret

Harte's poem 'The Heathen Chinee' carried such acts to the east coast: three song versions of the poem appeared in 1870–71 alone, with clichéd 'orientalized sounds' to denote the difference between Chinese and American music. The convention of the white singer appearing in yellowface, and talking a mixture of pidgin English and gibberish, began at this time:

> Like blackface, yellowface became a way for performers to comment . . . on Chinese immigrant inferiority – by inscribing stereotypes onto the performer's body. These actors usually wore a navy-blue or black tunic with loose-fitting pants, attire that was common among labourers from Southern China . . .

One subgenre of the 'heathen Chinee' craze was the farce, song or skit about the rivalry between Irish washerwomen and Chinese laundrymen, emphasizing how this traditional form of women's work had been taken over by less-than-masculine Chinese with dire economic consequences. The comedian John 'Chinee' Leach made a career out of this kind of material on the variety stage. His hit song 'Chun Wow Low' (1882) gives a flavour of his act:

> *Chun Wow Low – eatum chow,*
> *Chinaman a walla good likum bow wow,*
> *Litta Dog, litta cat, litta mouse, litta lat.*
> *Alla wella good for to makum me fat.*

One of the few popular comedies from that period which has survived as a written text is *Patsy O'Wang: An Irish Farce with a Chinese Mix-up* (1895, published 1900) by Thomas Stewart Denison – in which Chin Sum, hired as a cook by American sanatorium director Dr Fluke, by mistake drinks from a bottle containing 'Spirit of Hibernia' and turns into Patsy O'Wang.

> Whiskey, the drink of his father, transforms him into a true Irishman, while strong tea, the beverage of his mother, has the power of restoring fully his original Chinese character.

Dr Fluke desperately tries to transform Patsy O'Wang back into Chin Sum with copious quantities of tea, measuring his success by how servile and obedient Patsy has become, but Patsy declares he is determined to remain 'Irish for ever'. The play ends on the rousing chorus:

Me father was a Hooligan
me mother was Chinay . . .

In Moon's study, the third phase in the 'continual shifting and reworking of anti-Chinese types' – matching what was happening in legitimate theatre – was a series of songs and skits in which Chinese characters (sometimes by now *really* Chinese characters) became less problem subjects and more objects of desire, with songs about honeymoons and doomed love affairs (school of Puccini's *Madame Butterfly*, 1904), cuisine that was now-fashionable in America and dreamy nights out in Chinatown. If an interracial affair ended in tears, that was fine; if it succeeded, that was unacceptable. At the same time, the music business consolidated into Tin Pan Alley: 'Chinese instruments, orientalized operas and transcriptions of Chinese melodies were all important sources for American popular songwriters.' The socially marginal, as so often happens, had become the symbolical mainstream – and, having excluded the Chinese from settling in the United States, they returned on stage as objects of nostalgia, longing and fascination. The songs were long-lasting hits – for example, 'Chinatown, My Chinatown' (1910), which originally replaced a song called 'Apache Chinese' in a Broadway show, and which became a jazz standard, recorded over twenty-five times between 1928 and 1941:

Chinatown, my Chinatown
Where the lights are low
Hearts that know no other land
Drifting to and fro.
Dreamy, dreamy Chinatown.

And 'Chink, Chink Chinaman' (1909), a song about a Chinese immigrant who runs a chop suey restaurant in a white neighbourhood, but moves out because he cannot stand the locals' taste in music. In a black neighbourhood, he has the same experience. Eventually he realizes that in both cases his clientele insists on singing the well-known playground ditty 'Chink, Chink Chinaman'. There's no getting away from it.

The detailed studies by Wu, Williams and Moon all emphasize how the changing image of the Yellow Peril represented a combination and recombination of stage fictions: race as an 'act' or as performance. Whether the act was performed by Americans who had 'yellowed up their white bodies' or by Chinese vaudevillians who commented on the stage fiction by re-enacting it, the result was an artificial construct to be exploited and manipulated. The problem was that after years of repetition in different forms, as Moon puts it:

> White audiences who often saw Yellowface as authentic and true to life [came to expect] Chinese and Chinese Americans to reaffirm the caricatures that whites had previously produced in print media and on the stage.

Meanwhile, evil Asian masterminds – a more melodramatic form of 'stage act' embodying the Yellow Peril – were beginning to catch on, even before Fu Manchu arrived on the scene. Usually they played to the Genghis Khan myth of ruthlessness and savagery. The British equivalents were appearing in juvenile literature a little later, from the mid-1890s. There was Kiang Ho, a Harvard-educated seven-foot-tall Mongolian pirate who battles Tom Edison on and under the Yellow Sea, in *Tom Edison Jr's Electric Sea Spider* (*Nugget* dime novel, February 1892). He was followed by the aged sorcerer Yue-Laon, ruler of an empire in the middle of China, who has control over 'a hundred million people, body and soul' and who has designs on New York State, in *The Maker of Money* by Robert Chambers (July 1896). Perhaps the closest to Dr Fu Manchu, though, was Dr C. W. Doyle's *The Shadow of Quong Lung* (1900), five short stories about a graduate of Yale, Barrister of the Inner Temple and Tong leader ('besides being a Master of Arts, I am a Master of Accidents'), who rules San Francisco's Chinatown with extreme ruthlessness. In his preface to *The Shadow*, Doyle wrote acerbically: 'Of course the best thing to do with Chinatown would be to burn it down; but the scheme is too utopian to be discussed in a mere preface.' In the final story, 'The Seats of Judgement', the racketeer Quong Lung accidentally falls against an electric chair designed by a white Yale classmate called Ray, whom he has introduced to opium (for Doyle, as for Rohmer, the Chinese were immune from the evil effects of opium, while the white characters are highly susceptible) and supplied with pliant sing-song girls. The name Quong Lung was presumably a reference to the Qianlong Emperor, the one who snubbed Macartney.

But the novel which most dramatically and notoriously synthesized concerns about the Yellow Peril on both sides of the Atlantic *and* featured an Asiatic mastermind at the head of an avenging horde was Matthew Phipps Shiel's very popular *The Yellow Danger*, which appeared in eight separate editions between 1898 and 1908. Predictive war fantasies – usually involving the Germans, the

French or the Russians – with a message about Britain's unpreparedness *today* and the complacency of the military establishment during the late-Victorian and Edwardian arms race – were a fashionable subgenre following the huge success of *The Battle of Dorking* (1871) by the professional soldier George Chesney. They were usually written by retired military men, and first appeared in commuter magazines. There had been a handful of these predictive fantasies involving China before, but *The Yellow Danger* was something else.

Shiel had been commissioned by *Short Story* magazine to write a serial called *The Empress of the Earth* at the end of 1897 'when some trouble broke out in China', a reference to the killing of two German missionaries there in November 1897 and the Kaiser's aggressive response. The serial proved unusually popular – from February 1898 onwards – and within a few weeks C. Arthur Pearson was asking Shiel to make it last longer. Under its new title, *The Yellow Danger*, the ferociously aggressive book version made Shiel's name as a popular novelist. One of the reasons for its popularity is that it was very topical and Shiel kept up with current events in China – and with debates about the British navy – as the serial progressed. The seizure of the port city of Kiao-chan by Germany, as a reprisal; Russian aggression towards Port Arthur; the French occupation of Hainan – these were all cited on the first page as 'a conspiracy of the three great Continental Powers to act in concert in ousting England from her predominance in the East'. On the Chinese side, Li Hung Chang – mentioned by name – was already a very well-known figure, while the sinister Dr Yen How – doctor of the University of Heidelberg, medical practitioner in diseases of women and children in San Francisco, who studies in the British Museum – was evidently based on Dr Sun Yat Sen.

The main theme of the novel – which may have been written tongue in cheek: it is difficult to tell – is that unless the three great continental powers – Germany, France and Russia – can settle their differences over 'the scramble for concessions', the likelihood is that China and Japan will join forces, exploit European conflicts, divide and rule, fatally threaten 'the white races', drain Western exchequers and launch a full-scale race war, a 'yellow invasion', with Britain – standing alone – as the final enemy. Britain, of course, is the nation with the purest motives in China. It will be a global fight to the death: 'the yellow man is doomed *if* the white man is not'. It is a question of the survival of the fittest.

Throughout *The Yellow Danger*, political events are reworked in racial-ized terms. One big difference between Dr Yen How and Dr Sun Yat Sen is that, at the beginning of the serial, Yen How falls in love with the pretty Ada Seward on a London omnibus from Poultry to Fulham. She spurns his advances, on account of his race – 'I'll give you one lillee box of soap to wash your face' is her reaction – which leads to dire personal and political consequences. The bespectacled Dr Yen How is 'the son of a Japanese father by a Chinese woman', bringing together 'two antagonistic races in one man', which enables him to rise to senior positions in both nations and to launch his attack under Japanese leadership. He has an 'intellect like dry ice', is pugnacious, and can see with frightening clarity that the population of 'Christians' in the world may number millions, but that of 'non-Christians' numbers billions. Shiel seems to have a sneaking admiration for him as an Asiatic *Übermensch*:

> Dr Yen How's idea was this: that the cupidity and blind greed of the white races could be used by the yellow man as a means to the yellow man's triumph: the white races could be made to exterminate each other pre-paratory to the sweep, in hundreds of millions, of the yellow man over an exhausted and decimated Europe.

And so it might have been were it not for sub-lieutenant John Nelson Hardy, a handsome young man with a heart of oak who still believes that heroism and pluck are the answer, rather than necessarily the latest naval technology. Hardy impresses his superiors at the sea-battle of Shoreham, against the com-bined navies of France, Russia and Germany, the first of several increasingly large naval engagements (complete with drawings of battle-plans). Meanwhile, Dr Yen How becomes more and more ruthless:

> All his acts in the rousing and organisation of China were based on a profound knowledge of the Chinese character. The principal points of this character were an immeasurable greed, an absolute contempt for the world outside China, and a fiendish Love of Cruelty.

When Hardy and Yen How meet, in Peking, the civilities are at first observed. Etiquette remains strong in China, at least on the surface:

> In the colloquy which followed, one of these two men spoke an English as perfectly grammatical as that of Tennyson or Macaulay, though with

an intensely foreign something in his way of speaking it; the other spoke broken English. It was Yen who used the good, and John the bad, English.

As ever, when English is spoken *too* well, the speaker is likely to be a foreign villain. But soon Hardy is dragged to the torture chamber, where the refined cruelties of Sin-Wan and his water tortures put 'Chinese iron into his soul'. From now on, he believes profoundly that 'this bad race was wholly bad, wholly of hell'. Which explains his ruthlessness when he manages eventually to return home. After the final great sea-battle (he realizes there is no point in trying to match the locust-like Chinese hordes with their 'Tartar blood' on land), Hardy orders 100,000 barges full of 20 million captured Chinese prisoners of war to be towed into a Nordic whirlpool and sunk, sparing 150 Chinese soldiers who are injected with a deadly virus – 'more putrid than cholera' – and landed at seventy-five European ports, killing 'within three weeks . . . a hundred and fifty millions'.

> Europe was a rotting charnel-house . . . and still England found herself confronted with the long, and sometimes bloody, and always tedious task of clearing out of Europe nearly a hundred million yellow men.

The Yellow Danger ends with the words: 'We, then, for our part, believe, and cry aloud, and *prophesy* . . .' The idea of the Chinese diaspora as a carrier of disease was to have a very long shelf life.

The Yellow Danger is a shrill, obsessive, preposterous performance. Shiel particularly enjoyed writing about apocalyptic encounters and disasters, usually involving race wars. It is difficult, now, to recover his exact tone of voice. One suggestion is that Shiel's own background – born in the Leeward Islands to an Irish father (storekeeper and lay Methodist preacher) and a West Indian mother – may have had an influence on this. Shiel often referred to his Irish ancestry ('I am an Irish Paddy'), but never referred to his mother. Was he deeply conflicted about his own mixed-race origins? Might this have inflamed his venomous treatment of most non-WASP characters in his fiction? Where exactly *was* his authorial voice in stories such as *The Yellow Danger*?

Whatever his motivation, the serial and book made a significant impact, as well as making Shiel's name. It was the hit of the season, and remained by far his most popular work. The British juvenile magazine *Marvel* responded with another invasion fantasy: *London in Danger, or The Great Chinese Invasion*

(1900–1), in which the dreaded Captain Ching shrieks: 'We will destroy the capitals of every power which has waged war against our Emperor. Ere another noon, China will possess the whole world – that is certain!' The Allied army had just 'waged war' by relieving the Legations in Peking during the 'Boxer uprising'. Then *Chums* (1910–11) serialized *Terror from the East*, in which

> The Yellow Devil [China allied with Japan] that men had dreamt about had broken loose at last. Two nations, still obscured by the mists of barbarism, threw down a gauntlet . . .

In the *Chums* serial, which ran for six months, the Boy Scouts take on the 'hissing crew of Orientals' – who have landed on Brighton beach – and manage to defeat them. Both stories picked up on Shiel's mercilessly brutal treatment of enemy forces, this time for younger readers.

London in Danger involves invasion by a Chinese fleet of aerial balloons, and there was a precedent for this as well. Shortly after *The Yellow Danger*, another Irish author – Standish O'Grady, writing under the pseudonym of Luke Netterville – cashed in by publishing *The Queen of the World, or Under the Tyranny* (1900; serialized in 1899 as *The Tyranny*), this time set in December AD 2174, when aerial warfare has progressed well beyond 'gas for buoyancy and revolving wheel-blades for propulsion' to giant 'winged air-ships' – and the globe is under the iron control of 'powers exalted, unfriendly, alien, malignant, inquisitorial'. Readers are introduced to the 'prince of the Division', a South American branch of the World Empire:

> The creature, I can scarce call him a man, was short and thick, almost globular. His face was broad, yellow, clean-shaven and flat. To my surprise the set of the eyes was noticeably, though not remarkably, Mongolian. Before this wretch men of the freest and noblest races now grovelled upon the earth like whipped spaniels.

It turns out the Imperial race is, 'all over the world', 'of Chinese origin, or Chinese mixed with Russian'. In the early twenty-first century, the great 'Asiatic flood' – 'the colonization' – had begun to overrun Eurasia and America and 'the torpid and somnolent Mongolian intellect awoke now from its sleep of ages, nay, awoke like a giant refreshed, and put forth new and mighty powers and activities'. The hero, from Ireland, 'a noted hot-bed of sedition and rebellion', is particularly sensitive to various examples of 'inglorious servitude to another race which no-one in my time had regarded with any feeling but contempt'. There had been sporadic attempts to challenge the Empire – 'the Lords of the air, the slant-eyed Celestials' – and 'the Irish section of the races took, I am glad to tell, a great and sometimes leading part in the revolt'. One Captain Pollexfen (the unmarried surname of W. B. Yeats's mother), distinguished himself in the Anglo-Chinese War by leading 'an army of combined English and European soldiers against the Chinese in Hindustan'. But now, in 2174, it is time for *all* the 'subject races' to settle their differences and unite against 'the great Tyranny' under Alfred of Tanganyika, a distant descendant of the British royal family – from a base in Antarctica. In the twentieth century, the British Empire declined through decadence within and unpreparedness without. The Tyranny started with the bravery of individual warlords, but it too had long since declined into the decadence of 'pagans and polygamists'. After assorted air-battles – like medieval jousts involving knights of old among 'the police of the upper world' – Alfred and his allies succeed in defeating the Tyranny. But Alfred is killed in the final battle, shortly after bequeathing his throne to his daughter, the long-lost Princess Royal, 'the rare and radiant maiden' Leonore (shades of Poe's 'The Raven', 1845), who becomes the Queen of the World of the title, 'alone and undisputed', and who enjoys playing an Irish harp:

> A British cheer, wildly given – but more expressive, in its raucous force, of the victory of Anglo-Saxon freedom over the slavery of the Yellow Horror than the clashing of mighty cymbals or the beating of great drums – tore the air. It was finished.

O'Grady has been styled one of the fathers of the Irish Literary Revival. But his sympathies here seem to have been with Irish Home Rule under the British Empire – albeit a less decadent Empire than his contemporary one. The Irish heroes are notably loyal to the reformed British Empire, and a strong Anglo-Irish Alliance is the result. But the decadent Empire needs to remind itself of the deeds of the old bardic heroes – *and* of King Alfred the Great against the Vikings – as well as being more on its guard against the rising dragon in the East. As with Shiel's *Yellow Danger*, it is difficult to tell the authorial tone of voice O'Grady was adopting in his novel. He uses the vogue for Yellow Peril literature for his own purposes. Interestingly, he is prepared to cast the Chinese into the outer darkness in his single-minded allegory of Home Rule – and to present the issues in racial, rather than political, terms. Maybe

Sax Rohmer inherited, through his family, something of the Irish/Chinese tensions of the late nineteenth century – magnified through the fantasies of Shiel and O'Grady. One thing is for sure, though: Standish O'Grady knew a great deal less about aerial combat than H. G. Wells, and it shows.

Wells's *War in the Air* owes a great deal to *The Yellow Danger*. It was serialized in the *Pall Mall Magazine* from January 1908 – 'before the days of the flying machine' – and published as a book later that same year. Its scenario of total aerial warfare involves, among the five main alliances of international powers, the 'Confederation of Eastern Asia' – 'a close-knit coalition' of China and Japan. Wells refers to then-current ideas of the Yellow Peril but does not himself take sides in that particular debate: his concern is simply to describe, through the eyes of the down-to-earth London bicycle mechanic Bert Smallways, the German attack from the air, under the 'blond and virile' Prince Karl Albert, on the United States fleet, followed by total war which triggers the invasion of the American mainland by the Confederation. The main point of the story is that 'mechanical invention has gone faster than intellectual and social organization', and has made old-style thinking about warfare redundant. Bert, in common with everyone else in Britain, has 'a squittering succession of thinly violent ideas about German competition, about the Yellow Peril, about the Black Menace, about the White Man's Burthen . . .' These are, Wells notes, forms of patriotism 'perverted and distorted in the rush of the new times'. Then the Asian Confederation attacks, at first with lightweight machinery manned by Japanese samurai (for whom H. G. Wells seems to have had a strong admiration, following the Russo-Japanese War three years before).

> 'With this step,' said Tan Ting-siang, 'we overtake and pass the West. We recover the peace of the world that these barbarians have destroyed.'

> 'Every country was hiding flying-machines [summarises Bert's German friend Kurt]. They're fighting in the air all over . . . the world. The Japanese and Chinese have joined in. That's the great fact. . . . The Yellow Peril was a peril after all! They've got thousands of airships . . . now Asia is at us all, and on top of us all. . . . It's mania. China on the top. And they don't know where to stop . . .'

Eventually, the 'jerry-built' "modern" civilization of China' gives way under the strain of sustaining and resourcing a big invasion. Meanwhile, Bert muses about the penny-dreadful adventures he read 'when I was a kid' and how very out of date they have become. While Europe was 'all at sixes and sevens with our silly flags and our silly newspapers raggin' us up against each other', China had 'millions and millions of men only wantin' a bit of science, and a bit of enterprise, to be as good as all of us . . .'

Wells's point is not about unpreparedness, or about the *real* enemy being China: it is about how war seen from the skies, including the bombing of cities, is bound profoundly to transform the conflicts of the future. Wells is, as he put it, taking 'some developing possibility in human affairs and [working] it out so as to develop the broad consequences of that possibility'. In the process, Wells takes some of the simple-minded conventions of Shiel and others, and relocates them in a technological/progressive context.

A couple of years later, Jack London published his short story 'The Unparalleled Invasion' in *McClure's Magazine* (July 1910) – which picked up on the idea of 'war in the air', or rather war *from* the air, but used it for very different polemical purposes. The long-term result of the Russo-Japanese War is, contrary to expectations, 'the awakening of China': a newly confident Japan, 'dreaming a colossal dream of empire for herself', decides to develop China as a colony. Between the West and China, there is 'no common psychological speech', no common language of understanding; but between Japan and China there is, based on 'the common Mongol stock'. So Japan develops China's natural resources, her industries and her army. Eventually, by 1922, China is ready to throw off the shackles, and proceeds to invade Formosa, Korea and Mongolia. Then French Indo-China. The rest of the world is content to sit back and watch, because 'China was to be feared not in war but in commerce'. China seems to have no Imperial ambition, at least not in the traditional sense. The danger lies in 'the fecundity of her loins'. While other nations squabble, China's population grows to 1,000 million, and expatriate Chinese begin to take over the whole of Asia. Eventually, it is 1976 and America takes note; a humble New York scientist called Jacobus Laningdale comes up with the solution – to drop glass phials of various plagues onto the mainland Chinese population from the air. He easily persuades the President of the United States, and the 'unparalleled invasion' is the result. After most of the population of China has been wiped out, 'the world moved in' – guided by American democratic principles. The postponed bicentennial of the USA can now take place, and the countries of the world solemnly pledge themselves never to use biological warfare against each other. Jack London, the same writer and journalist as had written sensitive and perceptive accounts of life in the East End of London, in late-Victorian times, was now joining the sabre-rattlers who predicted the dire consequences of the renaissance of China. It is difficult to judge whether his story is intended to be a warning about biological warfare or a celebration of it. It is certainly a celebration of Yankee know-how, and a prediction of the American century. And it shamelessly played to middle-class anxieties about the Yellow Peril.

By 1909, P. G. Wodehouse was already satirizing Yellow Peril literature, and invasion novels in general, and their equivalents in juvenile magazines, in *The Swoop! or How Clarence Saved England: A Tale of the Great Invasion.* The Germans have landed in Essex; the Russians have occupied Yarmouth; the Mad Mullah has captured Portsmouth; and the Swiss navy has been sighted immediately westward of the bathing-machines at Lyme Regis:

> China, at last awakened, had swooped down upon that picturesque little Welsh watering place, Lllgxtplll, and despite desperate resistance on the part of an excursion of Evanses and Joneses from Cardiff, had obtained a secure foothold. . . .

> The Chinese especially had undergone great privations, having lost their way near Llanfair Pwlgwnngogogoch, and having been unable to under-stand the voluble directions given to them by the various shepherds they encountered. It was not for nearly a week that they contrived to reach Chester, where, catching a cheap excursion, they arrived in the metrop-olis, hungry and footsore, four days after the last of their rivals had taken up their station.

Only fourteen-year-old Clarence MacAndrew Chugwater, intrepid and bespectacled member of the Boy Scouts (founded in 1908, under the Boer War hero Robert Baden-Powell), seems to be taking the situation seriously. Most people are treating the nine-power invasion as a kind of World Cup for cricket-ers. Meanwhile, negotiations in London proceed slowly. General Ping Pong Pang tries to communicate in 'Chinese characters of the Ming period', which no one else understands. Eventually, the members of the alliance begin to argue among themselves and, this being 'the Music-Hall age', it is agreed that the only solution is for the invading generals each to be offered engagements in West End halls to deliver musical monologues about 'How I invaded England'.

The Boy Scouts, led by Clarence, successfully fight back with hockey sticks and catapults. *The Swoop!* ends with 'the nation's Proudest Possession – Clarence Chugwater' himself appearing on the stage and performing 'a few of those playground exercises which have made our Boy Scouts what they are'. In the suitably solemn Preface, written as from 'the Bomb-Shelter, London, W.', Wodehouse had announced to his readers:

> It may be thought by some that in the pages which follow I have painted in too lurid colours the hours of a foreign invasion of England. Realism in art, it may be argued, can be carried too far. I prefer to think that the majority of my readers will acquit me of a desire to be unduly sensational. It is necessary that England should be raised to a sense of her peril, and only by setting down without flinching the probable results of an invasion can this be done . . .

So, three years before the arrival of Dr Fu Manchu, written by his ex-bank colleague Arthur Ward, Wodehouse was unable to keep a straight face when reading hysterical predictions about the invasion of England by Chinese, and other, hordes. He saw them as the equivalent of music-hall turns: the public had an appetite for seeing outlandish sights – such as Invasion – 'and the music-hall provided the easiest way of doing it'. As the historian of science fiction I. F. Clarke points out in his study of invasion literature at this time, *Voices Prophesying War* (1970), it was the *solemnity* of such predictions – with endorsements from serious figures in the armed forces who wanted larger government grants – that was their most striking feature. Maybe Wodehouse thought – or hoped – that *The Swoop!*, by sending up the craze, would be the last word on the subject. If so, Sax Rohmer was about to prove him spectacularly wrong.

'But Smith, this is almost incredible!'

Sax Rohmer's description of the devil doctor at the beginning of *The Mystery* is given by Nayland Smith to the narrator Dr Petrie. Smith, we have learned, is an ex-District Commissioner, late of Burma, who now has

> a roving commission . . . not in the interests of the British government merely, but in the interests of the entire white race, and I honestly believe

– though I pray I may be wrong – that its survival depends largely upon the success of my mission.

He is 'a servant of the British government', armed with the highest possible credentials, now 'in the character of a detective'. From his surprise entrance onwards, he talks of himself in highly charged, bombastic language as 'a man who would arouse the West to a sense of the awakening of the East'. One of Dr Petrie's roles, on behalf of the reader, is sometimes to rein him in, or to ask him to explain what on earth he means. Smith is the only character in the early stories who constantly sees Dr Fu Manchu's criminal activities as more than just a local Limehouse-based case: he interprets the Doctor's every move on an Imperial and even global scale.

This largeness of perception hints at the origin of Smith's name. It is evidently from Wayland (or Weland or Weyland) the Smith, the mythical smith-god of the Saxons. Rohmer's most likely source was Rudyard Kipling's *Puck of Pook's Hill* (1906). The stories in *Puck* were intended 'to be read by children, before people realized they were meant for grown-ups'. In the first story, called 'Weland's Sword', two children are acting out their juvenile version of *A Midsummer Night's Dream* in an East Sussex meadow, when Puck manifests himself to them. He tells the children about the Old Gods and the Old Things who inhabited the area in ancient times, and he begins with the story of Weland the Smith.

Once upon a time, says Puck, Weland – 'not a gentle God' – arrived by sea with some Saxon warriors and 'began a long chant in his own tongue, telling me how he was going to rule England'. Puck predicts that, like all the Old Gods, Weland will one day fall from grace. 'Smith of the Gods . . . the time comes when I shall meet you plying your trade for hire by the wayside.' Sure enough, a long time afterwards, 'a year or two before the [Norman] Conquest' to be precise, at Weland's Ford, Puck comes across 'a white-bearded, bent old blacksmith in a leather apron' who creeps out from behind the oak and begins to shoe a horse. 'It was Weland himself.' Since the rise of Christianity, Weland has been forced to use his talents shoeing horses for a living. 'You foretold it, Old Thing. I'm shoeing horses for hire. I'm not even Weland now. . . . They call me Wayland-Smith.' When they need a horse to be reshod, local farmers leave a penny on a nearby stone, tie the horse to an oak-tree and call, 'Smith, Smith, here is work for you!' Then they come back the following morning to collect the horse. Only if some human being wishes Weland well, will he be released from this toil, which will enable him 'to get back to Valhalla'. A young novice monk called Hugh persuades a grumpy farmer to thank the smith – even though 'Wayland-Smith's a heathen' – which at last releases him. As a thank-you present, Weland crafts the novice a rare gift 'that shall do him good the wide world over and Old England after him': a sword. Back at his monastery, Hugh discovers the sword and in his excitement shouts 'Saxon battle-cries'. His abbot, convinced by now that the novice does not have what it takes to become a fully fledged monk, advises him to go into the wide world: 'go with your sword, and be as gentle as you are strong and courteous'.

Puck of Pook's Hill is partly about the rise and fall of Empire – a way for Kipling to keep pessimism about contemporary Britain at bay by regressing to childlike fantasies of old England set in the deep countryside. There is a sense of 'the once and future king' about his linked stories, and one of the symbols of this is Wayland-Smith and his sword of righteousness. Although *Puck* is set in East Sussex, 'Wayland's Smithy' was also – by long tradition dating back to before the Norman Conquest – a megalithic burial mound in Oxfordshire, named by the Anglo-Saxons, and still associated in folklore with the legend that if a horse is left by the Smithy overnight, with a silver sixpence, it will be reshod by morning.

There were equivalent stories of the exploits of Weland in Norse and North German sagas. The eighteen-year-old Adolf Hitler briefly fantasized about writing an opera about *Wieland der Schmied*, just after being rejected for a place at the Academy of Fine Arts in Vienna in 1908. He had discovered that Wagner had written a brief draft sketch for an opera libretto based on the Germanic legend of the master-craftsman Wieland – about 'the raw, uncultured folk of old' – and read about his exploits in a popular book called *Legends of Gods and Heroes: The Treasures of Germanic Mythology*, one of the few books he actually read at this time. For a few days, Hitler was apparently obsessed with the idea, then characteristically lost interest.

Sax Rohmer's Nayland Smith, with his strong, dogmatic sense of mission on an Imperial scale, is clearly intended to be a latter-day version of Wayland-Smith – Anglo-Saxon style. As befits an angry god, he is in a permanent state of frustration that no one will pay any attention to him. He is forever 'snapping' or 'rapping' or 'jerking' or 'crying' his speeches, rather than just speaking them, as if perpetually impatient with lesser mortals. He often reminds Petrie of the urgency of the situation ('Time is of the essence'), then loads his cracked briar pipe with 'broad cut Latakia mixture' and paces up and down tugging at the lobe of his left ear ('as was his habit in moments of perplexity') or beating his fist with his left palm. 'You must have worn tracks in more carpets than any man in England,' says one of his long-suffering colleagues. At times like this, Smith tends to reflect 'through clenched teeth' on the enormity of the task facing him – 'I am a child, striving to cope with a mental giant' – and to emphasize the encircling gloom. He wants to turn the tide, but it is usually ebbing not flowing.

Nayland Smith has a strong sense of the fragility of the British Empire, and always sees contemporary Britain through an Imperial prism. He is not an armchair detective, or a Scotland Yard policeman or a spy – like the other club-land heroes of Edwardian fiction – he is a *warrior*, trying against the odds to wield the sword of righteousness. The very first thing he does, when he appears to Dr Petrie at his surgery at the beginning of *The Mystery*, is to roll up his shirt sleeve and show him his latest battle-scar – a deep wound on the forearm made by 'a barb steeped in the venom of a hamadryad':

> 'There's only one treatment,' he continued, rolling his sleeve down again, 'and that's with a sharp knife, a match, and a broken cartridge. I lay on my back, raving, for three days afterwards, in a forest that stank with malaria, but I should have been lying there now if I had hesitated. Here's the point. It was no accident!'

> 'What do you mean?'

And so the story begins. Nayland Smith, in the early novels, seems to be able to command the protection of Scotland Yard, the support of the British Medical Association, the resources of His Majesty's Secret Service, the cooperation of the War Office – not to mention the backing of the Criminal Investigation Department, the India Office and the Royal Geographical Society. He is 'vested with powers which rendered him a law unto himself'. He has 'carte blanche', he raps, from the Commissioner of Police. He orders a police inspector to 'jump in a taxi, pick up two good men to leave for China at once' and the inspector does what he is told. He has a strong sense of fair play, even when it is to his own disadvantage: 'a servant of the Crown in the East makes his motto: keep your word . . .' He even asks Dr Fu Manchu to 'trust in the British sense of honour'. He is described as 'lean, agile, bronzed with the suns of Burma'; 'his long residence in Burma had rendered him spare and had turned his naturally dark skin to a coppery hue . . . his face so lean as at times to appear positively emaciated' – a model of masculinity at a time when fears of 'degeneration' were in the ether. At one point he despatches a giant poisonous centipede with 'one straight, true blow of the golf-club'. He is a model of British efficiency too. Amid all the coincidences, chance encounters, locked rooms, disguises, occult happenings, eavesdropped conversations, booby traps and escapes, it is Nayland Smith who makes sense of it all for us, who puts together the scattered pieces – by constantly reminding us, usually at the top of his voice, of the evil genius behind it all: Dr Fu Manchu. Mantra-like, he repeats the words 'Eastern', 'Yellow', 'Chinese', 'Chinaman', 'Oriental'. It is his way of linking the serialized, melodramatic action sequences and giving them the only available coherence: he, and he alone, turns them into a sequential narrative. Historian P. J. Waller, a specialist in the Edwardian period, sees Nayland Smith in such moods as

> one of the most surprising comic creations in modern literature: it always seems to me surprising as I read the books that he was not locked up, that people took him seriously. Most of his speeches in the books are delivered in a fever heat of hysterical denunciation of the villainy of Fu Manchu, and his self-proclaimed mission is to save the world as he knew it, and his mission is also of course to preserve the purity of the white race.

In the later Fu Manchu books, roughly from *The Drums* onwards, Sax Rohmer toned down his presentation of Nayland Smith – to the noticeable detriment of sales in England. But it is clear that Smith is meant to be *the* established authority, with a seemingly profound knowledge of Asia past and present – through which the reader always sees 'the other'. He is not just an expert on China, he knows all about Fu Manchu's alien networks as well: dope-pushers and impostors, secret societies, anti-British foot-soldiers such as Thuggees (breakaway worshippers of Kali, the Hindu goddess of death), dacoits (acrobatic Indian bandit-assassins who have fled to Burma) and Lascars: in later books, he also became an expert on Muslim fundamentalist sects. He knows about esoteric poisons, ancient tortures and of course Chinese characteristics. All subsumed – for him and for us – into 'the oriental mind'. Because, unlike in *The Yellow Danger* and its ilk, the threat is not military or even economic:

he must keep one step ahead of subversion and infiltration by always reading the signs. He must always be alert to the potential terror. Dr Fu Manchu spends his time bumping off or kidnapping specialists in Asian Studies of one kind or another who know enough to thwart his plans, so at one level the novels are about a struggle between the two over the *meaning* of the Orient, over its narrative, with Nayland Smith as the authorized version.

In the first book alone, these specialists include Sir Crichton Davey, who has held high office in India, and who is 'the only living Englishman who understands the importance of the Tibetan frontiers', enough to write 'an important book' about British interests there; the Revd J. D. Eltham, veteran of the 'Boxer uprising', who possesses information 'which has made him an object of interest to Young China' and who has been warned not to return to Nan-Yang by the mandarin Yen-Sun-Yat no less; Sir Lionel Barton, flamboyant orientalist and explorer, who makes Francis Younghusband of 1903 Tibet expedition fame look like a shrinking violet, and who has 'turned his attention to Tibet – thereby signing his own death warrant'; and Mr Graham Guthrie, British Resident in North Bhutan, whose work there is directing suspicion towards Dr Fu Manchu, something to do with 'secret influences at work to overthrow the Indian Empire, to place, it might be, the whole of Europe and America beneath Eastern rule'. What they have in common, says Smith, is that they are all in their different ways specially 'alive to the Yellow Peril'.

Dr Petrie, meanwhile, after total immersion in Smith's sermons, begins to think the same way:

> Since Nayland Smith's return from Burma I had rarely taken up a paper without coming upon evidence of that seething which had cast up Dr Fu Manchu. Whether, hitherto, such items had escaped my attention or had seemed to demand no particular notice, or whether they now became increasingly numerous, I was unable to determine.

He does, however, try to keep Smith under control, to act as a referee when his partner's fanaticism leads to unforgiveable breaches of etiquette. He mediates Smith's arrogance to us through a more conventional, less imaginative intelligence: this allows Smith to be understood without compromising his dogmatism. Smith's willingness to explain himself – albeit impatiently – to an 'ordinary, middle-class practitioner' seems something of a check on his misanthropy. Petrie maintains a respectful silence during Smith's tirades and, unlike

Dr Watson, does not in the end say, 'I did not pause to argue over this atrocious sentiment.' Petrie's first instinct is to interpret Fu Manchu's 'malignancy' in a different way to Nayland Smith: he diagnoses that 'the man is a dangerous homicidal maniac'. Smith will only accept half of that statement. 'Dangerous, yes, I agree,' he mutters; 'his existence is a danger to the entire white race.' Smith has no truck with medical or psychological explanations. And in the end, Dr Petrie goes with the flow.

Nayland Smith's battle for the meaning of the East is partly about what is now known as 'the Imperial Archive' embodied in British bureaucracy – paperwork, files, mapping: ways of making China legible and visible to British officials such as himself, a process which has been described as 'de-territorialization and re-territorialization' – the paper archive amassed by such organizations operating in China as the Imperial Maritime Customs, the Royal Asiatic Society, the Legation in Peking, the administration of the Treaty Ports and, outside the bureaucracy, by missionaries and teachers. All this information, which by late-Victorian times had filtered into non-specialist books such as *Chinese Characteristics* and *Things Chinese*, had become synonymous to British readers with 'China'. As an administrator stationed in Burma, Smith would have spent much of his time keeping the archive up to date. But what if the great game were to be turned *against* Britain? What if the chessboard was turning from 'white' to 'yellow'? Dr Fu Manchu is compiling a *rival* archive – by murdering British scholars and senior administrators in the field, kidnapping high-level scientists and medical researchers and taking them to China, taking revenge for the Opium Wars and the Allied reprisals after the 'Boxer uprising', and by combining his deep understanding of esoteric Eastern wisdom (which only 'adepts' in the West can begin to comprehend) with Chinese science and of course Chinese cunning. Dr Fu Manchu himself holds degrees from universities in Britain and Europe: he is using Western expertise against itself.

And he uses the great artery of the Empire, the River Thames, as 'his highway, his line of communication, along which he moved his mysterious forces'. Not just the dockland area around Wapping, Shadwell and Limehouse Reach – but out to the Estuary, and upstream to where he has a 'mansion' filled with *Chinoiserie* near Windsor Castle itself. Joseph Conrad's Thames, the crucible of adventure and Empire – with its East and West India docks, its warehouses and wharves – has become Fu Manchu's thoroughfare despite the best efforts of the River Police. When Smith and Petrie are trying to track him down, they 'circle upon the map a tract of country cut by the Thames'.

> Smith and I both had noticed how Fu-Manchu's activities centred always about the London river. Undoubtedly it was his highway . . . always he made his headquarters upon the river. It was significant . . .

Fu Manchu may be a Chinese Moriarty, but Nayland Smith is certainly not a Sherlock Holmes. The relationship between Dr Petrie and Smith in some ways resembles that between Watson and Holmes. But on closer inspection, their differences are more significant. Petrie's medical knowledge is – unlike Watson's – vague to say the least, and Smith is not a consulting detective or a freelance adventurer, but 'a plain Civil Servant', a representative of the state. Only later in the series does he become an Assistant Commissioner at Scotland Yard and a knight of the realm.

And Smith is not very good at playing the detective. He rarely solves a crime in time, never quite catches his man, usually falls straight into traps and needs help to extricate himself. While Dr Fu Manchu sits calmly in his lair on his cushioned throne, surrounded by his dragon draperies, Smith is constantly hailing cabs, running for trains and generally dashing from crime scene to crime scene when he is not lecturing Dr Petrie back at base. Whereas in the Sherlock Holmes stories the threat to the established order comes from homicides or burglaries or attempts at blackmail, in Rohmer's Fu Manchu novels it comes from the Yellow Peril. Since we know who-done-it, the interest shifts instead to the 'why' (oriental conspiracy) and the 'how' (How will Fu Manchu be thwarted this time round? How will he escape in the end?) – both focusing on the villain rather than the heroes. Unlike in the Sherlock Holmes stories, the narrators and their backgrounds change during the series, after the first three books: but not the points of view. Because Smith is so often caught on the back foot, the national sense of optimism and invulnerability which features so strongly in most Edwardian adventure and detective stories becomes, as one critic has put it, 'a grim racial fatalism'; a sense of standing on the darkling plain.

Smith often expresses his frustration that the powers-that-be do not understand the *scale* of the threat, and that – unlike his enemy – he has to contend with red tape and official apathy. In classic detective stories, because the identity of the criminal cannot be revealed until the final chapter, his or her character tends in important ways to remain hidden from the reader. That is part of the puzzle. In action thrillers, the villain is more likely to be centre stage, even if his appearances are carefully rationed. The writers of the more highbrow detective stories looked down on Sax Rohmer and his ilk. Ronald Knox, for example, one of the founders of pseudo-scholarship surrounding the Sherlock Holmes stories, codified the 'rules' of the detective story into 'Ten Commandments' in 1929, as a preface to a collection of that year's *Detective Stories*:

1. The criminal must be someone mentioned in the early part of the story, but must not be anyone whose thoughts the reader has been allowed to follow.
2. All supernatural or preternatural agencies are ruled out as a matter of cause.
3. Not more than one secret room or passage is allowable.
4. No hitherto undiscovered poisons may be used, nor any appliance which will need a long scientific explanation at the end.
5. No Chinaman must figure in the story . . .

These 'Commandments' could almost be a direct response to Sax Rohmer, as could the initiation oath devised by Knox for the Detection Club founded in 1932, at the peak of Rohmer's success, for writers of detective stories:

Do you promise that your detectives shall well and truly detect the crimes presented to them, using those wits which it may please you to bestow upon them and not placing reliance on, nor making use of, Divine Revelation, Feminine Intuition, Mumbo Jumbo, Jiggery Pokery, Coincidence or the Act of God . . .

Do you promise to observe a seemly moderation in the use of Gangs, Conspiracies, Death Rays, Ghosts, Hypnotism, Trap Doors, Chinamen, Super-criminals and Lunatics – and utterly and forever forswear Mysterious Poisons Unknown to Science?

Rohmer made regular use of every single one of these plot devices – except 'Divine Revelation' – up to and including 'Mysterious Poisons Unknown to Science'. Rohmer did write detective stories – for example, nine short stories and five novels featuring detective Paul Harley of Chancery Lane, and four novels featuring Gaston Max of the Paris Sûreté (first appearance in 1915: in some ways a prototype for Hercule Poirot), but for obvious reasons he was never initiated into the Detection Club. Occasionally, members of the Club would have a go at Rohmer in *their* stories. Carter Dickson (John Dickson Carr) in his locked-room mystery *The Plague Court Murders* (1934), the first of his Sir Henry Merrivale stories, has Sir Henry complain:

> Why, only last week they phoned up from the downstairs office and said an Asiatic Gentleman wanted to see me, and gave his name. I was so bloomin' mad I chewed the phone, and I yelled down and told Carstairs to chuck the feller down all four flights of stairs. And he did. And then it turned out that the poor feller's name really *was* Dr Fu-Manchu after all, and he came from the Chinese Legation . . .

If detective-story writers *did* make use of evil Chinamen, they tended to take the form of red herrings rather than yellow menaces. It has been said that the only detective/adventure writer of the interwar years who *didn't* include an inscrutable Chinese person at one time or another was Leslie Charteris of *The Saint* fame, and that was because he was half-Chinese! Where the classic practitioners of detective stories were concerned, Rohmer's stories were 'absolute rubbish' – the phrase used by Julian Symons in his study of the genre, *Bloody Murder* (1972).

The 'Mumbo Jumbo' in Rohmer's stories came from his interest in the occult, which tended to give his disjointed plots a dreamlike quality. One of the most distinctive features of the Fu Manchu stories is their blending of adventure and occult. He could not resist peppering the text with snippets of esoteric information, whether in character or not:

> It was in the ruins of Glastonbury Abbey that the adept Kelly, companion of Dr Dee, discussed, in the reign of Elizabeth, the famous caskets of St. Dunstan, containing the two tinctures . . .

> 'Only a gasworks,' came Smith's voice. 'But it always reminds me of a Mexican teocalli and the altar of sacrifice.'

As a young writer, Rohmer's highest ambition had been to write about the exotic East in the dreamy style of a Flaubert. In the Fu Manchu stories, this dreamlike qualify suffuses his approach to sex. While Nayland Smith represents manly action, Dr Petrie represents domesticity and sexual fantasies of 'the Orient'. From the moment he meets Karamaneh, Fu Manchu's Arab slave-girl, Petrie is in a state of high excitement at her heady mix of the erotic and the exotic. 'To our great good fortune, she has formed a sudden attachment, characteristically Oriental, for yourself,' observes Smith. Even though it is Karamaneh who regularly saves the intrepid pair from the clutches of Dr Fu Manchu, in the nick of time, Smith still does not trust her:

> You *know* that she is utterly false, yet a glance or two from those dark eyes of hers can make a fool of you! A woman made a fool of *me* once, but I learned my lesson. . . . You have failed to learn yours. If you are determined to go to pieces on the rock that broke up Adam, do so! But don't involve me in the wreck . . .

Petrie is not about to learn his lesson. His heart is 'fluttering like a child's' even though – or maybe particularly because – he notices at once that 'this beautiful stranger was not a child of our northern shores':

> The soul of Karamaneh was a closed book to my shortsighted Western eyes. But the body of Karamaneh was exquisite: her beauty of a kind that was a key to the most extravagant rhapsodies of the Eastern poets. Her eyes held a challenge wholly Oriental in its appeal; her lips, even in repose, were a taunt. And, herein, East is West and West is East.

For Petrie, that 'wholly Oriental' represents desire and sensuality. When Karamaneh visits him at home, he isn't sure whether he is awake or having a pleasurably erotic dream:

> She threw open her cloak, and it is a literal fact that I rubbed my eyes, half believing that I dreamed. For beneath, she was arrayed in gossamer silk which more than indicated the perfect lines of her slim shape; wore a jewelled girdle and barbaric ornaments; was a figure fit for the walled gardens of Stamboul – a figure amazing, incomprehensible, in the prosaic setting of my room. 'Tonight I had no time to make myself an English miss,' she said, wrapping her cloak quickly about her. You see me as I am.'

It was unusual – in Edwardian detective *or* adventure fiction – for the hero to fall in love with an 'oriental'. If he did, the relationship was almost certain to end in tears, *Madame Butterfly*-style. In plays, the Lord Chamberlain's office of censorship insisted on it. Thrillers were more likely to feature fragrant, plucky gals with floral complexions. But Karamaneh has hidden depths. She not only embodies Petrie's erotic dream of the Orient – an object of Petrie's contemplation – she embodies Nayland Smith's sadistic fantasies as well.

> 'You don't know the Oriental mind as I do. . . . If you would only seize her by the hair, drag her to some cellar, hurl her down and stand over her with a whip, she would tell you everything she knows, and salve her strange Eastern conscience with the reflection that speech was forced from her. . . . And she would adore you . . . deeming you forceful and strong!'
>
> 'Smith,' I said, 'be serious . . .'

Sax Rohmer clearly enjoyed writing about 'ivory skin' scarred by the whip. He even included a description of the practice in his monologue for the music hall 'The Pigtail of Li Fang Fu'. In his novel *Dope*, he attributes the fantasy to an impressionable Mayfair dope girl called Mollie Gretna:

> Mollie's eyes opened widely. . . . 'I have read that Chinamen tie their wives to beams in the roof and lash them with leather thongs until they swoon. I could die for a man who lashed me with leather thongs. Englishmen are so ridiculously *gentle* to women!'

Then again, Mollie Gretna is often prone to 'Chinatown' fantasies of this kind: 'I think there is something so magnificently wicked-looking about a pigtail – and the very name of Limehouse thrills me to the soul.' Karamaneh herself predictably, and depressingly, conforms to Smith's reading of 'the Oriental mind'. After all, he *is* the authorized version:

> If you will carry me off . . . so that I am helpless, lock me up so that I cannot escape, beat me, if you like, I will tell you all I do know. While he is my master I will never betray him. Tear me from him – by force, do you understand, *by force*, and my lips will be sealed no longer. Ah, but you do not understand. . . . I have said enough.

Dr Petrie is by now well out of his comfort zone:

> . . . it was dreadful to hear such words from a girl who, save for her singular type of beauty, might have been a cultured European.
>
> I clenched my teeth. Insane thoughts flooded my mind. For that creamy

skin was red with the marks of the lash. . . . I could not trust myself to speak for a moment.

Of another 'Eurasian' girl who is 'wickedly handsome', and rather less intoxicating, Dr Petrie writes:

> I use the word *wickedly* with deliberation; for the pallidly dusky, oval face . . . and her half-closed almond-shaped eyes, possessed a beauty which might have appealed to an artist of one of the more perverted schools, but which filled me less with admiration than with horror.

Belonging to the world of Edmund Dulac rather than 'the more perverted schools', Karamaneh is there to bridge the gap between Petrie's and Smith's perspectives. Smith is constantly resisting the lure of the eroticized East: it is as if he will be diminished as a warrior-hero if he allows himself to be seduced. His Orient is all about perils and plots, Empires and archives. Petrie, on the other hand, is in a constant state of erotic excitement. Karamaneh sends his senses reeling every time she meets him. But he never has physical contact with her. His Orient is feminized as an object of desire, not of performance. It is as if, like the incense-filled and opium-fuelled appearances of Dr Fu Manchu, she is happening in a dream. The doctor has a high opinion of Petrie's scientific knowledge: 'You shall be my honoured guest at my home in China. You shall assist me to revolutionize chemistry.' He is wrong about this – it is based on a misunderstanding – but it provides Rohmer with a direct link between Dr Petrie and *his* wet dreams, Fu Manchu and his drier ones.

Because, in addition to his giant intellect and cunning, the devil doctor is able to induce 'horrible phantasmagoria', 'waking dreams', hallucinations and 'dark fantasies' in his victims. Although he uses the opium trade as a 'front', he personally is immune from the drug. If anything, it sharpens his concentration. This, combined with his esoteric knowledge – of sorcery, Tibetan wisdom, ancient Chinese magic – leads Smith and Petrie into a confusion of fact and illusion, to the point where even their home turf of London seems to become a frightening and alien place. Much of the action takes place at night, in failing light, or in thick fog. Fu Manchu, it is clear, is playing a great game with *them*. On various occasions, Nayland Smith, thoroughly destabilized, begins to doubt his own sanity. In *The Mystery*, Dr Petrie spends half a chapter not knowing whether he is experiencing 'a strange dream', 'a delirium', or 'a waking nightmare':

That sense of fantasy, which claimed me often enough in those days of our struggle with the titanic genius where victory meant the victory of the yellow race over the white, now had me fast in its grip again. I was an actor in one of those dream-scenes of the whole Fu-Manchu drama.

Which leads to another distinctive feature of the series, the contrast between the perspectives of Smith and Petrie, and the down-to-earth reaction of the police. Rohmer's policemen, with their reassuringly homely names, invariably see the 'dream-scenes' in terms of the normal pattern of London dockland crime. This allows Fu Manchu to laugh at the amateurish and inept antics of his adversaries.

There is such a divine simplicity in the English mind that one may lay one's plans with mathematical precision, and rely on the Nayland Smiths or the Dr Petries to play their allotted parts . . .

In place of the detective story, Petrie presents us with a series of melodramatic situations strung together by Nayland Smith's explanations, and frequent repetitions of reassuring stylistic signature themes. Petrie will intone Smith's 'Yellow Peril incarnate in one man' speech at least once. Fu's voice will be described as 'sibilant' and 'guttural', Nayland Smith will 'rap' his staccato speeches. And Petrie will provide florid, over-written, expositions of the story so far. For the record, in the first three books, Nayland Smith 'snapped' ninety-six times, 'cried' seventy-seven times, 'rapped' fifty-nine times, 'muttered' twenty-six times and 'jerked' nineteen times. Rohmer may have written, in *The Mystery*, that 'there is no incidental music to the dramas of real life', but there certainly is in *his* stories. By 1917, Petrie's narratives have turned into a parade of 'allotted parts': the attempted murder or kidnapping of a prominent orientalist; a rant about the Yellow Peril by Nayland Smith; a scene in Shen Yan's or John Ki's opium den, a 'front' for Dr Fu Manchu's operations; a contrast between Smith's and Fu's codes of civilization; an elaborate machine of torture, described in meticulous detail, but seldom fully used; and so on, culminating in a final chase and Fu Manchu's 'death'.

There will be disguises – Smith as an oriental sailor, Fu as a professor working in the British Museum – and explanations of apparently occult phenomena: the devil doctor convinces potential buyers that a house is haunted by bell-ringing ghosts; Smith discovers the mice with bells tied to their tails which have been trained to run along the wainscoting. There will be dacoits and Thugs, mysterious poisons and sinister death-delivering agencies. The formula of the first three collections, consisting of twenty-nine stories, is a curious mixture of the reader's favourite box of chocolates – or so Rohmer hoped – and a deeply unsettling theme. Rohmer originally intended to finish the saga there, and for Fu Manchu's third 'death' to be permanent. Petrie and Karamaneh are married and settle down in Egypt and Smith wishes them well. The English Channel stands in for the Reichenbach Falls. Thirteen years and seventeen books later, following British serials and a Hollywood film, Rohmer began serializing *Daughter of Fu Manchu* in 1930 by popular demand . . .

At this point, Petrie ceased to be the narrator, making guest appearances with Karamaneh (by now Mrs Petrie) in *Daughter of Fu Manchu*, *The Bride of Fu Manchu* (1933) and *The Trail of Fu Manchu*. One advantage of Petrie's first-person narration in the first three books – and that of his successors in subsequent stories – over the three novels told in the third person (*Shadow of Fu Manchu*; *Re-Enter Dr Fu Manchu*, 1957; and *Emperor Fu Manchu*), is that we are presented with the fragmentation of a suburban, middle-class world – and its certainties – through the eyes of an identifiable personality who takes an active role in the proceedings. His relationships with Nayland Smith and Fu Manchu, and of course Karamaneh, are significant, as is his reaction to events. This enables us to share his perplexities, doubts and finally his acceptance of Smith's authority about what is *really* going on. It has been argued that the Fu Manchu stories share this sense of fragmentation and dislocation, of things falling apart, with Modernist novelists and poets of the period – but that instead of responding to the chaosmos with formal or linguistic innovations, they *racialize* the problem.

In such an analysis, Dr Fu Manchu becomes a deeply threatening version of 'the outcast of modern life' – the *flâneur* who treats the metropolis as his canvas. And Sax Rohmer's equivalent of a fragmented world where 'all that is solid melts into the air' is the dreamlike quality of his prose. He does not experiment with language (except to use archaisms) or with individual subjective experience; he does not write from different perspectives or play with the disjunction of form and content – but he *does* present a vision of the city where things apparently do not add up, where the Yellow Peril seems the *only* way to make sense of the chaos. So while Ezra Pound from 1913 onwards was finding 'imagistic' forms of beauty in the pictographs of classical Chinese poetry of the Tang dynasty, and James Joyce was including several references to the spectacular Edwardian light opera *The Geisha* (1896) in *Ulysses* (1922), Sax Rohmer was responding in his way to the alienating experience of trying to navigate the modern metropolis. For Joyce, music-hall songs were part of the repertoire of sights and sounds he could combine and recombine to evoke the cityscape. The Irishman Rohmer, however, was writing from *within* the music-hall tradition, and the view from there was very different.

Dr Petrie's various successors as narrators at least enabled Rohmer to present the stories through the eyes of someone who does not 'know' as much about Fu Manchu and the threat he poses as Petrie does by then, and who does not have to unlearn the cumulative lessons of the previous stories. This was always a problem with Dr Watson. *Daughter* brings not only a new narrator but a fresh villain in the form of Fu Manchu's rebellious daughter Fah Lo Suee, alias Madame Ingomar. She is his child by a Russian mother – a significant alliance – and her villainy serves to make Fu Manchu seem more human: 'In her, Sir Denis, I share the sorrow of Shakespeare's *King Lear*.' So the devil doctor is refreshed too, as is his appearance. The narrators come and go, but Fu Manchu – with a little help from his elixir of life – goes on forever. He is, after all, the top of the bill. Even when Nayland Smith at last has the opportunity to bring down the curtain on him, towards the end of the series in *Shadow*, he cannot bring himself to do it:

'Cease fire there!' he shouted angrily . . .

'You fool!' Nayland Smith's words came as a groan. 'This was no end for the greatest brain in the world.'

Sax Rohmer liked to say ruefully that long after he had been forgotten his creation Dr Fu Manchu would be remembered. He was right. In the year Rohmer died, 1959, P. G. Wodehouse published *A Few Quick Ones*, in which Bertie Wooster complains about his Aunt Dahlia:

This has shocked me, Jeeves. I wouldn't have thought such an idea would ever have occurred to her. One could understand Professor Moriarty, and possibly Doctor Fu Manchu, thinking along those lines but not a wife and mother highly respected in Market Snodsbury, Worcestershire.

It was a tribute, of sorts.

CHAPTER SIX

'The World Shall Hear from Me Again'

I Limehouse to Our House

In 1924, a ten-minute documentary film called 'Cosmopolitan London' – part of the series *Wonderful London*, based on some popular pictorial magazine articles – was doing the rounds. After offering viewers brief glimpses of Italians in Soho, 'negroes' in Whitcomb Street, Australian diplomats in the Strand, Eastern European traders off the Whitechapel Road, Irish shoppers in Tower Bridge Road and Lascars having their hair cut 'hard by Limehouse Pier', director Harry B. Parkinson and writer Frank Miller reached their destination:

> Now we are in sinister Pennyfields, where the Chink either shrinks away at the sight of the camera, or bursts into volleys of hysterical protest. But perhaps he has a reason for his dislike of publicity!

A shot of a narrow street corner, showing a woman with a pram and a little girl looking self-consciously at the camera. Men in suits walk by. The explanatory intertitles continue: 'Dun and mysterious is London's Chinatown – and in Limehouse Causeway one gets the tang of betel-nut, of bhang and of – opium.' A Chinese woman in an apron smiles, as she poses near a brick wall with a drainpipe, while holding a child – perhaps her son – dressed in a woolly coat. She looks tired and nervous: 'We managed to persuade these two to pose for us – but then, you see, they *are* half-English!' Cut to a shot of uniformed guardsmen marching on Horse Guards Parade, as well-dressed onlookers follow a military band:

> Yes, there are nicer places in London than Limehouse – and one is glad to get back to the centre of things and see something which reminds us that there is still something *British* in wonderful London!

'Cosmopolitan London' seems to want it both ways: it enjoys staring at the exotic, bustling cosmopolis at the centre of the Empire, and yet the facetious intertitles encourage viewers to be unsettled and even disgusted by what they are seeing. Except that viewers are not seeing what the intertitles say they are seeing. The cobbled street does not look remotely 'dun and mysterious'. The camera *can* lie, it seems. 'Cosmopolitan London' was released at a time when the *cinematic* image of Limehouse – through films such as *Broken Blossoms* (1919; released 1920) and *Cocaine* (1922) – had already become so well-established, in the wake of Thomas Burke's and Sax Rohmer's stories, that *Kinematograph Weekly* referred to 'the Limehouse melodrama' as a distinct category of films. The British Board of Film Censors was already concerned about the trend, and its association with now-banned drugs. Ironically, its President was none other than T. P. O'Connor, longstanding family friend of the Rohmers.

At much the same time, posters advertising the Stoll Picture Production of *The Mystery of Dr Fu-Manchu* (1923), all fifteen two-reel episodes of it, were to be seen at underground stations and on hoardings – Mrs Sax Rohmer clearly remembered the impact of these larger-than-life posters, which showed 'the leering visage and clutching hands of the Devil Doctor' as played by the gaunt Irish actor Harry Agar Lyons. In cinema foyers, there were graphic displays of Chinese lettering 'on panels' and usherettes dressed in suitably exotic traditional oriental costumes. No wonder those streets in Chinatown seemed so 'dun and mysterious'. *The Mystery* never mentioned Limehouse or even Chinatown by name. By that stage it did not need to. There had been unauthorized knock-offs of the earliest Fu Manchu stories circulating in cinemas well before this: *The Mysterious Mr Wu Chung Foo* (released in America at Christmas 1914 just two years after the original short stories had appeared in magazine form), *London's Yellow Peril* (1915), the serial *The Trail of the Octopus* (1919).

And Yellow Peril films went back at least as far as autumn 1900, when the popular British four-minute short *Attack on a Chinese Mission* – filmed in the garden of a derelict property called Ivy Lodge in Hove, Sussex – depicted 'nine Boxers in Chinese costumes of varied character' storming the compound of a Christian Mission, threatening the missionary and his family, until a party of bluejackets and marines, under the command of a mounted officer, arrives in the nick of time to overcome the marauding rebels and take them prisoner. The missionary has been killed; his wife and daughter are saved. According to the film's catalogue entry, 'This sensationalist subject . . . is everywhere greeted with great applause.' It had the most coherent narrative of *any* film made in England up to that time, featured cross-cutting and premiered at Hove Town Hall on 17 November 1900 – when the events it reconstructed were still happening in Northern China. In the same week, the Warwick Trading Company issued *Shanghai's Shops and Opium Dens*, a short actuality filmed 'in one of the worst sections of Shanghai':

> . . . showing numerous vile dens and shops, while hundreds of Chinamen are seen pulling their carts and carrying bundles, many appearing in a semi-nude state, all eyeing the camera operated by the 'foreign devil' with suspicion!

And there had been D. W. Griffith's dark, misty, gas-lit vision of Limehouse in *Broken Blossoms*. Most British critics observed that Griffith's 'Limehouse' was a great deal more colourful than the real thing, and treated it as a Hollywood fantasy: but it set the tone for cinematic depictions from then on, including British-made films. *Broken Blossoms*, which had the subtitle 'The Yellow Man and the Girl' and the working title 'White Blossom and the Chink', was based on Thomas Burke's short story 'The Chink and the Child' from his collection *Limehouse Nights*. It turned Burke's lowlife Cheng Huang into an idealistic Buddhist student-priest (Richard Barthelmess) who comes to London in the hope of 'bringing the glorious message of peace to the barbarous Anglo-Saxons of turmoil and strife' – reversing the logic of Empire – and changed the abused English girl from a twelve-year-old to a fifteen-year-old (played by the twenty-three-year-old Lillian Gish). Cheng Huang sometimes visits an opium den to dream of home – where he was esteemed as much more than 'just a Chink storekeeper'. As the empurpled intertitles put it (they are much more purple than Burke's prose): 'Chinese, Malays, Lascars, where the Orient squats at the portals of the West. . . . In this scarlet house of sin, does he ever hear the temple bells?' White women are there too, puffing away at 'the lilied pipe', and so are Chinese musicians. It is a scene out of Charles Dickens as much as Thomas Burke or Sax Rohmer and, like much of the film, it is shot in soft focus, a new experience for filmgoers. *Broken Blossoms*, marketed as a superior art film, was a box-office hit (cost $88,000, earned $700,000).

In the same year, from Germany, there had been Robert Reinert's *Opium*

(1919) – which had taken advantage of the post-war relaxation of censorship there to present in melodramatic, expressionist style the sinister, shuffling Nung Tschang (Werner Krauss) – in skullcap, dragon robe and pencilled eyebrows – who 'hates all Europeans' and introduces a benign German professor to the joys of opium-smoking in his well-appointed Chinese parlour – the pipe prepared by a tall Malay in a floppy turban – before getting his revenge on the professor and his family for apparently abducting his daughter Sin (later Magdalene) and taking her to Germany. *Opium* featured several Symbolist-inspired 'opium dreams' of randy blackface fauns chasing naked women clutching floral bouquets around a lakeside, and included some of the cast of *The Cabinet of Dr Caligari* (made the same year). China was described as 'the homeland of opium'; some of the action took place in India, where there was also an elaborate 'Opiumhöhle'; and the intertitles in the Nung Tschang sequences were presented in bamboo lettering.

And, in 1920, Stoll had produced a six-reel version of *The Yellow Claw*, based on the then-recent Sax Rohmer novel, in the company's first year of production, directed by American expatriate René Plaisetty. Most of the significant Yellow Peril movies at this time were made in England by American or European filmmakers, several of them émigrés. Reviews had complained that the story was 'peculiarly weak and futile', but that the scenes in an opium den and on the Thames had been well staged. But *The Mystery of Dr Fu-Manchu*, closely based on the first two Fu Manchu collections of stories, was altogether more ambitious. Stoll had realized that shorter subjects, in serial format, were his strongest suit. Thirteen and a half of the fifteen episodes have survived: they have the usual low-rent production values of Stoll pictures: cheap special effects (in the first episode, an ordinary lizard stood in for a giant poisonous centipede); painted drapes and dungeon for Fu Manchu's headquarters; the same dacoit in blackface falling from a great height at least four times. To compare *The Mystery* with Fritz Lang's *Dr Mabuse the Gambler* (1922) or even with Louis Feuillade's *Fantômas* (1913–14) is to compare cheap filmed theatre with *films*.

The individual episodes tend to be formulaic: Nayland Smith (Fred Paul) and Dr Petrie (H. Humberston Wright) are in Petrie's study above his sparse consulting room; news arrives of some orientalist dignitary who has been murdered/kidnapped/drugged; Inspector Weymouth of Scotland Yard (Frank Wilson, who was also one of the screenwriters) is contacted in his office;

Smith and Petrie hail a cab and rush to the scene of the crime, where there is some increasingly bizarre evidence of Fu Manchu's fiendish cunning; they go hunting for clues about the devil doctor in 'exotic' settings (an opium den – 'whatever you do, Petrie, don't inhale'; 'the Oriental Club – a page from the *Arabian Nights* within a few minutes of Piccadilly Circus'); Dr Fu Manchu is seen, raving, in his laboratory lair (a bamboo curtain, a gong, some painted *Chinoiserie*); following various coincidences, the heroes blunder in, are captured, Fu Manchu threatens to torture them, and all seems lost; the slave-girl Karamaneh comes to their rescue and asks them to trust her; they escape; Inspector Weymouth arrives, but Fu Manchu manages to get away and have the last laugh; the stolid Nayland Smith, in his three-piece tweed suit, will stride around while smoking his briar pipe and tugging at the lobe of his ear; the more mature Petrie will be a venerable surrogate for Dr Watson and will fall in love with Karamaneh; the short-fused Fu Manchu will cackle, grimace, roll his eyes, extend his claw-like fingers and gurn, as he throttles one of his victims or shouts 'I'll get you yet!' while standing beside the Thames at the end of an episode; the intertitles will turn into Chinese bamboo lettering at tense moments; and a spectral Fu will be superimposed between Smith and Petrie in one of the very few special effects. Harry Agar Lyons has slicked-down hair, pale makeup, is clean-shaven and has extended eyebrows. He wears a patterned floral mandarin robe and skullcap when he is at home; and a cloak, wide-brimmed hat, floppy bow-tie, spats and shiny shoes when he is on the street – like a pantomime villain. In summer 1924, after *The Mystery* had been released, Harry Agar Lyons visited the real Limehouse on a publicity stunt, in full regalia, and it was reported that 'he created great excitement among the genuine Chinese, who cheered whenever he triumphed in the story'.

Notwithstanding the repetitions and minimal production values, Stoll's *The Mystery of Dr Fu-Manchu* was and is a very faithful adaptation of the first two books in the series. Various elements from the novels were included – never to appear on screen in subsequent versions: the marmoset on Fu Manchu's shoulder; the clean-shaven villain; the Si-Fan secret organization for which Fu works; 'the dark Eurasian wildcat Zarmi' (Julie Suedo); above all, the interracial affair between Dr Petrie and Karamaneh (Jean Clarkson), a concept which Hollywood could not countenance until as late as *The World of Susie Wong* (1960) – unless the girl conveniently died of a broken heart before anything untoward could happen. Post the Production Code of 1930, if there was a hint of an interracial affair in a Hollywood movie, one of the partners *had* to die, even if the oriental was played by a yellowed-up American actor. Even if it just involved kissing. Strangely, for the period, Rohmer's racial insults are not much in evidence. Dr Fu Manchu 'pursues his devilish inscrutable sway', and Smith says at one point – in a direct quotation – 'pray God the river has that yellow Satan' – but it is made clear that the Chinese government wants nothing whatsoever to do with him.

In 'The Shrine of the Seven Lamps', the last of the series, Nayland Smith rather unsportingly shoots the fleeing Fu Manchu in the back and empties his gun into the body. The episode ends with a Chinese dignitary, in court dress, surrounded by officials, bestowing on Smith a decoration: 'in ridding the world of Dr Fu Manchu, you have earned the gratitude of the whole world'. Then Karamaneh and Petrie embrace at last, while Smith looks on and – a rare occurrence – smiles: '*My* reward . . . Karamaneh has consented to be Mrs Petrie.' The problem was that, in the absence of racial vituperation or political explanation, it was never made clear *why* Fu Manchu was being quite so beastly and why Nayland Smith was so obsessed with him. The critic in *Bioscope* noted that the stories made 'no attempt to be plausible, but depend entirely upon the appeal of lurid sensationalism'.

> The chief mystery about Fu Manchu is any possible motive for his career of crime, and the impunity with which this homicidal maniac goes about his deadly work without attracting the attention either of the police or the commissioners in lunacy.

Fu Manchu's motivation was to be supplied – literally, with a vengeance – in 1929 with the first Hollywood, and the first talking, adaptation, *The Mysterious Dr Fu Manchu*, also the first official step towards his Americanization. By then, Harry Agar Lyons had left Stoll to star in a six-episode serial about Dr Sin Fang for rival Pioneer Films, again opposite Fred Paul as the detective: he was already becoming typecast, and several 'oriental' parts were to follow, including a *singing* mandarin in Fred Paul's musical *In a Lotus Garden* (1931). But such an obvious example of plagiarism in 1928 showed, among other things, just how chaotic Sax Rohmer's business affairs had become. Since late 1927, he had been in dispute about royalty payments with his literary agent: he had simply asked his agent for cash when he needed it, and had no idea how his royalties were accumulating, or which rights had been sold and to whom. Pirate editions and unauthorized lookalikes were beginning to proliferate. *Hutchinson's Magazine* was shortly to run 'a sensational and thrilling serial by Sax Rohmer', with the instalments printed in the wrong order. Nobody noticed. Edgar Wallace, with *The Yellow Snake* (1926), featuring the devilish Fing Su, and Agatha Christie with *The Big Four* (1927), which locked Poirot's assistant Hastings in a Limehouse opium den, were busy getting in on the act.

Hollywood was ready for Fu Manchu. Serials, features, pulps and novels had already prepared the ground, albeit in diffuse ways. In May 1927, Grauman's Chinese Theatre had opened in Hollywood – with a thirty-foot stone dragon flying between huge red columns at the entrance: Anna May Wong, in a full-length silk Chinese cloak, had done the honours at the ground-breaking ceremony. Paramount Famous Players-Lasky Corp. purchased the film rights to the first trio of Fu Manchu books and – since the resulting films, directed by Rowland V. Lee, were made during the transition from silent to sound – turned them into stagey drawing-room melodramas with a lot of help from intertitles. But they *were* Hollywood's first-ever *series* of horror films, and the first one was in some ways a prototype for the Bela Lugosi *Dracula* (1931). They were also filmed at a time when the MPPDA (Motion Pictures Producers and Distributors of America) had recently promulgated a series of 'Don'ts and Be Carefuls' for the industry, including '[avoid] picturizing in an unfavorable light another country's religion, history, institutions, prominent people and citizenry', but somehow Dr Fu Manchu slipped through the net – as if he existed in a parallel universe.

The 'all-talking' *Mysterious Dr Fu Manchu* (it was filmed in both silent and sound versions) begins in Peking with the doctor as a genial family man, a specialist in oriental medicine who is 'dedicating my life to mankind'. During the rebellion of 1900, some retreating Boxers take refuge in his garden and use it as cover – 'Do not fear, the white men are kind and generous. They will not harm the house of Fu' – and the resulting collateral damage by trigger-happy Allies destroys Fu Manchu's beloved wife and son, and most of his house: 'God of my ancestors,' he cries, 'I have been blind. These whites are barbarous, devils, fiends.' He has been looking after Lia, the young daughter of the Revd Eltham (Jean Arthur) and he now vows to use her as his agent of revenge. He aims to kill an officer of the Allied Expeditionary Force for every bloodstained scale on his sacred dragon tapestry, and to destroy the Petrie family:

'The house of Petrie will atone for the house of Fu.' Twenty years later, in foggy Mayfair . . .

The filmed opened on 10 August 1929. Fu Manchu was played by the Swedish-born actor Warner Oland – who was not particularly tall, weighed fourteen stone, and came over as bovine rather than feline – but he did have vaguely 'Asiatic' features which were, he claimed, the result of 'the Mongol Invasion' via his Russian mother. So Warner Oland (born Johan Verner Ölund) had specialized in oriental villains since 1917. Most recently he had played Cantor Rabinowitz, the Orthodox Jewish father of Al Jolson, in *The Jazz Singer* (1927). Today, he is more fondly remembered for his many performances as the genial, pidgin-speaking, grammatically challenged, chubby Hawaiian detective with the sing-song voice, Charlie Chan – a part he played sixteen times between 1931 and 1938, when he died in the middle of shooting the seventeenth.

The Mysterious Dr Fu Manchu introduced the 'Fu Manchu moustache' for the first time, turned District Commissioner Nayland Smith into 'Inspector Nayland Smith of Scotland Yard – the greatest criminologist alive' (O. P. Heggie, later the blind hermit in *The Bride of Frankenstein*, 1935), defused the interracial romance of the books by having Lia Eltham – rather than Karamaneh – fall in love with Dr Jack Petrie, grandson of the Allied general. The film in fact jettisoned most of Rohmer's first book, making Fu Manchu himself – who appears too often – into a warm, chuckling character; but it did include Singapore Charlie's, now a gambling joint rather than an opium den. The devil doctor, on several occasions, draws attention in an arch way to the improbabilities of the plot and the clichés which the audience might already be expecting from this sort of film:

> I'm afraid my somewhat weird and oriental methods may have misled your occidental mind into believing that – er – this is nothing but a gigantic melodrama in which the detective's arrival at the last moment produces the happy ending.

At the end of *The Mysterious Dr Fu Manchu*, the doctor drinks from a cup of poisoned tea ('bring tea – the *guest* tea') – 'after all, Inspector, our story ends in the usual way' – but revives at the beginning of *The Return of Fu Manchu* (1930), made by the same team, after an elaborate funeral. As he explains, 'The theory is old – your Shakespeare used it in *Romeo and Juliet*.' The poison *simulates* death for a few days. And, as Nayland Smith adds, there was no autopsy 'out of respect for his religion'. *The Return* has little to do with Sax Rohmer's second collection of stories except for the names of the lead characters. There is more confident dialogue in this second film, and the action occasionally moves beyond the drawing room or dungeon. In the hurried last reel, Fu Manchu ('this is not the end of the story – only the end of another chapter') falls into the Thames as a grenade explodes in his hand.

The Return opened in America on 2 May 1930. After that, Fox signed Oland to play Charlie Chan. He was by then Hollywood's top 'oriental' performer. There had been three not-very-successful attempts to film the Charlie Chan stories since 1926, the year after he first appeared in print, and author Earl Derr Biggers was delighted that Oland was to 'try it at last'. He was apprehensive as well. '[I] hope to heaven he understands what sort of character Charlie is – not a sinister Fu Manchu.' Oland certainly *did* understand the difference. In his *New York Times* obituary on 7 August 1938, it was correctly noted that 'the hisses and grimaces of his long-nailed villainy were swiftly forgotten as Chan's traditional "so sor-ry" politeness, through Oland's reformed lips became now box-office magic'. The Charlie Chan films kept Fox solvent throughout the 1930s. When Warner Oland learned a bit of Mandarin Chinese and visited Shanghai in March 1936, he was given a hero's welcome. The Charlie Chan films had proved popular successes in China, too – the Nationalist government was pleased, maybe relieved, to permit the screening of films which presented such an unusually positive, if eccentric, image of a Chinese character – and audiences there seem to have forgiven him for the Fu Manchus – which in any case were never officially screened in China, though they could be seen in the Treaty Ports. He decided to give interviews in character as Charlie Chan and in costume: 'Visiting the land of my ancestors makes me so happy.'

With Warner Oland preparing *Charlie Chan Carries On* (1931), his first, over at Fox, by the time of *Daughter of the Dragon* (the third in the Paramount series, 1931), Fu Manchu as a character had been relegated to a guest appearance, not even appearing in the title. Sax Rohmer had sold the rights to *Daughter of Fu Manchu* to Paramount Publix Corp. on 23 March 1931 for $20,000, a year after it began serialization in *Collier's*. *Daughter* had also been serialized on radio (March–May 1930) in *The Collier Hour*, a variety programme on the NBC Blue network, in twelve fifteen-minute segments promoting the current issues of *Collier's*. But all the studio purchased for this large sum of money was, it seems, the word 'daughter'. The film bore no resemblance at all to the novel, which was published in book form that same year. *Daughter*, directed by Lloyd Corrigan, was released in the States on 5 September 1931, and cost $268,032.75. It jettisons Nayland Smith – instead, there is the more stuffy Sir Basil Courtney of Scotland Yard (Lawrence Grant, who was soon to play Sir Lionel Barton in *The Mask of Fu Manchu*, and the Burgomaster in *Son of Frankenstein*, 1939). It features a *different* daughter of Fu Manchu (Ling Moy rather than Fah Lo Suee). And it kills off the devil doctor – for real – a third of the way through the story. He arrives at Ling Moy's house, fatally wounded:

'. . . death lays his hands upon me and my sacred work is unfinished.
　　 Petrie still lives . . .'
'The blood is mine. The hate is mine. The vengeance shall be mine.'
'My flower daughter. The knife would wither your petal-fingers.'
'Father – I will be your son . . . I SWEAR.'
'Sovereign spirits, you have answered my deepest prayer. I have a son.'

So much for the *daughter* of Fu Manchu!

Princess Ling Moy, a celebrated Chinese dancer in Limehouse before she is fatally distracted by her father, was played by Anna May Wong: it was her comeback movie in Hollywood after she had left for Europe ('I was so tired of the parts I had to play – why is it that the screen Chinese is always the villain of the piece?') following the experience of *The Crimson City* (1928), when she found herself supporting Myrna Loy, who was made up in yellowface to play the Asian lead part; before that, she had played an assortment of doomed Butterflies, a Mongol slave-girl and a Native American. Following a couple of years in Europe, on stage and screen, and a stint in a Broadway version of an Edgar Wallace thriller, the first film part she could get was *Daughter*. The film did, however, result in a three-picture deal for her, and did make her the first Chinese-American to become a name above the title. The dashing, romantic Chinese detective Ah Kee, a character added to the story – perhaps on the rebound from Charlie Chan – was played by the Japanese-born actor Sessue Hayakawa (his stage name 'Sessue' means 'snowy island'), the best-known Asian-American leading man working in Hollywood in the silent days, who had been a major star since the mid-1910s. He, too, had left for Europe for a stint, in 1924, fed up with playing villains and forbidden lovers. Eventually, anti-Japanese feeling, and the strong views of the Hays Code on miscegenation, led him to leave again. *Daughter* was one of the first Hollywood films to feature two above-the-title Asian stars. It was Hayakawa's official 'talkie' debut – and his farewell as a Hollywood star. Unfortunately, there was little chemistry between Ling Moy and Ah Kee; throughout the story, her mind is on other things, as the echoing voice of her father Fu Manchu keeps reminding her.

This was not Warner Oland's finest hour as Fu Manchu. That had occurred in 1930, in a short segment of the portmanteau movie *Paramount on Parade*, one of those potpourri Hollywood showcases of contracted stars, dancers and musicians, which were fashionable at the time. Hosted by Jack Oakie, the segment was called 'Murder Will Out', and it featured the leading characters from Paramount's mystery movies: Dr Fu Manchu, Sherlock Holmes (Clive Brook), Philo Vance (William Powell) and Sergeant Heath (Eugene Pallette) – the dim policeman who is routinely humiliated by Vance. Oakie has apparently been murdered, with a note about destroying 'the lives of the foreign devils, father and son, into the third generation' pinned to his back and signed by Fu Manchu. Sergeant Heath enters and handcuffs Fu Manchu as the most obvious suspect. Then Philo Vance, debonair in top hat and evening wear, introduces himself and asks Heath in a supercilious way how he can be *sure* Fu Manchu was the murderer: after all, he hasn't 'mentioned the word "psychology"' and he hasn't bothered to spend screen time eliminating all the other suspects. Then Sherlock Holmes appears in a deerstalker and Inverness cape, says, 'Elementary, my dear Watson,' and orders everyone in the room to stand still: no one has mentioned 'the pearls'. 'Am I to be arrested or not?' asks an increasingly impatient Fu Manchu, as he whispers something to Sergeant Heath, who observes approvingly, 'Damn clever, you Chinese.' At which point Fu Manchu shoots Philo Vance in the bottom – he chivalrously pretends the bullet has hit him elsewhere – shoots Sherlock Holmes in the heart – he falls over gracefully – and says to the Sergeant, 'I had to do it. It was the only way I could convince them that I am a murderer.' He pushes a button, the corpse of Holmes disappears, he leaves the ground and flies offscreen like a caped crusader. Jack Oakie turns to the camera and laughs. Chorus of 'Who Killed That Man?' It was the only time in movie history that Holmes and Vance were shot dead, and Warner Oland clearly enjoys doing the deed – as well as sending up his oriental mastermind persona, just before moving on to play Charlie Chan. Fu Manchu's indestructability – and the edge he has over traditional detectives – were clearly thought by the studio to be his defining features. Like Holmes, he existed in audiences' minds well beyond the confines of his stories.

Sax Rohmer sold his next book, *The Mask of Fu Manchu*, not to Paramount but to MGM. By then, a daily comic-strip version of the first two novels, illustrated by Leo O'Mealia, had been appearing in various American newspapers, and would continue to do so until 1933 – to be reprinted by *Detective Comics* later in the decade, complete with a colour cover. The very first issue of *Detective Comics* featured a sinister full-face portrait of a Fu Manchu variant called Ching Lung. CBS was producing a series of thirty-one half-hour Monday evening radio shows based on Rohmer's first three Fu Manchu novels – plus a motivation for the devil doctor dating back to the time of the 'Boxer uprising' – for the season between September 1932 and April 1933, with the author giving a talk at the end of the opener: he was judged to be 'a delightful fellow possessed of charm and wit'. Each episode was complete in itself.

The Mask of Fu Manchu was serialized in *Collier's* from May to July 1932: Sax Rohmer was paid a reported $30,000 for the serialization rights alone. A reader's report for MGM, dated 18 May, recommended the book for 'purchase and production', but was concerned about 'the motivation for Fu Manchu's desperate attempts to gain the trophies taken from the tomb of El Mokanna', the ancient Masked Prophet. This was not made clear enough in the book, it was judged, the plot of which revolved around Sir Lionel Barton's discovery of El Mokanna's tomb in Persia and Fu Manchu's plot to acquire the contents in Cairo – to use them to lead an anti-Western uprising. Despite these misgivings, by July MGM had purchased the rights. The studio announced that it was determined to ring the changes. 'A new Fu Manchu,' crowed the publicity, 'not to be confused with the Fu Manchu of other pictures.' *One hundred million readers* had already enjoyed the novels, it claimed, and this would be the film for them. Boris Karloff, who was loaned for the occasion to MGM by Universal – fresh, if that is the word, from *Frankenstein* (1931), *The Old Dark House* (1932) and eight other films in 1932 alone – arrived at the studio and found himself sitting in the makeup chair on 6 August (the makeup – pointed ears, slanting eyebrows, thin-shell front teeth, long moustache – took two and a half hours to apply each morning), not having seen a script. In fact, there wasn't one. When he asked for a copy, he recalled, 'I was met with roars of laughter.' This was his most vocal part to date in a horror movie – beyond expressive grunts – and he needed to learn his lines. Karloff was handed a few sheets of paper, which were then taken away and substituted with a few more – including 'some scenes written in Oxford English, others in God knows what!'

"Imagine a man, tall, lean and cat-like, with long, strange, magnetic eyes, the brow of Shakespeare and the face of Satan . . . invest him with the cruel cunning of an entire Eastern race, with all the resources of science, and vast wealth—imagine that awful being, and you have DR. FU MAN-CHU, the Yellow Peril incarnate in one man!"

The Second of this Amazing Series of Nayland Smith's Fights with the Yellow Group. The Most Weird and Eerie Mystery Stories Every Written. Each Narrative is Complete in Itself

The Si-Fan Mysteries
By Sax Rohmer

This Story Tells of Petrie's Visit to John Ki's Shop—

—And the Amazing Discoveries in that Den by Thames-side

13

Wooden tables, their surfaces stained, were ranged round the place. They accommodated groups of nondescript nationality

TOP LEFT: American newspaper comic-strip version of *The Mystery of Dr Fu-Manchu* (a.k.a. *The Insidious . . .*), drawn by Leo O'Mealia in 1931 and often reprinted. **TOP RIGHT:** The first American illustration of Dr Fu Manchu, based on Rohmer's original description, from the *Collier's* serialization of 1913. **ABOVE:** *The Si-Fan Mysteries* serialization in the weekly *Chums*, the official journal of the Boy Scouts, 'in response to requests from readers' (1923–24).

American Avon comic-book version of *The Mask of Fu Manchu* (1951), with artwork by the celebrated Wally Wood.

ABOVE: Promotional card from the 1940s for the Fu Manchu Restaurant and Bar at Miami Beach, Florida.
RIGHT: Box cover of a Fu Manchu magic board game from the 1960s.
BELOW: Ironic 'Fu Manchu ashtray and match-holder', made by Chinese and sold in Hong Kong in the mid-1990s.

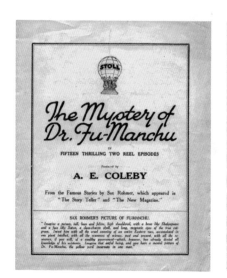

Pressbook of the Stoll Picture serial *The Mystery of Dr Fu-Manchu* (1923), the first official film version.

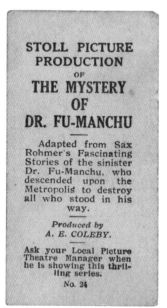

Trade cards (front and back) issued to promote the 1923 Stoll serial.

Austrian poster for Robert Reinert's expressionist film *Opium* (1919), which features the sinister Nung Tschang (Werner Krauss), peddling erotic opium dreams. **OVERLEAF:** Boris Karloff in his laboratory, concocting new tortures, in MGM's outrageously racist extravaganza, *The Mask of Fu Manchu* (1932).

TOP LEFT: Studio portrait of rotund Swedish actor Warner Oland as Hollywood's first all-talking lord of strange deaths, in *The Mysterious Dr Fu Manchu* (1929). TOP RIGHT: Spanish-language poster for the action-packed Republic serial *The Drums of Fu Manchu* (1940), with Berlin-born Henry Brandon in the title role. ABOVE: West German still from *The Face of Fu Manchu* (1965), with the doctor's sadistic daughter (Tsai Chin) enjoying herself.

FU MANCHU

FOR MAYOR

THIS ADVERTISEMENT WAS PAID FOR BY THE CITIZEN'S COMMITTEE TO ELECT FU MANCHU FOR MAYOR.

Promotional subway poster for the New York release of *The Face of Fu Manchu* in 1965, successfully exploiting a concurrent mayoral election.

Charles Starrett, who was cast as the young Terry Granville (Shan Grenville in the book, Barton's dashing future son-in-law), remembered that 'they changed the script from day to day', sometimes from morning to afternoon, and that there was a lot of expensive waiting around on the MGM set. Filming began without a completed script, under the direction of Charles Vidor, only to stop on the third day, then to resume on 11 August with a new screenplay. By a week later Vidor had been fired – to be replaced by the Liverpool-born Charles Brabin. In the end, filming took two and a half months and cost $322,627.

The studio files are full of draft screenplays, panic-stricken memos from the producer and increasingly outlandish ideas about how best to adapt Sax Rohmer's novel while keeping faith with his readymade audience. There is the sense that the studio could be on to a *very* good thing, if only it could find a sensational way of enhancing this presold property and riding the wave of the books' incredible popularity. *And* improving on the Paramount versions. The initial (incomplete) screenplay, dated 3 August, relocated the main action of the novel from Persia and Cairo to some mountains on the edge of the Gobi Desert and Shanghai. El Mokanna turned into the more recognizable Genghis Khan. Fu Manchu was presented as 'the reincarnation of Evil, and yet at all times diabolically suave and gallant'. Where the motivation issue was concerned, the screenplay strongly emphasized 'the revolution of the Asiatics against the white man' – much more strongly, and with a more specifically *Chinese* emphasis, than in Sax Rohmer's original.

> I dare say you've heard of Genghis Khan, the Mongol whose yellow horde overran all of Asia and Eastern Europe in the thirteenth century ... swept right up to the gates of Vienna ... nearly destroying all white civilisation, all the white race ... and with his death died also the last great threat of the yellow race against the white.

When Sir Lionel Barton explains this, he is in a foul mood, because he has had an argument with the Chairman of Trustees of the British Museum about whether 'the Gypsies might be Semitic instead of Aryan', a subject on which he has apparently written the definitive monograph. He has, he confides, located the lost tomb of Genghis Khan, and it is *imperative* that 'the sword of Genghis Khan must never fall to the yellow race', because he remains 'the symbol of an undying race hatred'. Enter Fu Manchu, who reasons that 'with the mask and sword; I will wipe your whole white race off the face of the earth'. This was the screenplay Vidor started filming on 6 August. By the end of August, it had been decided that Fu Manchu should become increasingly insane as the story progressed, 'turning into a character something like "the Phantom of the Opera" – a slinking, fast-moving madman. . . . All his suavity and oily characterization gives way to this new shading.' At least this finally gave Karloff something to get those thin-shell front teeth into.

It had also been decided to emphasize Fu Manchu's elaborate tortures. Producer Hunt Stromberg, in one of his production memos, wrote 'check on the book *Torture Garden*'. The pioneering journalist Irene Kuhn, who had worked for a time on the Shanghai *Evening Star*, who was said to be the first woman ever to broadcast on radio in China (1928), and who had recently written the narration for the documentary *The Amazon Head Hunters* (1932), had been called in specifically to improve the scenes set in the devil doctor's palatial hiding-place, buried beneath Wang Loh's curio emporium with sing-song shop and opium den ('with a certain eerie atmosphere') attached. The tortures – all to be presented in MGM's usual brightly lit, glittering deco style by design manager Cedric Gibbons – included a huge temple bell ('copied from a Chinese original in the British Museum' trumpeted the studio publicity) which through percussion and repercussion shatters Sir Lionel's eardrums ('You enjoy the chimes of your beautiful English cathedral?' taunts Fu, and later offers the victim a drink – 'Oh, I forgot to tell you it was *salt*!'); the steel spikes which slowly join together, with Nayland Smith or perhaps Sir Lionel's daughter Sheila or perhaps the archaeologist Von Berg between them (in one early version which was filmed, Nayland Smith slumps forward at the dénouement, 'his body run through with a thousand spikes'); and the pit full of hungry crocodiles, with Smith strapped to a seesaw above it as a sand weight pours away. Other possibilities included, at one stage or another, 'garden of poison flowers for Terrence?', 'The Well of Tears (if we finally use the water gag)' and 'the pit containing the snakes – the chain set – the hour glass etc.' Also the whipping post, which gives Fah Lo See (Myrna Loy, who in those days still specialized in oriental vamps – this was to be her last) the chance to reveal her true colours as she squeals at her minions, 'Aïee! Faster! Faster! Faster!' Myrna Loy was to recall:

> I was at an age when I had just discovered Freud etc., and had a number of incompletely digested theories about psychology, and was appalled

to find that not only was I supposed to have a pet python, but that I used to have my father's male victims turned over to me for torture, stripped. I then whipped them myself, uttering sadistic cries. I went to see the producer Hunt Stromberg, and said 'This is awful. The girl is a sadistic nymphomaniac.' 'Oh,' he said, 'hold on,' and disappeared into an inner office where he kept his dictionaries. In the end the Princess's worst excesses were toned down – as I remember, I no longer did the whipping myself, and I became quite friendly with the python . . .

Fah Lo See (as the name was spelled in the film) does indeed have a pet python, which she fondles suggestively with her 'ivory fingers'. But when Nayland Smith sees her caressing the drugged Terry, Stromberg wrote on 3 August, 'I see the same effect here as though Smith would have discovered him in an open den lying on a bunk with a naked woman.' Hunt Stromberg was convinced, for some reason, that the love triangle of Fah Lo See, Terry and Sheila should become the pivot of the plot: 'if this doesn't violate Sax Rohmer's readers too much'. Fu Manchu, understandably, views his daughter in a somewhat differ-ent light: 'Her skin is like the creamy lotus blossom – her body is like a young willow. She is a poem by Li Po.' Nevertheless, he *is* prepared to offer her to the kidnapped Sir Lionel Barton, in exchange for information about the where-abouts of Genghis Khan's tomb:

FU MANCHU: Even my daughter – even *that* for you!
SIR LIONEL: Fu Manchu, I'm not for sale – and damn your yellow hide, I draw the colour line.

By the time of the final version, Sir Lionel's reply had been excised. But at the end of August, Hunt Stromberg was worried about some of the footage that *had* already been shot, including the kidnapping of Sir Lionel in the Egyptian Room of the British Museum, by dacoits secreted in mummy cases: 'almost as putrid a scene as any I've ever seen'. Although he mentioned possible retakes, the scene survived intact into the finished film.

But it was the climax of the film, after Fu Manchu has acquired the sword and mask, which exercised the producer and writers for the longest time, right up to the last minute. One of the writers suggested that there should be a robotic clockwork effigy of Genghis Khan, which Fu Manchu would wind up to create the impression that the sword of the great raider was being handed on to him by the ghost of the man himself. This survived, unexplained, in the finished film. And there was the idea that in the final scene Sheila would be sold at auction to the highest bidder in the Hall of the Gods: 'lecherous lust of the tribal warriors . . . (mixing of white and yellow blood a dialogue point)'. Should Fah Lo See turn against her father, and help the good guys, out of love for Terrence? Or should the heroes substitute her for Sheila on the sacrificial couch at the last minute? If Smith and Granville came onto the stage, in front of the angry mob, how on earth would they manage to escape? In the end, the writers simply fell back on that old stalwart the death ray or 'deadly lightning thrower': 'Yes,' says Smith, 'they make them in Berlin.'

How *do* the heroes manage to find their way to the electric ray gun, asked Stromberg? Nayland Smith has somehow escaped from the crocodiles, Von Berg has extricated himself from the silver fingers and Terrence has recovered from a fiendish hypnotic serum. Too late to worry about all that . . . And about the fact that Fah Lo See simply disappears from the story. Meanwhile, Fu Manchu's words in the Hall of the Gods were finally signed off:

Fu Manchu (as Sheila is carried onto the stage, in a 'sacrificial bridal bed'): 'The sacrifice to our god! Would you all have maidens like this for your wives?'

Loud cheers from the assembled crowd of frenzied Orientals.

'Then conquer and breed! Kill the white man, and take his women!'

Loud cheers. The robotic effigy of Genghis Khan leans forward and seems to present the sword to Fu Manchu.

'Aïee! In the blood of Shiva's bride, I baptise this sword.'

Then the electricity strikes . . .

According to Elizabeth, Sax Rohmer did not much care for *The Mask of Fu Manchu*. Too crude, he thought, and Dr Fu Manchu was too *obvious*: Karloff was physically all wrong for the part (which did not prevent him from playing a good-hearted Chinese bandit-general called Fang in *West of Shanghai* (1937) and the polite, soft-spoken detective Mr James Lee Wong six times between 1938 and 1940). When the film opened on 2 December 1932, some newspaper critics agreed: they were more comfortable with Warner Oland's more genial, less demented Fu Manchu. When MGM made noises about filming a follow-up Fu Manchu, the Chinese Consulate at Los Angeles lodged a formal protest, channelling the views of the new National Board of Film Censors in Nanking and of Chinese-Americans who had complained. At a time when the USA was alarmed by the territorial ambitions of Japan – following the invasion of Manchuria in 1931 – China might well be needed as an ally in the future. MGM cancelled the production. But they did authorize the merchandising of a paper mask with 'The Mask of Fu Manchu' emblazoned on the forehead. Boris Karloff later judged that the protest had been 'utterly ridiculous': the film had a cartoonish plot and pantomime atmosphere and he had deliberately overplayed the part in a stylized way. *The Mask of Fu Manchu* grossed $625,000, domestic and foreign.

It is still very controversial, and for some critics the most blatantly racist mainstream Hollywood film – in the literal sense – ever made. In May 1972, it was reported that the Japanese-American Citizens League had written to MGM asking the company to remove *The Mask* from its back catalogue forthwith.

> . . . [it] falsely depicts Asians as a mindless horde blindly worshipping the bloody activities of Genghis Khan and Fu Manchu. When United States foreign policy is reaching out for understanding of Asian people, this rehash of Yellow Peril cannot be tolerated by any patriotic American.
>
> Fu Manchu is an ugly, evil homosexual with five-inch fingernails while his daughter is a sadistic sex fiend.

MGM did not delete the title, but *The Mask of Fu Manchu* was not released on video until the end of 1992, ten years after equivalent back-numbers from MGM/UA. A minute of racial vituperation had been trimmed from the original print for the video version. Out went 'son of a white dog', some of 'Faster! Faster!', 'entering your Christian heaven together', 'the first white martyrs to perish at the hands of Genghis Khan', 'I will wipe out your whole accursed white race' and of course 'Would you all have maidens like this for your wives? . . . Kill the white man, and take his women!' Television prints in Britain retained these cuts. They have all been restored on the latest DVD release.

Critic Frank Chin – who styles himself 'Chinatown Cowboy' – interprets *The Mask* in terms of the way it assaults Asian masculinity:

> Unlike the white stereotype of the evil black stud, Indian rapist, Mexican macho . . . the Chinese is a sexual joke glorifying white power. Dr Fu, a

man wearing a long dress, batting his eyelashes, surrounded by muscular black servants in loin-cloths, and with his bad habit of caressingly touching white men on the leg, wrist and face with his long fingernails, is not so much a threat as a frivolous offence to white manhood . . .

For all these reasons – and more – *The Mask of Fu Manchu* has come to epitomize the worst aspects of American sinophobia: the character of Fu, the iconography of silk robe and mandarin fingernails, the tortures, the mindless mass of 'orientals', the sexual joke, the deep horror of miscegenation. Walter Cronkite featured a clip on a television piece about American attitudes, just before Nixon's visit to China in February 1972. In the classic American documentary about the Vietnam War, *Hearts and Minds* (1974), director Peter Davis cut from an ex-marine in a wheelchair admitting 'I nailed one of them. . . . I wanted more because they were the opposition, the enemy' to Nayland Smith in *The Mask* asking 'will we ever understand these Eastern races?' then to Bob Hope making a wisecrack in *The Road to Hong Kong* (1962), then to Fu Manchu in *The Mask* being described as 'you hideous yellow monster', then to a Vietnamese witness observing 'Americans can say that Vietnamese are just slant-eyed savages: the Vietnamese have five thousand years of history – it's not *we* who are the savages'.

Shortly after *The Mask* was released, over in England Anna May Wong was starring in *Tiger Bay* (1934), set in a port somewhere in South America, where 'all the riff-raff of the seven seas' gather in the café-bar owned by Lin Chang (Wong). Originally, the script had been set in a Chinese restaurant near Shadwell's 'Tiger Bay', but the British Board of Film Censors had insisted on the change of locale. They had had enough of Limehouse melodrama: 'The whole story is an exact replica of the worst type of American gangster film with the scene laid in London amidst low and sordid surroundings.'

The remake of *Broken Blossoms* (1936) *was* still set in Limehouse, although a sequence was added to the original in which a coach party arrives in Limehouse, to gawp at the inhabitants. By this stage, 'Chinatown' – such as it was – had become a tourist attraction for the coach trade. 'See Chinatown by night' promises the placard in the film, while a pompous bowler-hatted tour guide explains that 'it is the very portal of the mysterious East'. The film ends – in a more extreme version of the original film's finale – with an angry mob, whipped up by Battling Burrows, smashing the windows of the 'curio and antiques' shop run by Chen Huan and setting fire to it – in ways that must have chimed with audiences who had recently read about the rise of Oswald Mosley's British Union of Fascists, and the behaviour of Nazi thugs wrecking shops in Germany. The new *Broken Blossoms* failed to impress the critics or the public. The spoken dialogue made it seem even more melodramatic than the original, and it has become very dated. Limehouse as an exotic setting was going out of fashion. In Humphrey Jennings's documentary *Fires Were Started* (1943), the new recruit Barrett is looking for the fire station in Limehouse, and approaches a man standing in a cobbled street of terraced houses in a woollen overcoat and trilby, lighting a cigar. There are some peeling posters in the background. 'Excuse me, could you tell me where the fire station is?' 'Yes . . . through the corner here.' And the man points. The fact that he is Chinese is treated as part of everyday London life; not worth a mention. Limehouse, or 'what's left of it', was no longer part of exotic London.

In 1937, MGM in Hollywood made some amends for *The Mask of Fu Manchu* – for hard commercial reasons – by filming Pearl Buck's Pulitzer-prize-winning novel *The Good Earth* (1931), the story of Wang Lun, a hardworking Chinese peasant farmer in Nanxuzhou, and his noble, long-suffering, servile wife O-lan (she dies with the words 'forgive me' on her lips), showing their courageous struggle for existence against bad harvests, famine, hail-storms, a swarm of locusts, difficult childbirths, the temptations of life in the city, the bloody reaction of Manchu troops in 1911 to the revolution, looting, and finally their mutual recognition of each other's strengths. As Wang buries O-lan by the tree they grew together, he says, 'O-lan – you are the earth.' Fadeout. The book had been a huge success, eventually selling 2 million copies (it was *the* best-selling work of fiction in the USA for 1931 and 1932), and the film rights were sold to MGM for a record $50,000 – the most money ever paid by a Hollywood studio for a book, up to that time. Journalist and political scientist Harold R. Isaacs has justly written:

> Book and film together, *The Good Earth* almost singlehandedly replaced the fantasy images of China and the Chinese held by most Americans with a somewhat more realistic picture of what China was like, and a new, more intimate and more appealing picture of the Chinese them-selves. Indeed *The Good Earth* accomplished the great feat of providing faces for the faceless mass. . . . The Chinese girl in the story, O-lan, bride,

mother and grandmother, and the man, Wang, dogged, strong, weak and sometimes sinning, are certainly the first such individuals in all literature about China with whom literally millions of Americans were able to identify warmly. . . . Pearl Buck did not write about Chinese in relation to foreigners, but about Chinese in relation to one another.

The book appeared when Japan was invading Manchuria; the film appeared when Japan was waging a full-scale war against China – and American sympathy was with the Chinese. The adversities facing Wang Lun with his smallholding also chimed with dust bowl, Depression America. The book was criticized by a few for sentimentalizing the noble peasant couple, and for infantilizing the people it was celebrating, but there was no doubt that it made a profound impact at that time. Pearl Buck, who had spent most of her life in China, and knew its rural society intimately, was keen that the film be cast with Chinese actors and shot on location in the villages described in the novel. After all, this was to be a prestige production, and the most favourable to ordinary Chinese people in the history of Hollywood. The screenwriter Frances Marion and the Chinese Vice-Consul of Los Angeles worked through a synopsis together for five months, off and on, cutting out all references to opium, bound feet, bandits, warlords and rural superstition – associated by the modernizing Kuomintang Nationalist government with the benighted Manchu regime. A location crew left for Northern China in December 1933, thinking that the permissions granted by the Chinese Embassy in Washington would be enough – only to discover on arrival that they also needed permits from Central Kuomintang Headquarters in Nanking. And these would only be issued if certain demands were met: a change of title to uncouple the film from the novel (MGM refused); the acceptance of 'any and all changes . . . suggested by the interested Chinese authorities'; the collaboration of official Chinese representatives in 'all stages of the production'; a written on-screen prologue explaining that the film 'does not follow exactly the text of the novel called *The Good Earth*' but has instead followed the advice of 'qualified experts'; and finally that 'the entire cast of actors and actresses employed in the production of the motion picture shall be Chinese persons'. Needless to say, this attempt by a foreign government to censor a Hollywood film not just in China but in America as well went down badly with senior film people *and* diplomats. But still, a formal contract was drawn up on the basis of it, to which MGM agreed. They had to, if they wanted location exteriors to be filmed and props to be purchased – '390 packing cases' of them, according to MGM's publicity department. The formal contract included the clause: 'It is the intention and hope of the studio to produce this picture with a complete Chinese cast.' Chinese officials were indeed present during the production process – but as to the casting, the hope proved impractical as MGM, no doubt, anticipated. Some location footage was duly shot in the Yangtze Valley – about ten minutes' screen time – and eventually *The Good Earth* was released in China virtually uncut.

Anna May Wong had desperately wanted the part of O-lan, but once it was decided to cast Paul Muni as Wang, a Chinese actress playing his wife became out of the question, by Production Code rules. Wong was screen-tested for the part of Lotus, the sensual sing-song girl and the villain of the piece, but either MGM thought she was too mature for the part – and not pretty enough – or she turned them down (as she was to claim). She did not want to play yet another no-hope prostitute. The Austrian ex-ballerina Tilly Losch was cast instead. Several other Chinese actors were tested for key roles, but – in an extraordinary statement – it was announced that they did not fit the audience's 'conception of what Chinese people looked like'. They did not look MGM Chinese. But sixty-eight non-principal, small, speaking parts *were* cast with oriental actors – Chinese, Korean and Japanese. Paul Muni spoke gibberish which *sounded* vaguely Chinese, and Losch is said to have modelled her dances on Anna May Wong's routines, which must have added insult to injury. The part of O-lan went to Austrian actress Luise Rainer, who was under contract to MGM, so at least the principal female accents were fairly consistent. Paul Muni, too, was born in Austria, but had by then lost his accent . . .

The slow-burn romance between Wang and O-lan and the love interest with Lotus moved centre stage, and the character of O-lan herself – seemingly a dull drudge but with hidden spiritual depths – turned out to be more Hollywood than Buck. But at least there was no doomed miscegenation, no sacrificial suicide in the last reel, no denigration of 'Chinese culture' by Western heroes. And, of course, no pigtails and bound feet. It was Luise Rainer, rather than the intense Paul Muni, who won the Oscar that year, in competition with Greta Garbo and Barbara Stanwyck – the first time anyone had won Academy Awards two years running. American actors who managed to play 'oriental' in the sound era clearly appealed to the Academy: H. B. Warner was nominated for *Lost Horizon* (1937), set in Tibet; Aline MacMahon for *Dragon*

Seed (1944, based on another Pearl Buck novel, of 1942, about the Japanese war with China); and Gale Sondergaard for Anna and the King of Siam (1946). Shortly before Luise Rainer started preparing for *The Good Earth*, her husband Clifford Odets was writing the dialogue for his first screenplay, *The General Died at Dawn* (1936). The two films were made almost simultaneously. But over in Nanking *The General* – unlike *The Good Earth* in its finished form – was considered 'entirely offensive' to Chinese sensibilities, and in November 1936 was banned outright as a film which had the 'deliberate intention of insulting China'. For a time, the renamed Central Motion Picture Censorship Committee even threatened to ban *all* Paramount productions in reprisal, until Adolph Zukor, Paramount's chairman, undertook never again to be disrespectful to 'the sensibilities, characteristics and customs of foreign countries'. The film censors in Nanking had reacted equally badly to *The Bitter Tea of General Yen* (1932), with Danish-born, Swedish-raised Nils Asther as Yen, and had issued a similar threat to Columbia; in this case, the compromise involved the insertion of a written prologue on prints of the film circulating in China.

> [This] picture represents a mere literary fancy devised by its author, and it does not in any way pretend to depict actual conditions in the real life of China.

When *China Sky* was made into a film by RKO in 1945, based on yet another Pearl Buck novel (1941), the character of the anti-American collaborator with Japan was changed from Chinese to Korean – a move which must have been well received by the Chinese government.

The Good Earth was a prestige production, given roadshow treatment at $2 a ticket on first release, with a trailer which claimed – to the sound of trumpets, and in spite of the contract with the Chinese authorities – that 'line by line, page by page, chapter by chapter – this production *is* the book'. Sax Rohmer's novels belonged more to double-bill land. He had sold his first three Fu Manchu novels to Stoll, a different three to Paramount, *The Mask* to MGM and in 1939, the year of its publication, he sold *The Drums of Fu Manchu* to Republic, further down the market, for serialization. There had been three other Fu Manchu novels since *The Mask* was filmed. Serials, with their weekly chapterplay format, thrived on the exaggerations of stereotypical villains, and larger-than-life Chinese bad guys were already – not surprisingly – a staple ingredient: in the mid- to late 1930s Emperor Ming the Merciless

(Charles Middleton) was battling it out with *Flash Gordon* (1936, 1938, 1940), Quong Lee, underworld king, was being thwarted by Buster Crabbe as *Red Barry* (1938), the Dragon was mobilizing for Manchurian independence in *Ace Drummond* (1936) and Bela Lugosi, his career on the slide, played a mad Eurasian scientist who attempts to destroy the Los Angeles Chinatown – with the help of sliding panels, trapdoors, a hypnotism machine and mind control – in *Shadow of Chinatown* (1936).

The Drums of Fu Manchu was made shortly before China became a formal ally against Japan – at which point Japanese spy networks took over from Chinese conspiracies. It took most of its plot from the film *The Mask of Fu Manchu*, with sequences from the first trio of novels in the series and insistent, beating drums ('his death signal') at the end of each chapter to justify the title. It was, said the credits, 'suggested by stories by Sax Rohmer' – six writers were credited – and, unlike the novel on which it was nominally based, made no attempt to be topical. The fifteen chapters were filmed between December 1939 and February 1940, with the first episode released on 15 March. The devil doctor was played by Berlin-born Henry Brandon, with bald rubber skullcap, drooping moustache, raised eyebrows, Joan Crawford shoulders and – of course – a robe embroidered with dragons. His accent, deliberately flat, resembled Laurence Oliver's later *Richard III* (1955) until Fu Manchu became hysterical. He clapped his hands a lot. Co-director William Witney, a stalwart of serials, candidly referred to his style of filmmaking as 'in a door, into a fight, out a door, into a chase', which just about summed up the structure of *Drums*. The basic plot was about using the sacred sceptre of Genghis Khan – misspelled as 'Ghengis' – to lead an uprising in Holy Year and ultimately to the conquest of Asia: 'to sweep every white enemy from the continent of Asia'. Fu Manchu, from his base in California, uses a gelatinous dart, 'the Seven Gates of Paradise', a magic screen, a 'cryptograph frequency tabulator', plastic surgery, a bomb detonated by a telephone, a scented pillow and a poisonous lizard, a magic crystal which magnifies the power of the sun – and in chapter two he feeds the hero to a giant octopus. His army consists of vampire-fanged dacoits with jagged latex lobotomy scars across their foreheads. As Nayland Smith helpfully explains, 'Fu Manchu . . . is an adept brain surgeon: by operating on the frontal lobe he kills that part of the mind controlling the will.' Smith himself is billed as 'of the British Foreign Office', 'of Scotland Yard', 'on official business for the Foreign Office', and he speaks 'in the name of the English

Commonwealth of Nations' – the scriptwriters can't make up their minds – and in the final chapter the venerable High Lama, on the side of the angels, concludes that 'the prophecy of the Holy Year is fulfilled – the holy sceptre of Genghis Khan reposes with the English officers'. Fu Manchu survives, and in an epilogue set in the tomb of the Khan, solemnly vows that there will be 'another day of reckoning . . . this I pledge you'.

The Drums of Fu Manchu is the only Republic serial in which the villain survives the final curtain. Clearly, the studio was planning a sequel, but the Chinese Consulate in Los Angeles made representations to the State Department, and the sequel was quietly shelved. A sixty-nine-minute feature version was, however, released in November 1943 with a new ending: this time, Fu Manchu died in a car crash rather than living to fight another day. When asked, years later, about the protests from Chinese officials in America about *The Drums of Fu Manchu*, Henry Brandon replied that he had 'played countless heavies of various nationalities' – including Native American chiefs in *The Searchers* (1956) and *Two Rode Together* (1961) – and had never once felt he was 'maligning any race by doing so'.

There were no film adaptations of Sax Rohmer's novels in wartime, for obvious diplomatic reasons. The CBS radio serial of fifteen-minute episodes, *The Shadow of Fu Manchu*, came off the air in September 1940. Ten years later, a television pilot for NBC – with Cedric Hardwicke as Nayland Smith and John Carradine as the devil doctor – was made, but could not find a sponsor or a satisfactory script. But in 1955, Republic paid Sax Rohmer $4 million – or so it was reported – for all film, television and radio rights to the Fu Manchu novels. The resulting television series – *The Adventures of Dr Fu Manchu*, made by a subsidiary of Republic – previewed in February 1956 (filmed between June and December 1955), one of the few television series at the time to star a villain. Seventy-eight half-hour episodes were planned, but the series was cancelled after just thirteen. Three feature films were planned too, but they never materialized either. They were to have been based on the first three Fu Manchu novels. Sax Rohmer was quoted by *Picturegoer* (July 1955) as saying excitedly that he hoped these films would be strong on *atmosphere* – 'from the shadows, a terrified face, a hand . . . that's what works with the public' – and not be too *obvious* in their effects: 'It's not enough just to show Fu Manchu. He ought, on the contrary, to remain mysterious and not allow himself to be seen except at very rare moments.'

In film, less was more. The devil doctor's charisma depended on his absence as much as his presence. Each episode of the television series began with Dr Fu Manchu (Glen Gordon) in full mandarin rig and resembling a stockier version of Henry Brandon, playing chess to camera:

> Black and white, life and death, good and evil, two sides of a chess game – it is said that the devil plays for men's souls; so does Dr Fu Manchu.

Set in Macao and Hong Kong – with stock footage inserts of both – the explicitly racial aspects of the stories were downplayed in favour of Cold War concerns: Dr Petrie, now American, was assigned to the Surgeon General's Department; his friend Nayland Smith, 'late of Scotland Yard', was now a kind of secret agent working undercover; Fu Manchu had become a middleman, selling nuclear arms/chemical weapons/Second World War secrets/gold reserves to 'the Reds' beyond the Bamboo Curtain – but with his own freelance plans for destruction as well. The chess game, rather than being about 'good and evil', was really about American influence in Asia. When Dr Fu Manchu escapes, he is said by Nayland Smith to have been 'swallowed up by the teeming millions that make up Red China' – though it is never explained how he manages to be 'swallowed up' while wearing his traditional Manchu outfit. In one episode, he expresses his admiration for Hitler as a fellow world-dominator, and tries to resurrect him on an operating table.

After the cancellation of *The Adventures*, there were no further adaptations of the Fu Manchu novels until 1963, when buccaneering producer Harry Alan Towers purchased 'the rights of all the Fu Manchus' (as he put it) – or perhaps just the 'character rights' – from Mrs Sax Rohmer for the princely sum of £2,500. Towers, an experienced radio producer – his greatest success had been with the 'character rights' to Harry Lime – who had also worked in British television, had decided to become a film producer when he discovered that the rights to Edgar Wallace's Africa-set novel *Sanders of the River* (1911) were available, unlike Wallace's London thrillers, which belonged to Rialto Films, a Danish–German company. Edgar Wallace, he was to recall, was still a magic name to German cinema goers – and 'I am a great believer in going back to the classics':

> When you've got an author's name you've got your feet on pretty solid ground. And, provided the subject is dealt with originally and isn't too

repetitive, you get all the advantages – a good deal should be presold by the author's name, title and story.

So Towers turned to another famous and memorable 'author's name', a name that sold books in Germany – and that had just featured on a series of successful early 1960s paperback reprints (by Pyramid) in the United States. In Britain, the name was instantly recognizable as well: in *The Party's Over* (1963), one of the art students (Katherine Woodville) greets a friend at the door of her room, while wearing a high-collared silk robe. 'Dr Fu Manchu, I presume,' says the friend. The reference needs no explanation at all. *The Face of Fu Manchu*, with a script by Peter Welbeck – nom de plume of Harry Alan Towers – started filming in and around Dublin on 15 February 1965, with a budget of £175,000. Kilmainham Gaol stood in for forts in China and Tibet, there was a car chase around the docks, the Museum of Oriental Studies was Government Buildings in Merrion Street – deserted, because filmed on the day the remains of Roger Casement were belatedly brought to Ireland – and interiors were filmed in the large rooms at Kenure House just north of Dublin. This was the first Fu Manchu film in colour, and the first to be set in 'period'. The period details, however, were wobbly – 1930s plane bombs 1920s car, which when it crashes becomes a 1930s car – but they at least served to distance the story, to some extent, from present-day sensitivities.

The plot involved the kidnapping of eminent scientist Professor Muller, who has discovered how to distil a deadly poison from the juice of the Tibetan black hill poppy: Muller and his entourage are all played by German actors – part of the co-production deal with Constantin Film, rival of Rialto, Towers's partner on his two *Sanders* films. Fu Manchu wants to use the poison to further his plans for world domination. Eventually they all find themselves in Tibet, where Assistant Commissioner Nayland Smith of Scotland Yard hides a detonator in a chestful of poppy seeds and blows Fu Manchu and friends – plus all the inhabitants of the fort, regardless – to smithereens. Fu's face is superimposed on the burning building: 'The world shall hear from me again.' This was not based on any of Sax Rohmer's novels, though it did contain some of his favourite elements: the kidnapping of an expert; Fu Manchu's hidden headquarters in Limehouse; the display of elaborate tortures – in this case whipping, slow drowning in a water-chamber which releases its victim into the Thames ('another suicide'), and suicide by dagger while under hypnosis; the agile red-sashed Burmese dacoits who use Tibetan prayer scarves to strangle their victims and who believe 'every ritual murder is a passport to heaven'; Nayland Smith as a ramrod-straight, imperturbable military man (Nigel Green, fresh from playing Colour-Sergeant Bourne in *Zulu*, 1964); connections with the Younghusband expedition to Tibet; museum and archaeological settings; the climactic events in Tibet; the brisk pacing to cover the illogicalities of the plot. On the main credits, the title was given as 'Sax Rohmer's The Mask of Fu Manchu' . . . written in 'Chinese' lettering. 'Based on characters created by Sax Rohmer.' Sometimes, the script – unusually well-written for Harry Alan Towers – shows moments of self-awareness. Dr Petrie (Howard Marian Crawford) says to the dogmatic Nayland Smith, 'Not the Yellow Peril again . . . you *are* overtired.' The film begins with the apparent execution of Fu Manchu 'in the name of Imperial China' – therefore pre-1912; then it transpires, many years later, that the victim was really a famous Chinese actor called Lee Toy, hypnotized by Fu – so the opening sequence is an elaborate confidence trick *and* a reference to the devil doctor's resurrection for the first time in film since 1940. Maybe also a knowing reference to the fact that Fu Manchu had *never* been played by 'a famous Chinese actor', on screen or off. But on the whole *The Face of Fu Manchu* is content to combine *Boy's Own Paper* heroics with a low-budget attempt to create chop suey James Bond (including a rerun of the aerial attack on Fort Knox from *Goldfinger* (1964), with just one plane this time – and a vintage car chase).

When I met director Don Sharp, shortly before he died, I asked if he was concerned about the racist implications of resurrecting Fu Manchu – albeit in a distanced 1920s setting?

> I grew up with the Yellow Peril and the Japanese, in Tasmania. And I do remember when I was walking to school there, aged about six or seven, and going past a Chinese shop run by Chinese people and all the school-children singing 'Chinky, Chinky Chinaman'. But, strangely, I didn't project any of that onto Fu Manchu. I don't know why, but it didn't seem like that: anti-Chinese. He was like a James Bond villain. People are so used to super-villains and there's no special nationality attached to him.

Did it occur to anyone to cast a Chinese actor? Such as Burt Kwouk, who appeared as a henchman in three sequels to *The Face* – and who in Britain was everyone's favourite actor 'of East Asian appearance', as Kwouk himself put it?

No, and not Burt Kwouk. He doesn't quite have the stature. But of course Fu Manchu's daughter Lin Tang *was* played by Tsai Chin. . . . She caught on very early that the thing about Lin Tang was to be totally still and concentrated, and just to watch. And you knew *exactly* what she was thinking and what she would love to do with that person. And there was the contrast between Chris Lee and Tsai: I wanted Fu Manchu not to be cruel for the sake of cruelty – he wanted power and he had to kill someone or torture them to get it. But he would not necessarily enjoy it. Whereas his daughter – 'Let me do it, father.' You couldn't have them both in the same mould, I thought.

Christopher Lee was cast early on. He had already played Hong Kong organized crime boss Chung King in *The Terror of the Tongs* (1960), from a very Rohmerish script ('Have you ever had your bones scraped, Captain?'). Lee had also played Hong Kong Chinese detective Ling Chu, helping Scotland Yard, in *The Devil's Daffodil* (1961, a West German production with a narcotics theme). So did *he* have any qualms about playing Dr Fu Manchu?

Well, I agreed because as a young man or boy I'd read almost every book written by Arthur Sarsfield Ward. And I had one important physical qualification: I am tall. . . . I tried to present an old-fashioned Chinese mandarin, a noble man, a man of dignity – a brilliant brain and a man of enormous power. With one gesture of the finger would be death. Mad, I suppose, by most people's standards. I did my best not to offend anyone, not to play Fu Manchu in any way that the Chinese could find offensive. A few members of the Chinese community were not very happy. A few. In Hong Kong [when we made *The Vengeance of Fu Manchu*, the third film, in 1966], all the extras were Chinese and Cantonese, and none of them objected as far as I know. . . . There were some objections in San Francisco and other cities with large Chinese populations. What I *can* understand is that the Chinese object to the character being referred to as 'the Yellow Peril'. But not to the character as I played him.

It must have been strange, acting the part of Fu Manchu surrounded by Hong Kong Chinese in the Shaw studio?

I was staying on the Hong Kong side at the Hilton, and I was made up on that side – with the moustache, the eyes – that epicanthic fold on the edge of the eye which became the plastic eye-lids I had to wear – the bright colours. To get over to the Kowloon side and the Run Run Shaw studio, we had to take the Star Ferry to get across. I had a hat on, and dark glasses. I couldn't do much about the moustache, though, and I was getting curious looks from some of the Chinese people on the ferries. They looked at me, then whispered among themselves. Then one of them got up, bowed and said, 'Excuse me, sir; we're all fascinated. What is your oriental background?' 'I'm an actor and I'm playing a Chinese character. This is not real, it is makeup.' Then I removed my glasses: the makeup was by Tom Smith, one of the great makeup artists. And there in front of this man was a Chinese played by a Western actor in this makeup. 'Sir, what is your name?' I said 'Lee!', which of course is also a Chinese name, Li. All of them nodded their heads! This used to happen quite often!

Was it in any way difficult to act 'Chinese' with Tsai Chin on the set?

We used to have a lot of laughs. I never quite found out if she was happy about it – because she *is* Chinese and her father was a very famous actor and singer, Qi Lintong. I didn't think it was appropriate to ask, because you cannot let people lose face in the Orient. Whether she thought she was in a sense caricaturing Chinese people and their habits and customs – particularly in the case of the sort of character I was playing, because she was supposed to be my daughter . . . I never found out . . .

Tsai Chin herself, in retrospect, did have strong views on the subject. She had been the first-ever Chinese student at the Royal Academy of Dramatic Art. She had subsequently appeared several times on the satirical television show *That Was the Week That Was* (1962–63), in pointed sketches about early-1960s British attitudes towards Chinese people. In one sketch, called 'The World of Suzi Smith', she played a Chinese general, with Jacqui Chan as her colonel, members of a Chinese occupation force in London, brandishing riding crops, who were surprised that the natives sometimes showed signs of affection and even of intelligence. In her memoir *Daughter of Shanghai* (1988), Tsai Chin recalled:

I myself have had to live down the disquieting feeling that at one point in my career I let my race down. For my sins, I was Fu Manchu's daughter five times, with Christopher Lee as my father.

By the mid-1960s, when *The Face of Fu Manchu* was made,

> the subject matter was still . . . very racist. So I had to search my con-
> science all the time. . . . You know as an ethnic actor you are not offered
> as many roles as say a Caucasian actor . . .

Even Myrna Loy had a better written part in *The Mask of Fu Manchu*, as Fah
Lo See:

> All I had to do in these films was to follow my father around and say a
> few banal lines while trying to look evil. . . . At least Myrna Loy was
> allowed to be a nymphomaniac, which I find infinitely more interesting.

For Tsai Chin, the stereotypical roles – the one-dimensional characters – were
still very much around:

> In early cinema . . . Chinky, Chinky Chinamen wore pigtails and shuf-
> fled their feet when they walked. If they were not actively evil, they were
> invariably seen serving white masters. Such images have changed to an
> extent, but often to be replaced with subtler forms of racial stereotyp-
> ing. In the Sixties . . . yellow men suggested the violent activities of the
> secret societies. Even today, I watch TV advertisements that rely on racial
> cliché to make their point. One way or another, we are not presented as
> real people.

What did she think of the 1960s Fu Manchu films? 'I haven't seen any of them.'

Burt Kwouk – born in Warrington, raised in Shanghai –appeared with
Tsai Chin in *The Brides of Fu Manchu*, *The Vengeance of Fu Manchu* (uncredited) and *The Castle of Fu Manchu* – as well as playing the smooth Mr Ming
who is murdered by the Red Dragon Tong with a hatchet in his heart in *The
Terror of the Tongs*. He tends to disagree:

> If you are offered a part in a Fu Manchu film, what do you expect? Do
> you expect it to present a sympathetic picture of Chinese people? You
> don't expect a Fu Manchu film to be a biography of Sun Yat Sen . . . !

Douglas Wilmer, who took over from Nigel Green as Nayland Smith in
The Brides and *Vengeance* – and who never felt comfortable in the part – would
perhaps have agreed. When cast in *The Brides*, he was more used to playing
Sherlock Holmes, a very different character:

Frankly, I did it because even actors have to eat! Nayland Smith and Dr Petrie are like Holmes and Watson, and Fu Manchu is like an Oriental representation of Moriarty, except that Fu Manchu is the better part. Fu Manchu is the *only* part worth playing in the film: I do all the donkey work and he rides off. Nayland Smith was a sort of poor man's filleted Sherlock Holmes – I couldn't make the character stand up. I wasn't happy with my performance. Couldn't bring him to life. What I do remember is working with some very objectionable German actors. . . . The films were extremely dull and boring to do. They did not make an indelible mark on my mind.

The Face of Fu Manchu puzzled the British Board of Film Censors, though not because of any sensitivities about the depiction of Chinese people, or about the film being 'very racist' from the point of view of a Chinese living and working in England. When the film was submitted to the Board in black and white without a full soundtrack, on 20 April 1965 – under the title *The Face of Dr Fu Manchu* – at first they proposed a 'U' for ('Universal') certificate, provided some cuts were made: these included some shots, in the opening sequence, of the corpse's head being taken away in a basket and of the decapitated body; some pruning of the fistfights in Professor Muller's laboratory, the museum and the warehouse; removing all the 'preparations (tying up, baring of back, handling of lash) for the flogging of the Chinese girl'; removing all shots 'of the Chinese girl from the moment she is put into the water-chamber'; excising 'shots of corpses in Fleetwick, and especially remove the one hanging upside down'; and toning down the language of the soldiers there (a couple of 'bloodys'). Then John Trevelyan, the President, said he was surprised at the recommended 'U' certificate as he thought the makers were producing 'a horror film with perhaps an "X" or at least an "A" in mind'. The assessor replied in a memo that it had been rated 'U' 'as a *Boys Own Paper* story but could certainly raise the certificate to "A" with only a few cuts'. Initially, Hallam Productions, Towers's company, said that *they* 'were surprised [at the "U"] and had not made the film with that category in mind'; then – presumably with the widest possible distribution in mind – let it be known by the Board that 'they would after all prefer "U"'. But there were still concerns within the Board about the possible impact of the film on young children. The assessor reiterated, in replying to these:

We treated this as a BOP [*Boy's Own Paper*] story and I don't think it would worry children of, say, 11 or over. It sounds as though the children in this case were considerably younger. . . . I hope that, in fact, the cut version was shown.

So *The Face of Fu Manchu* (as it was now called) went on release passed 'U', as a BOP romp. Presumably the assessor was of an age to remember when the Yellow Peril featured prominently in children's comics. Towers was pleased, on reflection, with the decision to have been awarded a 'U' – even though it might put off the horror crowd. The Board had been much tougher a few years before, on Hammer's *The Terror of the Tongs* and on the bizarre Albert Zugsmith film *Confessions of an Opium Eater* (1962), known in Britain as *Evils of Chinatown* – with Vincent Price as Gilbert De Quincey, grandson of Thomas (the film was cheekily billed as 'Thomas De Quincey's classic'), wandering dreamily into a Tong war in 1910 San Francisco's Kowloon Alley. The film had featured an opium den, a curio shop as a front, white slavery, a girl auction, a libidinous Chinese lady midget, drug barons, hatchet men, dope fantasies, trapdoors and secret passageways, and it ended on a raft in a sewer – the lot. When first they saw the film – under its original title – on 17 June 1963, members of the Board – including the President – reacted strongly against it:

> We did not like this film and propose to start by insisting on a minimum of cuts without any promise of eventually passing the film. If it is eventually passed, the film will be an 'X'.

The title *Evils of Chinatown*, by the way, seemed much more acceptable than the original. So when the film was finally released under that title, there were no shots of a captive girl being beaten with a silken whip, or of a girl being drowned in a glass-sided water-chamber. Both, of course, had their equivalents in *The Face of Fu Manchu*, which was deemed suitable for 'children of, say, 11 or over'. Because *Confessions* did not come over as a story out of an old children's comic – rather, as a dreamlike piece of pop-surrealism ('was it a dream of the poppy or was it reality?') – it was judged to be far the more offensive.

The Face of Fu Manchu turned out to be a surprise hit in the United States. In New York, the film's release coincided with mayoral elections in November 1965, and a provocative publicity campaign placed 'Fu Manchu for

Mayor' election posters on the walls of 500 subways. The success of *The Face*, thanks in part to unusually wide distribution for a Towers film, encouraged the producer to proceed with the sequels *Brides* (shot in Ireland again), *Vengeance* (Hong Kong), *Blood* (Brazil) and *Castle* (Barcelona and Istanbul). By the end of the cycle, in 1969, the devil doctor was well beyond his sell-by date and *The Blood of Fu Manchu* was retitled *Kiss and Kill* in the USA. The name had lost its box-office appeal. *Castle* scarcely achieved distribution at all. Even the 'magnificent locations', said Christopher Lee wistfully, were wasted.

Undaunted, eleven years after the last of Harry Alan Towers's cycle – the most substantial Fu Manchu series ever – Peter Sellers (alas) appeared in the final film before he died of a heart attack, *The Fiendish Plot of Dr Fu Manchu*, which opened in August 1980. He had already parodied Charlie Chan in *Murder By Death* (1976). *The Fiendish Plot* had been on the stocks as a project for some time. In May 1976 it was announced in the trade press that Michael Caine would play Nayland Smith in an updated comedy version of 'the famed Sax Rohmer stories'. The producer was seeking a major star to play opposite Caine. In the event, Sellers played *both* characters. *The Fiendish Plot* seems at some stage to have turned into a belated attempt to relive the glory days of 1950s *Goon Show*, with Sellers doing his 'dotty colonel' voice as Nayland Smith, and his 'pukka Chinese' voice as Fu Manchu. If so, it was seriously out of time, and showed Sellers's lack of judgement about his own performances. There were limp jokes about Chinese food, China tea, pidgin English, Chinese laundries and 'they all look the same'. The plot involves the 168-year-old devil doctor – 'around 1933' – desperately trying to capture the ingredients of the elixir of life – a precious diamond, the Crown Jewels, a mummy, a rare plant and so on. In the final sequence, Fu Manchu, at last revived, does an Elvis Presley impersonation in fringed, Las Vegas buckskins while singing 'Rock a Fu, man'. His latest weapon to take over the world is to be rock 'n' roll. Sellers looks very ill in both his roles. The British Board of Film Censors found 'watching this on the day Sellers's death was announced was painfully ironic, for it is truly terrible . . . very far-fetched and really quite unlikely to suggest itself as a model'. *Variety* called *The Fiendish Plot* 'a misfire from beginning to end'. Various interest groups in America picketed the film. It had taken four directors – including Peter Sellers himself – and Playboy Productions to bring it to the screen. It was the devil doctor's last screen appearance. A tacky swan-song for 'the greatest brain in the world'.

There have been rumours of revivals. In the early 1970s, there was talk of a Fu Manchu musical on Broadway. In February 1993, the stage farce *Face Value* – written by David Hwang, who had created the successful gender-bending *M. Butterfly* – opened in Boston, set against the background of a Fu Manchu-like Broadway musical; it was itself intended for Broadway, but died after only eight previews. Marvel Comics, between 1973 and 1983, featured Fu Manchu as the evil father of the superheroic kung fu master Shang-Chi in a series of oedipal comic-books which tapped into the craze for martial arts films in the post-Vietnam era. The series ran for 118 issues, and was then cancelled, apparently because the rights to the name and character 'Fu Manchu' had not been renewed by Marvel. The Shang-Chi series harked back to Yellow Peril comics of the Cold War 1950s. But Iron Man continued to battle his arch-enemy The Mandarin, descended from Genghis Khan, from the same stable – introduced in 1964 and still, half a century later, planning schemes for world domination with the ten magic rings on his fingers. In the blockbuster film *Iron Man 3* (2012), The Mandarin was played by Ben Kingsley – only in *this* version, he is not really Chinese at all, he is a British actor called Trevor Slattery who is *pretending* to be Chinese. The producers did not want to be accused of pandering to the Fu Manchu stereotype. Critic Frank Chin had written abrasively, way back in 1974, of the transition from Sax Rohmer to kung fu and superheroes:

> In 40 years, apes went from a naked, hairy King Kong, gigantic with nitwit sex fantasies about little human women, to a talking chimpanzee leading his fellow apes in a battle to take over the planet [in the *Planet of the Apes* series, 1968–73]. We've progressed from Fu Manchu, the male Dragon Lady of silent movies, to Charlie Chan and then to *Kung Fu* on TV. We've made no progress at all . . .

The latest guest appearance of the devil doctor by name in a feature film was in one of the 'false trailers' – directed by one Rob Zombie – interrupting Quentin Tarantino's *Grindhouse* (2007). The trailer is for a Z-movie called *Werewolf Women of the SS*, and it shows Nicolas Cage as Fu Manchu, in full mandarin regalia with beard and moustache, shrieking madly about revenge, with a swastika behind him and flames burning in front of him. He has evidently become as 'transgressive' as the Nazis – the stuff of low-grade grindhouse movies, which are camp and surreal or deeply offensive, depending on your point of view. Meanwhile, the producers of the remake of the sabre-rattling *Red Dawn*

(2012), about a surprise attack by Chinese forces on the United States, changed the military livery in post-production into symbols of North Korea instead. It had been decided that it would be a big mistake to antagonize the lucrative Chinese market. As for the actors – Chinese, North Korean, what's the difference? Kim Jong-un, where Hollywood is concerned, has become the new brand of Yellow Peril. I mean, who in North Korea will pay to see Hollywood movies? Harry Alan Towers, to his dying day in summer 2009, talked of resurrecting Fu Manchu and producing a new film in his series: he had been worried, he said, that the director of *The Castle of Fu Manchu* had made such a lousy film that he'd 'done something that was impossible – he'd successfully killed Fu Manchu'. But there was hope . . . Christopher Lee, on the other hand, reckons that the franchise was 'all right at the time. I think it's out of date now.' Tsai Chin agrees. She has written that Fu Manchu must surely have made his last appearance on the screen: 'At least, I hope so.'

II Chinatown, Whose Chinatown . . . ?

On the 'Surrealist Map of the World', published in the Parisian journal *Variétés* (June 1929) as an alternative to the brazenly Imperialist maps displayed in school classrooms, China was depicted as a third of the size of Alaska, England did not feature at all, and the Southern hemisphere was dominated by the Pacific Islands, notably Easter Island; Tibet belonged to China, and Japan did not exist. The idea was that the scale of these territories would match their contemporary artistic significance – in the eyes of late-1920s Parisian Surrealists, at any rate, who much enjoyed making charts and lists, and who loved founding new niche magazines. So China was not rated very highly – the old story about a culture stranded in the past – but *fantasies* of China, gleaned from pulp series, scored much better among the Surrealists. Indeed, the cultural theorist Siegfried Kracauer, in his essay 'Boredom' (1924), had likened the whole experience of going to the darkened space of the cinema and consuming images there to human beings 'squatting like a fake Chinaman in a fake opium den'.

In some of their Paris-based magazines, such as *Documents* and *Minotaure*, the Surrealists celebrated the improbabilities of plot and characterization, the bizarre coincidences, the larger-than-life characters, the lack of logic, the apparent disregard of bourgeois values, and the general air of *surreality* in popular thrillers, penny dreadfuls, low-budget weekly serials, and the novels and Louis Feuillade films featuring the super-villain and master of disguise Fantômas, and his superiority over the dogged and unimaginative Inspector Juve: artefacts in which distinctions between 'the real' and 'the fantastic' completely broke down, and everyday life seemed very strange indeed. They also celebrated the stars of the music hall, for similar reasons. And filmmaker Fritz Lang's serial super-villain Dr Mabuse the Gambler – based on a novel by Norbert Jacques – another master of disguise who specializes in corrupting healthy young men through a heady mixture of hypnotism and cocaine, games of chance, beautiful women in thrall to him, blackmail and high finance: the abrupt changes of locale, the chases at high speed, the improbabilities, the revelling in nightlife decadence while presiding over the social chaos of Weimar Berlin, all had Surrealist appeal. In one key sequence, Mabuse (Rudolf Klein-Rogge) hypnotizes his fellow card-players by casting a spell over them through some Chinese mumbo-jumbo he calls 'Tsi-Nan-Fu'.

The pope and dogmatist of the Surrealist Movement, André Breton, in his semi-autobiographical novel *Nadja* (1928), remembered watching an American adventure serial

> in which a Chinese who had found some way to multiply himself invaded New York by means of several million self-reproductions. He entered President Wilson's office followed by himself, and by himself, and by himself; the President removed his pince-nez. This film, which has affected me more than any other, was called *The Grip of the Octopus*.

It was indeed called *The Grip of the Octopus* in France, but in America – where it was released in fifteen episodes in 1919 – it was *The Trail of the Octopus*. The evil Chinese 'with tentacles like an octopus' was called Wang Foo, the good guy was Carter Holmes, master criminologist, and 'President Woodrow Wilson' did indeed make a guest appearance. The convoluted plot was about nine sacred daggers from an ancient Egyptian 'temple of death', which when reunited with the cursed 'Devil's Trademark' – a large jewel – and with the symbols inscribed on the archaeologist Dr Reid Stanhope's arm, will give the owner all sorts of magic powers. *The Trail of the Octopus* contained many Sax Rohmerish elements, without acknowledgment, above all the super-villain Wang Foo.

But André Breton's memory was playing tricks. In the final episode, called 'The Yellow Octopus', President Wilson (in some newsreel footage) visits *San Francisco*, while in the same city Wang Foo – 'dreaming of world dominion' – is busy cloning himself (complete with embroidered mandarin robe, black cap and long moustache) with an 'atomic replicator' in his laboratory within the House of Shadows: a succession of identical 'Wang Foos', 'all controlled by one mastermind', emerges from a sealed chamber in puffs of smoke. Carter Holmes keeps thinking he has defeated the yellow octopus, but it turns out on closer inspection to have been one of his clones. Wang Foo also has the power, now that he possesses the lost daggers, to 'project his astral, or atomic, body any place'. 'With this power called "Dynolife" and the chemical gas "Raido Atomite",' explains one of the characters when he is arrested, 'Wang Foo could destroy the white race . . .' In the end, Carter Holmes and the fragrant Ruth Stanhope receive the personal congratulations of the President (this time a lookalike) in the White House. 'You have rendered your country a service by ridding it of this terrible menace, this gigantic octopus.' The End. Wang Foo never meets the President, in the White House or anywhere else. He operates from San Francisco not New York. But still, the fantasy of an American city being invaded by endless Chinese clones was certainly a memorable one. It picked up on the invasion literature of the previous decade. And it was the most blatant Fu Manchu derivative so far to reach the screen.

The Transylvanian photographer Brassaï experienced something of the surreal, disorientating shift of register between the mundane, familiar street, and the magic neon-lit interior of a bar – seen in countless descriptions of London's Limehouse – when in 1931, during one of his nocturnal prowlings around Paris in search of 'eccentric human behaviour', he was escorted by the son of a wealthy industrialist to 'an opium den', not in 'the Chinese enclaves of Paris, little Pekings, full of retired Colonels, where "puffing bamboo" was commonplace – but on the high-class avenue Bosquet'. There was the dreamlike contrast between the bourgeois exterior of the street and the artificiality of the den's interior, which in this case was distinctly 'oriental':

> . . . diwans, sofas covered with brocades and velvets, and low Chinese tables bearing trays loaded with pipes, lacquered boxes, and ceramic bowls; oil lamps gave off a subdued light – all the panoply of an opium den. My eyes took in Chinese vases and statues of Buddha . . .

Brassaï photographed a tray of artfully arranged equipment, a smoker preparing pipes for his partner, an habituée lying on a divan smoking a pipe and another sleeping it off. He was told by his companion Achille that

> in the old days, *cangari* – Chinese servants – prepared the pipes with an Asiatic ceremony. Unfortunately, we don't have *cangari* any more, and each smoker has to do it for himself.

And he made a self-portrait photograph wearing a gold brocade ritual gown, looking down on an opium pipe, 'so as to blend with the atmosphere'.

This was the year that *Le Docteur Fu-Manchu* was first published in France, to be followed in 1932 by *Le diabolique Fu-Manchu* and a year later by *Le masque de Fu-Manchu* (which confusingly was the second adventure, *The Devil Doctor*). The success of these three publications, all part of the *série noire* publisher's collection 'Le Masque', explains why Marcel Carné's film *Drôle de Drame* (Bizarre, Bizarre) (1937), written by the poet Jacques Prévert, relocated several scenes from the original thriller on which it was based – *His First Offence* (1934) by the Scots novelist and antiquarian J. Storer Clouston – from Hammersmith to Limehouse. *Drôle de Drame* reworks the gentle comedy of *His First Offence* into an out and out Surrealist farce. It is set in an absurd version of turn-of-the-century London. The 'Chinese Quarter' near the docks is 'the end of the world' where one of the characters says 'all hotels look alike' and where a Chinaman, touchingly, hits a top-hatted drunk on the head to steal the flower from his buttonhole. It is also the hiding-place of William Kramps (Jean-Louis Barrault), a mild-mannered vegetarian serial killer who murders and dismembers butchers ('I love animals with passion, you see') and always manages to escape on his bicycle. For all sorts of complicated reasons, detective-story writer Felix Chapel (Michel Simon), who is *really* a respected botanist in disguise, and who is suspected of murdering his wife, similarly goes to ground in Limehouse, where 'in the street at night people often kill each other a little. So it does get a little noisy.' What film and book have in common is a fascination with an eccentric British establishment figure who feels the need to repress his love of detective stories; and a sense of the mad logic of pulp fiction. *Drôle de Drame*, though made in 1937, was not properly released until 1951, when it soon became a cult success. Around the same time, a former teacher of literature and minor novelist called Jean-Marie Maurice

Schérer arrived in Paris, changed his name to Rohmer in homage to Sax's adventure novels, which had become fashionable among sophisticated intellectuals – and partly to put his disapproving family off the scent – and became the filmmaker Eric Rohmer.

Meanwhile, across the Atlantic, Jack Kerouac, in Mexico City, was fantasizing with William Burroughs about a 'Doctor Sax', an alchemist in a black cape and slouch hat who tries to defeat 'the great world snake'. Unfortunately, Doctor Sax is not successful. His fantastical exploits were eventually published in 1959. 'Sax' had made the journey from Edwardian adventure fiction to the druggy underground, and was 'hip' with some of the Beat generation. It is even possible that Burroughs's concept of a 'blade-runner' originated in the name Sax Rohmer – the wandering blade.

Farcical treatments of Sax Rohmer's fictional universe started earlier in Britain with Jack Harrison's nine-minute surreal puppet-film in the *Little People Burlesques* series, 'The Limejuice Mystery, or Who Spat in Grandfather's Porridge?' (1930), a spoof of Rohmer and of the recent Clive Brook film *The Return of Sherlock Holmes* (1929). 'The Limejuice Mystery' is mainly set in an opium den, where a Fu Manchu lookalike in a long moustache and shiny mandarin robe tries to have his wicked way with a Chinese girl, a fiendish bearded barman with a long pigtail hits people over the head with a wooden barrel, four clodhopping bobbies from the 'Flying Quad' (Keystone-style) fall down the stairs, and master of disguise/drag artiste Herlock Sholmes comes to the rescue in the nick of time. The music, by Philip Braham, consists of his popular 'Limehouse Blues' (1922, first performed and made famous by Gertrude Lawrence), rearranged as if for steamboat Mickey Mouse – with the barman playing bells which are suspended around an opium bunk, and pigtails being plucked as if on a double bass. Eventually, the villain gets his pigtail caught in a chandelier.

'Limehouse Blues' refers in its lyric to:

> . . . *Limehouse*
> *Where the yellow chinkies love to play* . . .
> *Poor broken blossom and nobody's child,*
> . . . *right here in orange blossom land.*

It left no cliché unturned. When Fred Astaire in Chinese 'coolie' makeup danced to it in the 'dramatic pantomime' sequence of *Ziegfeld Follies* (1944, released 1946) – gas-light, an opium-smoker, a curio shop, an opium den, a fan dance, a willow-pattern chorus – the line was changed to 'Where Orientals love to play . . .' By then it had become a jazz standard in the United States and Britain. In 1932, the music-hall comedian George Formby was to have his first hit record with the parody 'Chinese Laundry Blues' – about a lovelorn Mr Wu, who is feeling 'Kind of Limehouse Chinese Laundry Blues'. Later, Mr Wu would become a window-cleaner, with the usual voyeuristic results.

By 1938, over in Hollywood, one of Warner Bros' *Merrie Melodies*, called 'Have You Got Any Castles?', was featuring Fu Manchu, together with Dr Jekyll, the Phantom of the Opera and Frankenstein's creature, performing a dance one winter's night in a library – while the characters of fairytale and children's literature also come to life from the books on the shelves and applaud them. Sax Rohmer's creation, in cartoon-land at any rate, was on a level with the greats of Gothic literature. In the late 1930s, thanks to films, magazine stories and best-selling books, it certainly must have looked like that.

A curious cocktail of satire, melodrama and affection for a gas-lit Edwardian London – with a large dash of music hall added for good measure – was the signature of The Goons on BBC radio in the 1950s, especially when the scripts were written by Spike Milligan. The Goons were obsessed, one way or another, with pushing the clichés of the Imperial past to their illogical conclusion with a surreal abandon that could only work on radio. Inevitably Sax Rohmer was a regular target. When the show became a national institution, Peter Sellers, Harry Secombe and Spike Milligan liked to josh each other in telegrams and letters written in character. Secombe to Milligan, 11 March 1957: 'I see that Sax has reared his ugly head stop remember all men eat but few men chu stop'.

As the show gathered momentum, and began to consist of full-length stories rather than short sketches, there were regular send-ups of books – in episodes such as *Confessions of a Secret Senna-Pod Drinker* and *King Solomon's Mines* – the Fu Manchu novels among them. 'China Story', first broadcast in January 1955 and often repeated, concerned an attempt to assassinate General Kash-Mai-Chek with an exploding upright rosewood piano with brass candleholders: 'You Chinese are very damned clever people,' says Neddie Seagoon as the band strikes up 'There'll Always Be an England'; there are jokes about Mr Ah Pong who works in The Teahouse of the August Goon ('Knock 6,000 times and ask for Ah Pong.' 'We are Ah Pong till 11 o'clock'); and about the

'Ying-Tong period' in Chinese history (a reference to the hit Goons' song which began 'Ying-tong-yiddle-i-po'). Milligan provided the 'Chinese' voices.

The Goons followed up with 'The Terrible Revenge of Fred Fu Manchu' (announced on air as 'Fred Fu Manchu and his Bamboo Saxophone'), written by Spike Milligan and broadcast in December 1955. The most direct send-up of Sax Rohmer's writings, it begins in 1895, at the international heavyweight saxophone contest in the Crystal Palace. Fred Fu Manchu is competing with Major Dennis Bloodnok who wears 'a turban made out of our glorious Union Jack', and although Fred is by far the better musician, he loses ('Vast cheers. Crowd singing "There'll Always be an England"'). He vows *terrible revenge* on white man' for these dirty tricks at the Crystal Palace, and creates a devilish exploding liquid within 'a life-sized reproduction of the Kremlin' in Outer Mongolia. Back in Hyde Park, Bloodnok finds a bottle of spiked whisky:

> BLOODNOK [Sellers]: What do you want, you fiendish yellow devil carrying a bamboo saxophone? Are you one of those Boxer villains?
>
> FU MANCHU [Milligan]: Pardon?
>
> BLOODNOK: Have you never heard of the Boxer Rising?
>
> FU MANCHU: Only after the count of ten.
>
> BLOODNOK: I don't wish to know that.
>
> FU MANCHU: Now listen kind fliend, will you do honable flavour for me, please?

So Bloodnok points his exploding finger at a passing police constable. Eventually, Fu Manchu succeeds in blowing up 27,000 saxophones in an attempt to 'finish Britain as a saxophone-playing nation', and to show off his skill appears for one night only at the Adelphi Theatre as 'Jim Fu Manchu, amazing oriental conjuror. No relation to naughty Fred', before fleeing to Dewsbury – leaving a trail of noodles behind him. There, the elderly forces' sweetheart Minnie Bannister (Milligan) – the last remaining player of a metal saxophone in Britain – gives a solo rendition of 'The Yellow Rose of Texas'. Enter Fred Fu Manchu, who points his 'explodable finger' at the entire cast, including the announcer, and ends up giving a recital as 'the world's *only* bamboo saxophonist'.

By then, the BBC transcription service was preparing episodes of *The Goon Show* for broadcast overseas, but they made an exception with 'The Terrible Revenge', which might not have gone down well in Asian territories.

It was, however, adapted as a fifteen-minute episode of the second series of *The Telegoons*, broadcast on BBC television in August 1964. The episode was featured in the Parisian Surrealist film magazine *Midi Minuit Fantastique* in June 1966. Spike Milligan's 'Chinese' impersonations were simultaneously satirizing gung-ho Imperial adventure stories – and the attitudes which went with them, at a time when the Empire was in serious decline – and using funny voices to raise a laugh. The attitudes were to be recalled by a fellow humourist, the illustrator Ronald Searle, when he described how, at the age of twenty-two as a sapper in the Royal Engineers, he found himself posted halfway across the world to fight the Japanese during the Second World War: 'For all of us the Japanese were – what – Fu Manchu. I mean we had no idea . . . they were slit-eyed, couldn't shoot straight, yellow dwarfs . . . That's how it was.' He soon revised his opinion of their incompetence when he was captured and made to work on the 'hell on earth', the Burma railway. The Fu Manchu novels provided an off-the-shelf image of 'orientals' of all descriptions for impressionable draftees in wartime England.

Thomas Pynchon's vast, sprawling, postmodern novel *Gravity's Rainbow* (1973) opens in the same historical period – in London, December 1944, during the V2 rocket attacks – and includes among its many surreal allusions to then-contemporary popular culture, and to assorted conspiracy theories, a series of references to Sax Rohmer's novels. Some of the Americans, in their quest for the secret device unknown to science made of an unknown plastic – which has been developed at the rocket research centre in Peenemünde – think of Fu Manchu. There's a silly song about a 'little chink' with 'his ass just as yellow as Fu Manchu'; a fantasy about being abducted by Burmese dacoits and 'used for unspeakable purposes'; a quotation from a book published by 'the Nayland Smith Press'; and a character called Pointsman, who researches Pavlov's conditioned reflexes at a top-secret military establishment, is a Sax Rohmer fan, and periodically hears voices in his head:

> 'East and West, together in the same bloke? You can not only be Nayland Smith, giving a young lad in a funk wholesome advice about the virtues of work, but you also, at the same time, get to be *Fu Manchu*! eh? . . . How's *that*? Protagonist and antagonist in one. I'd jump at it if I were you.' . . . 'Yang and Yin,' whispers the Voice . . .

Pointsman owns a matched set of all the books in Sax Rohmer's great Manichaean saga, and is apt these days to pop in at any time ... and actually *stand* there, in front of the toilet, reading aloud a pertinent text.

In the context of 1944, such references are instantly recognizable. For Pointsman, the Fu Manchu stories are not so much about race as about a cosmic battle between 'wholesome advice' (or is it?) and world domination, at a time when incomprehensible rockets are landing in London, fired by another tyrant who seems to have stepped out of some 'Manichaean saga'.

S. J. Perelman's essay 'Why, Doctor, What Big Green Eyes You Have!', first published in *The New Yorker* in September 1950 and collected in *The Ill-Tempered Clavichord* (1952), reminisces about how the author was first introduced to *The Mystery of Dr Fu-Manchu* as a twelve-year-old on his summer holidays in 1916. At the time, it encouraged him to take some extreme precautions at night: barricading the doors with a chest of drawers, sprinkling tacks along the windowsills and strewing crumpled newspapers about the floor to warn of approaching footsteps.

A casual reference to Thuggee over the breakfast oatmeal leads him to find out that his *daughter* is now reading *The Mystery*. He confiscates the book, reacquaints himself with it, and is surprised to discover that it is really 'as abrasive to the nerves as a cup of Ovaltine'. The plot, he now sees, is 'engagingly simple and monstrously confused'. He can now appreciate 'how lightly the laws of probability weighed on Sax Rohmer', how when in doubt he flings 'a shower of adjectives in the reader's face' and how, 'if there was one branch of literary hopscotch Rohmer excelled in, it was avoiding dénouements'. So none of the excursions of Nayland Smith and Dr Petrie, in their pursuit of the devil doctor, ever actually leads anywhere.

There is only one thing to do. Perelman finishes the book, makes sure his daughter is asleep, slips downstairs and consigns 'the lord of the fires to his native element' by chucking the book into the flames:

> As he crumbled into ash, I could have sworn I smelled a rather rare essential oil and felt a pair of baleful green eyes fixed on me from the staircase. It was probably the cat, though I really didn't take the trouble to check. I just strolled into the kitchen, made sure there was no trapdoor under the icebox, and curled up for the night. That's how phlegmatic a chap gets in later life.

Perelman's essay is about how yesterday's best-selling thrills become today's clichés; about how *dated* Rohmer's style of hyperbole has become; about grown-up tastes and childish anxieties; and having said all this – about how Fu Manchu has *still* not 'retired to the limbo of the second-hand book-shop'. He lives in books that are still read, comic-book lookalikes (Fu Manchu himself had appeared in *Detective Comics* in 1938), films that are still in circulation, radio serials – and in the 'popular imagination'.

Perelman was right when he wrote that Fu Manchu still lived. Twenty years later, when President Nixon made his historic visit to China in February 1972, Walter Cronkite presented a news item on television about 'the American conception of the Chinese': it included a clip from *The Mask of Fu Manchu*, of the devil doctor in his laboratory injecting Terry Granville with a serum which will make him 'a reflection of my will', and another from a Charlie Chan movie. His point was that for at least two decades the American people had been unable to see any other images of *contemporary* China: perhaps the President's visit, with huge press corps in tow, would at last make available some images of a *living* culture, to counteract the stereotypes.

The *National Lampoon* issue of February 1972 celebrated Nixon's uncharacteristic decision with 'The Thoughts of Chairman Fu-Manchu' by Henry Beard – one of the founders of the magazine. It tells of Dr Petrie and Nayland Smith meeting again, for the first time for twenty years, in the Embargo Club in Singapore, after Smith has sent Petrie the enigmatic summons: 'What has green eyes and hamadryads?' Nayland Smith rushes into the Club in time-honoured fashion, and tells Petrie that he must finish his whisky on the stairs, such is the urgency. Having dodged a dacoit with a poisoned rope, an envenomed dart and a taxi-driver who cannot make head or tail of Smith's garbled instructions ('It's been a long time,' he admits), they reach a certain Chinese restaurant called Jimmy's Gate of the Heavenly Eggroll. Smith, now pretending to be an American tourist, explains that the devil doctor is, despite all evidence to the contrary, still very much alive:

> The dozens of Chinese-born scientists, seized with the sudden urge to leave their well-stocked laboratories and return to China. The cleverly arranged purges of American scholars learned in Chinese studies. The mysterious suicide of an American Secretary of Defense who had seen the peril. . . . And now the sudden activity, the Ping-Pong tour, a

trade agreement, the issuance of a vague invitation for the American President to visit Peking, its dramatic acceptance, and finally the U.N. debacle. Petrie, it's all of a pattern, and the hand on the loom is that of Dr Fu-Manchu!

There have been other strange happenings, adds Smith. The crushing of the Red Guards and the disappearance of nine of the most powerful leaders in China, in a plane crash just inside Mongolia; troop movements, the grounding of the air force – all on the eve of the President's visit. It points to one thing, which has

> more significance than anything that has taken place since the War, perhaps since the beginning of the century! For Mao is dead, Chou En-lai is none other than Dr Fu-Manchu and Chaing Ching is his daughter!

At this point, a noxious greenish gas emanates from the fortune cookies in the restaurant, and the now-paralysed pair are taken by motor-junk to a waiting submarine. They are unconscious for nearly three weeks, throughout Nixon's visit, and wake up in the Forbidden City, Peking. Premier Chou En-lai enters:

> He was wearing not the customary blue Mao suit, but a rich silk jacket, and on his head sat the black silk cap of the Mandarin order. But, as he drew closer, some subtle change seemed to come over his features, for, with every catlike step he took, his face seemed less like that of the austere-looking man in the wirephotos and more like the one which occasionally appeared in my worst nightmares, a face in whose high brow and sharp, Satanic features were joined at once the ancient cunning and the fathomless cruelty of the yellow race. It was Dr Fu-Manchu.

The Premier takes his 'guests' on a little tour. First stop is a balcony overlooking Tiananmen Square, where an animatronic Chairman Mao intones, 'Death to the imperialists and all their running dogs.' The devil doctor explains that Walt Disney, the victim of 'death-simulating drugs', is now 'a tool in the hands of Fu-Manchu'. He has advised on the animatronics. Next stop is an ancient dungeon, where President Nixon is a captive. A lookalike has just been sent back to the United States. Will anyone notice the difference? When 'Mr Nixon' destroys the American economy, divides her people and diminishes her role in the world, he will surely be acting just like his predecessor. No change there. Thus China will be served and 'restored to glory' by vassals prostrating themselves before the Dragon Throne like in the old days. Having shared his thoughts, Fu Manchu offers Nayland Smith and Petrie a comfortable retirement in China – or death by acupuncture. Petrie chooses retirement in a 'little palace built by a minor Ming emperor for his favourite concubine'. Smith does not display equal wisdom. 'The mind of the occidental is inscrutable,' says Petrie. And Fu Manchu laughs.

'The Thoughts of Chairman Fu-Manchu' is a clever parody of Sax Rohmer's early stories – Henry Beard evidently knew them well – as well as being a satire on the dominant images of 'China' shared by most Americans. It plays, in its conclusion, to anxieties about the decline of the American Empire and the rise of the Chinese. The Imperial nostalgia of *British* satires is absent.

Nostalgia for Victorian London was, on the other hand, strong in the *Dr Who* series of February–April 1977, *The Talons of Weng-Chiang*, part of the fourteenth season. This brought together the Whitechapel murders and Sax Rohmer's stories, and the main villain was Weng's agent Li Hsen Chang (John Bennett), whose day job was as a stage magician and hypnotist; he works with a ventriloquist's dummy called 'Mr Sin' who comes to life. Dr Who (Tom Baker), in a deerstalker, accompanied by Leela (Louise Jameson), tracks him down ('I rather hoped we'd catch Little Tich'), is attacked by a giant mutated rat in the sewers beneath the music hall – Weng-Chiang's lair – and eventually unmasks Weng as a war criminal from the future: 'Haven't I met you somewhere before?' asks the Doctor, to which Li replies wearily, 'I understand we all look the same.'

Series producer Philip Hinchcliffe intended to take 'a literary convention . . . borrow the trappings of it, and then re-dress that up within the Doctor Who format'. In this case, the Gothic novel and Fu Manchu. *The Talons* was full of Rohmerish elements: 'inscrutable Chinks', the death of a thousand cuts, ancestor worship, opium addiction, a super-villain known as 'the Yellow One', his control over the Tong of the Black Scorpion, a death ray. It elicited special criticism from Mary Whitehouse's National Viewers' and Listeners' Association for its 'racism, violence and sexuality' (Leela wears wet-look Victorian knickers), and for its tendency to corrupt younger viewers. Today, the racism of the series is more problematic – as was the episode of *Sherlock* (2010) partly derived from it, which involved sinister goings-on in a contemporary Chinese circus. Unlike 'The Thoughts of Chairman Fu-Manchu', *The Talons* attempted to reclaim the literary conventions of Yellow Peril literature as an eccentric *British* phenomenon. At one point, Tom Baker even begins to recite 'The Green Eye of the Yellow God'.

Instead of revisiting Victorian Limehouse in a Tardis, Alan Moore's words and Kevin O'Neill's illustrations in chapter three of the graphic novel *The League of Extraordinary Gentlemen* Vol. I (1999) – 'Mysteries of the East' – conjure a steampunk version of docklands, populated with a dense network of characters and environments out of Victorian and Edwardian popular fiction which have taken on a life of their own. As O'Neill told me: 'I looked at photos of old Limehouse and the docks and they looked nothing like the fantasy version. Ours was a Limehouse of the imagination.'

The story is set in July 1898, the year after Queen Victoria's Diamond Jubilee, and a league of literary characters, all with personal problems – Allan Quatermain (from *King Solomon's Mines*, 1885), Dr Jekyll, Griffin the Invisible Man and Wilhelmina Murray (from *Dracula*, 1897) – is on the track of the gravity-cancelling alloy Cavorite (from H. G. Wells's *First Men in the Moon*, 1901). A jovial *Boy's Own Paper*-style introduction by Mr S. Smiles alerts readers to the 'many serious, morally instructive points that are within the narrative' – including the conviction that 'the Chinese are brilliant, but evil'. Britain rules most of the world, and the time is one of troubled supremacism. The clues lead 'down East' to Limehouse, a dockside rabbit-warren of wood-clad opium dens, brothels, low dives lit by colourful Chinese lanterns, reached by Escher-like stairs and walkways. The first destination is the tea shop of Quong Lee, where the proprietor speaks in seemingly obscure riddles. Quong Lee was a wise old man in some of Thomas Burke's poems and stories. Then to Shanghai Charlie's – a wooden pagoda-like structure built on stilts – located within Shen Yan's barbershop, to talk with someone called Ho Ling: Shanghai Charlie's is Singapore Charlie's from *The Mystery of Dr Fu-Manchu*, where Shen Yan's shop also famously appeared; Ho Ling was another character in Thomas Burke's Limehouse fiction, the boss of a fantan parlour. In a room behind Charlie's opium den, lit by the reddish reflection of a bubbling cauldron, the 'unnamed' crime king of London's East End – known as 'the Doctor', the 'wily Chinese', 'the devil doctor' or 'the lord of Limehouse' – is busy torturing Ho Ling, by painting a calligraphic message onto his body, in Chinese characters, with acid:

A man without scars

Is an unwritten book

'That room was very much like hell,' says Quatermain, 'and he was very much like Satan.' Apparently, the devil doctor 'grew up during the Opium Wars in China, and therefore abhors the British with a vengeance'. He has a catlike green eye, is tall and lean, has a moustache and a long pigtail. It transpires that the lord of Limehouse is experimenting with a 'flying warship' powered by Cavorite, a terrifying 'weapon of the new electric age', in a disused tunnel beneath the recently opened Rotherhithe Bridge . . .

Alan Moore admitted to me that the Chinese super-villain was unnamed for reasons of copyright: the brand 'Fu Manchu' had been licensed by the estate's representatives for appearances in comics. But the clues were obvious enough: there's even the name 'Rohm–' written between 'Poe' and 'Stevenson' on the wall of a Chinese-run shelter for the homeless. *The League* sets up a fantasy world of late-Victorian and Edwardian high Imperialism, in order to confront and undermine its assumptions. Again, there is a playful nostalgia for the popular fictions and myths of a century before, but there is also serious criticism. Moore has rightly said that the legacy of Empire still haunts English society, at a deep level. Was he worried about reviving Sax Rohmer's stereotypical 'Chinee'?

> '. . . a Chinese-American wrote to me saying that people might complain about Fu Manchu as a Chinese stereotype, but that he thought of Fu Manchu as a positive, powerful – all-powerful in fact – role model! Much better than a young man in spectacles studying cybernetics.'
>
> 'Or a laundryman . . .'
>
> 'Yes.'

The speech bubbles of the characters in Shanghai Charlie's, and in Fu Manchu's den, are written in simplified modern Standard Chinese, and are not translated. The doctor's disciples are in fact saying mundane things like 'The boss needs more brushes'. How did Kevin O'Neill manage with the language? 'I went to my local Chinese takeaway, to get the words translated. The man there asked "Who *is* this?" And I heard myself saying "Fu Manchu"!'

In *The League of Extraordinary Gentlemen Black Dossier* (2007), Kerouac's 'Doctor Sax' becomes the great-grandson of the devil doctor. In the film version of *The League* (2003), the Fu Manchu sequences disappeared completely, presumably because they might offend a lot of paying customers. Fu Manchu has since made guest appearances in Kim Newman's postmodern vampire novel *Anno Dracula* (1992) – as 'an ancient Chinaman' or 'the Lord of Strange Deaths', a member of the Si-Fan and associate of Dr Nikola – and in Paul Magrs's *Something Borrowed* (2007), where his widow Sheila Manchu, who owns the cheesy Hotel Miramar in Whitby in Yorkshire and dresses in a 'silken oriental outfit – which strains all over her curves', reminisces about her surprisingly successful marriage to the man she called 'Mu-Mu Manchu', once he had agreed to give up 'his various schemes to conquer the world': he was 'ninety-two years older than me' when they met, but there were compensations; '*look* how wide his brow was'. The cosy world of Whitby bed and breakfasts, and tea shops, is about to become the site of 'infernal rites'. But Fu Manchu is long gone, she says: 'He died in 1977. During a street party for the Silver Jubilee. A fit of anti-British apoplexy.' Sheila sighed. 'I always told him he'd do himself a mischief, one of these days.'

This book has been many years in the making and has accrued along the way many obligations to other writers, critics, scholars, commentators and friends. In order to keep its length within reasonable bounds, however, it has been possible to cite only the most direct debts – and significant matters arising – in the notes that follow. In particular, specific references have not been supplied for all the discussions of Sax Rohmer's Fu Manchu stories. Those readers new to the exploits of the devil doctor, and wishing to pursue him further, will find (at the time of going to press) paperback or e-book reprints of the first nine volumes in print – for better or worse.

Numbers refer to page numbers.

Preface
9 …a BBC radio documentary series… The BBC Radio 4 series was called *Print the Legend* and it was broadcast in autumn 1995. Quotations by Said are from the unedited taped interview for the series.

11 …Franz Fanon's book… Said referred to this, in print, in his essay 'Jungle Calling', reprinted in Edward Said, *Reflections on Exile and Other Literary and Cultural Essays* (London: Granta Books, 2001), pp. 327–36.

14 …Yunte Huang's book… See Yunte Huang, *Charlie Chan: The Untold Story* (New York: Norton, 2010); the quote from Keye Luke is on p. 265. Against Huang's thesis, see Jessica Hagedorn (ed.), *Charlie Chan Is Dead: An Anthology of Contemporary Asian American Fiction* (New York: Penguin, 1993), especially the preface by Elaine Kim, pp. ix–xiii.

15 …*The Fu Manchu Complex*… David York, *The Fu Manchu Complex* (2013), performed at the Ovalhouse, London, 1–19 October 2013.

16 …the name 'Fu Manchu'… On the impossibility of this name, see, among other commentators, Leslie Charteris in Robert E. Briney (ed.), *Rohmer Review* 6 (1971), p. 19, and *Rohmer Review* 9, p. 15.

Introduction The Setting of the Sun
19 It felt like the last day… This account of the Hong Kong handover is based on Jonathan Dimbleby, *The Last Governor: Chris Patten and the Handover of Hong Kong* (London: Little, Brown, 1997), pp. 395–426; Piers Brendon, *The Decline and Fall of the British Empire, 1781–1997* (London: Vintage, 2008), pp. 635–56; Peter Moss, *Hong Kong Handover – Signed, Sealed and Delivered: A Visual Record* (Hong Kong: FormAsia, 1997); and a videotape of the BBC television coverage of 30 June–1 July 1997.

22 …*Ripley's Believe It or Not*… Reproduced in Harold R. Isaacs, *Images of Asia: American Views of China and India* (New York: Harper, 1992), p. 100. Original title was *Scratches on Our Minds* (1958). The illustration dates from 1929–34.

23 …'The "Fu Manchu" Problem…' See James R. Lilley, 'The "Fu Manchu" Problem', *Newsweek* 129:8 (24 February 1997).

24 …where did information about China come from…? On this, see in particular Isaacs, *Images of Asia*, pp. 70–72, 109–41.

24 'Hasty conclusion easy to make…' On Chan's aphorisms, see Harvey Chertok and Martha Torge (eds), *Quotations from Charlie Chan* (New York, Golden Press, 1968); Huang, *Charlie Chan*; and Ken Hanke, *Charlie Chan at the Movies: History, Filmography, and Criticism* (Jefferson, NC: McFarland, 1989). The Chertok and Torge volume is presented in the form of a little red book, Mao-style.

25 Even distinguished Harvard researchers… See Samuel P. Huntington, 'The Clash of Civilizations?', *Foreign Affairs* 72:3 (summer 1993), pp. 22–47.

25 A guide written for Americans going East… Paul S. Crane, *Korean Patterns* (Seoul: Holym Corp., 1967): 'a popular handbook by a long-time medical missionary…intended to help the newcomer understand Korean culture and psychology'. See *Rohmer Review* 3 (August 1969), p. 31.

25 'There is an old tradition…' Lilley, '"Fu Manchu" Problem'.

25 …the sentiments of the hero-diplomat… Douglas Hurd and Andrew Osmond, *The Smile on the Face of the Tiger* (London: Fontana, 1971), p. 189.

26 When I asked Chris Patten… Author's interview with Lord Patten of Barnes, October 2007, from which the following quotations are taken.

28 …Jonathan Spence…or…Lucian Pye's… See Jonathan D. Spence, *The Chan's Great Continent: China in Western Minds* (New York: Norton, 1998), especially pp. 122–44 ('China at Home') and 165–86 ('An American Exotic?'); and Lucian W. Pye: *The Spirit of Chinese Politics: A Psychocultural Study of the Authority Crisis in Political Development* (Cambridge, MA: MIT Press, 1968), especially pp. 36–49 ('Politics Without Modern Men') and 67–84 ('The Discovery of Hate'). Also Raymond Dawson, *The Chinese Chameleon: An Analysis of European Conceptions of Chinese Civilization* (London: Oxford University Press, 1967), especially pp. 65–89 ('Eternal Standstill'), 90–105 ('East Is East and West Is West'), 106–31 ('Aesthetic Appeal') and 132–52 ('The Heathen Chinee'); and Colin Mackerras, *Western Images of China* (Hong Kong and Oxford: Oxford University Press, 1989), especially pp. 91–100 ('Images of China's Past') and pp. 111–24 ('Lack of Change').

29 The original Palace had been sacked… See Brendon, *Decline and Fall*, pp. 106–8; Robert Bickers, *The Scramble for China: Foreign Devils in the Qing Empire, 1832–1914* (London: Allen Lane, 2011), pp. 77–112; and Harry G. Gelber, *The Dragon and the Foreign Devils: China and the World, 1100 BC to the Present* (London: Bloomsbury, 2008), pp. 184–93.

29 First of all, replied Dr Fang… Author's lecture visit to Tsinghua University, April 2009. The conversation with Dr Fang Xiaofeng took place during an architectural tour of the Summer Palace.

31 …the maybe too casual use of language… On *American* slang about Chinese people, see Arthur Bonner, *Alas! What Brought Thee Hither?: The Chinese in New York, 1800–1950* (Madison, NJ: Farleigh Dickinson University Press, 1997), p. 16.

33 A Record of National Humiliation… On the 'literature of humiliation' in general, see William A. Callahan, *China: The Pessoptimist Nation* (Oxford: Oxford University Press, 2010), pp. 2–30, 35–45 (on school textbooks) and 82–89 ('national humiliation days'). On just one of these 'humiliations', see Robert A. Bickers and Jeffrey N. Wasserstrom, 'Shanghai's "Dogs and Chinese Not Admitted" Sign: Legend, History and Contemporary Symbol', *The China*

Quarterly 142 (June 1995), pp. 444–66.

34 …a scaly serpentine dragon… On modern Western iconography of China, see Christina Larsen and Adam Minter, 'It's Time to Retire the Tiger and the Dragon', *Foreign Policy* (20 September 2010), pp. 1–3.

34 …Showdown: Why China Wants War… Jed Babbin and Edward Timperlake, *Showdown: Why China Wants War with the United States* (Washington, DC: Regnery Publishing, 2006).

35 …The Coming China Wars… Peter Navarro, *The Coming China Wars: Where They Will Be Fought and How They Can Be Won* (Upper Saddle River, NJ: FT Press, 2007).

36 The third book which caught my eye… Sax Rohmer, *The Fu-Manchu Omnibus: Volume 1* (London: Allison and Busby, 1998), containing the first three novels in the series.

Chapter One Sax and the Single Chinaman

39 …Elizabeth Sax Rohmer… The author's visit and conversation took place in June 1971. All the following quotations by Mrs Sax Rohmer date from this visit, and have been compared with the book she co-authored with Rohmer's protégé Cay Van Ash, *Master of Villainy: A Biography of Sax Rohmer* (London: T. Stacey, 1972).

40 …unfortunate choice of advisers… On one of these, a literary agent, see *The Author* 40:2 (January 1930), pp. 40–43; and the Society of Authors Archive in the British Library, vol. CCXXVIII (Additional MSS 56791 and 63433). This particular 'misunderstanding' ended up in court.

42 …£1,047 and 16 shillings. See Robert Bickers, 'Ward, Arthur Henry [Sax Rohmer] (1883–1959', *Oxford Dictionary of National Biography* (Oxford: Oxford University Press, 2004), pp. 278–79.

42 …'The Village Green Preservation Society'… See Nick Hasted, *The Story of the Kinks: You Really Got Me* (London: Omnibus, 2011), pp. 123–33.

43 'Let's give our crime…' Anthony Shaffer, *Sleuth* (London: Marion Boyars, 2009), p. 31.

44 'Take a look at yourself, Andrew…' Shaffer, *Sleuth*, p. 90.

44 …always to drink Bollinger… Anthony Shaffer, *So What Did*

You Expect?: A Memoir (London: Picador, 2001), p. 20, and on Sax Rohmer's detective stories, pp. 207–8.

44 'with regard and affection' Shaffer, *Sleuth*, p. 5.

44 …memories of Sax Rohmer… See John Pearson, *Alias James Bond: The Life of Ian Fleming* (New York: Bantam, 1967), pp. 267–68 and 280–86; C. F. Snelling, *James Bond: A Report* (London: Panther, 1965), pp. 161–66; Ben Macintyre, *For Your Eyes Only: Ian Fleming and James Bond* (London: Bloomsbury, 2009), pp. 15, 110–12, 183 and 205; Sheldon Lane (ed.), *For Bond Lovers Only* (London: Panther, 1965), pp. 10–28 and 114–25; and Colin Watson, *Snobbery with Violence: Crime Stories and Their Audience* (London: Eyre & Spottiswoode, 1971), pp. 244–45.

45 'Dr No was at least six inches taller…' Ian Fleming, *Dr No* (London: Pan Books, 1960), p. 127.

46 …a most improbable 'Miss Taro'… See Matthew Field, 'Remembering Zena Marshall', *Cinema Retro* (2012), movie classics special on *Dr No*, pp. 69–70.

47 …the parallels with Fu Manchu were *too* close See Cubby Broccoli and Donald Zec, *When the Snow Melts: The Autobiography of Cubby Broccoli* (London: Boxtree, 1999), pp. 158–59. Also Christopher Frayling, *Ken Adam: The Art of Production Design* (London: Faber & Faber, 2003), pp. 95–96, and Adrian Turner, *Goldfinger* (London: Bloomsbury, 1998), pp. 139–40.

47 Harry Alan Towers… Harry Alan Towers, *Mr Towers of London: A Life in Show Business* (Albany, GA: BearManor Media, 2013), pp. 56–58; Cy Young filmed interview with Harry Alan Towers, BECTU History Project interview no. 608 (held at the BFI); John Exshaw, 'Face to Face with Fu', *Cinema Retro* 5:15 (autumn 2009), pp. 26–33; Jonathan Rigby, *Christopher Lee: The Authorised Screen History* (London: Reynolds & Hearn, 2001), pp. 107–8, 112–16, 120 and 123; Jonathan Sothcott, *The Cult Films of Christopher Lee* (Lewes: Eaton, 2000), pp. 85–89; and Christopher Lee, *Lord of Misrule* (Orion, London, 1997), pp. 267–70.

58 'The Fu Manchusical'… D. R. Bensen, 'The Fu Manchusical', *Ellery Queen's Mystery Magazine* 53:6,

whole no. 307 (June 1969), pp. 147–50.

59 'So vehement and repetitive…' Watson, *Snobbery with Violence*, p. 118–19.

60 The Sins of Séverac Bablon. On this serial, see Robert E. Briney, 'Sax Rohmer: An Informal Survey', in Francis M. Nevins, Jr (ed.), *The Mystery Writer's Art* (Bowling Green, OH: Bowling Green University Popular Press, 1970), pp. 58–59, and Sax Rohmer, *The Sins of Séverac Bablon* (London: Cassell, 1914).

60 …an article in the New Yorker… Reprinted as 'The Doctor's Blade' in *Rohmer Review* 9 (August 1972), pp. 19–21.

62 He also wrote, very revealingly, in January 1938… In one of a series of autobiographical 'Pipe Dreams', *Manchester Empire News*, 30 January 1938, p. 11. See also Van Ash and Rohmer, *Master of Villainy*, pp. 183–84.

64 Having failed the Civil Service entrance examinations… Mrs Sax Rohmer also handed me – as corroborating evidence – a copy of an anonymous article, entitled 'Master of Menace' (*MD Literature* (October 1969), pp. 171–76), that covered in outline some of the ground of her *Master of Villainy*, which was shortly to be published. The *MD Literature* article confidently states that 'one of his fellow employees was P. G. Wodehouse'.

65 Which took the story up to when they met… Van Ash and Rohmer, *Master of Villainy*, pp. 21–26 and 40–46, covers the early life together of Sax and Elizabeth.

66 '…Sax knew him well, for several years…' See also Mary Tich and Richard Findlater, *Little Tich: Giant of the Music Hall* (London: Elm Tree, 1979), pp. 7 and 118, and on Tich's act, pp. 3–7; Rohmer, 'Pipe Dreams', 13 March 1938, p. 13; Van Ash and Rohmer, *Master of Villainy*, pp. 78–84; and *Little Tich: A Book of Travels (and Wanderings)* (London: Greening and Co., 1911), ghost-written by Sax Rohmer.

67 According to one version… See Rohmer, 'Pipe Dreams', 30 January 1938, p. 11. Other versions – among many – include Sax Rohmer, 'The Birth of Dr Fu Manchu', *Daily Sketch*, 24 May 1934, reprinted in *Rohmer Review* 17 (August 1977), pp. 1–4; Van Ash and Rohmer,

Mastery of Villainy, pp. 72–77; and Sax Rohmer, 'Meet Dr Fu Manchu', in Cecil Madden (ed.), *Meet the Detective* (London: George Allen & Unwin, 1935).

68 ...the plots of *The Yellow Claw* and *The Golden Scorpion*... Sax Rohmer: *The Yellow Claw* (Methuen, London, 1915); Sax Rohmer: *The Golden Scorpion* (Methuen, London, 1919) and Sax Rohmer: *Yellow Shadows* (Doubleday, New York, 1926), especially pp. 25–32 ('Yvette Goes East') and pp. 56–64 ('Behind the Curtain').

69 The very innocence of the shopfronts... On the wider significance of this cliché, see John Seed, 'Limehouse Blues: Looking for Chinatown in the London Docks, 1900–40', *History Workshop Journal* 62:1 (autumn 2006), pp. 68–71 and 76–81.

69 H. V. Morton, for example... H. V. Morton, *The Nights of London* (London: Methuen, 1926), pp. 44–48 ('Fan-Tan'), 73–77 ('White and Yellow') and 102–107 ('Charlie Brown's').

70 ...the author as intrepid, tough-minded adventurer... See, for example, Jack London, *The People of the Abyss* (London: Journeyman, 1978); George R. Sims (ed.), *Living London: Its Work and Its Play, Its Humour and Its Pathos, Its Sights and Its Scenes*, 3 vols (London: Cassell, 1901–3), especially the article by Count E. Armfelt, 'Oriental London' (vol. 1, pp. 81–86); and James Greenwood, *In Strange Company: Being the Experiences of a Roving Correspondent*, 2nd edn (London: Vizetelly & Co., 1883); Rohmer on 'Charlie Brown knew much about Limehouse' and Sax Rohmer: *Limehouse Memories* (*Daily Sketch*, 3 April 1934, p. 4).

70 'Charlie Brown knew much about Limehouse...' and Sax Rohmer, 'Limehouse Memories', *Daily Sketch*, 3 April 1934, p. 4.

70 'Chief Inspector Yeo...' Rohmer, 'Pipe Dreams', 30 January 1938, p. 11.

70 ...the Billie Carleton case... The best single account of this is in Marek Kohn, *Dope Girls: The Birth of the British Drug Underground* (London: Lawrence & Wishart, 1992), to which I am indebted.

71 Rohmer wrote indignantly... Letter to the press, reproduced in manuscript

and print in *Rohmer Review* 9 (August 1972), pp. 16–17.

72 '...something in the conversation...' Rohmer, 'Pipe Dreams', 13 March 1938, p. 13.

73 ...the writer Thomas Burke... On Burke's biography, see Anne Veronica Witchard, *Thomas Burke's Dark Chinoiserie: Limehouse Nights and the Queer Spell of Chinatown* (Farnham: Ashgate, 2009), pp. 6–7, 162–65, 117–32. See also Seed, 'Limehouse Blues', pp. 77 and 79, for the two Thomas Burke quotations; and Thomas Burke, *Out and About: A Note-Book of London in War-Time* (London: George Allen & Unwin, 1919), pp. 34–41 ('Chinatown Revisited').

73 ...some kind of caveat... See Rohmer, 'Pipe Dreams', 30 January 1938, p. 11, and Sax Rohmer, 'The Birth of Fu Manchu', *Daily Sketch*, 21 May 1924.

74 'At the time I did them...' See Seed, 'Limehouse Blues', p. 77, and Thomas Burke, *The Real East End* (London: Constable, 1932), pp. 62–75.

74: A spirited exchange of letters... Revd R. J. Powell, Rector of Limehouse, letter to the *Daily Mail*, 18 October 1929, and reply from Thomas Burke, in Tower Hamlets Local History Library and Archive, cuttings file.

74 ...one of his autobiographical articles of 1938... Rohmer, 'Pipe Dreams', 30 January 1938, p. 11.

75 Rohmer's last utterance on the subject... Sax Rohmer, 'Limehouse Rhapsody', *The Saint Detective Magazine* (British edn) 5:2 (December 1958), pp. 25–40, especially pp. 32 and 39.

76 ...very interested in the occult... See Van Ash and Rohmer, *Master of Villainy*, pp. 161–68 and 185, and Rohmer, 'Pipe Dreams', 13 February 1938, p. 11.

76 ...Houdini was, apparently, much impressed... On Rohmer and Houdini, see Rohmer, 'Pipe Dreams', 27 March 1938, p. 11, and Van Ash and Rohmer, *Master of Villainy*, pp. 121–25 and 134–40.

77 ...the Hermetic Order of the Golden Dawn... For a summary of the Order's history, see David V. Barrett, *The Atlas of Secret Societies: The Truth Behind the Templars, Freemasons and Other Secretive Organizations* (London: Godsfield, 2008), pp. 102–21.

78 ...experimenting...with a ouija board... See Van Ash and Rohmer, *Master of Villainy*, p. 63; Sax Rohmer, 'The Birth of Fu Manchu' (*Rohmer Review* 17, p. 3); and Anon., 'Master of Menace', p. 174.

78 ...'psychic detective' called Moris Klaw... On Moris Klaw, see Briney, 'Sax Rohmer: An Informal Survey', pp. 57–58, and Sax Rohmer, *The Dream Detective* (London: Jarrolds, 1920).

78 'Opium in my case...' See also Rohmer, 'Pipe Dreams', 30 January 1938, p. 11.

79 ...an 'oriental' perfume called 'Honan'... Van Ash and Rohmer, *Master of Villainy*, pp. 112–16; Rohmer, 'Pipe Dreams', 30 January 1938, p. 11.

80 ...a bizarre postscript to her Limehouse adventure... See Van Ash and Rohmer, *Master of Villainy*, pp. 116–18. Compare Rohmer, 'Limehouse Rhapsody', pp. 33–40, and Rohmer, 'Pipe Dreams', 30 January 1938, p. 11.

83 ...*The Rohmer Review*... Edited by Robert E. Briney from issue 5 onwards, the *Rohmer Review* ran from 1968 to 1981, and was originally the journal of the Sax Rohmer Society. It was a bound, typescript journal, with articles by and about Sax Rohmer, and reviews of books and films.

***Chapter Two* Charles Dickens and Princess Puffer**

87 ...Dickens wrote to Sol Eytinge... See Madeline House and Graham Storey (general eds), *The Letters of Charles Dickens* (Oxford: Clarendon Press, 1965–2002), vol. 12, *1868–1870*, pp. 354–64, and Walter Dexter (ed.), *The Letters of Charles Dickens, Volume 3: 1858–1870* (London: Nonesuch Press, 1938), pp. 725–27.

87 'Among the most memorable...' See James T. Fields, *Yesterdays with Authors* (New York: AMS Press, 1970, reprint from 1900 edition), pp. 202–6.

87 ...according to an investigative journalist... See Frederic G. Kitton, *The Novels of Charles Dickens: A Bibliography and Sketch* (London: Elliot Stock, 1897), pp. 228–31, and James Platt, 'Chinese London and the Opium Dens', *The Gentleman's Magazine*, 279 (1895), pp. 272–82.

88 ...'Chinese Amazons'... See Matthew Sweet, *Inventing the*

Victorians (London: Faber, 2001), pp. 95–103, to which I am indebted.

88 ...he had published an article about it... J. C. Parkinson, 'Lazarus, Lotus-Eating', *All the Year Round*, 12 May 1866, pp. 421–25.

90 ...Colonel the Honourable Frederick Wellesley... Frederick Wellesley, *Recollections of a Soldier-Diplomat*, ed. Sir Victor Wellesley (London: Hutchinson, 1941), pp. 74–76.

90 ...Charles (or Charley) Frederick Field... See Philip Collins, 'Inspector Bucket Visits the Princess Puffer', *The Dickensian* 60 (1964), pp. 88–91; Philip Collins, *Dickens and Crime* (London: Macmillan, 1962), pp. 206–11; Charles Dickens, 'On Duty with Inspector Field', *Household Words*, no. 64 (14 June 1851), pp. 265–70, reprinted in Michael Slater (ed.), *Dickens' Journalism* (London: Dent, 1994–2000), vol. 2, *The 'Amusements of the People' and Other Papers: Reports, Essays and Reviews, 1834–51*, pp. 356–69; and Kate Summerscale, *The Suspicions of Mr Whicher; or, The Murder at Road Hill House* (London: Bloomsbury, 2009), pp. 53–55.

92 According to Virginia Berridge... Virginia Berridge, 'East End Opium Dens and Narcotic Use in Britain', *The London Journal* 4:1 (May 1978), pp. 4–5.

92 ...descriptions of opium-smoking... See Berridge, 'East End Opium Dens', pp. 3–29, and Virginia Berridge, 'Victorian Opium-Eating: Responses to Opiate Use in Nineteenth-Century England', *Victorian Studies* 21:4 (summer 1978), pp. 437–61. Also, more generally, Virginia Berridge and Griffith Edwards, *Opium and the People: Opiate Use in Nineteenth-Century England* (London: Allen Lane, 1981), pp. 195–205; the appendix 'Opium in the Nineteenth Century' in Barry Milligan's edition of Thomas De Quincey, *Confessions of an English Opium-Eater and Other Writings* (London: Penguin, 2003), pp. 247–54; and Sweet, *Inventing the Victorians*, pp. 97–103.

92 ...a journalist in July 1868... Anon., 'East London Opium-Smokers', *London Society: An Illustrated Magazine of Light and Amusing Literature for the Hours of Relaxation* 14 (1868), pp. 68–72.

95 ...another account of...an East End opium house... 'In an Opium Den',

The Ragged School Union Magazine, no. 237 (September 1868) pp. 198–200. See also George Dolby, *Charles Dickens as I Knew Him: The Story of the Reading Tours of Great Britain and America (1866–1870)* (London: Everett & Co., 1912; originally 1885), pp. 419–20.

95 ...the Pharmacy Act was passed... On the Act, its genesis and consequences, see Berridge, 'Victorian Opium-Eating', pp. 450–54; Berridge and Edwards, *Opium and the People*, pp. 173–94; and Mike Jay, *Emperors of Dreams: Drugs in the Nineteenth Century* (Sawtry: Dedalus, 2000), pp. 72–80.

97 ...Dickens's weekly journal *Household Words*... See 'Opium Chapter the First', *Household Words*, no. 384 (1 August 1857), pp. 104–9, and 'Opium: Chapter the Second', *Household Words*, no. 386 (22 August 1857), pp. 181–85. On the context for these, see Brendon, *Decline and Fall*, pp. 99–110; Gelber, *Dragon and the Foreign Devils*, pp. 184–193; and Bickers, *Scramble for China*, pp. 77–112. On Dickens and China, see also Witchard, *Thomas Burke's Dark Chinoiserie*, pp. 34–50.

98 ...John Forster wrote in his *Life of Dickens*... See John Forster: *The Life of Charles Dickens*, ed. A. J. Hoppé (London: Dent, 1966), pp. 365–75. Also E. Beresford Chancellor, *The London of Charles Dickens* (London: Grant Richards, 1924), pp. 258–59, which has a similar view.

98 ...'an important influence...' In addition to Dickens's own experiences, see, for example, Sweet, *Inventing the Victorians*, p. 89.

98 ...strong views about Chinese culture... Dickens's article on 'The Chinese junk', *The Examiner*, 24 June 1848, is reprinted in Slater (ed.), *Dickens' Journalism*, vol. 2, pp. 98–102. According to Dickens, it was moored 'in a corner of a dock near the Whitebait House at Blackwall'. He also made remarks about a freelance Chinese exhibition, coinciding with the Great Exhibition in Hyde Park of 1851, in *Household Words*, no. 83 (8 November 1851), reprinted in Slater (ed.), *Dickens' Journalism*, vol. 3, *'Gone Astray' and Other Papers from Household Words, 1851–59*. Dickens returned to the symbolism of the junk in 'Our Phantom Ship', *Household Words*, no. 66 (28 June 1851), pp. 325–31. On the junk *Keying*,

see Bonner, *Alas! What Brought Thee Hither?*, pp. 2–3.

98 *Edwin Drood* begins... Charles Dickens, *The Mystery of Edwin Drood*, ed. David Paroissien (London: Penguin, 2002), p. 7. See also Wendy S. Jacobson, *The Companion to the Mystery of Edwin Drood* (London: Allen & Unwin, 1986), pp. 22–30, 174–80.

99 ...Henry Mayhew had referred to rumours among prostitutes... See Henry Mayhew, *London Labour and the London Poor* (New York: Dover, 1968), vol. 4, pp. 231–32. I am indebted to Benjamin Hervey for this reference, and to his D.Phil. thesis, 'Late Victorian Horror Fiction' (University of Oxford, 2002).

100 When he returns there... Dickens, *Edwin Drood*, pp. 256–57.

100 ...in the heart of England, no less... Dickens, *Edwin Drood*, pp. 270–71.

101 ...Sir John Bowring... See House and Storey (eds), *Letters of Charles Dickens*, vol. 3, *1842–1843*, pp. 521–22, vol. 9, *1859–1861*, p. 333, and vol. 12, *1868–1870*, pp. 520–21. Also Dexter (ed.), *Letters of Charles Dickens*, p. 775; Sweet, *Inventing the Victorians*, pp. 76–89; and Kitton, *Novels of Charles Dickens*, p. 230.

101 ...'In the Court' and 'Sleeping It Off'... See Jane R. Cohen, *Charles Dickens and His Original Illustrators* (Columbus, OH: Ohio State University Press, 1980), pp. 221–28, for Luke Fildes's contribution.

102 'An Opium Den in the East End of London' Also known as 'Opium Smoking: The Lascar's Room in Edwin Drood', Doré's image was originally printed in Gustave Doré and Blanchard Jerrold, *London: A Pilgrimage* (London: Grant and Co., 1872), in the chapter 'Whitechapel and Thereabouts' (between pages 146 and 147), to illustrate a visit to 'the room in which *Edwin Drood* opens'.

102 ...a giant centipede crawling up his leg... See Berridge, 'East End Opium Dens', p. 8.

103 American essayist James Platt... Platt, 'Chinese London'. The same volume of *The Gentleman's Magazine* also included, by way of contrast, W. H. Gleadell, 'Night Scenes in Chinatown, San Francisco': vol. 279 (1895), pp. 576–84.

103 'Even in Courts of worst repute...' See Harry Jones, *East and West London: Being Notes of Common*

Life and Pastoral Work in St James's, Westminster, and in Saint George's-in-the-East (London: Smith, Alder & Co., 1875), pp. 239–40.

104 ...a rather less charitable view of the opium-masters... See Joseph Salter, *The Asiatic in England: Sketches of Sixteen Years' Work Among Orientals* (London: Seeley, Jackson and Halliday, 1873), pp. 19–37 ('Sketches of Sixteen Years' Work Among Orientals'), pp. 200–17 ('The Chinese') and pp. 272–85 ('Dissolution of the Opium-Smoking Rooms'). Also Salter's later *The East in the West; or, Work Among the Asiatics and Africans in London* (London: S. W. Partridge, 1896), pp. 26–31 ('Chinese Opium Dens') and pp. 32–36 ('Chinese Amazons').

114 The journalist George R. Sims... See, among other contributions, George R. Sims (ed.), *Living London*, vol. 1, pp. 81–86 on 'Oriental London'.

114 ...'Li Ting of London'... George R. Sims, *Li Ting of London and Other Stories* (London: Chatto & Windus, 1905), pp. 7–23.

115 ...amid articles about opium-growing in China... *The Friend of China: The Organ of the Anglo-Oriental Society for the Suppression of the Opium Trade*, 6 April 1883 (on the effects of opium-*smoking*), May 1883 (a House of Commons debate), July 1883 (poppy culture in Yun-nan). The Piercy letter is in the September 1883 issue, pp. 234 and 239–42, with a follow-up in October 1883, p. 267.

116 An Inspector for the London County Council... See Berridge, 'East End Opium Dens', pp. 6–8.

117 ...'Limehouse Blues'... Seed, 'Limehouse Blues', p. 76.

117 ...Confessions of an English Opium-Eater... Thomas De Quincey: *Confessions of an English Opium-Eater and other writings* (ed. Barry Milligan), Penguin, 2003, pp. 3–88.

118 'I know not whether others...' De Quincey, *Confessions*, p. 80.

119 'I was stared at, hooted at...' De Quincey, *Confessions*, pp. 81–82.

119 ...justifying...British intervention in China... Thomas De Quincey, *China: A Revised Reprint of Articles from 'Titan'* (Edinburgh: James Hogg, 1857), especially pp. 12 and 25. See also Robert Morrison, *The English Opium-Eater: A Biography of Thomas De Quincey* (London:

Weidenfeld & Nicolson, 2009), pp. 386–90, and John Barrell, *The Infection of Thomas De Quincey: A Psychopathology of Imperialism* (New Haven and London: Yale University Press, 1991), pp. 147–56. On the critical debate about De Quincey's posterity, see Witchard, *Thomas Burke's Dark Chinoiserie*, pp. 61–64. On the context of opium-eating, see Alethea Hayter, *Opium and the Romantic Imagination* (London: Faber & Faber, 1968), pp. 101–31 and 226–54.

121 Lord George Macartney's 'pacific' mission... On the two contrasting images of China, see Isaacs, *Images of Asia*, pp. xi–xiii. On the Macartney mission, see Gelber, *Dragon and the Foreign Devils*, pp. 160–73; Brendon, *Decline and Fall*, pp. 100–102; and Bickers, *Scramble for China*, pp. 21–24 and 77. I am indebted to conversations with Matthew Turner about the connections between the mission and the British perceptions of Chinese export design.

123 'Mutual misunderstanding...' Brendon, *Decline and Fall*, p. 101; De Quincey was much exercised by the gift of the state coach in his 'The English Mail Coach' (see pp. 195–96 of the Penguin edn of *Confessions*).

123 ...a celebrated hand-coloured etching by James Gillray... See Richard Godfrey and Martin Myrone, *James Gillray: The Art of Caricature* (London: Tate Publishing, 2001), p. 96, which prints two impressions of the 'Pekin' etching.

125 ...George Otto Trevelyan... See Brendon, *Decline and Fall*, p. 103.

125 'East London lay hidden...' Charles Booth, in Charles Booth (ed.), *Life and Labour of the People of London* (1889), vol. 1, *East London*, pp. 591–92. See also in the same volume Beatrice Potter, 'The Docks', pp. 184–208.

126 ...Wilde complained to Arthur Conan Doyle... In a letter of April 1891. I am grateful to Benjamin Hervey for this reference.

126 ...a similar complaint in...The Soul of Man... See Oscar Wilde, *The Soul of Man under Socialism*, in G. F. Maine (ed.), *The Works of Oscar Wilde* (London: Collins, 1948), pp. 1018–20.

126 The description of Dorian's journey... See Oscar Wilde, *The Picture of Dorian Gray*, ed. Robert Mighall (London: Penguin, 2003),

pp. 135, 174–84, and 'Introduction', pp. ix–xxix. The following quotations come from this text.Thanks to Benjamin Hervey, who suggested this interpretation to me.

128 The Sherlock Holmes story 'The Man with the Twisted Lip'... See Arthur Conan Doyle, *The Adventures of Sherlock Holmes and The Memoirs of Sherlock Holmes*, ed. Ed Glinert and Iain Pears (London: Penguin, 2001), pp. 113–36, and notes pp. 521–23.

129 'A night in an Opium Den'... Carlson Kernahan, 'A Night in an Opium Den', *The Strand Magazine* 6 (June 1891), pp. 624–27.

129 '...in Ratcliffe Highway...' On the geography of these fictitious opium dens, see Bernard Davies, 'Limehouse Blues', in Roger Johnson and Heather Owen (eds), *The Sherlock Holmes Journal Diamond Jubilee Supplement* (London: Sherlock Holmes Society, 2011), pp. 28–31.

131 ...'The Yellow Face'... See Conan Doyle, *Adventures and Memoirs of Sherlock Holmes*, notes pp. 535–36.

132 '[This house] which appears to have been...' Platt, 'Chinese London', pp. 281–82.

132 'The masters of the opium-smoking dens...' Joseph Salter, *Asiatic in England*, pp. 272–85.

132 ...some tips for 'the casual seeker'... Article in *What's On*, week ending 4 April 1908, in Tower Hamlets Local History Library and Archive, cuttings file 'Limehouse'.

133 ...Platt contributed his own article to *Notes & Queries*... James Platt, 'The Chinese in London', *Notes & Queries* 6, no. 134 (21 July 1900), pp. 42–43; see also *Notes & Queries* 6 no. 137 (11 August 1900), pp. 114–15.

133 ...the phrase 'Yellow Peril'... See Witchard, *Thomas Burke's Dark Chinoiserie*, pp. 94–97 and footnote on p. 185.

Chapter Three At the Sign of the Swinging Cymbal

137 ...interview given to the *New Yorker*... See also Rohmer, 'Pipe Dreams', 10 April 1938, p. 11.

138 ...later attributed by biographers to Robey... See biographical details in James Harding, *George Robey and the Music Hall* (London: Hodder & Stoughton, 1990).

138 ...a 'preparatory note'... Sax Rohmer and George Robey (both anonymous), *Pause!* (London: Greening & Co., 1910), 'prefatory note', unpaginated. See also Van Ash and Rohmer, *Master of Villainy*, pp. 64–65.

139 ...sacrifice by the Aztecs... *Pause!*, pp. 39–40.

139 '...Alma Tadema'... *Pause!*, pp. 59, 108–110.

139 ...school of Kenneth Grahame... *Pause!*, pp. 126–27.

139 Three passages were... particularly prescient... *Pause!*, pp. 126, 59, 55.

140 'If you think music hall "art"...' George Robey, *My Life up Till Now* (London: Greening & Co., 1908), pp. 127–28.

140 ...large collection of blue-and-white Chinese porcelain... See Harding, *George Robey and the Music Hall*, pp. 60–63.

140 '...it reached me...by registered mail...' See Van Ash and Rohmer, *Master of Villainy*, p. 62.

141 ...'came from the pen of Sax Rohmer...' See, for example, George Robey, *Looking Back on Life* (London: Constable, 1933), pp. 164 and 214. On Robey's act, see, among other sources, John Major, *My Old Man: A Personal History of Music Hall* (London: HarperPress, 2012), pp. 151–58, and Harding, *George Robey and the Music Hall*, pp. 35–41.

141 'Shakespeare: Waggish Will of Avon' Sax Rohmer's songs written for George Robey, Little Tich and others, unless otherwise stated, were consulted in the British Library's Sheet Music Collection.

142 Rohmer always claimed that it was inspired... See, for example, Van Ash and Rohmer, *Master of Villainy*, p. 62.

144 Writers and intellectuals began to take music hall seriously... For the transition of music halls into variety, and accompanying nostalgia, see W. Macqueen-Pope, *The Melodies Linger On: The story of Music Hall* (London: W. H. Allen, 1950); Raymond Mander and Joe Mitchenson, *British Music Hall* (London: Gentry, 1974), especially pp. 148–59; Ronald Pearsall, *Edwardian Popular Music* (Newton Abbot: David & Charles, 1975), pp. 46–73; and especially (ed.) Benny Green, *The Last Empires: A Music Hall Companion* (London: Paulson, 1986), a rich anthology of contemporary writings.

146 ...Robey's writers was Joe Tabrar... See W. Macqueen-Pope, *Melodies Linger On*, pp. 420–21.

146 ...during one of his meandering *Nights in Town*... See Green (ed.), *Last Empires*, p. 218.

147 'I will sacrifice everything...' See Green (ed.), *Last Empires*, p. 61.

147 ...*The Exploits of Captain O'Hagan*... Sax Rohmer, *The Exploits of Captain O'Hagan* (London: Jarrold, 1916), pp. 9–48 ('He Patronises Pamela').

148 Another source of income for lyricists and songwriters was pantomime... See Harding, *George Robey and the Music Hall*, pp. 53–59 and 105–6; Witchard, *Thomas Burke's Dark Chinoiserie*, pp. 31–40 and 68–76; and Green (ed.), *Last Empires*, pp. 141–48.

149 ...a fairytale, topsy-turvy China. See especially Witchard, *Thomas Burke's Dark Chinoiserie*, pp. 31–40.

150 Originally called 'The Chop Waltz'... See Krystyn R. Moon, *Yellowface: Creating the Chinese in American Popular Music and Performance, 1850s–1920s* (New Brunswick, NJ: Rutgers University Press, 2005), pp. 100–105.

150 ...a series of...musical comedies... See Witchard, *Thomas Burke's Dark Chinoiserie*, pp. 80–88; Brian Singleton, *Oscar Asche, Orientalism, and British Musical Comedy* (Westport, CT: Praeger, 2004), pp. 10–16 and 17–26; Pearsall, *Edwardian Popular Music*, pp. 18–23; and Moon, *Yellowface*, pp. 145–51.

151 ...Max Reinhart opened...the modernist *Sumurun*... See Julie Hankey, *A Passion for Egypt: A Biography of Arthur Weigall* (London: I. B. Tauris, 2001), pp. 211–12.

151 ...in his study of *Propaganda and Empire* (1984)... See John M. MacKenzie, *Propaganda and Empire: The Manipulation of British Public Opinion, 1880–1960* (Manchester: Manchester University Press, 1984), pp. 40–66, on 'the theatre of Empire'.

152 The most successful of them all was *Chu Chin Chow*... See Singleton, *Oscar Asche*, pp. 109–37, for a detailed analysis of this phenomenon.

154 ...Siegfried Sassoon, in his poem '"Blighters"'... On this, see Hankey, *Passion for Egypt*, p. 231.

154 ...the spread of 'oriental departments'... See Sarah Cheong, 'Selling China: Class, Gender and

Orientalism at the Department Store', *Journal of Design History* 20:1 (2007), pp. 1–16.

155 ...also saw Chinese food... See J. A. G. Roberts, *China to Chinatown: Chinese Food in the West* (London: Reaktion Books, 2002), pp. 53–81, 82–95 and (on the South Kensington menu) 140–42. Also Ng Kwee Choo, *The Chinese in London* (London: Oxford University Press, 1968), pp. 27–29; and, for America, Bonner, *Alas! What Brought Thee Hither?*, pp. 96–107.

155 Sax Rohmer continued to do this... See Rohmer, 'Pipe Dreams', 30 January 1938, p. 11.

156 ...the fashion for Pekingese lapdogs... See Sarah Cheong, 'Women, Pets and Imperialism: The British Pekinese Dog and Nostalgia for Old China', *Journal of British Studies* 45:2 (April 2006), pp. 359–87; the reference to Cixi's book is on pp. 371–72. For 'Looty', see Royal Collection photograph RCIN 2105644 (dated 1865) and Brendon, *Decline and Fall*, pp. 106–8. Also, on loot, see James L. Hevia, *English Lessons: The Pedagogy of Imperialism in Nineteenth-Century China* (Durham, NC: Duke University Press, 2003), pp. 74–118.

157 ...wrote at length about Loki... See Agnes and Egerton Castle, *Our Sentimental Garden* (London: William Heinemann, 1914), pp. 3, 220 and 300. Also Cheong, 'Women, Pets and Imperialism', pp. 384–85.

157 ...with productions now costing so much... See Pearsall, *Edwardian Popular Music*, pp. 18–23.

158 ...a 'musical adventure' called *Round in Fifty*... Sax Rohmer, Julian Wylie and Lauri Wylie, *Round in Fifty* (1922), in British Library Lord Chamberlain bound manuscripts, vol. 6, licence no. 4103, 2.3.1922. It was never published. See also R. E. Briney, 'Sax Rohmer, George Robey and "Round in Fifty"', *Rohmer Review* 8 (March 1972), pp. 11–17, and Harding, *George Robey and the Music Hall*, pp. 108–11. Sax Rohmer's other unpublished attempts at writing plays include *The Eye of Siva*, Lord Chamberlain bound manuscripts 1923/18, 19.7.1923, and *Secret Egypt*, 1928/366, licence no. 8471, 3.8.1928.

158 In his short story 'The Green Spider'... A. Sarsfield Ward, 'The Green Spider', *Pearson's Magazine*

18, no. 106 (October 1904), pp. 428–35, reprinted in *Rohmer Review* 3 (August 1969), pp. 3–15.

159 ...a musical adaptation of the Captain Kettle stories... See Rohmer, 'Pipe Dreams', 10 April 1938, p. 11.

159 ...Hans Christian Andersen's fairytale 'The Chinese Nightingale'... *The Chinese Nightingale: A Musical*, book and lyrics by Michael Martin-Harvey and Sax Rohmer (Prince's Theatre Programme, and A music-hall archive, Blythe Road, Hammersmith). See also the *New York Times* review (17 July 1947) of the show, reprinted in *Rohmer Review* 18 (spring–summer 1981), p. 16.

169 'Kelly's Gone to Kingdom Come' See Van Ash and Rohmer, *Master of Villainy*, pp. 68–69.

171 ... roaring actor Bransby Williams... See J. S. Bratton, *The Victorian Popular Ballad* (London: Macmillan, 1975), pp. 37–88; Harding, *George Robey and the Music Hall*, pp. 99–100; Robey, *Looking Back on Life*, pp. 153 and 291; John E. Carroll, 'The Imperial Dragon', *Rohmer Review* 10 (March 1973), p. 6; and Bransby Williams, *Bransby Williams by Himself* (London: Hutchinson, 1954), pp. 45–47, 109 and 129.

171 ...'The Green Eye of the Yellow God'... J. Milton Hayes and Cuthbert Clarke, *The Green Eye of the Yellow God; or, Mad Carew* (London: Reynolds & Co., 1911).

172 ... comedian Billy Bennett... See Williams, *Bransby Williams by Himself*, p. 47, and John Fisher, *Funny Way to be a Hero* (London: Frederick Muller, 1973), pp. 28–33.

175 ...'Little Tich' as he came to be known... On Tich's act, see Major, *My Old Man*, pp. 142–50; Green (ed.), *Last Empires*, pp. 130–37; Harding, *George Robey and the Music Hall*, pp. 71–73; Tich and Findlater, *Little Tich*, pp. 3–7; and Rohmer, 'Pipe Dreams', 13 March 1938, p. 13.

176 The publisher Arthur Greening... The result was Little Tich, *Little Tich: A Book of Travels (and Wanderings)* (London: Greening & Co., 1911).

177 ...'My Chinese Correspondent'... Little Tich, *Little Tich*, pp. 128–31.

177 ...'My Impression of the Great Pyramid'... Little Tich, *Little Tich*, pp. 110–15. See also Rohmer, 'Pipe Dreams', 27 February 1938, p. 11, on

Rohmer's real-life travels in Egypt – after he had ghost-written *Little Tich*.

177 ...*Little Tich* had been a book... Sax Rohmer, 'Pipe Dreams', 13 March 1938, p. 13.

178 By far the most successful of these was 'Chung Ling Soo'... See Will Dexter, *The Riddle of Chung Ling Soo* (Bideford: The Supreme Magic Company, 1973), pp. 13–25 (on his act), 40–43 (on Ching Ling Foo), 55–57 (on the rivalry), 68–70 (on other 'Chinese' acts) and 154–69. See also Sidney W. Clarke's 1928 article, 'Oriental Conjuring', reprinted in Dexter, *Riddle of Chung Ling Soo*, pp. 212–17.

179 ...'DEFYING THE BULLETS'... See Christopher Frayling, 'Sax Rohmer and the Devil Doctor', *London Magazine* 13:2 (June–July 1973), pp. 65–80, and Dexter, *Riddle of Chung Ling Soo*, pp. 13–25 and 154–69.

180 Fu Manchu was born in the Edwardian music hall For earlier, summary versions of this thesis, see Frayling, 'Sax Rohmer and the Devil Doctor', and Christopher Frayling, 'Fu Manchu', in Kim Newman (ed.), *The BFI Companion to Horror* (London: Cassell, 1996), pp. 131–33.

182 Economist J. A. Hobson famously wrote in 1901... See Mackenzie, *Propaganda and Empire*, pp. 40–66.

183 In his novel *The Yellow Claw*... Rohmer, *Yellow Claw*, pp. 136–39.

184 'We used to return by train...' Van Ash and Rohmer, *Master of Villainy*, pp. 78–79 and 82–83, and Rohmer, 'Pipe Dreams', 13 March 1938, p. 13.

Chapter Four 'A Little Amusement...'
187 ...a trawl through the archives... Thanks to Claire Twinn, archivist of the HKSB, for her exhaustive search through the files.

187 All he ever said about it... See Van Ash and Rohmer, *Master of Villainy*, pp. 20–22, and Anon., 'Master of Menace', p. 174.

188 ...both clerks would send off articles... See N. T. P. Murphy, *A Wodehouse Handbook: The World and Words of P. G. Wodehouse* (London: Popgood and Groolley, 2006) (Vol. 1, *The World*; Vol. 2, *The Words*), pp. 15 and 66–67, and Van Ash and Rohmer, *Master of Villainy*, pp. 23, 25, 30–31 and 296.

188 ...the huge expansion of print journalism... See Rohmer, 'Pipe

Dreams', 13 March 1936, p. 13; Kate Jackson, 'The *Tit-Bits* Phenomenon: George Newnes, New Journalism and the Periodical Texts', *Victorian Periodicals Review* 30:3 (Fall 1997), pp. 201–26; and Clive Bloom, 'West Is East: Nayland Smith's Sinophobia and Sax Rohmer's Bank Balance', in Clive Bloom (ed.), *Twentieth Century Suspense: The Thriller Comes of Age* (London: Macmillan, 1990), pp. 22–36.

189 ...'intense distaste for banking'... See Van Ash and Rohmer, *Master of Villainy*, pp. 21ff. for this early phase of Sax Rohmer's career.

189 'wholesome and harmless entertainment...' See Jackson, '*Tit-Bits* Phenomenon', pp. 201 and 221.

190 'Oh, you may call it cheap journalism...' See Jackson, '*Tit-Bits* Phenomenon', pp. 220–21.

190 ...the 'light reading supplied by *Tit-Bits*... A complete run of *Tit-Bits*, *The Globe* and *Answers* for this period was consulted at the British Library's Newspaper Collection, Colindale. The articles on the Great Japanese Exhibition appeared on 28 May and 4 June. In general, references to these titles and dates are contained in the main text.

192 '...George Robey Confesses to a Particular Weakness...' *Tit-Bits*, 3 September 1910, p. 600.

192 'Drug Maniacs in Society...' *Tit-Bits*, 31 December 1910, p. 405.

192 ...'The Opium Dens of London'... *Tit-Bits*, 1 January 1910, p. 395.

194 ...the 'Houndsditch Murders'... For a lively recent account of these murders and their significance, see Clive Bloom, *Victoria's Madmen: Revolution and Alienation* (Basingstoke: Palgrave Macmillan, 2013), pp. 270–73.

197 ...'the honour of having popularized venomous insects...' Rohmer, 'Pipe Dreams', 20 March 1938, p. 11.

197 ...the scoop of the autumn... *Tit-Bits*, 26 October 1911, headlined '£50,000 for Rebel's Head', p. 166. See also J. Y. Wong, *The Origins of an Heroic Image: Sun Yatsen in London, 1896–1897* (Hong Kong and New York: Oxford University Press, 1986), pp. 21–45 (on the kidnapping), 45–63 (on its construction as a 'sensation') and 114–43 (on the creation of Sun Yat Sen's international image). On the historical background to this, see Jonathan D. Spence, *The Gate of*

Heavenly Peace: The Chinese and Their Revolution (London: Faber & Faber, 1982), pp. 1–26.

199 At the time of the kidnapping... See Wong, *Origins of an Heroic Image*, pp. 179–80.

200 ...the Revd E. J. Hardy... *Tit-Bits*, 2 December 1911, p. 292.

201 ...the popular and influential Chinese Characteristics... Arthur H. Smith, *Chinese Characteristics*, 5th edn (Edinburgh: Oliphant, Anderson and Ferrier, 1900), pp. 35–40 (on 'politeness'), 90–97 ('absence of nerves'), 98–106 ('contempt for foreigners'), 107–14 ('absence of public spirit'), 115–24 ('conservatism'), 144–51 ('physical vitality'), 152–61 ('patience'), 194–216 ('absence of sympathy'), 242–65 ('mutual suspicion') and 265–86 ('absence of sincerity'). On Smith's book, see Robert Bickers, *Britain in China: Community, Culture and Colonialism, 1900–49* (Manchester: Manchester University Press, 1999), pp. 26–27 and, for context, pp. 22–63. Also V. G. Kiernan, *The Lords of Human Kind: European Attitudes Towards the Outside World in the Imperial Age* (Harmondsworth: Pelican, 1972), pp. 155–79, on old China hands and their sweeping estimates of the 'Chinese character'.

203 J. Dyer Ball's *Things Chinese*... The edition used here is J. Dyer Ball, *Things Chinese; or, Notes Connected with China*, 5th edn (Shanghai: Kelly and Walsh, 1925).

206 ...he cautioned against using the word 'Chinaman'... Smith, *Chinese Characteristics*, 'Introduction', p. 10.

206 ...old China hands... See Kiernan, *Lords of Human Kind*, pp. 155–66.

206 ...a Christmas parody of boys' adventure stories... *Tit-Bits*, 16 December 1911, p. 352. On some of the stories being parodied, see Ross G. Forman, 'Peking Plots: Fictionalising the Boxer Rebellion of 1900', *Victorian Literature and Culture* 27 (1999), pp. 19–48. For a recent, balanced account of the 'Boxer uprising', see Diana Preston, *A Brief History of the Boxer Rebellion: China's War on Foreigners, 1900* (London: Robinson, 2002); also Bickers, *Scramble for China*, pp. 337–73; Gelber, *Dragon and the Foreign Devils*, pp. 232–38, and Hevia, *English Lessons*, pp. 186–240.

207 ...children's comics and magazines of the Edwardian period... See Kathryn Castle, *Britannia's Children: Reading Colonialism through Children's Books and Magazines* (Manchester: Manchester University Press, 1996), pp. 134–57 (on comics) and 123–30 (on history textbooks); E. S. Turner, *Boys Will Be Boys: The Story of Sweeney Todd, Deadwood Dick, Sexton Blake, Billy Bunter, Dick Barton, et al.* (London: Michael Joseph, 1948), pp. 74–76, 149–53, 198–201 and 204–9; and Frank Richards, *The Autobiography of Frank Richards* (London: Charles Skilton, 1952), pp. 36–39.

208 'Ten Little Manchus'... *Tit-Bits*, 20 January 1912, p. 499.

209 ...'the refinements of torture'... *Answers*, 5 December 1908, p. 100.

210 ...'The East End after Dark...' *Answers*, 24 December 1910, p. 191; follow-up article, 31 December 1910, p. 216.

211 ...its focus shifted from...London to Cardiff... *Answers*, 28 January 1911.

212 ...articles headed 'China in England'... *Answers*, 1 May 1911, p. 3; 13 May 1911, p. 29; 20 May 1911, p. 58.

214 ...'Is the Anglo-Saxon Race decaying...?' *Answers*, 24 August 1911, p. 422.

215 A community of print See Jackson, '*Tit-Bits* Phenomenon', pp. 206–9.

215 ...high anxiety about the Chinese in Britain... See P. J. Waller, 'Immigration into Britain: The Chinese', *History Today* 35:9 (September 1985), pp. 8–15; P. J. Waller, 'Racial Phobia: The Chinese Scare, 1906–1914', in the Junior and Middle Common Rooms of Wadham College (ed.), *Essays Presented to C. M. Bowra* (Oxford: The Alden Press, 1970), pp. 88–100; Robert Winder, *Bloody Foreigners: The Story of Immigration to Britain* (London: Abacus, 2005), pp. 358–59 and 395–98; J. P. May, 'The Chinese in Britain, 1860–1914', in Colin Holmes (ed.), *Immigrants and Minorities in British Society* (London: Allen & Unwin, 1978), pp. 111–24; David Parker, 'Chinese People in Britain', in Gregor Benton and Frank N. Pieke (eds), *The Chinese in Europe* (Basingstoke: Macmillan, 1998), pp. 67–95; Bickers, *Britain in China*, pp. 1–17 and 51–54; and Mukti

Jain Campion, *Chinese in Britain* (BBC Radio 4 documentary series, especially episodes broadcast 30 April and 1 May 2007).

215 Admiral Lord Fisher... Waller, 'Immigration into Britain', p. 14.

216 J. A. Hobson... Waller, 'Immigration into Britain', pp. 12–13.

216 ...the most patient and hardworking of the pack-ponies... Waller, 'Immigration into Britain', p. 14.

216 ...the General Election of January 1906... See Waller, 'Racial Phobia', p. 156; Witchard, *Thomas Burke's Dark Chinoiserie*, pp. 94–103.

217 ...the Special Commissioner of the *Sunday Chronicle*... Waller, 'Racial Phobia', pp. 93–94.

218 ...in London's docklands... This account – of labour disputes and public disturbance in Limehouse, between May 1908 and April 1912 – is based on research into the files of the *East London Advertiser*, the *East End News* and the *East London Observer* in the 'Limehouse' archive of the Tower Hamlets Local History Library and Archives.

221 ...Graham Wallas shrewdly observed... Waller, 'Immigration into Britain', p. 14.

222 Census returns for this period... These statistics are derived from the collection of census returns for Stepney and Poplar 1901–11, and of *Kelly's Directories* for London 1897–1928, housed in Tower Hamlets Local History Library and Archives. See also Seed, 'Limehouse Blues', pp. 62–68.

223 According to sociologist Ng Kwee Choo... See Ng Kwee Choo, *Chinese in London*, pp. 11–12 (sex ratio), 12–15 (occupations), 15–16 (Chinatown) and 16–20 (early immigrants).

224 ...yet another report by the London County Council... Berridge, 'East End Opium Dens', pp. 6–9, and May, 'Chinese in Britain', pp. 113–14.

225 'If there were twenty Chinese...' Lao She, *Mr Ma and Son*, trans. William Dolby (Melbourne: Penguin Australia, 2013), p. 15.

225 ...campaigning journalist Walter Besant... Walter Besant, *East London* (London: Chatto & Windus, 1903), pp. 202–7.

***Chapter Five* 'The Yellow Peril Incarnate in One Man'**
229 ...the locked-room mystery...

For background, see Ian Ousby, *The Crime and Mystery Book: A Reader's Companion* (London: Thames & Hudson, 1997), pp. 70–72.

230 As the critic D. J. Enright has observed… See D. J. Enright, 'Introduction' to *The Mystery of Dr Fu-Manchu* (London: Dent, 1985), pp. vii–viii.

231 "'Mysterious enough for you?" he laughed…' See Sax Rohmer, *The Mystery of Dr Fu-Manchu* (London: Corgi, 1967), p. 5.

232 The crime writer Julian Symons… Julian Symons, 'The Ups and Downs of Fu-Manchu', *Sunday Times*, 24 December 1972, p. 33. In his *Bloody Murder: From the Detective Story to the Crime Novel: A History* (London: Faber & Faber, 1972), Symons dismisses Rohmer's Fu Manchu novels as 'absolute rubbish' (p. 217).

233 Crime writer Colin Watson… Watson, *Snobbery with Violence*, p. 118.

234 …Professor Moriarty… See Conan Doyle, *Adventures and Memoirs of Sherlock Holmes*, p. 492.

236 P. G. Wodehouse…made the connection… P. G. Wodehouse, *Cocktail Time* (London: Herbert Jenkins, 1958), p. 154.

236 Dr Nikola… Guy Boothby, *Dr Nikola, Master Criminal* (Ware: Wordsworth Editions, 2009), includes both *A Bid for Fortune* and *Dr Nikola* (1896). The description of Dr Nikola quoted below is from *A Bid for Fortune*, p. 9.

237 'Chang Yu Sing the Chinese Giant'… See Bridget Telfer, Emma Shepley and Carole Reeves (eds), *Re-framing Disability: Portraits from the Royal College of Physicians* (London: Royal College of Physicians, 2011), pp. 44–46, and Bonner, *Alas! What Brought Thee Hither?*, p. 33.

237 …a Chinese…managed to gatecrash… See Witchard, *Thomas Burke's Dark Chinoiserie*, pp. 43–46. There is a group portrait of the Grand Opening Procession in the British Galleries of the Victoria and Albert Museum, including the mysterious mandarin.

238 …the history of the cat… See Sax Rohmer, *The Green Eyes of Bâst* (London: Cassell, 1920); Rohmer, 'Pipe Dreams', 13 February 1938, p. 11; also Juliet Clutton-Brock, *The British Museum Book of Cats* (London: British Museum, 1994), pp. 26–57.

239 …the last canto of the *Inferno*… See Michael Keevak, *Becoming Yellow: A Short History of Racial Thinking* (Princeton, NJ: Princeton University Press, 2011), pp. 9–13; also J. R. Christopher, 'Dantean Allusions in the *Trail of Fu Manchu*', *Rohmer Review* 5 (August 1970), pp. 27–30.

241 …'Character Reading from Foreheads and Eyes'… *Tit-Bits*, 18 March 1911, p. 21.

241 According to Pamela Kyle Crossley… See Pamela Kyle Crossley, *The Manchus* (Oxford: Blackwell, 1997), pp. 187–94.

242 …the changing significance of Chinese torture… Timothy Brook, Jérôme Bourgon and Gregory Blue, *Death by a Thousand Cuts* (Cambridge, MA: Harvard University Press, 2008), p. 28. See also review article by Glen Newey in *London Review of Books*, 29 January 2009, pp. 11–13, and Hevia, *English Lessons*, pp. 231–40.

243 …Octave Mirbeau's *Le Jardin des Supplices*… Octave Mirbeau, *The Torture Garden*, trans. Alvah C. Bessie (San Francisco, CA: RE/Search Publications, 1989), pp. 9–112.

246 …racialized the anxieties of more Modernist writers… See, for example, Urmila Seshagiri, 'Modernity's (Yellow) Perils: Dr Fu-Manchu and English Race Paranoia', *Cultural Critique* 62 (2006), pp. 162–94, and Hevia, *English Lessons*, pp. 123–55, on 'constructing the archive'.

247 …the dispossessed ancien regime… On the changing politics of Fu Manchu, see Jim Pobst, 'The Politics of Fu Manchu', *Rohmer Review* 10 (March 1973), pp. 9–14. And for bibliographical background, see Robert E. Briney, 'The Early Chronicles of Fu Manchu', *Rohmer Review* 15 (September 1976), pp. 9–22, and Robert E. Briney, 'Fu Manchu Checklist', *Rohmer Review* 7 (August 1971), pp. 21–24. See also my entry on 'Fu Manchu' in Newman (ed.), *BFI Companion to Horror*, pp. 131–33.

249 …the peacock historically represented the *third rank*… Ball, *Things Chinese*, p. 365.

250 …Dr Fu Manchu promotes himself… See Frayling, 'Sax Rohmer and the Devil Doctor'.

251 …a visit to Calvin Coolidge… See Frank Luther Mott, *A History of American Magazines* (Cambridge, MA: Belknap Press, 1938–68), vol. 4, *1885–1905*, p. 471.

252 …the phrase 'yellow peril'… On this phrase, see Michael Balfour, *The Kaiser and His Times* (Harmondsworth: Penguin, 1975), pp. 142–43 and 209–40; Keevak, *Becoming Yellow*, pp. 124–44; Jenny Clegg, *Fu Manchu and the 'Yellow Peril': The Making of a Racist Myth* (Trentham: Stoke-on-Trent, 1994) – a guide for teachers; William F. Wu, *The Yellow Peril: Chinese Americans in American Fiction, 1850–1940* (Hamden, CT: Archon, 1982), which treats Fu Manchu as a largely American phenomenon; David Glover, 'Die Gelbe Gefahr, le Péril Jaune, the Yellow Peril: The Geopolitics of a Fear', in Kate Hebblethwaite and Elizabeth McCartney (eds), *Fear: Essays on the Meaning and Experience of Fear* (Dublin: Four Courts Press, 2007), pp. 47–59, especially pp. 49–52; and David Shih, 'The Color of Fu-Manchu: Orientalist Method in the Novels of Sax Rohmer', *Journal of Popular Culture* 42:2 (2009), pp. 304–17.

253 …another version of the image… See John D. Squires, 'M. P. Shiel and the Emergence of Modern China', in A. Reynolds Morse (ed.), *Shiel in Diverse Hands: A Collection of Essays by Twenty-Nine Students of M. P. Shiel* (Cleveland, OH: Reynolds Morse Foundation, 1933), pp. 249–301.

253 …the chromatically inaccurate colour 'yellow'… Keevak, *Becoming Yellow*, centres on this thesis.

253 Comte Arthur de Gobineau… See Glover, 'Die Gelbe Gefahr, le Péril Jaune, the Yellow Peril', pp. 51–52; Gregory Blue, 'Gobineau on China: Race Theory, the "Yellow Peril," and the Critique of Modernity', *Journal of World History* 10:1 (1999), pp. 93–139; and Arthur de Gobineau, *The Inequality of Human Races*, trans. Adrian Collins (Heinemann, London, 1915), pp. 77–97 (on 'civilizations') and 205–12 (on 'the three great races – black, yellow and white').

254 Critic William F. Wu's study… See also, for different perspectives, Michael Diamond, *'Lesser Breeds': Racial Attitudes in British Popular Culture, 1890–1940* (London: Anthem, 2006), pp. 12–33 and 36–57; Robert G. Lee, *Orientals: Asian Americans in Popular Culture* (Philadelphia, PA: Temple University

Press, 1999), pp. 67–68 ('John Chinaman') and 113–17 (Fu Manchu 'consolidating the oriental'); and Bonner, *Alas! What Brought Thee Hither?*, pp. 40–47.

255 …the image of Chinese people in American *drama*… See Dave Williams, *Misreading the Chinese Character: Images of the Chinese in Euroamerican Drama to 1925* (New York: Peter Lang, 2000), pp. 1–11, 54–72 (during the Opium Wars), 73–95 (in California) and 145–51 (idealizations at the end of the nineteenth century), and Dave Williams (ed.), *The Chinese Other, 1850–1925: An Anthology of Plays* (Lanham, MD: University Press of America, 1997).

256 Historian Krystyn R. Moon… Moon, *Yellowface*, pp. 12–29 (imagining China), 38–51 (Bret Harte; towards Exclusion), 105 (Chopsticks and 'Chinatown, My Chinatown') and 116–20 (costume).

257 One of the few popular comedies… Thomas Stewart Denison, *Patsy O'Wang: An Irish Farce with a Chinese Mix-up*, in Williams (ed.), *The Chinese Other*, pp. 125–48. I am also indebted to Fintan O'Toole, 'From Patsy O'Wang to Fu Manchu: Ireland, China and Racism' (a talk for RTÉ radio, 2009).

259 …evil Asian masterminds… Michael Diamond, *'Lesser Breeds'*, pp. 36–57; Jess Nevins, *Heroes and Monsters: The Unofficial Companion to the League of Extraordinary Gentlemen* (London: Titan, 2006), pp. 63–74 and 193–204; and William F. Wu, *Yellow Peril*, passim.

259 …*The Yellow Danger*… M. P. Shiel, *The Yellow Danger* (London: Grant Richards, 1898). On predictive war fantasies, see I. F. Clarke, *Voices Prophesying War, 1763–1984* (London: Oxford University Press, 1970), pp. 30–63 (the Battle of Dorking) and 64–106 (late-Victorian and Edwardian), and I. F. Clarke (ed.), *The Tale of the Next Great War, 1871–1914: Fictions of Future Warfare and of Battles Still-to-Come* (Liverpool: Liverpool University Press, 1995). For Shiel's *The Yellow Danger*, see M. P. Shiel, *China in Arms* (the final version of *The Yellow Danger*); facsimile of the first edition of *The Yellow Danger*, annotated by Shiel (Kettering, OH: Vainglory Press, 1998); and, in the same volume, John D. Squires, 'The Yellow

Danger Revisited: An Afterword', pp. 353–56. On Shiel, see Sandra Kemp, Charlotte Mitchell and David Trotter (ed.), *The Oxford Companion to Edwardian Literature* (Oxford: Oxford University Press, 1997), pp. 360–61. For bibliographical details of *The Yellow Danger*, see A. Reynolds Morse and M. P. Shiel, *The Works of M. P. Shiel: A Study in Bibliography* (Los Angeles, CA: Fantasy Publishing, 1948), pp. 40–43 (*The Yellow Danger*), 72–74 (*The Yellow Wave*) and 88–90 (*The Yellow Peril* or *The Dragon*).

261 'I'll give you one lillee box…' Shiel, *The Yellow Danger*, p. 7.

262 …London in Danger…Terror from the East… On these, see Castle, *Britannia's Children*, pp. 134–57. In children's literature, the best-known *heir* to Fu Manchu – first appearing the year after the serialization of *The Mystery of Dr Fu-Manchu*, the year of its book publication, in *The Brotherhood of the Yellow Beetle* (1913) – was Prince Wu Ling, adversary of Sexton Blake, sometimes operating from a base in Cardiff docks. Sexton Blake was another Alfred Harmsworth production. See William Vivian Butler, *The Durable Desperadoes* (London: Macmillan, 1973), pp. 43–50.

263 …The Queen of the World… Standish O'Grady, *The Queen of the World, or Under the Tyranny* (London: Lawrence and Bullen, 1900).

265 Wells' *War in the Air*… H. G. Wells, *The War in the Air*, ed. Patrick Parrinder (London: Penguin, 2005).

266 …'The Unparalleled Invasion'… Jack London, 'The Unparalleled Invasion', reprinted in Clarke (ed.), *Tale of the Next Great War*, pp. 257–70 and 373.

267 …satirizing Yellow Peril literature… P. G. Wodehouse, *The Swoop! Or How Clarence Saved England: A Tale of the Great Invasion* (Cirencester: The Echo Library, 2005), pp. 9, 13 (the Chinese in Wales), 22–25 (war as music hall) and 41–42 (epilogue in the Palace Theatre).

269 …the origin of Smith's name… See Rudyard Kipling, 'Weland's Sword', in his *Puck of Pook's Hill* (Ware: Wordsworth Editions, 1994), pp. 13–30, and Martin Seymour-Smith, *Rudyard Kipling* (London: Papermac, 1990), pp. 341 and 353–56.

On Nayland Smith, see also Bloom, 'West is East'.

270 The eighteen-year-old Adolf Hitler… Ian Kershaw, *Hitler, 1889–1936: Hubris* (London: Allen Lane, 1998), pp. 36–41.

272 …'one of the most surprising comic creations…' P. J. Waller, in *Cockney John Chinaman*, a television documentary for Channel 4, produced and directed by Anthony Shang (a Chinese Broadcasting Production, 1987).

273 …specialists in Asian Studies… On this, see Seshagiri, 'Modernity's (Yellow) Perils', pp. 165–67; Hevia, *English Lessons*, pp. 123–55; James L. Hevia, 'The Archive State and the Fear of Pollution: From the Opium Wars to Fu-Manchu', *Cultural Studies* 12:2 (April 1998), pp. 237–48 and 250–54; and Shih, 'Color of Fu-Manchu', pp. 307–9.

274 …the great artery of the Empire… See John E. Carroll, 'Limehouse and the River Police', *Rohmer Review* 5 (August 1970), pp. 13–20.

276 Ronald Knox, for example… For the 'Ten Commandments', see Ousby, *Crime and Mystery Book*, pp. 66–67; and for the initiation ceremony into the Detection Club, see H. R. F. Keating (ed.), *Crime Writers: Reflections on Crime Fiction* (London: BBC, 1978), pp. 76–77.

277 …the first of his Sir Henry Merrivale stories… Carter Dickson (John Dickson Carr), *The Plague Court Murders*, chap. 22, quoted in *Rohmer Review* 14 (July 1976), p. 17.

277 'absolute rubbish' Julian Symons, *Bloody Murder: From the Detective Story to the Crime Novel: A History* (London: Faber & Faber, 1972), p. 217.

278 …Petrie is in a state of high excitement… On Karamaneh and slave-girl fantasies, see, among others, Watson, *Snobbery with Violence*, pp. 156–58, and Frayling, 'Sax Rohmer and the Devil Doctor', pp. 68–72.

281 …Nayland Smith 'snapped' ninety-six times… See John Harwood, 'The Man Who Never Said Anything', *Rohmer Review* 6 (February 1971), p. 20.

282 …a fragmented world… See Seshagiri, 'Modernity's (Yellow) Perils', pp. 167–71; and, on James Joyce and *The Geisha*, Weldon Thornton, *Allusions in Ulysses: An*

Annotated List (Chapel Hill, NC: University of North Carolina Press, 1968), pp. 94, 217, 281, 341 and 412.

283 'This has shocked me, Jeeves...' P. G. Wodehouse, *A Few Quick Ones* (London: Everyman, 2009), p. 82.

Chapter Six 'The World Shall Hear from Me Again'

286 ...'the Limehouse melodrama'... On this, see Jon Burrows, 'A Vague Chinese Quarter Elsewhere: Limehouse in the Cinema', *Journal of British Cinema and Television* 6:2 (summer 2009), pp. 282–301; Shannon Case, 'Lilied Tongues and Yellow Claws: The Invention of London's Chinatown, 1915–1945', in Stella Deen (ed.), *Challenging Modernism: New Readings in Literature and Culture, 1914–45* (Aldershot: Ashgate, 2002), pp. 17–34; and, for comparison, Sabine Haenni, 'Filming "Chinatown": Fake Visions, Bodily Transformations', in Peter Feng (ed.), *Screening Asian Americans* (New Brunswick, NJ: Rutgers University Press, 2002), pp. 21–52.

286 ...Stoll Picture Production... Thirteen and a half of the original fifteen episodes of *The Mystery of Dr Fu-Manchu* have been rediscovered, and are in the BFI's National Film Archive. On background to the production, see John T. Soister, *Up from the Vault: Rare Thrillers of the 1920s and 1930s* (Jefferson, NC: McFarland, 2004), pp. 9–28.

286 ...Attack on a Chinese Mission... See John Barnes, *The Beginnings of the Cinema in England, 1894–1901* (Exeter: University of Exeter Press, 1997), vol. 5, *1900*, pp. 39 and 47–54, and Terry Staples, *Film in Victorian Britain: A Teaching Pack for Primary Schools* (London: British Film Institute, 1997), pp. 39–40.

287 ...Shanghai's Shops... See Barnes, *Beginnings of the Cinema in England*, vol. 5, pp. 151–53.

287 ...D. W. Griffith's...Broken Blossoms... Richard Schickel, *D. W. Griffith and the Birth of Film* (London: Pavilion, 1984), pp. 377–80, and 389–95; Gina Marchetti, *Romance and the 'Yellow Peril': Race, Sex, and Discursive Strategies in Hollywood Fiction* (Berkeley, CA: University of California Press, 1994), pp. 10–45; Lee, *Orientals*, pp. 127–36; and, of course, Thomas Burke, 'The Chink and the Child', in his *Limehouse Nights: Tales of*

Chinatown (London: Grant Richards, 1916), pp. 18–37.

287 ...Hollywood fantasy... I have found useful background to this part of the chapter in Matthew Bernstein and Gaylyn Studlar (eds), *Visions of the East: Orientalism in Film* (London: I.B. Tauris, 1997), especially on 'romance'; James Robert Parish (ed.), *The Encyclopedia of Ethnic Groups in Hollywood* (New York: Facts on File, 2003), pp. 154–275; Isaacs, *Images of Asia*, pp. 109–58, especially on public attitudes; Bickers, *Britain in China*, pp. 43–54; Kim Newman, 'Fu Manchu', in Phil Hardy (ed.), *The BFI Companion to Crime* (London: Cassell, 1997), pp. 138–40; and the American Film Institute's Catalog of Motion Pictures, 1921–1930.

291 Anna May Wong... See Graham Russell Gao Hodges, *Anna May Wong: From Laundryman's Daughter to Hollywood Legend* (New York: Palgrave, 2004), and the film documentary by Elaine Mae Woo, *Anna May Wong: Frosted Yellow Willows* (Woo Neimann Productions, 2007).

291 ...'Don'ts and Be Carefuls'... See Hye Seung Chung, *Hollywood Asian: Philip Ahn and the Politics of Cross-Ethnic Performance* (Philadelphia, PA: Temple University Press, 2006), pp. 87–119, on the various production codes; the quotation is on pp. 89–90.

293 ...attempts to film the Charlie Chan stories... See Huang, *Charlie Chan*, especially pp. 247–58; Chung, *Hollywood Asian*, pp. 59–86; Otto Penzler, *Earl Derr Biggers' Charlie Chan* (New York: Mysterious Bookshop, 1999); Newman (ed.), *BFI Companion to Horror*, pp. 76–78; and Hanke, *Charlie Chan at the Movies*, for a full filmography.

294 ...played by Anna May Wong... See Hodges, *Anna May Wong*, pp. 109–17; and pp. 81–82 and 92–96 (on 'Piccadilly'), 119–124 (on 'Shanghai Express'), 142–143 on ('Tiger Boy') and 143–144 (on 'Chu Chin Chow').

296 ...a daily comic-strip version... See the collected reprint, *Sax Rohmer: Fu Manchu – Two Complete Adventures*, illus. Leo O'Mealia, ed. Tom Mason (Newbury Park, CA: Malibu Graphics, 1989).

296 ...Monday evening radio shows... See Ray Stanich, 'Radio Fu Manchu', *Rohmer Review* 12 (September 1974),

pp. 11–15; the Sax Rohmer entries in Frank Buxton and Bill Owen, *The Big Broadcast, 1920–1950* (Lanham, MD: Scarecrow, 1997); Vincent Terrace, *Radio Programs, 1924–84: A Catalogue of Over 1800 Shows* (Jefferson, NC: McFarland, 1999); John Dunning, *Tune in Yesterday: The Ultimate Encyclopedia of Old-Time Radio, 1925–1976* (Englewood Cliffs, NJ: Prentice-Hall, 1976); W. O. G. Lofts and R. E. Briney, 'SH-H-H! Dr Fu Manchu Is on the Air', in *Rohmer Review* 11 (December 1973), pp. 9–16.

296 The Mask of Fu Manchu was serialized... The studio archives – memos, reports, scripts, synopses, cutting continuities – are in the MGM Collection, University of Southern California Doheny Library, where I researched them. Also very useful were Gregory William Mank, *Hollywood Cauldron: Thirteen Horror Films from the Genre's Golden Age* (Jefferson, NC: McFarland, 2001), pp. 53–88; Cynthia Lindsay, *'Dear Boris': The Life of William Henry Pratt, a.k.a. Boris Karloff* (London: Nick Hern, 1995), pp. 62–63; Scott Allen Nollen, *Boris Karloff, A Gentleman's Life: The Authorized Biography* (Baltimore, MD: Midnight Marquee Press, 1999), pp. 54–57; William Black, 'Interview with Charles Starrett', *Paragon Papers* 6 (1975), pp. 14–15; Raymond Durgnat, 'Spies and Ideologies', *Cinema* 2 (March 1969), pp. 10–13; and AFI Catalogue 1931–40.

309 ...assaults Asian masculinity... Huang, *Charlie Chan*, pp. 280–83.

310 ...Originally, the script had been set... Jeffrey Richards, *The Age of the Dream Palace: Cinema and Society in Britain, 1930–1939* (London: Routledge & Kegan Paul, 1984), p. 112.

311 ...British Union of Fascists... See Burrows, 'A Vague Chinese Quarter Elsewhere', pp. 295–301.

311 ...The Good Earth... See Chung, *Hollywood Asian*, pp. 87–119; Hilary Spurling, *Burying the Bones: Pearl Buck in China* (London: Profile, 2010), pp. 204–23, 230–38 and 254–256; Isaacs, *Images of Asia*, pp. 155–58; and author's interview with Luise Rainer, 1 February 2010.

314 ...The General Died at Dawn... For political background, see Chung, *Hollywood Asian*, pp. 87–119. Also John Baxter, *Von Sternberg*

(Lexington, KY: University Press of Kentucky, 2010), pp. 142–51, on *Shanghai Express*.

314 ...*The Drums of Fu Manchu*... Jeff Walton, 'The Drums of Fu Manchu', *Serial World* 28 (fall 1981), pp. 6–9 and 12–15; Jean-Claude Romer, 'Fu-Manchu à l'Écran', *Midi Minuit Fantastique*, no. 14 (June 1966), pp. 33–46; and Jack Mathis, *Republic Confidential* (Barrington, IL: Jack Mathis Advertising, 1999), vol. 2, *The Studio*.

316 ...'played countless heavies...' See Nollen, *Boris Karloff*, p. 62.

316 ...*The Adventures of Dr Fu Manchu*... See Darrell Y. Hamamoto: *Monitored Peril: Asian Americans and the Politics of TV Representation* (Minneapolis, MN: University of Min-nesota Press, 1994), pp. 111–12, and Mathis, *Republic Confidential*, vol. 2.

317 ...buccaneering producer Harry Alan Towers... Exshaw, 'Face to Face with Fu'; Lee, *Lord of Misrule*, pp. 267–70; Cy Young filmed interview with Harry Alan Towers, BECTU History Project interview no. 608 (held at the BFI); Towers, *Mr Towers of London*, pp. 56–58.

319 ...director Don Sharp... Interview with the author, November 2007.

320 'Well, I agreed because as a young man...' Interview with the author, May 2007.

321 Tsai Chin...did have strong views on the subject... Tsai Chin, *Daughter of Shanghai* (London: Corgi, 1990), pp. 185–89 and 201; and extras on the Blue Underground DVD releases of *The Blood of Fu Manchu* and *The Castle of Fu Manchu*.

322 Burt Kwouk... Interview with the author, 18 November 2010, following a lecture at the Cinema Museum, Kennington.

322 Douglas Wilmer... Interview with the author, June 2008, and Douglas Wilmer, *Stage Whispers: The Memoirs* (Tenbury Wells: Porter Press, 2009), pp. 168–70.

323 ...The British Board of Film Censors... BBFC Files, 'The Face of Fu Manchu', 20 April, 20 June, 5 July, 7 July and 5 August 1965, and 2 March 1966.

324 ...*The Terror of the Tongs... Confessions of an Opium Eater*... BBFC Files, 'The Terror of the Tongs', 26 March and 18 August 1960; 'Evils of Chinatown', 17 June, 26 June and 28 August 1963.

325 ...announced in the trade press... *Screen International*, 22 May 1976, pp. 16–17.

325 ...'watching this on the day Sellers's death...' BBFC Files, 'The Fiendish Plot of Dr Fu Manchu', 24 July 1980.

326 Marvel Comics... *Shang-Chi, Master of Kung Fu, and Fu Manchu* (New York: Marvel Comics, August 1979–June 1980). See also the earlier *The Yellow Claw* 1–4, by Al Feldstein and Jack Kirby (New York: Marvel Comics, October 1956–April 1957), reprinted in *Marvel Masterworks* (New York: Marvel Comics, 2009), pp. 131–233.

326 ...Frank Chin had written abrasively... Chung, *Hollywood Asian*, p. 31.

326 ...the remake of the sabre-rattling *Red Dawn*... See Donald Clarke, 'Hollywood Reveals Its True Colours in Use of Yellow Peril', *Irish Times*, 9 March 2013, p. 14.

327 ...the 'Surrealist Map of the World'... Dawn Ades, *Dada and Surrealism Reviewed* (London: Arts Council, 1978), p. 464.

327 ...they celebrated the improbabilities... Ades, *Dada and Surrealism Reviewed*, pp. 279–89 and 336–45. Much has been made of the Fantômas connection.

328 The pope and dogmatist...André Breton... Peter Stanfield, 'American as Chop Suey: Invocations of Gangsters in Chinatown, 1920–35', in Lee Grieveson, Esther Sonnet and Peter Stanfield (eds), *Mob Culture: Hidden Histories of the American Gangster Film* (Oxford: Berg, 2005), pp. 238–40.

329 ...Brassaï experienced something of the surreal... Brassaï, *The Secret Paris of the 30's*, trans. Richard Miller (London: Thames & Hudson, 1976), 'An Opium Den' (final chapter), from Brassaï, *Paris de nuit* (1932), a series of studies of 'the city and its eccentricities of human behaviour'.

332 ...'Have You Got Any Castles?'... See Steven Lloyd, 'Looney Tunes Golden Collection, Vol. 2', *Video Watchdog*, no. 123 (January–February 2006), pp. 18–29.

332 ...The Goons on BBC radio... See Graham McCann, *Spike and Co: Inside the House of Fun with Milligan, Sykes, Galton and Simpson* (London: Hodder & Stoughton, 2006), pp. 47–77 and 181; Roger Wilmut, *The Goon Show Companion:*

A History of Goonography (London: Robson Books, 1976), pp. 16–40 (especially p. 31) and 56–57; Peter Eton (ed.), *The Book of the Goons: Incorporating a New Selection of Spike Milligan's Goon Show Scripts and...the Authentic, Unexpurgated Inter-Goonal Correspondence...* (London: Robson Books, 1974), pp. 24–29 (for the correspondence) and 77–90 (for the script of 'The Terrible Revenge of Fred Fu Manchu'); and Humphrey Carpenter, *Spike Milligan: The Biography* (London: Hodder & Stoughton, 2003), p. 163, for a Third Programme *Critics* discussion of 'China Story'.

333 ...'The Terrible Revenge of Fred Fu Manchu'... The episode has been reissued as part of *The Goon Show, Volume 25* (BBC Audiobooks, 2008).

334 ...the illustrator Ronald Searle... On *Desert Island Discs* (BBC Radio 4, 31 March 2006).

334 ...*Gravity's Rainbow*... Thomas Pynchon, *Gravity's Rainbow* (London: Vintage, 1995), pp. 13, 68, 83, 278 and 631.

335 ...'Why, Doctor, What Big Green Eyes You Have!'... The *New Yorker*, 30 September 1950, reprinted in S. J. Perelman, *The Ill-Tempered Clavichord* (London: Reinhardt, 1953), pp. 31–40.

336 ...'The Thoughts of Chairman Fu-Manchu'... Henry Beard, 'The Thoughts of Chairman Fu-Manchu', *National Lampoon*, vol. 1, no. 23 (February 1972), pp. 67–71.

338 ...*The Talons of Weng-Chiang*... Jean-Marc Lofficier, *The Doctor Who Programme Guide, Vol. 1* (London: Target, 1981), pp. 101–2, and John Tulloch and Manuel Alvarado, *Doctor Who: The Unfolding Text* (London: Macmillan, 1983), pp. 112–13, 158–59 and 213.

339 ...*The League of Extraordinary Gentlemen*... See also George Khoury, *The Extraordinary Works of Alan Moore* (Raleigh, NC: TwoMorrows, 2008); 'An Afternoon with Alan Moore', *Mustard* 6 (January 2006); Nevins: *Heroes and Monsters*, pp. 63–74; author's interview with Alan Moore and Kevin O'Neill, 2 June 2009, at the ICA, London.

341 ...'an ancient Chinaman'... Kim Newman, *Anno Dracula* (London: Titan, 2011), p. 88.

341 'He died in 1977...' Paul Magrs, *Something Borrowed* (London: Headline Review, 2007), p. 22.

ACKNOWLEDGMENTS

My warm thanks go to (in order of appearance) Edward Said, Chris Patten, Rose Elizabeth Sax Rohmer, Piers Brendon, Luise Rainer, Jimmy Sangster, Christopher Lee, Douglas Wilmer, Burt Kwouk, Don Sharp – who talked with me, in some cases at considerable length, about aspects of *The Yellow Peril*. Thanks, too, to my friends Jeffrey Richards, John Exshaw, Louise Swan, Kim Newman, Fintan O'Toole, Penny Sparke, Arthur Pulos, Cy Young, John Baxter, Matthew Sweet and Kevin Jackson, who helped me along the way. Matthew Turner gave advice on Chinese design and Benjamin Hervey on Oscar Wilde. David Drummond provided materials on the music-hall. Dr Fang Xiaofeng, of Tsinghua University Beijing, showed me around the Summer Palace and gave me many insights into the Chinese side of the story. The design teams at Tsinghua and at Shanghai Institute of Chemical Technology – when I was teaching there – added others. Assorted Royal College of Art postgraduate students provided translations into English. The artist Grace Lau encouraged me, when first I mentioned the book in print. Her photographic project depicting passers-by from Hastings amid 'Chinese' props and in formal poses – as if they were exotic Chinese photographed by Westerners in an 1850s Shanghai studio – has made oblique comments on Imperialist ways of seeing, by reversing the usual roles; it is based on her research into vintage photographic portraits of Chinese 'types'. She wrote to me:

> Please will you go ahead and write this essential book soon? Because although we are noted for keeping our humble heads down in the formerly-powerful ex-colonialist society of Britain, sometimes our Confucian patience is worn thin by continued uninformed media cover-age of our culture. For example, the 'World News' page of the *Times*, 25 February 2006, states
>
>> 'Chinese give cat food a whole new meaning . . . thousands of cats are transported to Southern China, not destined to become pampered pets of the country's new rich, but to be served up at the dinner table . . .'
>
> You must be aware of these racially negative implications for you to suggest the book, but I would say that despite China's presently high profile, there still exists a level of hostility bubbling beneath the surface

which is inherited from former Victorian Imperialism. . . . My question is 'Has anything really changed?'

She wrote this in July 2006. 'Soon' proved to be more than a tad optimistic. But I was very gratified that Grace, and other individuals from the Chinese community in Britain, were so supportive at early stages. Thanks, too, to the staff of Cambridge University Library (especially the West Room), at Blythe House Archive and Reading Room (V&A), the British Library, the British Library's Newspaper Division at Colindale, New York Public Library, Tower Hamlets Local History Library (and some of the elderly inhabitants of Tower Hamlets with long memories), Ned Comstock at the University of Southern California Doheny Research Library (MGM film files) and UCLA (Fox film files), and to the first editor of *The Rohmer Review*, the late Robert E. Briney, whom, despite various attempts, I never managed to meet in person. And, of course, to Lucy Edyvean, who deciphered my handwriting – which is how I still draft my books. Warm thanks to Maria Ranauro and Karin Fremer at Thames & Hudson, and Kit Shepherd who edited the text with such an eagle-eye. Earlier versions of parts of this book, when they were still work-in-progress, appeared in the *London Magazine* (June–July 1973) and the *BFI Companion to Horror* (1996). Some of the music-hall material was included in *The Lord of Strange Deaths: The Fiendish World of Sax Rohmer* (2014).

SOURCES OF ILLUSTRATIONS

Unless otherwise noted below, all photographs appear courtesy of a private collection. a = above / b = below / c = centre / l = left / r = right

2 *The Mask of Fu Manchu* (1932). Directors Charles J. Brabin and (uncredited) Charles Vidor. Production MGM. Courtesy Everett Collection/Rex Features. **8** Buyenlarge/SuperStock. **18** Richard Jones/Rex Features. **49a** The British Museum, London, inv. 1851,0901.619. **49b** Courtesy FormAsia Publishers. **51** *The Coming China Wars: How They Will Be Fought, How They Can Be Won*, Peter Navarro. FT Press (Financial Times Press, an imprint of Pearson), 2006. **52a, 52b, 53a, 53b, 54** Collection Grace Lau. **55** The Royal Collection. Photo 2014 Her Majesty Queen Elizabeth II/Bridgeman Art Library. **106–7** D. W. Griffith Productions/courtesy Ronald Grant Archive. **108** City of London/Heritage Images/ TopFoto. **109a** Collection Grace Lau. **109b** North Wind Picture Archives/Alamy. **110a** Library of Congress, Prints and Photographs Division, Washington, DC (LC-USZ62-62503). **110b** David Low, 20 February 1932. © Solo Syndication. **111** *The English Illustrated Magazine*, vol. 23, no. 2 (July 1900), p. 301. Victoria and Albert Museum, London. **112** Library of Congress, Prints and Photographs Division, Washington, DC (LC-G403-BN-0383). **161b** Bryan Wharton/The Times/ NewsSyndication.com. **163** *Little Tich: A Book of Travels (and Wanderings)*, London: Greening and Co., 1911. **164, 165bl** Victoria and Albert Museum, London. **166al** A. L. Burt Company, 1920 (reprint 1928). **166ar** Methuen, 1916. **166bl** Cassell, 1925. **166br** Popular Library no. 217, 1950. **167al** Methuen, 1913. **167ar** A. L. Burt Company, 1913. **167bl** Allan Wingate, 1977. **167br** A. L. Burt Company, 1917 (reprint 1920s). **168** Doubleday Doran, 1931. **186** Topical Press Agency/Getty Images. **228** Cassell, 1922. **284** The Blood of Fu Manchu (1968). Director Jess Franco. Production Ada/Commonwealth/Constantin. **298** Courtesy the Wallace Wood Estate, www.wallacewoodestate.com. **302** *The Mask of Fu Manchu* (1932). Directors Charles J. Brabin and (uncredited) Charles Vidor. Production MGM. **303al** *The Mysterious Dr Fu Manchu* (1929). Director Rowland V. Lee. Production Paramount. **303ar** *The Drums of Fu Manchu* (1940). Directors John English and William Witney. Production Republic. **303b, 304** *The Face of Fu Manchu* (1965). Director Don Sharp. Production Hallam/Constantin.

Captions for the chapters' opening illustrations are as follows:
8 'Aladdin's Procession', from *Aladdin and the Wonderful Lamp*, set in an imaginary China as was traditional, illustrated by Walter Crane (1874). **18** The Union flag is finally lowered during the British handover of Hong Kong, June 1997. **88** Portrait of the author Sax Rohmer, complete with pipe and the shiny Egyptian robe he wore for publicity photographs. **86** The most influential visual image of an opium den in Victorian England: 'An Opium Den in the East End of London' (also known as 'Opium-Smoking: The Lascar's Room in Edwin Drood'), an engraving by Gustave Doré for the book *London: A Pilgrimage* (1872). **136** Sheet-music cover of 'Somebody's Got to Go Through It!', words by Sax Rohmer, performed by the music-hall superstar George Robey (1910). **186** London's 'Chinatown': two Chinese men meet on a street corner in Limehouse in 1911. **228** Characteristically lurid book jacket of Sax Rohmer's collection of short stories, *Tales of Chinatown* (first British edition, 1922). **284** Christopher Lee as the devil doctor on his throne – with crumpled dragon tapestry – in the period adventure *The Blood of Fu Manchu* (1968).